THIS YEAR'S GAME

*One Couple's Annual Pursuit of College Football
Rivalry and Revelry*

A Fourteen-Year True Story

To Philip H. Knight,

The Man in the Arena.

By Sean and Valerie McMahon

Written by
Sean J. McMahon

Sean & Valerie McMahon
www.thisyearsgame.com

Library of Congress Control Number:2019916465 ISBN:978-0-578-59351-7

This Year's Game.

Printed in the United States of America

Cover football image courtesy of Wilson Sporting Goods Co.

Book design by Jerry Wiant, www.wiantdesign.com

To the devoted individuals inside arenas
across this great nation of ours.

"It is not the critic who counts; not the man who points out how the strong man stumbles, or where the doer of deeds could have done them better. The credit belongs to the man who is actually in the arena, whose face is marred by dust and sweat and blood; who strives valiantly; who errs, who comes short again and again, because there is no effort without error and shortcoming; but who does actually strive to do the deeds; who knows great enthusiasms, the great devotions; who spends himself in a worthy cause; who at the best knows in the end the triumph of high achievement, and who at the worst, if he fails, at least fails while daring greatly, so that his place shall never be with those cold and timid souls who neither know victory nor defeat."
    – Theodore Roosevelt

THIS YEAR'S GAME

	YEAR	GAME	LOCATION
1.	2000	Texas | Oklahoma *Chilling Start to a Wonderful Quest*	Dallas, TX
2.	2001	Army | Navy *Schwarzkopf Rocks*	Philadelphia, PA
3.	2002	Florida | Tennessee *Swamped in Knoxville*	Knoxville, TN
4.	2003	Miami (FL) | Virginia Tech *Welcome to the Terrordome*	Blacksburg, VA
5.	2004	Michigan | Ohio State *Fans and Formations*	Columbus, OH
6.	2005	California | Stanford *The Big Game*	Palo Alto, CA
7.	2006	Auburn | Alabama *Fear the Thumb*	Tuscaloosa, AL
8.	2007	West Virginia | Oklahoma *Fiesta Time*	Tempe, AZ
9.	2008	Georgia | Florida *World's Largest Cocktail Party*	Jacksonville, FL
10.	2009	Texas | Texas A&M *Midnight Yell*	College Station, TX
11.	2010	Yale | Harvard *The Fight in the Dog*	Cambridge, MA
12.	2011	Texas Christian | Air Force *Flight and Fight*	Colorado Springs, CO
13.	2012	South Carolina | Clemson *A Sobering Affair*	Clemson, SC
14.	2013	Southern California | Notre Dame *Keeping the Faith*	South Bend, IN

CONTENTS

PREFACE

By Valerie McMahon

Meeting up with Sean and his former college football buddy in the lobby of a hotel, the thought of a decades-long annual pursuit never entered my mind. Let alone, writing a book about it. We were simply on vacation and taking in a passion so deeply ingrained in our pasts that it's become an integral part of our marriage.

Nevertheless, the stories began to accumulate and as each season approached, friends and family members would ask, "Hey, what's this year's game?"

After traveling to some of college football's most storied rivalries – along with participating in many of its most outlandish traditions – someone suggested we write a book. We dismissed this encouragement with "yeah, we should," but never did anything about it.

Then, following an intrastate showdown in the South, the idea for this book started to take shape. And not because we had witnessed another amazing game with amazing players in an amazing arena. But because, (once again!) we experienced a slice of the many rituals that unfold every fall Saturday in this great country – along with their silliness and surprises.

That was in 2012.

We decided that Sean would write our story and I would provide color commentary (to use sports announcing parlance), prompting him with "remember when . . ." anecdotes from each adventure. He started to write, but it was slow going. Life got in the way, and suddenly the few pages he wrote in his spare time on weekends sat unfinished.

A few years later (and with a few idle threats from me that if he didn't finish it, I would), Sean diligently sat in our TV room, our cat Freya by his side, and wrote.

The result is a labor of love.

This marvelous journey of ours compelled me to think about why I love college football – and one team above all others.

It started on Thanksgiving weekend in 1977. My older sister was at the movies with a friend. *Star Wars* had made its way to the smaller screens across America and she was in Miami seeing it for the first time. Miami is pronounced "My-AMM-uh," by the way, and was the closest "big city" to the ranch I grew up on, five miles outside the town of Vinita, Oklahoma.

On that Saturday afternoon, I tried to find some semblance of entertainment on one of the four TV channels we received in this rural part of the state. I settled on a football game: the Texas Longhorns versus Texas A&M. What began as a close contest soon got away from the Aggies. Even though they were playing at home, A&M was no match for the Longhorns, losing 28-to-57.

By game's end, I was captivated with everything "burnt orange."

I loved the silly outfits worn by the University of Texas' marching band – no self-respecting cowboy would ever wear *that* chin-strapped hat or *that* fringed jacket. I loved how skilled their football players were. And, I loved that the team had a cow as its mascot!

Having spent my early years surrounded by annoying fans of the team from the University of Oklahoma, I easily warmed up to the Longhorns. They were winners. And they weren't OU.

My sister eventually returned home from Luke and Leah's battle with the Dark Side and asked me who won the game. I remember telling her, Texas won and that they have a really good player, a running back, some guy named Earl. A few weeks later, that guy named Earl collected the Heisman Trophy for his contribution to the Longhorns' undefeated regular season.

At that time, I didn't know that the "Tyler Rose," as Earl Campbell was affectionately called, would lead the nation in both rushing (1,744 yards) and scoring (19 touchdowns) during that 1977 season. What an eye for talent I had, at such a young age! Unfortunately, his Longhorns' unblemished season came to end – losing to Notre Dame in the 1978 Cotton Bowl Classic by the score of 10-to-38.

Even with my discovery on that impressionable Saturday afternoon, I had no plan to enroll at the University of Texas at Austin after graduating from high school – and I certainly was not going to attend the University of Oklahoma.

My first memory of Sooner fandom came when I was a young girl. Driving with my family into town, a white Chevrolet Impala (with red interior) drove up behind us at a high rate of speed. After tailgating for several miles, the driver finally had enough of *going the speed limit* and passed us on the narrow road. Our fear turned to dismay when we realized he was our neighbor from the ranch across the way; a man who, before that day, never drove faster than 15 miles per hour on that same stretch of country highway.

I guess when you're late for a game in Norman, you find the gas pedal and throw caution to the wind.

Ever since, I have pondered why I continue to dislike a football team from the state where I haven't lived for more than three decades. The answer is, they still seem to be forced upon me every time fall rolls around. Preseason football polls almost always have the Sooners listed in their top-10. The team seems to get a pass whenever they lose. From my perspective, sports commentators talk them up to a point of bias. And then there's "Sooner Magic," – that moment in the game when you think OU is beaten and, yet, they somehow find a way to win. Usually in the most incomprehensible fashion.

I admit it, the Sooners are worthy adversaries. I acknowledge they have a history of winning and I probably cannot be objective when it comes to the Longhorns. Still, beating OU – or just watching them lose – is so much fun!

This book is about our travels across this beautiful country, sitting alongside fellow Americans and experiencing their college football traditions – some comical, some not so – and cheering just as loudly as they did for their team, their family members, and their beloved school.

The questions Sean and I are most-often asked about our quest are, "Who were the best fans?" "What was your favorite campus bar?" and "What was the best rivalry you experienced?"

It would be unwise for me to tell you who we perceive to be the best fans. Because, if you happen to root for the rivals of that school; you most certainly won't agree!

Our favorite watering hole? The one we accidentally stumbled upon and found great food, frosty beers, and wonderful camaraderie.

As for the best game, I have my favorite, but Sean will tell you it's *this year's game!*

CHAPTER ONE
Chilling Start to a Wonderful Quest
2000 Oklahoma | Texas

"TEXAS! --- FIGHT! TEXAS! --- FIGHT!"

Back and forth, this chant reverberates off the underbelly of Cotton Bowl Stadium. An undulating belly rivaling the size of the arena leads the call. Confidently striding in the wake of this University of Texas fraternity brother are a dozen or so undergrads, each dressed in long-sleeve white button-downs and starched Wrangler jeans. Several wear cowboy hats comically large enough to have come from the movie *City Slickers*. The noisy posse cuts a swath toward the opening to the venerated stadium.

It's a little before 10 a.m. More than 75,000 adrenaline-fueled fans – half draped in burnt orange, half in crimson and cream – stream beneath an enormous waving cowboy known as "Big Tex," the 52-foot-tall animatronic cowhand that's stood watch at this gateway to the Texas State Fair since 1952. At the far end of this sprawling carnival, an interstate football rivalry is scheduled to kick off in less than an hour.

Today is the 95th gridiron meeting between the Texas Longhorns and the University of Oklahoma Sooners.

As in most years, this highly (some might say manically) anticipated scrimmage will likely set the tone for the second half of the season for both programs, and also, quite possibly, the race to the 2000 Bowl Championship Series (BCS) national title. Ranked 10th in the nation, with an unblemished four-game record, the Sooners are slightly favored over their 11th-ranked rival, who comes into this contest with only one loss, a hard-fought 24-to-27 defeat at Stanford University.

Valerie and I are jostled liked pinballs as we head toward the turnstiles. Palpable hostility exudes from the slowly compacting mob. As furtive glances pass between distinctly-clothed revelers, we can feel pent-up energy – and mutual animosity – from each fan base. The battle on the field may not yet have started, but make no mistake: the determined horde surrounding us is engaged in their own form of combat.

My introduction to full-contact football was at age 9. From that time as a Bengal in Santa Barbara's Youth Football League through high school, I spent every summer preparing for the upcoming slate of games. My senior season at San Marcos High was filled with familiar experiences that predictably play themselves out every year across our nation. Obligatory two-a-day practices. Pep rallies. Pregame meals. Team bus rides and Friday night victory parties.

Early in the season, however, we ran into a buzz saw. On a chilly night (for Southern California), Randall Cunningham threw a 60-yard bomb in the waning seconds of the game. Victorious, the future Philadelphia Eagle and four-time All-Pro NFL Quarterback was carried off the field by his fellow Santa Barbara High School players.

During the summer before my first year of college, I set my sights on becoming a Cowboy . . . by walking-on the varsity football team at Oklahoma State University. As did another aspiring young player from the southwest corner of the Sooner State. Even though we shared this same ambition, we traveled very different paths to the arid practice field outside Lewis Field (as the Stillwater stadium was called at the time).

I first met James Kruger during my inaugural visit to the Oklahoma State campus in the summer of 1980. He was a tough-as-nails country kid whose father was a colonel at Fort Sill Army post in Lawton. After his senior season as starting defensive end for the undefeated Eisenhower High School Eagles, James looked to prove he was just as gristly as his older siblings. Sharing the dream of big-time college football, he and I instantly hit it off as we prepared for tryout weekend that sticky summer in Stillwater.

At the end of our freshman year – much to my dismay – James announced he was enrolling at the University of Oklahoma. In the years following – much to my disgust – he became a dyed-in-the-red Sooners fan.

Even so, I still consider him a friend.

Last week while visiting family in Oklahoma, Valerie advised me to pack light; it's been in the low-90s and is even hotter in Dallas on this first weekend in October. With the clothes on my back and a couple extra t-shirts, I leave our home in Eugene, Oregon for the heart of Big XII country.

Valerie and I acknowledge three critical elements keep our wonderful marriage together: 1. my love of college football, 2. her love of college football, and 3. our mutual disdain for the Sooners from "Norman Junior College." Thus, it's easy to discern who we're rooting for on this contentious weekend in the Lone Star State.

As the age-old saying goes: "The enemy of my enemy is my friend." And, this weekend, that friend is wearing an oversized Stetson.

"Better dead than Sooner red!"

This I yell as James pulls his Chevy SUV into the loading zone. I also give him a bear hug. He's just made the three-hour trip from his home in Norman, Oklahoma to Dallas.

For the past few years, my close friend has also organized a promotional package at the Crowne Plaza Hotel featuring nightly cocktail parties, radio broadcasts from the lobby, and chartered bus rides to and from the game for fans residing in his home state. This year, despite the given that we will be apostates, Valerie and I have been invited.

Entering the hotel lobby, I'm immediately struck by the obnoxious arrangement we've signed up for. The first of what will be more than a quarter of a million monotonous shrieks (calculated at one per second over the next three days) bombards us as we step to the check-in counter.

"BOOMER!"

Bile involuntarily surges to my throat.

"SOONER!"

I wince in disgust, even though I knew this Pavlovian bark would follow.

Unfortunately, my friendship with James means we will not only be surrounded by insufferable Sooners throughout this entire weekend; we'll be verbally reminded of this fact every day. All day. And all night.

Valerie, who arrived earlier this morning, greets us in the lobby with, "I hear there's a Motel 6 a few miles down the road."

Sooners are cheaters, as we learned in elementary school.

Way back in 1889, President Benjamin Harrison opened land that's now Oklahoma for settlement beginning at noon on April 22nd of that year. The evening before, nefarious individuals ("moonshiners" they were called since their disreputable deeds were conducted in the middle of the night) snuck into the soon-to-be-occupied state. Most hid in bushes and ditches waiting for the sanctioned land-rush. At the sound of the starting pistol, the moonshiners popped out from these hiding places and staked their claim hours before the arrival of legitimate settlers.

The now-familiar name for these underhanded land-grabbers – and proud team name of the school locking horns with Valerie's alma mater today – comes from *Proclamation 288*. This "sooner clause" decreed that individuals entering the Indian Territory before the designated start were to be denied a claim to the homestead land.

Ever since their inaugural scrimmage in 1900, seven years *before* Oklahoma joined the United States, this rivalry has been held in Texas. That first year, the varsity squad from Oklahoma, known then as the Rough Riders, traveled 500 miles by train to the game. Even though Dallas is slightly less than 200 miles due south, the rail lines of the day stretched the trip to more than 17 hours.

Arriving on the morning of the contest, the fledgling team from the Indian Territory was thoroughly dominated by the varsity squad from Austin. Fittingly, the *Austin American-Statesman* referred to it as a "practice game" since many starting Texas players sat out the contest.

Over the past several decades, the Red River Shootout has kicked off at the cobwebs-in-the-head time of 11:00 a.m. Knowing this, Valerie and I set out for a relaxing patio dinner at a Tex-Mex restaurant on this unusually warm Friday evening. With James entertaining his fellow moonshiners back at the hotel, we casually enjoy several rounds of salt-encrusted libations. These should help us get a good night's sleep in the Sooner Asylum tonight.

That optimism is instantly dismissed as we open the lobby door.

"BOOMER!"

Ugh.

It's 6:30 a.m.

We can hear Sooners gathering for breakfast and carousing with fellow boosters. As true football fanatics, we usually wake early every Saturday in the fall for ESPN's College GameDay with Chris, Kirk, and Lee. Just not *this* early.

Today's midmorning clash is one of several "border wars" that take place every year across the college football landscape, including Ohio State versus Michigan, Georgia versus Florida, and the University of Kansas versus the University of Missouri. The actual border in *this* war is formed by the Red River, a major tributary of the Mississippi that derives its name from the brick-colored soil in this region.

Valerie and I make it to the lobby, where the smell of sizzling pork products hangs over the now empty breakfast tables. I'm in jeans, an Oregon Ducks Football t-shirt, and a black Longhorns hat. Valerie is discreetly clad in burnt orange. Looking out the windows, we realize we're in for a far greater challenge than being surrounded by Sooner fans: during the night, a wet cold front unexpectedly moved into the state.

It's not until we step out the door to make our way to the bus that we feel its full impact – forty-four spirit-dampening degrees. Made even more insufferable by my apparel.

I grimace and say to Valerie, "I think we're in for a long day."

The bus lurches away from the hotel. We're sitting a couple rows from the back overlooking two red and white columns of enlivened fans. James is standing in the middle of the aisle shouting the times of our arrival and departure. Vigorously rubbing my hands between my legs to bring a modicum of warmth to my fingers, the incessant droning begins.

From the left column, "BOOMER!" Followed instinctively by the right, "SOONER!"

"Y'all sure y'all are on the right bus?"

The question comes from a large crimson-draped individual sitting across the aisle from Valerie. The guy takes a slug from a shiny 16-ounce can.

"This year," he says, "we're gonna restore order to this rivalry and make up for the last three! Texas ain't prepared for what's gonna hit 'em today. Kinda like how y'all ain't prepared for the weather!"

He lets out a guttural laugh and, to punctuate these sentiments, adds, "Texas sucks!"

Having accepted our fate during the earliest moments of our arrival at the Sooner-occupied hotel, we expected this taunting on our ride to the Texas State Fair. Neither of us, however, anticipated the drizzling streaks on the windows.

Starting with the first game between these rivals (which ended with the Rough Riders scoring a safety to narrowly avert a 28-point shutout), until the 90th meeting in 1995, when the nation's second-ranked Longhorns defeated Oklahoma 45-to-12, this annual scuffle was known as the Red River Shootout. The following year, the politically-correct powers that oversee such naming decided to act in the best interest of our safety by officially changing it to the Red River Rivalry.

To me, it will always be the Red River Shootout. To Valerie, it's simply OU-Texas.

Each season on this weekend, tens of thousands of hungry Big XII football fans meander through the State Fair of Texas to Cotton Bowl Stadium. Alumni and supporters typically enjoy carnival games, school-colored cotton candy, flying swing rides, and deep-fried everything as they make their way toward the massive arena. On this unanticipated blustery morning, however, fans of both schools are only stopping at one booth.

And, Valerie and I are laser-focused on making it to that booth.

The single-sided temporary structure is about the size of a semi-truck. Individuals in two conspicuous colors, six or seven rows deep, push and yell in an attempt to purchase additional layers of any sort for the next four hours in the soggy stands.

"At this point, I don't care which logo is on it, I'm buying the warmest thing I can get my hands on!" I shout at Valerie, though who knows if she hears me? The place is a zoo.

After 15 minutes, we make it to the front of the crowd, only to discover all men's jackets and rain slickers are sold-out. According to James earlier this morning, our seats are located under an overhang. Let's hope. I immediately turn my attention to anything warm. The only items left at all are five extra-large sweatshirts on the back wall.

"Charge me any price you want," I tell the vendor. "Just give me one."

By the time we turn away from the booth, the sweatshirts have been sold.

I may not have a jacket. And my jeans don't offer much in the way of protection from the rain. But at least I have a cap on my head and a long-sleeved sweatshirt with arching white letters that scream "TEXAS." I also managed to grab the last women's windbreaker for Valerie. The burnt orange jacket has a white Longhorns logo over the pocket and adds a welcomed layer atop her thick gray Texas sweatshirt.

We continue our advance to the enormous, ashen stadium. "TEXAS! --- FIGHT!" from the procession of fraternity brothers is swiftly drowned out by the obnoxious back and forth "BOOMER! --- SOONER!"

Passing shoulder-to-shoulder through the noisy tunnel, we see that our seats are on the opposite side of the venue. Not lost on either of us, however . . . they do appear to be under the overhang of the upper section.

Cotton Bowl Stadium, with its buttressed walls, narrow passageways, and bare metal benches, is by no means a modern sports arena. Constructed in 1937 at a cost of $328,000, its initial 46,000 capacity was increased with the addition of an upper deck on the west side in 1948 and a similar addition the following year on the east side, resulting in its current 75,000 seats.

A few minutes before kickoff, the walkway above the lone tunnel leading onto the field becomes an intimidating pinch point. Unlike most contemporary stadiums, which typically have each team enter through separate passageways, the Depression-era Cotton Bowl has only one tunnel onto the field.

Prior to the early 1990s, this annual contest featured both teams parading side-by-side through the single underpass. This ill-conceived tradition led to numerous pregame scuffles between the bitter rivals, cementing "tunnel walk" as one of the most notorious entrances in all of college sports. Today, even though each team runs onto the field at separate intervals (the designated home team enters first), it's still a frenzied experience for players and fans.

Signaled by an exploding cannon boom and a burst of "Texas Fight" from the Longhorn Band, the burnt-orange-numbered white jerseys race through the corridor, across the Sooners' end zone, and onto the sodden field. Throngs of crimson-clad fans violently shake the head-high chain-link fence erected above the tunnel to (ineffectively) protect players from being pelted with beverages, nachos, or other objects of disrespect.

Just ahead of us is an enormous, scruffy-bearded individual in a clear plastic poncho carrying a soggy tray of concession-stand food. "Everybody slow down! Stop pushing! He shouts. "Quit your gaawwd-damn pushing!"

The four of us can feel the surge of adrenaline surrounding us. We also quickly become aware we're being pressed into each other at this midpoint in the south end. As the ever-growing throng clamors to participate in the bombardment above the tunnel, rowdy supporters of both teams attempt to rush to opposite sides in time for the imminent kickoff.

In a frightening instant, I can no longer move. Panic hits Valerie when she sees the terror in my eyes. I hear her scream she's being crushed. With each second, the mass compresses even tighter.

"Go up!" I yell. "Try to squeeze your way on top of the crowd!"

Fearing we're about to be trampled or suffocated, I grab Valerie around the waist and attempt to lift her above the compacting swarm. Just then, as quickly as the mob packed together, the outer edge frees itself and we are thrust against the cement wall of the walkway. Like a pulling guard on an end-around, James takes the lead and speedily navigates us away from the spontaneous mayhem erupting above the notorious tunnel.

With hearts still pounding, we make it to our unsympathetic metal seats several rows under the east deck.

Settling into the covered section at about the 35-yard-line, James points to another unique facet of this annual showdown. Rather than sitting across from each other along each sideline, the Red River Rivalry crowd is precisely segregated at the 50-yard-line. A linear crash of burnt-orange and deep-red runs perpendicular to the grassy field.

Even though the Longhorns – who came into this season with 18 returning starters – are slight underdogs today, they're arguably the frontrunner to win the South Division of the Big XII Conference. The only real question, as the football travels through the south end zone after leaving the foot of Oklahoma's kicker, is which quarterback head coach Mack Brown will choose to steward the team down the field.

Junior gunslinger Major Applewhite, returning co-offensive Big XII Player of the Year gets the nod over highly-touted sophomore Chris Simms (son of NFL quarterback Phil Simms). Both signal-callers, along with their senior tailback Hodges Mitchell, who led the conference in rushing yards last season have contributed to the team's 41.5 points averaged in their first four games.

As the seasoned quarterback approaches the line in his all-white uniform, James hollers, "I hear his middle name is 'Mistake!'" This, from a fan whose team has lost the three most recent Shootouts and eight of the last 11 meetings between these contentious rivals.

Coming into this 2000 season, the University of Oklahoma – for some reason also known by the dyslectic initials "OU" – was ranked No. 19 in the Associated Press national poll. A year ago, the team notched seven wins and played to a last-second field goal loss against Ole Miss in the Independence Bowl. Directed by second-year head coach Bob Stoops, the Sooners are now on the cusp of cracking the top-10 national rankings.

It's worth noting that their flawless record in September of this year came through the following gauntlet on their home field: the Miners from the University of Texas-El Paso, the Indians from Arkansas State, the Rice University Owls, and perennial Big XII cellar-dweller Kansas Jayhawks.

The Longhorns open with a paltry 2-yard dive into a host of crimson jerseys. More concerning than this flaccid first play, a 5-yard false-start penalty is called prior to the next snap. Following the infraction, all three defensive linemen converge on Hodges Mitchell in the backfield. On third and 15, Applewhite completes a short pass to All-Conference receiver Roy Williams. Forced to punt, Kris Stockton shanks a wobbly kick that's fair-caught on his opponent's 43-yard-line.

Valerie looks displeased but optimistic. "Let's hope Mack Brown has his defense ready," she says, "because our offense looks about as prepared as your buddy on the bus said *you* are!"

A minute and 16 seconds later, the Sooners crush her optimism.

On this chilly Dallas morning, with less than 2 minutes removed from the game clock, Oklahoma's senior quarterback Josh Heupel (pronounced "hy-pull") opens with a 10-yard screen-pass to running back Josh Norman (who, with this last name, all but *has* to play for OU). Valerie, fully aware our mutual arch-enemy is currently averaging 44 points per game this season, winces as the University of Oklahoma band belches forth what will soon become the most nauseating sound of the day.

As most fans of any opposing team can attest, there's one thing this state school does exceptionally well. Regardless of the sport – be it football, women's basketball, or rowing – the university's band has the amazing ability to repeat their absurdly intricate "Boomer Sooner" fight song. Every 30 seconds. For the entire event.

Four plays following this successful first play from scrimmage, Heupel drops back in the pocket and throws a perfect arc over the head of sophomore cornerback Roderick Babers. Wide receiver Andre Woolfolk glides into the end zone for a stunning 29-yard touchdown. The crimson side of the stadium erupts as the band plays the abhorrent four syllables over and over. Three-and-a-half-minutes have ticked from the Cotton Bowl scoreboard and it feels as if the temperature has dropped 10 degrees.

On their second offensive series, Texas continues to unveil just how unprepared they are for the onslaught of speed and chaos being released by linebackers Rocky Calmus and Torrance Marshall. This stunted 7-play series, which includes 4 negative rushing yards, one incomplete pass, and another false start penalty, results in a fair-catch by the Sooners on their 23-yard-line.

With a time-out on the field, Valerie exclaims, "Look at the difference between the offensive linemen and our players!"

This observation is not lost on James or me. As both teams line up for Oklahoma's second possession, it's as if we are looking at a prototype of modern football players compared to overweight, poorly conditioned throwbacks from the past. The offensive linemen are tall and lean with broad shoulders, relatively thin waists, and muscular butts and thighs. The linemen for Texas have large bellies and thick legs. While these plodding physiques may have worked well against wishbone formations of past eras, today it's obvious: they're no match for the agility of the players in dark red helmets and jerseys.

The Sooners resoundingly verify Valerie's observation as they pick apart the defense on an 11-play, 77-yard drive featuring a seamless pass from Heupel to tight end Matt Anderson for 20 yards and another screen-pass to running back Quentin Griffin, which gains an additional 25 demoralizing yards. In a little more than 4 minutes of play, Oklahoma scores another 7 points on an option pitch to their diminutive running back.

Standing 5'7" (in cleats) and weighing 190-pounds (if one were being generous), Griffin appears to be an improbable star of this year's border clash. Much like the mismatch created by the impressive frames and superior conditioning of his linemen however, Texas has no answer for the running back's speed and elusiveness. It's 14-to-0 with 3 minutes left in the first quarter of the 2000 Red River Rivalry.

After another feeble 3-play series, Texas again punts. Starting on his 43-yard-line, Heupel swiftly maneuvers his offense down the field. Uncontested in the backfield, he slices the secondary with a 19-yard pass to his wide receiver, followed by a scramble to the 13-yard-line. But wait! On the next play, cornerback Quentin Jammer makes a spectacular interception in the corner of the end zone. Vexingly, pass-interference is called on the burnt orange defender for pushing off receiver Andre Woolfolk.

The ball is placed on the 2-yard-line. Heupel quickly hands off to Griffin for his third consecutive touchdown. In less than 2 minutes, the score is 21-to-nothing. And, even though Valerie's new windbreaker provides some protection from the blustery conditions, this performance by her team offers nothing but discomfort.

The Longhorns' offense adds (once again) to this distress with two incomplete passes and a sack by blitzing linebacker Marshall. Forced to punt (again), after taking only a minute off the clock, it's obvious Mack Brown has no solution for the assailing crimson-and-cream. This perception is (again) instantly confirmed as T.J. Thatcher catches the 41-yard kick and races along the sideline to the 11-yard-line. Even a personal-foul penalty after this return is no deterrent to the overpowering team from the former Indian Territory. Two plays and 24 seconds later, Griffin plunges over the goal line (again) to make the score 28-to-0.

James hugs his girlfriend as the repetitive excuse for a fight song blasts from the south end. I should be happy for them, but I'm not. I am not at all happy. I am hoping that, as bad as this unfolding drama is for the Texas faithful, it is not going to get any worse.

It gets worse.

On the third play of the ensuing attempted drive by the Longhorns, which includes an incomplete pass and another false start, Rocky Calmus (who, I begrudgingly admit, has a pretty impressive he-man name for a middle linebacker) intercepts the pass thrown by newly inserted quarterback Chris Simms. Playing with a wrist-high cast due to a broken left thumb, Calmus scrambles 41 yards to illuminate the scoreboard 35-to-0. Precisely one minute has ticked off the game clock since his team's last touchdown.

Texas follows this disastrous interception with yet another 3-play series, featuring yet another false start and a punt to the dominating OU offense. For the fifth successive time in this mismatch, the podgy defense is unable to stop Griffin and his exceptionally fit offensive line. Even with the inclusion of a twelfth player, the formerly heralded team from Austin allows the spritely running back to gain 9 yards.

After the penalty for too many Longhorns on the field, wide receiver Curtis Fagan takes the ball from Heupel on an end-around sweep. Charging through a hole wide enough for the 1,800-pound live steer mascot known as Bevo (who is standing in the far corner) to run through, Fagen effortlessly crosses the goal line. It's 42-to-nothing, with almost 5 minutes left in the second quarter.

Valerie notices at this point that my usually enthusiastic in-stadium demeanor has vanished. James, on the other hand, is the beau of the ball. Not only is he cooing with his girlfriend; he's also rambunctiously interacting with every fan in our section. High fives are extended all around us. Sarcastic jabs along the lines of, "I guess that orange really is getting burnt today, isn't it!" are directed at Valerie's new windbreaker and my damp sweatshirt.

For the final offensive series of this half, Major Applewhite is back on the field after the debacle by Simms during the previous set of downs. Aided by two pass-interference calls, the ginger-headed junior from Baton Rouge somehow directs his teammates to the 7-yard-line, where he finally connects with running back Mitchell in the back of the end zone. The normally triumphant blast from "Smokey the Cannon" fired after each Longhorns touchdown sounds subdued against the gray expanse of the Cotton Bowl.

As both teams funnel into the lone tunnel, the chilling reality of 42-to-7 begins to set in. Along with the intercepted pass for a touchdown by Calmus, the Sooners scored on all five possessions in the first half. These six touchdowns are more than the number of first downs achieved by their opponent. Their total points almost equal the 44 points the Longhorns have given-up during their first four games this season, *combined*.

In these initial 30 minutes, the top-10 ranked scoring offense in the nation from the home state has gained 13 net rushing yards, incurred seven penalties, and crossed the 50-yard-line only once. As I process this, and as if on cue, a very cold droplet of water drips from a crack in the ancient overhang and runs down the side of my neck.

As feared, the third quarter commences exactly like the first two.

Less than a minute after the soggy intermission, Applewhite is once again intercepted, this time by senior defensive back J.T. Thatcher. Eighteen seconds and two unimpeded plays later, the score increases to 49-to-7, courtesy of another 3-yard plunge by Griffin. James and his girlfriend hug each other (again) as the crimson side of the stadium erupts with yet another stirring rendition of "Boomer Sooner."

A second splash hits the back of my neck.

Mack Brown sends Chris Simms in for the second offensive series, presumably thanks to Applewhite opening this half with an incomplete pass and the crushing interception for a touchdown. Irrespective of the reason, Simms proceeds to throw three consecutive incomplete passes, takes a total of 23 seconds off the clock – and gains zero yards.

Slightly more than 11 minutes later in the game, Griffin

punches through the sponge-like defense to take the score to 56-to-7. There's still 1:26 left in the third quarter when, once again, a sound as pleasant as a caterwauling infant is emitted by the Sooners' band. A diminutive white prairie schooner – OU's traveling spirit wagon that's pulled by two miniature white ponies – travels across the south end zone.

I turn to Valerie, only to see tears welling up in her eyes. The frustrations of the day have overwhelmed her as she screams, "Somebody stop that little Sooner!" Only, the word she screams is not "Sooner." I wrap my burnt orange arm around her shoulder in sympathy, and for warmth.

At the start of the fourth quarter of this historic Red River blowout, the Longhorns manage to score their second and final touchdown, nudging the score to 14-to-56. Another drip from the overhang splatters on my right shoulder. Even the old Texas stadium appears to be crying.

"Well, at least it's not a *total* rout!" James says to me, feigning sympathy and failing by a mile.

Fittingly, Oklahoma is not done. With a little more than 9 minutes left in the fourth quarter, Griffin scores his school-record sixth rushing touchdown of the game to extend the score to a near-inconceivable 63-to-14. The Longhorns never mount a threat during the remainder of this dreary final quarter.

Nate Hybl, the transfer quarterback from the University of Georgia, enters the game for mop-up duty along with his fellow second and third-string crimson-clad teammates. As the final gun sounds, only one of the two horseshoes in the Cotton Bowl has retained its original color. The other has bled from burnt orange to concrete gray.

With the three-game losing streak in the Red River Rivalry coming to a resounding end, several Oklahoma players run victory laps around the drenched field. From under the dark overhang, Valerie and I watch one of the triumphant Sooners plant a massive spirit flag onto the Red River logo at midfield. I congratulate James with a shivering handshake and laughingly add, "Boy, I'm sure looking forward to the bus ride back to our hotel!"

The fairgrounds are an abandoned theme park. Carnival rides are motionless. No fans stop at the fried-food booths or kewpie-doll games. My oversized sweatshirt is not only damp; the letters on my chest are not quite so loud. Shouts of "Boomer!" followed by "Sooner!" are heard at random intervals as Valerie and I brave the rain back to the bus, soon to be filled with jubilant Sooner fans.

They have a right to be jubilant: today's 49-point massacre is the second greatest margin of victory by either team in this rivalry since the 50-to-0 shutout by Oklahoma in 1908.

Ninety-two seasons later, Texas managed only 10 first downs and finished the day with negative 7 rushing yards, as compared to OU's 28 first downs and 245 rushing yards. The Sooners gained a total of 534 yards, while their foe from the Lone Star State managed only 158 yards from the line of scrimmage. More humiliating, Texas was forced to punt eight times whereas OU only had to punt once.

The stingy defense from Norman intercepted *both* besieged quarterbacks and recovered a fumble. The Longhorns did neither. Their defense did, however, allow Oklahoma to cross the goal more times than any other offense in the history of this interstate contest.

Valerie and I are first onto the bus. Shrinking into the back row, we brace for the ride to the Crowne Plaza. Red and white-draped fans clamor aboard. I place a consoling hand on Valerie's knee and whisper, "As painful as it is to say, they have every right to gloat."

"At least we can say we were at a *historic* game," she whispers back.

Yes, historically *depressing* for hundreds of thousands of Longhorns students, faculty, alumni, and fans around the globe.

As victorious Sooners steadily fill the rows in front of us, a dejected first-year petty officer aboard an aircraft carrier somewhere in the Indian Ocean with a recent degree from Austin angrily clicks off the radio. Four portly patrons in over-sized burnt orange jerseys decide to order another round to drown their sorrows in a downtown Chicago tavern. A recently transplanted member of the University of Texas Alumni Association (known as "Texas Exes") commiserates with fellow former coeds at a long table in the Victoria Sports Bar and Grill on the outskirts of London. The maverick founder of a Houston-based oil exploration conglomerate curses something about the size of his donation to the athletic foundation. And a five-star recruit from Permian High School starts to rethink his verbal commitment.

How do we know of their dejection? Because we talked with all these people about the game. Not on this day, but in the months and years that followed. The heartfelt connection individuals have for their alma mater is one of the remarkable aspects of college football that makes a lopsided loss such as this felt far beyond the cold damp walls of a 70-year-old stadium.

College football reaches into the hearts of fans arguably further than any other American sport. While geographic pride tends to be the determining factor for fans of professional teams, college football boosters forge their allegiance through connections that transcend time and space. Every year, young men from small towns, rural communities, and big cities aspire to make the varsity roster at colleges and universities of all sizes. Cheerleaders, drill team partners, marching band members and coaching staffs all have the same dream, one shared by family members sometimes many times generations deep.

These connections become a way of life.

From the rear of the bus, Valerie's thoughts meander to when she was a young girl on a dusty country road in northeastern Oklahoma. The indelible dint left by a slow-poke neighbor in a white Impala during her years of adolescence only adds to the look of disappointment on her face . . . and in her heart. It's true that sometimes a precocious child can indeed be very impressionable at an early age.

As the wet-smelling transport fills with jovial passengers, I reflect upon how this scene will repeat itself hundreds of times today and every Saturday during every college football season to come. Across the country, elated fan bases will marvel at the performance by their winning team and verbally replay highlights with family and friends. Regardless of the margin of victory; regardless of the color of the jerseys, regardless of whether we win or lose (though winning is greatly preferable!), we love college football.

The exultation reaches its peak as the bus doors shut with a thump. At least the outside chill is starting to dissipate. Then, something reminds me that sometimes the simplest gesture lets us see others in a new light.

With the early start to today's contest, most of our fellow passengers do not have celebratory libations for this return trip.

After a couple minutes on the highway, James somehow convinces our driver to stop at a roadside liquor store. Given our dampened mood and very damp clothes, Valerie and I stay on the bus. As the rambunctious riders retake their seats with 12-packs, 18-packs, and even 24-packs of variously labeled (but same tasting) light beers, the noise level again reaches a fevered pitch.

The bus lumbers back onto the highway and a woman with shiny red beads around her neck lets out a cackle and shouts "BOOMER!"

This time, however, as the exhaustion of the morning begins to take hold, I watch the back-and-forth volley of this mundane cheer as a simple observer of this extraordinary pastime called "college football in America." Valerie, also watching with a now insouciant eye, quotes the opening line from an Elvis Costello song we both loved as undergrads.

"Oh, I used to be disgusted, now I try to be amused," she says.

At the exact same time, a round-faced passenger across the aisle in a double-XL sweatshirt affably asserts, "Y'all look like you could use a pick-me-up . . . here, y'all might as well join in."

Handing the tepid Bud Light to Valerie, I convey our appreciation and add, "Well, you know what they say . . . if you can't beat 'em."

With a bellowing laugh, he replies, "Yup . . . and every year, ya get another chance!"

And that, I realize, is one of the reasons this pastime has such an enduring hold upon millions of Americans.

Even if you have to sit through more than four hours of esteem-crushing misery at the hands of your intolerable rival, followed by 364 days of jeering and jabbing from their pompous fans, *there's always next year*. And *there's always next year* begins on the way home from hundreds of stadiums across this great nation on every Saturday of every season.

The now-not-so-loathsome, jolly-faced fan sitting next to us asks, "Where y'all from?" Come to find out, he grew up in Craig County, Oklahoma, less than 30 miles from Valerie's hometown.

CHAPTER TWO
Life, Liberty, and Pursuit
Our Annual Quest

There's no "s" at the end of the team name for Tulsa University athletics. Of 129 schools competing in the Football Bowl Subdivision (FBS, and formerly known as Division I-A), only 13 share this distinction. Valerie *was* a Golden Hurricane, as the athletic squads at Tulsa are known. After her freshman year, however, she transferred from this private university to the University of Texas at Austin.

Upon arrival, it didn't take long for her to realize that everything really *was* bigger in Texas. The university's campus stretches for miles. Texas Memorial Stadium is an enormous concrete edifice. The famed library tower reaches more than 300 feet into the sky. Big Bertha, named after a massive World War I howitzer, is claimed to be the largest marching band drum in all of college football. An imposing Civil War artillery cannon is fired after every Longhorn touchdown. And the school's mascot truly does weigh almost a ton.

Valerie also quickly discovered the seemingly larger-than-life university was more of a serious academic institution than "party school." (Nonetheless, as she can attest, it *does* know how to throw a party.) While impressed with this commitment to learning, she also admired the pride most everyone connected with the school exuded. And especially their adoration for its football program.

Saturdays at Darrell K Royal Stadium weren't just athletic competitions; they were formal events. Collegiate gentlemen in western-cut blazers, burnt orange ties, and ostrich-skin boots escorted sorority debutantes and Southern belles to each home game. Valerie was moved and delighted by this reverence for tradition, and though she could not know it then, it would leave a lasting imprint.

In 1984, she and her roommate eagerly awaited the annual Red River Shootout. Much like the first game of our annual quest at Cotton Bowl Stadium in 2000, the skies over Dallas dumped rain the entire game.

In contrast to our washed-out misery, however, Valerie and her roommate paid little attention to the deluge as they cheered for their No. 1 team in the nation. With No. 2 clinging to a soggy 3-point lead, Texas quarterback Todd Dodge threw a desperation third-down pass into the corner of the end zone. Safety Keith Stanberry intercepted the errant throw. And yet! Several seconds after it was snatched by Stanberry, the officials declared him out-of-bounds.

Incomplete pass!

Ask anyone – other than a Texas fan – who was close to the field, or watching on television, or has seen the replay (as I have, more than once), this inexplicable ruling on a play which would have sealed the game for the team with the little white ponies appeared to be based on something other than evidence.

Following this highly questionable call, and with only 3 seconds left on the scoreboard, head coach Fred Akers elected to kick a 32-yard field goal. The 15-to-15 contest remains one of only five ties in the history of the Shootout.

Barry Switzer, in his twelfth year as head coach, stormed off the drenched Astro-Turf in his "Beat Texas" cap without so much as an attempt to congratulate Akers. Offensive coordinator, Mack Brown, trailed hastily behind his steaming head coach. All the while, Valerie and her fellow students laughingly cheered as their team performed impromptu belly-slides on the saturated field.

Four years before this sodden clash in Dallas, James Kruger and I were pursuing our dreams of playing Division I college football.

To better my chances, I attempted to make myself known to the coaches. Several days before walk-on weekend in Stillwater, I ambled into the offices behind Lewis Field with my high school highlights tape and informed the attractive girl at the front desk that I was there to see the head coach. Looking up from her Physiology textbook, she casually asked if I had an appointment.

"My coaches in California encouraged me to give my tape to your staff," I told her. "I was hoping to meet your head coach and hand it to him." I'd waited a few minutes in what passed for the lobby, a couple orange couches and a coffee table featuring an oversized Big Eight Conference logo, when a stocky, somewhat short, round-faced man with a helmet-sized head of hazel hair came barreling toward me.

"What can I do for you, son?" he asked.

Standing before me in a white OSU polo shirt and light brown Sansabelt slacks was the former starting nose guard for the 1964 National Championship team from the University of Arkansas, future head coach of the 1987 University of Miami National Championship team, future two-time NFL Super Bowl Champions Dallas Cowboys, and immensely popular Fox Sports television personality; Jimmy Johnson.

Knowing nothing of his past and possessing no clairvoyance (then or now), I informed Coach Johnson that I would be trying out for the team and hoped he would review my tapes. He said if he had the time he would; or at least, pass them to one of his assistant coaches. I thanked him and shook his hand. I also gave the young receptionist a smile. Hey, she was cute. Plus, who knew? Maybe she'd be the one in charge of passing along my highlights.

Walk-on weekend turned out to be two grueling days in the heavy humidity that hangs across the plains of Oklahoma every mid-July. Of the approximate 120 just-out-of-high-school athletes who competed for a position that muggy Saturday and Sunday, 11 made the team. I was one of those chosen and so was James Kruger, my then-roommate and future lifelong friend. Being of average size coming out of high school, I was quickly moved to pulling-guard on scout team.

Every day, my "dummy O" team lined up against our starting

defensive squad.

Unfortunately for me, our defensive tackle was Dexter Manley, future two-time All-Pro with the Washington Redskins. I can still recall the bursts from his oversized nostrils, much like an angry hippopotamus breaching a river's surface, every time we snapped the ball. At an imposing 6'3" 235-pounds and able to easily bench-press my body weight more than 30 times, Dexter steadily pounded my enthusiasm for the game into the synthetic turf of Lewis Field.

To this day, however, both my former roommate and I consider it an honor to have dressed-out for an Oklahoma State varsity game.

On that crisp November 8th morning, after experiencing the exhilaration of pregame warm-ups on the hard plastic turf, we stood side by side, in our orange jerseys and bright white pants, on the unsteady bench along the sideline. With the sun in our eyes, we cheered our 42-to-7 victory over the hapless Buffalos from the University of Colorado. My pants stayed pristine and I never once took off my helmet the entire game.

During our locker room celebration, I stood in awe of the effort it took to be victorious at the collegiate level; in what seems to be a simple game of moving a leather ball against an opposing 11-man squad.

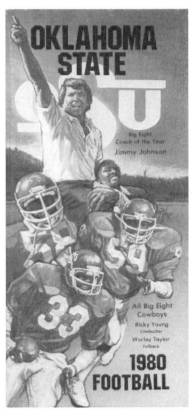

From my envious vantage point, there was more going on than exuberant 18 and 19-year-olds snapping towels and singing in the showers. There were untold hours of weight room workouts. Early morning wind-sprints. Practice squads and blocking dummies. Stadium steps and blocking sleds. Athletic dorms and team meals. Training tables and whirlpool baths. Daily ankle tapings and groin stretches. Equipment assignments for players of all sizes and proportions. Coaching hires. Coaching fires. Recruiting trips. Game tickets for family members. Travel arrangements to games halfway across the country. And dreams, not just of continuing to play the game we all love, but dreams of being the next Michael Singletary, Earl Campbell, or Tony Dorsett.

Things I couldn't know that day: that our starting quarterback Houston Nutt will go on to be head coach at both the University of Arkansas and the University of Mississippi, that Dexter Manley will become known in the NFL as the "Secretary of Defense," that our dummy-O quarterback Rusty Hilger will be drafted by the Los Angeles Raiders in the sixth round of the 1985 NFL draft, that defensive line coach Dave Wannstedt will become head coach at the University of Pittsburgh and NFL assistant coach for the Dallas Cowboys, Chicago Bears, and Miami Dolphins, that receivers coach Butch Davis will soon be on his way to become head coach at the University of Miami, University of North Carolina, and the Cleveland Browns, and that head coach Jimmy Johnson will become one of the best-known faces of football, ever.

What I *did* know that day, as I peeled the white OSU sticker from the side of my black helmet for a memento, was that I was walking out of a locker room for the last time.

Upon graduating from the University of Texas, Valerie moved to Stockton, California to pursue her master's degree at the University of the Pacific. A month after she arrived, a classmate invited her to a costume party at an apartment complex across town. Several months earlier, I'd moved to the same apartments, following my graduate degree from Saint Louis University.

To this day, when friends ask how we met, Valerie tells the following story:

> *At this boring Halloween party with people I barely knew, I was on the phone in the kitchen trying to get*

more of my classmates to come over when in walks this guy wearing a full Viking costume: gray tunic, long blond braids, and a horned helmet. As he burst through the front door, he exclaimed, "We're going to drink and pillage and burn this village!" Finally! I thought, the life of the party had shown up! Naturally, I wanted to talk to this Norseman and find out if this was his real hair color, when I overheard him say he was the representative for Anheuser-Busch while at Oklahoma State. That's right, B.M.O.C. – Bud Man on Campus. Here I was, a thousand miles from home, and I meet someone who not only went to OSU but who'd been at events I attended in Stillwater while visiting my sister, who also went to OSU. Being the Bud Man, he'd even coordinated parties with my sister's boyfriend at his fraternity!

After several years of courtship, we moved together to the lush green college town of Eugene, Oregon. Fortuitously, during our initial four years as Oregonians, we lived directly across from Autzen Stadium, home of the University of Oregon Ducks. As a then middle-of-the-road team, great seats could be had from the ticket booth minutes before kickoffs.

On Saturday mornings, we'd walk out our front door and immediately be in the midst of exciting Pacific-10 (as the conference was known then) football games, including the opening-day 48-to-14 upset victory over Michigan State in 1998, the five-hour triple-overtime win over Southern California the following season with James Kruger in attendance, and, in 2006, the one-point defeat of his beloved Sooners following a perfectly executed (he and others might argue otherwise) onside kick.

Did James fume in the stands? Yes, he did. But did I gloat? Nah. Well, maybe a little.

Shortly after our arrival in Eugene, Valerie accepted a part-time position with the University of Oregon Alumni Association. In her first couple months, the Ducks surprisingly earned a bid to their fourth-ever Rose Bowl after finishing 7-and-1 in conference play during that 1994 season. For the trip to this prestigious bowl game – the first since Oregon was defeated 7-to-10 by the Ohio State Buckeyes in 1957 – her department was tasked with coordinating alumni packages and event activities and receptions in Pasadena. And she got to bring a guest.

Sitting in the luxurious sunshine with more than 102,000 fans, this 81st Rose Bowl Game was the first out-of-state game Valerie and I attended since our marriage eight months earlier.

On Penn State's first play, running back Ki-Jana Carter took the hand-off from Kerry Collins at the 17-yard-line and shot like a rocket along the Oregon sideline, dramatically putting the first of five touchdowns on the scoreboard for the Nittany Lions. Though the Ducks tied the game early in the third quarter on a pass from Danny O'Neil to wide receiver Cristin McLemore, Penn State ultimately cruised to a 38-to-20 victory. Due in part to this dominating performance, Carter would go on to be to the first player selected in the 1995 NFL Draft.

That trip to the "Granddaddy of All Bowl Games" was our first strike of the anvil.

On the short flight back, my new bride and I marveled at how very few other pastimes capture the connection of communities and the heart-swelling pride the way college football does. In 1869, the Scarlet Knights of Rutgers College (now known as Rutgers University) vanquished the Tigers from the College of New Jersey (recognized today as Princeton University), by the score of 6-to-4. Ever since, generations of students, alumni, and fans across the nation – and the world – have annually come together to passionately support their teams on the gridiron.

Along with this loyalty, arguably, no other American sport boasts as many social rituals as college football with each team's unique customs serving to tie together fans and families for generations.

Ask a Crimson Tide booster why the University of Alabama has an elephant as its mascot. She'll tell you the answer. Ask alumni from the state school in Ames, Iowa why the Cyclones have a red cardinal on their football helmets. They'll tell you. Ask a Longhorns fan how their live steer mascot got its name. He'll tell you. Ask a pigskin-loving graduate from Yale University if she knows which university was the first in America to have a live animal as their mascot and you will get your answer. Ask followers of Stanford University how a dancing tree became their team's official mascot. If they're honest, they will inform you that, first, their school does not have an official mascot, and second, that they have no idea why a costumed pine tree maniacally runs around during each Cardinal football game.

In addition to wonderful traditions, another (rarely recognized) aspect adds to our fanaticism for this sport: players from a wide spectrum of shapes, sizes, and skills are critically important to a football team's success.

Where else can a 5'8" 175-pound speedster, a 6'5" 210-pound gazelle, and a 6'0" 330-pound brick wall not only play on the same team, but also be standout athletes? In what other sport can those who can scamper through an off-tackle hole, or leap almost 4 feet for a fade pass, or deliver unyielding backside protection in the pocket play on the same team?

It's this combination of varied sizes and talents that adds up to the wholeness, harmony, and radiance of a winning college football team.

Early in our union, Valerie and I came to appreciate the widespread attraction of college football, both how much it has in common with and contributes to the traits that make our country great. Individual contribution. Hard work. Teamwork. Pride. And winning. Entire towns – even entire states – rally around this year's team; pinning their hopes on both returning starters and new players. Whether in boardrooms or barbershops or bakeries or bars, every year as fall approaches, talk turns to college football.

Talk between the two of us also centered around this national pastime. As we became more and more aware of our shared passion, we also recognized an intriguing phenomenon throughout the fan bases of most college teams. While allegiance to one's alma mater is typically formed during impressionable collegiate years, the decision to embrace a school's athletic teams often doesn't occur until sometime after graduation.

Perhaps this is because the first few years following college are full of major events such as establishing a career, finding a mate, and starting a family. As we get further and further away from the liberating days of school, we tend to nostalgically wish for their return. This may be why so many of us attempt to revisit these days every August as the first game of the season kicks off.

I think the values associated with this sport and the joy it brought during our undergraduate days are why we've chosen our delightful pursuit each fall. Both Valerie and I share these values; they enrich our union every day. And, having chosen to not have offspring of our own, seeing the commitment, effort, and achievement put forth by the young men and women on collegiate fields of competition is rewarding in and of itself; whether we have a place in our heart for a specific team or not.

Equipped with these insights and with the understanding of just how ingrained the game is becoming to our marriage (especially after our excursion to the now infamous Red River Shootout!), Valerie and I have set our sights on what we hope will be a rollicking and fascinating tradition. What better way to experience the cultures and customs across our nation than to attend a college football rivalry each season? To pursue the ultimate tailgate experience. To explore our values, eccentricities, and shared humanity. And, to see Americans as they really are – irrespective of the color of their face paint.

CHAPTER THREE
Schwarzkopf Rocks
2001 Army | Navy

By mid-June, Valerie and I are ready to select the first connecting link in our newly hatched plan. It had better be a game for the ages, one that will get rid of the lingering bitter taste from last season.

After humiliating Valerie's alma mater in the Red River Rivalry and then squeaking past the Cowboys in a 12-to-7 slugfest in Stillwater, the Sooners finished with an improbable unblemished regular-season record. The aftertaste did not abate when Josh Heupel atoned for his second-place finish in the Heisman Trophy race (behind Florida State's quarterback Chris Weinke) by throwing more than 200 yards and smothering the third-ranked Seminoles in the inaugural BCS Championship Game.

In search of this much-needed palate cleanser, we decide upon the always-impassioned Army-Navy game. Given our direct lineages to combat veterans – Valerie's father, a West Point graduate, served two tours in Vietnam; my father, a World War II Marine, fought through the island battles of Iwo Jima, Saipan, and Tinian – our excitement grows as we plan our excursion to this celebrated clash on the gridiron.

Knowing the popularity of "America's Game" (as this historical annual showdown is referred to), we begin our pursuit of tickets early. I ask my father if he knows any ticket holders within his military or professional networks. We hope he can also secure tickets for Valerie's sister Julie and husband Gary.

Fully in support of our mission, my father enlists the help of LTC (RET) Charles F. Bliss, III, a longtime friend in Muskogee, Oklahoma. Field Officer Bliss comes through with flying colors! Being a former starting football player at West Point, not only does he procure four adjacent seats; he puts us five rows from the sideline, in the middle of the Army letterman section. Wow!

We can't know at the time these seats, normally reserved only for former players and military dignitaries, will thrust us into a once-in-a-lifetime experience . . . and into history.

The United States Naval Academy first fielded a football team ten years after the groundbreaking scrimmage between Rutgers College and the College of New Jersey. A year later, Army Cadet Dennis Mahan Michie accepted a challenge by the Midshipmen to a gridiron contest at the United States Military Academy.

Legend has it this overture was instigated by Cadet Michie through taunts sent to his friends at Annapolis. Whether or not this is true, Michie's persistence convinced his superiors to sponsor the inaugural game and also to pay half of Navy's travel expenses. More than 270 Army cadets ponied up the exorbitant sum of 52-cents apiece for the train ride up the Hudson River and the ferry crossing to West Point.

Once ashore, the midshipmen realized they needed a mascot to represent their team along the sideline. Passing the Non-Commissioned Officers quarters, they caught a glimpse of a spirited goat tugging at its tether. Seizing the moment, the officers-in-training commandeered the feisty animal and led it to the main parade ground. To this day, a charging goat named "Bill" is the symbol of Navy athletics. And ever since 1953, Army cadets attempt to clandestinely "borrow" the live mascot prior to their showdown with the sailors from Annapolis.

At the time of this foundational game in 1890, the United States Military Academy did not have an intercollegiate sports program of *any* sort. Thus, not only did the newly cobbled squad receive no money from the West Point administration, Cadet Michie had to assume the roles of coach, field captain, trainer, and even team fundraiser. Because of his valiant efforts during these first years, the field at the Academy in upstate New York bears his name to this day.

Unfortunately for the Cadets on that cold November morning, their unfamiliarity with the relatively new game resulted in a 24-point shutout at the cleats of the Midshipmen. The first-ever crowd, approximately 500 fellow soldiers and friends, were not, however, wont for action.

In addition to Navy's reliance on the "flying wedge" – an offensive play directly tied to military strategies of old whereby players link arms to form a wall that protected the ball carrier and inflicted significant carnage upon opposing players – fistfights erupted throughout the contest. Cadet Kirby Walker was knocked out four times, with the final blow sending him to the hospital after he failed to regain consciousness.

Fittingly, the following season, the Black Knights of the Hudson delivered their own retaliatory blow through a surprising 32-to-16 victory. A spectacular touchdown run by Cadet Michie bolstered their winning effort.

On the morning of September 11, 2001, the upcoming 102nd Army-Navy football game is one of the furthest thoughts from our minds. For only the second time in history, the United States of America has been attacked by foreign invaders, this time by terrorists who possessed an irrational ideology and a hatred for our way of life. The world, as we know it, changes forever.

With all military branches on highest alert, and given that our armed forces headquarters is severely damaged by one of the hijacked planes, the decision to play this year's game between the academies remains uncertain for more than a month after this cowardly attack. Nonetheless, realizing the game's symbolic importance, and embodying the tremendous resolve of our nation, the high brass of both institutions concur it is to be played as scheduled.

Terrorism, by its very definition, is an attempt to alter behavior through force and fear. Our country chooses not to cower to this attempt.

Seventy-five days after that heinous morning, Valerie and I

touch down in "The City of Brotherly Love." We see instantly that this isn't going to be a usual college football weekend. "America's Game" is being held at Veterans Stadium in decidedly urban south Philadelphia. Also known as "The Vet," this multi-purpose stadium is home to two professional sports teams, the NFL Eagles and the Major League Baseball Phillies.

Situated nearly equidistant from both academies, it's also a decidedly unadorned municipal arena surrounded by lots of concrete and city streets. A makeshift jail resides under the stands to deal with overly rowdy fans. Precisely the antithesis of rolling campus hills and fraternity and sorority houses that come to mind when we think of football in late fall.

Arriving at our downtown hotel, we become aware of just how atypical this vacation is going to be.

Parked at the entrance are three identical white panel vans with blacked-out windows and government license plates. Stenciled in white on the rear window of each conspicuously non-descript vehicle is a name: Beno, Rudy, and Kevin. A hive of dark-suited, serious-faced men and women scurry in and out of the well-worn lobby. Approaching the front desk, Valerie asks if we're lodging with the President, who is scheduled to attend this weekend's scrimmage. To our astonishment, the young receptionist conveys she can neither confirm nor deny this. She does say that the Secret Service teams responsible for securing Veterans Stadium – and their elite bomb-sniffing co-workers – *are* staying at the hotel!

Entering the elevator, we're met by a stout, soldierly individual wearing a heavily pocketed black jacket and matching pants. In his right hand is the operative end of a leather leash. On the business end is a very alert and very controlled, dark-sable-colored dog with very big ears and a very big mouth. Upon making eye contact with the paramilitary-clad handler, Valerie sweetly asks, "Is this Rudy or Beno?" Visibly startled, the Secret Service agent snaps, "How would you know to ask that question?"

Valerie politely informs him that we noticed the matching white vans and deduced one of the names on the windows must belong to our four-legged passenger. Satisfied with her response, the handler in all-black tells us this is actually Kevin and he is, in fact, staying at our hotel.

She also asks if Kevin is a German Shepherd. We're informed he and his two highly trained counterparts are a similar breed called Malinois. During our brief ascent, we also learn these Belgian shepherding dogs are extremely obedient, constantly alert, easy to train, and ideal bomb-sniffing partners.

After the kind of good night's sleep that only comes from lodging with Secret Service dogs, Valerie and I meet Julie and Gary at day-break. Our plan is to be at Veterans Stadium before 9:00 a.m. Today's historical matchup is scheduled to kick off at 12:30 this afternoon. Even so, we know that to *truly* experience an Army-Navy game, we need to arrive at its venue by 0900 hours.

Crossing The Vet's vast parking lot, we notice an inordinate number of dark SUVs and nondescript vans circumnavigating the massive structure. Security personnel with black assault rifles stand at each entrance. Drawing closer, we see the silhouettes of several two-man teams strategically located along the uppermost rim of the stadium.

Once through the extended security line, we're hit with the unexpected sound of rapidly approaching sirens. From across the entrance of the main parking lot, a cavalcade of State Police motorcycles, Highway Patrol cars, and black SUVs escort three luxury motor coaches, and then *another* three luxury motor coaches, at a significant rate of speed to the south side of the stadium. The sight of these three team buses of each academy brings a cheer from the swelling crowd outside the gates.

It's been said all Americans should attend an Army-Navy game to fully appreciate what it means to live in this free nation. Our coveted tickets secured by lieutenant colonel Bliss provide front-row evidence to us that this is so. With the mid-morning sun creeping into the stadium, the Corps of Cadets progress with military precision across the field. Walking to our seats, we watch hundreds of ruddy-cheeked 20-somethings march to a solitary drumbeat.

As the seemingly never-ending procession fills the field, the magnitude of where we are hits us. I'm on the aisle at the far left of our row, aligned with the 40-yard-line. Surrounding us are former players and coaches who in our eyes are all heroes. And, unequivocally, some truly *are*.

Two rows down from us is Glen Davis, the speedier half of the famous duo known as "Mr. Inside and Mr. Outside," who played on the National Championship teams fielded by Army from 1944 through 1946. The other half of this unstoppable backfield, Felix "Doc" Blanchard – Mr. Inside – won the Heisman Trophy in 1945. Twelve months later, Mr. Outside won this most prestigious individual award in all of sports.

That 1946 Heisman-winning season for Davis included what many historians call the "game of the century," a knockdown grudge match against the Notre Dame Fighting Irish at Yankee Stadium that ended in a scoreless tie. It also saw Davis finish without losing a single game – for the third consecutive year.

In an era dominated by stifling defenses and low-scoring games, Davis rushed for nearly 3,000 yards, caught for another 850 yards, and even threw – from his halfback position! – for an additional 1,172 yards. All punctuated by just how challenging it was for teams to move the ball during this decade. (Army gave up a total of only 46 points during the entire 1945 season and shut out five of nine regular-season opponents.)

To our immediate right, a flood of officers-to-be quickly transforms the entire lower quarter of the stands into a rolling sea of dark gray overcoats. As we watch the fledgling personnel settle into their seats, I spot John Wooden a few rows down from us. Given that the legendary college basketball coach served almost three years as a lieutenant in the Navy during World War II, we surmise he must be a guest of a former Black Knight.

With kickoff more than an hour away, Gary and I set out for photo opportunities along the Army sideline. Walking at field-level toward the end zone, we come upon two large brown letter A's on the ass end of two large brown asses. Sitting atop each freshly shaven beast of burden is a sharply dressed cadet wearing a long dark trench coat and a gray service cap.

As official mascots of the United States Military Academy, two mules attend all home games and this annual battle in Philadelphia. This year's pair, Traveler and Trooper, come from a long line of donkey-horse offspring.

In 1899, an officer stationed at the Philadelphia Quartermaster Depot realized the team needed a mascot to rival Navy's live goat. The strong, stubborn mounts were an obvious choice given their storied past as pack animals for the Calvary. Since 1936, seventeen representatives from the U.S. Mule Corps have assumed the role of mascots. All have been male except Buckshot, who in 1964, was a gift from the United States Air Force Academy in exchange for a ceremonial sword.

Making our way past the alliteratively-named equine, we find ourselves amid the Army cheerleading squad. Handing my camera to Gary, I wrap my arm around their costumed medieval mascot, who looks a lot like Darth Vader. At the same time, a pixyish cheerleader hands me her spirit sign, with "GO" on one side and "ARMY" on the other. I pose for a few shots with the faux leader of the Dark Side and then spontaneously raise the sign overhead. I am immediately met with a resounding "ARMY!" from the gray overcoats in the lower section.

After several more blaring responses to my improvisational fandom, Gary and I realize players are entering the field for pregame warm-ups. Heading back to our seats, we are hit with a sound so deafening it shakes the walls of the now capacity-filled stadium. It escapes no one that evil rained down upon the unsuspecting streets of New York City less than two months earlier, and our minds race to the unthinkable.

Gary and I instinctively turn toward the explosion, just in time to see the glistening tail wings of two U.S. Navy F/A-18 fighter jets disappear over the rim of Veterans Stadium.

Relief floods through me, and I'm guessing everyone else, too, as the entire arena roars at the precision fly-over by the four Hornets zooming at seemingly stadium-height from the Army side to the Navy side. Catching my breath, I turn to Gary, only to be whipped around again by another tumultuous crash from above.

This time, blasting over the brim from the Navy side and directly towards us is the ear-splitting beat of five U.S. Army Apache attack helicopters. With tears of terror and amazement and gratitude, I'd like to report I screamed to Gary, "That was really great!" but, in fact, the words were a bit more colorful.

It's been a challenging season for the Middies, as Navy's football squad is sometimes known.

The Black Knights can hand the team from Annapolis their tenth straight loss in this final game of the season, a fact not missing from the spirit-videos on the in-stadium big screens: "Two tickets on the fifty-yard-line: $300.00. Matching Army sweatshirts: $90.00. Navy's first winless season since 1948: Priceless!" Other lighthearted vignettes created by students at both academies feature a montage of "Beat Navy" flags from posts around the globe, numerous animated skits depicting inter-branch superiority, and today's crowd favorite, a real-life night-vision "kid"-napping of the Navy mascots in the back of a Humvee.

Both teams proceed to the tunnels following pregame warm-ups. Army is in their home team solid black jerseys, gold pants with a black stripe down the sides, and matching gold helmets. Navy wears traveling white jerseys, pale gold pants, and solid gold headgear. The restless stadium fills to standing-room-only, which seems appropriate given that the white-capped Navy underclassmen and the gray-suited Army cadets will stand for the entire game.

On this unusually warm first day of December, the game officials position themselves at midfield. Following the lead of the lettermen surrounding us, we look to the brilliant blue sky. Slowly drifting into view, several black dots begin to swirl into yellow and blue rectangles. As they grow larger, "SEALS" in oversized block letters can be seen across each canopy.

Gliding into the vast opening of Veterans Stadium are members of the Navy Parachute Display Team. Each has more than five years of jumps on the Navy Parachute Team, cleverly called the Leap Frogs. With the game ball in his pouch and the Stars and Stripes trailing behind him, the final flying amphibian lands on the Army-Navy logo next to the officials. The approving roar from the crowd signals that kickoff is just a few minutes away.

In the wake of a few booming compositions by the Naval Academy Marching Band, including the instantly recognizable "Anchors Aweigh," several hundred midshipmen stretch into two parallel lines, barely 5 feet across from each other, at the opening in the far end zone. The future naval officers, dressed in matching Service Dress Blue uniforms, form a narrow corridor at the entrance. As their fellow soon-to-be-officers dash through the passageway, the underclassmen wildly pound each player's shoulder pads.

At the same time, in the corner to our right, the gold-helmeted combat-officers-to-be funnel through an identical human corridor created by bluish-gray overcoats. The Stars and Stripes leads the streaking procession. Senior defensive tackle Brandon Perdue follows a step behind with a black and gold "ARMY" flag. A black POW/MIA flag also flutters ahead of the Black Knights.

Approaching the ceremonial coin toss, Army co-captain and middle linebacker Brian Zickefoose is well aware that even though the team he is about to face hasn't won a single game, neither has *his* senior year gone exactly as envisioned.

The 5'10" 210-pound inside linebacker from Bridgeport, West Virginia and his fellow Black Knights come into this final game touting a paltry 2-and-8 record. Their only wins (both at Michie Field) came against the winless Cougars from the University of Houston and the three-win (and wonderfully named) Tulane Green Wave. Even so, a victory on this emotion-filled afternoon would certainly cap the four-year linebacking career for the future Army Ranger.

With millions of Americans watching – including military personnel, families, and friends around the globe – the almost 70,000 fans in Veterans Stadium eagerly turn their attention to the center of the timeworn field.

A small entourage in gray business suits makes its way from the Navy sideline directly across from our seats. Wearing a non-biased red tie and blue blazer, the current Commander in Chief of the American Armed Forces greets both team captains at midfield and asks Navy's quarterback, senior Ed Malinowski, for his choice of sides. No. 10 in white and gold answers, "Heads, sir."

Ten weeks earlier, Brian Zickefoose and his Army teammates conducted practice as usual, as billowing smoke from the World Trade Center was clearly visible to all at the Academy. The young men on West Point's practice field that day understood, as do all players on both sides of the field today, that the virtues of courage, perseverance, and unwavering respect for liberty make our country the most revered in the world. No attempt, no matter how horrific, to strike a blow upon these virtues was going to change their way of life.

They also understand, because of the orders just a few days ago by the man holding the commemorative coin at midfield, they'll be standing on real battlefields in the months following this battle today.

The Black Knights may have won 6 of the last 10 meetings, but the two most recent have been won by the squad from Maryland. Last season, the Naval Academy vanquished their rivals in a 30-to-28 nail-biter inside Baltimore's PSINet Stadium.

Nevertheless, it's obvious to the four of us – Valerie and Julie in matching gold scarves, Gary in street clothes, and me with a white "Army Football" cap – that the players from West Point are easily a step faster than their counterparts.

For the entire first 15 minutes of play, which seems to have zoomed by at the speed of the pregame fly-overs – and unsurprising, given both teams' propensity for running the ball – the Zickefoose-led defense shuts down every attempt by Navy to navigate the field. Earlier this season, Army's senior tight end Clint Dodson professed that his fellow co-captain Zickefoose is "the toughest dude I'll ever know."

Dauntingly, Army scores on each of their first two possessions: a slashing 60-yard off-tackle sprint by freshman running back Ardell Daniels, and a surprising 42-yard pass from quarterback Chad Jenkins to his senior wide receiver, Brian Bruenton. The scoreboard shows the Black Knights ahead, 13-to-0. A missed extra-point is the only exploit that gives the Naval Academy reason to cheer. Each soon-to-be-officer in the section behind the bright yellow "BB-64 GO NAVY" banner slams together blue and gold sound-makers as the ball sails wide of the goalpost.

Except for this errant extra-point-try, the cadets in gray are enjoying every moment of this first quarter. The rolling chant of "Gooooo . . . You Mighty Army, Goooo!" swells from the rollicking section to our immediate right and quickly fills the entire stadium. A dark trench coat with a skinny soldier-to-be inside is tossed over the heads of the shouting cadets.

Their boisterousness spikes when Navy is forced to punt deep in their own territory. The bull rush converges at the foot of the Midshipmen's kicker and bats the ball to the ground.

Following this disruptive turnover, Army defiantly moves into the "red-zone" with 13 seconds remaining until halftime. The

Cadets' head coach, Todd Berry, sends his field goal team onto the synthetic field for another successful 3 points. The Midshipmen only have one field goal to show for their effort as they head to the locker room. The scoreboard reads: Army 16. Navy 3.

A slight commotion develops in front of our section as a small podium is swiftly rolled into place along the sideline.

Just as swiftly, an Army cadet positions himself with his back to me in the aisle to my left. With continued precision, two gray-coated undergrads rush to face each other on every step, effectively creating a human wall on each side of the aisle. Without any indication of what's about to take place, the mass of trench coats to our right begins a low rumbling chant that quickly ascends to a repetitive, "Schwarzkopf Rocks! Schwarzkopf Rocks! Schwarzkopf Rocks!"

Turning to look over my left shoulder, I see the broad,

assenting face of General Norman Schwarzkopf, the commander of the United States Central Command who led all coalition forces during the Persian Gulf War. Wearing a blue civilian blazer and a solid black turtleneck sweater, the larger-than-life officer strides confidently in a procession of high-ranking military officials descending the aisle toward the now-crowded sideline.

As the highly decorated officer passes, I impulsively shout, "Sir!" This instantly causes the career military leader to snap his head in my direction. Now, I've done it. I ratchet up my courage and say, "Thank you, sir!"

I am sincere. And, I bet he knows it. Because he assertively grins, gives a thumbs-up, and replies, "You're welcome."

With the world watching, Stormin' Norman (a nickname he reportedly is not fond of) proceeds to deliver one of the most confidence-instilling declarations in the history of this country. Using today's clash of gridiron forces as a backdrop, he alerts all nations across the globe that the full might of the United States Military will seek out those who conspire to eradicate our freedoms. At the culmination of each inspiring sentence, both sides of the field cheer with unbridled resolve. We are all on our feet. Patriotic tears well up. As he finishes his brief but powerful oration, the entire stadium erupts with a booming ovation.

Across the field, another small procession of dark suits makes its way down the aisle to our immediate left. Every year, the President of the United States spends the first half of this contest on the Navy side of the stadium and the second half on Army's. (The Commander in Chief of all branches of our military doesn't want to be perceived as playing favorites, even in the stands.)

Keeping with custom, and after navigating the ceremonial gauntlet of midshipmen, the procession stops midfield to greet representatives from the mule-riders' sideline. The affable letterman sitting next to Valerie informs us that, in addition to this showing of neutrality, the Navy assemblage passes the "football" to the top brass of the United States Army.

The "football" he's referring to is the nuclear football – a 45-pound, over-sized black leather briefcase carried by a rotation of military aids from one of our five service branches.

This emergency satchel functions as a mobile command center should the President be called upon to authorize a nuclear missile strike while away from the White House Situation Room. The contents of this ominous "football" include a black book featuring more than 75 pages of retaliation options and procedures, a manila folder with instructions for the Emergency Broadcast System, a pamphlet identifying classified missile sites, and the all-important 3-by-5-inch card of launch codes adorably called "the biscuit."

Following the cordial exchange of pleasantries (and annihilation codes) at midfield, the entourage escorts the commander of our armed forces toward the Army sideline. As the small procession strides with a high-ranking male cadet on the President's right side and an equally-ranked female midshipman on his left, we realize the procession is swiftly making its way to the cadet-lined aisle in our section.

Three resolute faces, obviously Secret Service agents given their nondescript suits and obligatory earpieces, lead the pack. As each pair of nervous cadets stiffens to attention, I struggle to catch a glimpse of the single-file line. Several Army commanders, who appear to be brigadier generals and higher, closely follow the no-nonsense agents. One stadium step behind, dressed in an all-black Army uniform with three gold stripes on each sleeve, is the designated carrier of the "football."

Protruding from the top left corner of the leather-encased attaché is a small black antenna. The gravity of its contents hits me when Valerie points to the metal shackle on his wrist.

Immediately behind the sport-named satchel, just a few rows below us is the President of the United States of America.

Presently, George W. Bush's youngest twin daughter, Jenna, is a sophomore at the University of Texas. Graduating from Austin High School in 2000, "Twinkle" (her Secret Service code name) became a member of her mother's sorority Kappa Alpha Theta at UT Austin early this year. (Her older sister from the same birth, Barbara, is clandestinely called "Turquoise"). Concurrent with today's events, the No. 3 team in the nation from Jenna's school, the Longhorns, will be battling the No. 9-ranked University of

Colorado Buffalos in the annual Big XII Championship Game in Texas Stadium this afternoon.

As Twinkle's father swiftly approaches, Valerie and I quickly switch places so she's in the first seat of our row, up against the backside of the gray-suited cadet. Wearing the burnt orange windbreaker purchased outside Cotton Bowl Stadium before last year's dreary Red River Rivalry, she surreptitiously snaps a picture of the atomic football as it passes by at ankle height.

The most important leader on the planet advances on our row. I furtively lean between the two cadets abreast each other, hold up the two-finger Longhorns hand sign, and abruptly yell, "Hook 'em Horns, Mr. President! Hook em' Horns!"

George W. Bush whips his head in my direction. At this point, one can only imagine the number of well-trained professionals poised on the brim of the stadium silently repeating, "Just give me a reason, buddy . . . just give me a reason."

As the startled 55-year-old President attempts to process my advances, I impulsively point to the bright white Longhorn logo on Valerie's jacket. After an instant of thought, the 43rd Commander-in-Chief replies, "Hey, that's right! We have a big game today, don't we!"

Reaching out to shake my hand, he adds, "Good luck with that!" and turns to hastily rejoin the single-file procession leading him to his seat on our side of the field.

After the few remaining dignitaries make their way to their seats, the parallel walls of cadets begin to disperse. The lanky soldier-in-training, whose back was to us during this unexpected exchange with his ultimate boss, gives both Valerie and me a big hug, and exclaims, "Thank you! This has been one of the most wonderful experiences of my life!"

The exhilaration of halftime immediately carries over to the start of the second half.

Omari Thompson catches the opening kickoff on his 4-yard-line, careens off a glancing blow from the first cover-man and explodes up the field. The 5'7" 160-pound wide receiver streaks past the line of helmeted Cadets along the sideline, leaving all 11

Midshipmen on the gridiron in his wake. He crosses the goal in a blur for a scintillating 96-yard touchdown. The roar from the gray trench coats to our right hits us like the blast from the pregame Apache helicopters.

This blazing runback by the senior from Miami, Florida is the second-longest kickoff return in the 102-year history of the Army-Navy game. Only a runback during the 1901 game by Army's Charles Daly is longer (and only by 2 yards). The graduates in our prestigious section jubilantly high-five each other – and the four of us interlopers – as Army's placekicker extends his team's lead to 20 points. Only 7 seconds have ticked off the game clock.

This explosive return instantly takes the wind out of Navy's sails and propels the Black Knights into a commanding position for the rest of the game. The Midshipmen do however, close the gap on a pair of field goals from kicker David Hills; the first a career-best 47 yards and the second a 20-yard chip-shot.

With the score now 23-to-9 heading into the fourth quarter, the defenses of both teams dig in to make it tough sledding on the outmoded artificial turf. Another field goal by the Cadets early in this final quarter advances their lead 3 more points.

With less than 3 minutes left in the game, Navy attempts to strike quickly. Malinowski, unexpectedly, throws three consecutive down-field passes for 36 yards. On his fourth pass, the senior signal-caller fails to account for Zickefoose dropping back in coverage and fires the ball directly into the linebacker's arms at the 17-yard-line. Only 2:19 remains on the game clock. Injured during this interception, this will turn out to be the final play in a Navy uniform for the triple-option quarterback from Pittsburgh, Pennsylvania.

Unfortunately for the Naval Academy, the Middies are only able to cross the goal line once during the entire scrimmage; a too-little-too-late touchdown pass by third-string quarterback Craig Candeto to Steve Mercer with only 23 seconds remaining in the battle. After a successful two-point-conversion, the 17-to-26 score makes the game look a lot more competitive to anyone not in the stands.

Following a failed onside kick, with the final seconds ticking off the clock, the Black Knights proudly line up in "victory formation." The imposing gray section to our left cheers with deafening approval. Having led the entire game, the now victorious Cadets celebrate along the sideline by dousing their second-year head coach with an obligatory Gatorade bath. Co-captain Brian Zickefoose leads the orange bucket brigade.

The character of the greatest fighting forces in the world reveals itself as military officers and team guests pour onto the field inside Veterans Stadium. With the dark shadow of late afternoon descending upon both sections of the still full-to-capacity stands, we watch as one of the greatest spectacles in sports takes place directly in front of us.

Each time these service academies compete against each other, players on both teams stand before the losing student section and sing their vanquished opponent's fight song. This wonderful tradition is then immediately followed by both teams assembling before the winning section to sing the victor's fight song. Though it's a magnificent showing of mutual respect, the goal is to always sing second.

On this first day in the final month of 2001, however, this exhibition takes an unexpected – and unprecedented – turn.

On about the 40-yard-line, the teams have come together to offer congratulations and heartfelt appreciation to their brothers-in-arms by forming what looks like a human yin-yang symbol. The bright Navy uniforms compress into the dark jerseys of the Black Knights. As a cool shadow fills the entire stadium, the teams remain huddled together in this ancient Chinese design.

Rather than race over to each student section to deliver their alma mater, they turn as a group and stand at attention. Facing the victor's side of the stadium, each Midshipman has his right hand over his heart. Solemnly, they sing their fight song alongside the respectful Cadets in black and gold. Army's senior defensive back, Brent Dial, and Navy's fourth-year quarterback, Malinowski, stand side by side in the middle of the bifurcated cluster. Both are immediately flanked by Army's coach Berry.

The triumphant Knights immediately follow with their alma

mater as tears stream down the faces of the winless Midshipmen. Tears roll from the eyes of the victors, as well.

For almost four hours today, the soldiers from these two branches fought valiantly against each other during this one-sided contest. Very soon, they'll be fighting alongside each other in a much more serious theater of war.

Todd Berry turns to Navy's head coach, Charlie Weatherbie for a final handshake. Clint Dodson sprints over to the Corps of Cadets. The senior linebacker climbs atop the stadium wall and into the arms of his ecstatic fellow underclassmen. Valerie's eyes, for the second year in a row on our quest, well up in response to the spectacle on the field. However, this year, it's because of much different emotions.

Settling onto a rickety barstool in a downtown Philadelphia corner bar, I await the kickoff to the annual Civil War between the Oregon State Beavers and the University of Oregon Ducks. The talking heads on Sports Center mention that today's Army-Navy game was the most-watched game of all college football contests in the past ten years.

Valerie, Julie, and Gary have opted for a celebratory dinner at a restaurant down the street rather than watch the grudge match about to take place in a downpour in Eugene.

Just as the Pacific Northwest rivalry is about to start, three spirited revelers enter the quaint single-room neighborhood tavern and sit to my immediate right at the long, mahogany bar. I notice a temporary Army tattoo on the left cheek of the golden-haired young lady as she orders a drink. Keenly, I ask if she and her friends attended today's game at The Vet. She readily replies they *did*; and, that they had a great time. She follows by asking me the same question.

"Not only did I have a tremendous time," I exclaim, "I got to shake hands with the President of the United States at halftime!"

"No WAY! THAT was YOU!" shouts her boyfriend sitting to her right. "We were in the stands and I hollered for my girlfriend to look at the Jumbotron because some couple just stopped the President with their Texas Longhorns jacket!"

The following morning, *The Baltimore Sun* runs an article chronicling how players from both military squads proclaimed they were fully aware the world was watching.

"You could feel it, before the game," said Navy's placekicker Hills. "The country rallied around us. The week before, at Notre Dame, as we got off the bus, people were clapping and cheering for a 0-8 team. It wasn't a good-luck-on-the-field cheer, but a deep-in-the-gut cheer because of what was to come."

Zickefoose, who played far beyond his slight (for Division I-A) size and who led his defense in holding Navy to only 97 rushing yards and 142 passing yards, put it this way: "Everyone had this big sense of patriotism. It made you feel great; but it also gave you a sense of, 'Hey, don't screw this up.'"

His co-captain on offense, Clint Dodson, added, "I must have done three or four [media] interviews every night for two weeks before the game. It was really intense. We saw the game as a rallying cry for both the military and America. We said, 'Let's show them the character of the people who are going to lead this country.'"

CHAPTER FOUR
Swamped in Knoxville
2002 Florida | Tennessee

The *Art of War* identifies five factors that determine the outcome of any battle. In this famed Chinese military strategy book, written in the second century BC, general Sun Tzu states how each – *mission, weather, terrain, leadership*, and *strategy* – is inextricably linked to one another in warfare among armies and nations. The same holds true for clashes between football squads.

And, in both types of combat, none may have a greater impact upon the others than *weather*.

College football is an all-weather sport. There's almost no meteorological condition in which it has not been played. In 1950, The Ohio State Buckeyes hosted the Michigan Wolverines in one of the coldest games on record. Along with 5 inches of snow on the frozen turf, blizzard-force winds howled throughout the stadium. The thermometer peaked at 10 degrees Fahrenheit. Despite gaining only 27 yards – and zero first downs – the visiting team beat their abominable rival 9-to-3, in what's become known as the Snow Bowl.

A more recent clash was possibly even more severe. With a kickoff temperature of 5 degrees below zero, the 2013 Football Championship Series (FCS, and formerly known as Division I-AA) second-round playoff game between the Coastal Carolina Chanticleers and the Montana Grizzlies may have witnessed the most inhospitable conditions in the history of the sport. Suffice it to say, this FCS playoff game was not hosted by the Chanticleers from Conway, South Carolina, whose fabulous team name – a chanticleer is a large, flamboyant rooster – adds to its cocky appeal. Even more remarkable than the high of 3 face-stinging degrees in Missoula, the ornately-feathered team from the South upset the fourth-ranked home team 42-to-35.

During my senior year at Oklahoma State, an also later-to-be appropriately-named severely inclement game took place inside Lewis Field. In 1985, the Oklahoma Sooners (who, by now, should be acknowledged to be on par with root canals, tax audits, and Brussels sprouts) arrived in Stillwater for the final regular-season game for both teams. As I walked across campus, the temperature hovered around 32 degrees. By halftime, a freak Arctic blast dropped it to a numbing 20 degrees with a wind-chill of 4 below zero. Did I mention the freezing rain? The entire stadium – the aluminum benches, the handrails, the playing field – glazed over with almost a quarter-inch of ice. All in less than 30 minutes.

Possessing the intestinal fortitude of a college senior – and an intestinal tract fortified with malted "antifreeze" – there was no way I was *not* going to stay until the end of this frozen contest.

As could be expected, the icy field offered little traction – and just as little scoring. The Sooners fumbled six times and the Cowboys five. Spencer Tillman, OU's junior halfback, scored the only touchdown. Two field goals put the 13-to-0 game on ice for the Sooners. The glistening layer wasn't the only extraordinary phenomenon that night. Thunder and lightning accompanied the sleet throughout the entire contest. We are talking apocalyptic weather!

According to school records, attendance that night was a little more than 44,000 fast-approaching frostbit fans. By halftime, less than a quarter remained; and by the end of what would become known as the Ice Bowl, no more than a few hundred brave (as in, foolish like me) individuals huddled in the inhospitable stands, made even more inhospitable by the final score.

College football, by its design, produces some of the most unexpected feats in sports. Twenty-two athletes racing toward each other at full-speed inevitably will result in unpredictable if sometimes unimagined outcomes. The very shape of the ball makes for weird bounces and bobbles, which at times seem directed by fate. However, no other element contributes more to the volatile nature of the game than Mother Nature herself.

With a nod to Sun Tzu, this is about to affirm itself in spades during our next cross-country pursuit of rivalry and revelry.

As the 2002 season approaches, the high-scoring Gators from the University of Florida and the hard-nosed Volunteers from the University of Tennessee are the top teams in the powerhouse Southeastern Conference, known almost universally as the SEC. Both also have produced national championship teams and nationally recognized players during the past decade.

Led by Heisman Trophy-winning senior quarterback Danny Wuerffel, the 12-and-1 Gators capped the 1996 season with a 52-to-20 victory in the Sugar Bowl over their archnemesis Florida State, to be crowned National Champions. Comparably, in the inaugural year of the BCS, the 1998 Volunteers conquered all 13 foes to win the American Football Coaches Association National Championship Trophy, succinctly known as the Coaches Trophy. This improbable perfect season in Knoxville came one year *after* senior quarterback Peyton Manning graduated to the NFL.

Last year's game in this rivalry was scheduled for September 15, 2001. However, due to the inconceivable acts four days earlier, the conference matchup was moved to the first weekend in December. This final game of the regular season was well worth the wait. The Volunteers, ranked fifth in the nation, beat the second-ranked Gators in a 34-to-32 shootout in Gainesville, Florida. Tennessee followed this victory at "The Swamp" (as Florida's home field is ingeniously referred to) with a disappointing loss to Louisiana State University in the Conference Championship game.

Nonetheless, the Vols avenged this second loss of their season with a crushing defeat of No. 17-ranked Michigan Wolverines in the Florida Citrus Bowl. Just as impressively, the Gators from Gainesville rebounded from their loss to Tennessee with a beatdown of the sixth-ranked Terrapins from the University of Maryland in the Orange Bowl.

As we sit down to select this year's game, it's the team that won the National Championship last season I want to see: The University of Miami, who is ranked No. 1 heading into this season as well. I suggest to Valerie that we go to the Hurricanes' sixth contest of the season versus their archrivals. In mid-October this year, the Florida State Seminoles (who are also highly-ranked) travel to Miami's Orange Bowl Stadium.

Valerie, however, would much rather see the team that had the inside track to the BCS Championship Game last season until their rude awakening against the Volunteers at The Swamp. And she politely lets me know it. Having never seen the Florida Gators in-person, nor been to the massive stadium in Knoxville, she really doesn't have to twist my arm much!

The University of Tennessee was established as a state agricultural college when a federal land grant set aside 300 acres along the Tennessee River in 1879. Appropriately, the new learning institution drew upon the official state nickname for its athletic teams. It's said "The Volunteer State" moniker originated from the many residents who willfully fought in the three-year conflict with Great Britain known as the War of 1812.

The newly founded university in Knoxville formed its first varsity football team in 1891. Unfortunately, the Volunteers' maiden scrimmage resulted in a 24-point shutout at the paws of the Tigers from Sewanee: The University of the South. Two other games also stood out during these early years.

In 1905, the nascent team opened the season with a resounding 10-point victory over the Tennessee School for the Deaf. This now pre-kindergarten through grade-12 school still has a football team; the mighty Vikings currently compete in the Tennessee Secondary School Athletic Association. In the second game of that season, fans witnessed Tennessee's greatest margin of victory ever. The Volunteers defeated American Temperance University 104-to-nil.

As most anyone who's attended a modern-day game in Knoxville can attest, the founding mission of this second vanquished opponent utterly failed to take hold in The Volunteer

State. Established during the 1890s in a rural valley approximately 40 miles west of the Volunteers' campus, American Temperance University was to be the cornerstone of a planned prohibitionist community originally called Temperance Town. Today, it's known as Harriman, Tennessee, and sits not far from the Whiskey Trail, which features 25 different distilleries.

In the storied history of the sport, only 40 teams have ever captured a National Championship title. Tennessee has five. Some argue six.

In 1967 – the final year that the National Championship was decided prior to the bowl games – the Southern California Trojans finished atop the AP poll with 36 of 49 first-place votes. The Volunteers finished second with 11, even though they had a perfect 6-and-0 record against fellow SEC teams, while USC had a loss in their conference to the pesky Beavers from Oregon State University.

Though the number of National Championships at this institution in the Great Appalachian Valley is disputed, its had only one official combination of school colors since the original farmland was bestowed by the state. And what a combination it is!

In 1889, the president of the university's athletic association chose the unmistakable pairing of sherbet orange and bright white to represent its athletic teams. Charles Moore is said to have selected these distinctive shades because of his love of the wild daisies that dotted the campus every spring. If that doesn't strike fear into opposing teams, nothing will.

On the weekend before this third game of our quest, Valerie's alma mater is battling the Tar Heels from the University of North Carolina under the lights in Kenan Memorial Stadium. Seizing the opportunity to double our gridiron pleasure, we arrive in Raleigh on the eve of this showdown.

The following night, however, it doesn't take long for the team in outstanding white uniforms to turn out the lights on the home squad. Texas scores on all three of their first possessions. Not quite the homecoming the locals wanted to give their former head coach. Mack Brown, who restored prominence to this renowned basketball school, was the second-winningest football coach in its history, stewarding the Heels to six consecutive bowl games before leaving for the rolling hills of Texas.

With this evening's game well in hand, many starting players loiter alongside the bench late in the fourth quarter. Recognizing No. 4, I holler from our seats, "Hey, Roy!" The junior wide receiver from Odessa, Texas, snaps his head to the stands. "Beat OU!" I shout. Somewhat taken aback, Roy Williams smiles and flashes "Hook 'em Horns" in our direction. Much to Valerie's satisfaction, her team closes-out their performance with three scores in the final quarter to beat Mack Brown's former team 52-to-21.

Even though this weekend's conference clash in Knoxville is between top-10 teams, the state universities didn't necessarily consider each other rivals for most of their existence. In the 85 years since their first game in 1916, they've met only 31 times. Before 1990, the two SEC members had only played a total of 19 contests. Since then, what a rivalry it has become!

Steve Spurrier, the confident (some might use a more ardent adjective) head coach at the University of Florida, grew up approximately 100 miles east of Knoxville in Johnson City, Tennessee, where he was an All-American quarterback for the fabulously named Hilltoppers from Science Hill High School. Upon graduating, Spurrier chose *not* to attend the University of Tennessee, heading instead to the University of Florida in Gainesville. This was due in large part to wanting to play on a team that did not operate from a run-dominated, single-wing formation. It was a wise choice. In 1966, Spurrier became the first Gator to win the Heisman Trophy. He was hired as his alma mater's head coach in December 1989.

In Spurrier's first season, his undefeated Gators traveled north to face the undefeated Volunteers. For the first time, both teams were ranked in the AP top-10. The final score revealed that only one deserved to be. Turning the ball over six times in the second half, the visitors were handed their largest margin of defeat since the beginning of the century. Florida 3. Tennessee 45.

Five years later, both teams again entered the contest undefeated and ranked in the top-10. Led by four-year head coach Phillip Fulmer, sophomore quarterback Peyton Manning put 30 points on the board in the first half to stun the fans at The Swamp. However, Sun Tzu's critical factor contributed greatly to the outcome. At the start of the second half, a torrential downpour erupted above Florida Field. The home team erupted just as violently. In a certified Category 5 storm, Spurrier's squad scored 48 unanswered points in the contest 62-to-37. His Gators scored more points against the Vols than any other football team *ever*.

In 1996, the "Ol' Ball Coach," as Spurrier came to be known, won his fourth consecutive SEC Championship and his first and only National Championship. During this impressive run by the Gators, Tennessee was relegated to the Citrus Bowl. Never one to let a good ribbing pass by, Spurrier famously quipped during a booster dinner the following season, "You can't spell Citrus without U-T!"

He followed this classic one-liner by derisively commenting on Peyton Manning's decision to not enter the NFL draft and return for his senior year. "He wants to be a three-time Citrus Bowl MVP," he said. That season, Spurrier handed Fulmer his fifth consecutive loss. Tennessee would go on to win the 1997 SEC Championship. Florida ended up playing Penn State to a victory in the Citrus Bowl.

We spend a couple of relaxing days alongside the Outer Banks following Mack Brown's victory in Chapel Hill, then head due west through the Great Smoky Mountains (which really do appear covered in gray smoke as the early morning fog settles into the valleys) and into Tennessee.

Arriving in the home city of the Volunteers two days before their scrimmage with the much-reviled reptiles, it quickly becomes apparent Knoxville is very much aware of this contest. Every fast-food marque, tavern sign, and store window is emblazoned with "Beat Florida!" and seemingly every other vehicle flies a miniature flag or sports an orange sticker.

We initiate our pursuit of revelry by making our way to the

"The Strip." This obligatory cluster of college bars and fast-food restaurants, properly known as Cumberland Avenue, runs west-to-east alongside Neyland Stadium.

First stop: a surely soon-to-be-defunct hole-in-the-wall. We ask our part-time server/part-time student if there's any particular tradition we should experience during this Florida-Tennessee weekend. Without hesitation, she exclaims we *must* try fried alligator! Armed with her culinary recommendation, we depart for a well-known establishment a couple blocks north.

Named "Best Bar in America" by *Playboy* magazine just a year ago, Barley's Taproom is a converted 19th-century feed store with a massive selection of draft beers, an upstairs billiard room, and a vast patio overlooking the lights of downtown. As anticipated, the immense red brick establishment is packed with college football fans, most dressed in the logoed apparel of one school. On this pleasant evening – temperatures today were in the mid-80s – the orange-clad patrons spill onto its expansive terrace.

After a couple regional malt beverages, our deep-fried "gator bites" arrive. Ask anyone from this part of the country and they'll tell you – whether they've tried the prehistoric reptilian meat or not – cooked alligator "tastes like chicken." With a wince, Valerie states, "If Southerners consider this an accurate description, they're eating barn fowl raised on mud." The tough, sinuous strips of breaded tetrapod may be a novel attraction, but one bite is more than enough to understand why they're only on the menu this weekend. Another malt beverage to wash away the taste and we're good.

Though the game kicks off at 3:30 tomorrow, we end our evening a little before midnight so we can be up early for Knoxville's acclaimed tailgate activities.

Built in 1921, Neyland Stadium is nestled just a few hundred yards from the north bank of the winding Tennessee River. Following the construction of the colossal arena, residents soon realized this navigable waterway was a convenient route to home games. Over the years, an armada grew and soon came to be known as the Volunteer Navy.

Several days before each home game, vessels of all shapes and sizes moor together for "sailgating" across from the monolithic stadium. Ranging from dinghies to luxury yachts, the collection of boats can be a dozen rows deep across the placid channel. Overseen by a loosely organized group called the VOL Navy Boaters' Association, the unofficial flotilla must abide by this published code of conduct while docked outside the arena:

> Dockage is on a first come, first serve basis. No reservations required. The only protocol is for the larger boats to moor up to the docks; the smaller boats tie off from them. When you arrive, you simply identify a preferred boat to tie up to (one that would match your length or be slightly larger) and slowly approach. If the boat you choose is occupied, the owners will certainly see you and come out to help. If the boat is unoccupied, do not hesitate to simply tie up to them (no one will mind, and you will make great friends).

In addition to the spectacle of sailgating, we're looking forward to several vaunted campus activities, including Volunteer Village, which features local radio broadcasts, interactive games, and live bands before the game. Also on our list is Vol Walk, the team's traditional procession from Torchbearer statue in Circle Park to Neyland Stadium, and Band March; the time-honored parade to the stadium that includes a "salute to the Hill" along the way, "the Hill" being the relocation site of the university in 1828. All this SEC pageantry is to be punctuated by the nationally televised ESPN countdown-to-kickoff show from outside the home field.

We awake at 7:00 a.m. and are immediately hit with a sense of déjà vu. From our hotel window, we see the skies releasing a deluge of mythical proportions. The local news informs us we can expect very heavy rain (an actual meteorological term for precipitation falling at a rate of between half-an-inch and two inches per hour) throughout the entire day. And it's not expected to stop until this evening.

The oversized raindrops pounding our rental car show no sign of abating as we approach the stadium.

Cautiously navigating alongside the Tennessee River, we realize there will be no Volunteer Navy today. There will be no sailgating. Pulling into the deserted parking lot, we also realize there will be no Vol Walk. No Band March. No salute to the Hill. And, most disappointingly, no tailgating. The rain is beating the desolate pavement so fiercely, we actually contemplate heading back to our hotel.

Having committed to being a part of College GameDay, however, we make a dash toward a large overhang outside Thompson-Boiling Arena. Small clusters of fans sporting team-orange apparel congregate between each concrete layer of the multi-level parking garage next to this arena. With the temperature in the low-70s, it's not necessarily cold, but the incessant rain falling perpendicular to the gray mezzanine does have most of the two hundred or so GameDay fans huddling in the covered garage.

ESPN's GameDay first aired in 1987 as an in-game update hosted by Tim Brando. Not until six years later did it evolve into the phenomenon it is today. In 1993, the show was broadcast outside Notre Dame Stadium in South Bend for the showdown with the top-seeded Florida State Seminoles. This celebrated No. 1 versus No. 2 matchup catapulted its ratings. Today's contest is expected to capture a similar-sized audience and is the fifth time the countdown-to-kickoff TV show has been to Knoxville.

Under a large clear-sided tent, the three horsemen of college football pregame sit alongside each other: the program's host since 1990, Chris Fowler; commentator and former Ohio State starting quarterback Kirk Herbstreit, and the only remaining original cast member, Lee Corso.

With their set relocated to an upper-level mezzanine, Fowler comments over the loudspeakers that Mother Nature is sure to have a hand in the outcome of today's highly-ranked matchup. Corso adds something about "Good Ol' Sloppy Top," a subtle attempt at humor based on the Volunteers' adopted fight song. (First recorded in 1967 by the Osborne Brothers, "Rocky Top" was officially licensed to the university upon the death of its songwriters.)

Today's weather-challenged broadcast culminates with Corso wearing a raccoon-skin cap and holding a Volunteers' musket.

Walking in the drizzle along Fraternity Park Drive, we see a small group of brethren holding shiny cans on the porch of a four-columned fraternity house. Hoping to pick up a local custom, I ask the members if their school has a recognized hand sign, something akin to the two-fingered "Hook 'em Horns" of Texas. To my surprise, four right hands instantly raise with index fingers, ring fingers, and pinkie fingers pointed straight up, their middle fingers touching the tip of their thumbs. When looking at the hand gestures from left to right, each spells "V-O-L." We smile in approval and head toward today's venue.

Outside the huge arena, two young Africa-American kids – obviously brother and younger sister – shout to passing fans, "LINE UP . . . FIFTY CENTS! LINE UP . . . FIFTY CENTS!" At that price, whether we need a list of the starting players or not, it's easy to support the energetic entrepreneurs.

Neyland Stadium, the largest of all stadiums in the SEC (and the sixth largest non-racing stadium in the world), is slowly filling to capacity as we stop at a concession stand for impromptu rain ponchos. (Optimists that we are, Valerie and I have again not packed foul weather gear.)

Named for legendary coach Robert Neyland, who commanded the Volunteers for three stints (1926-34, 1936-40, 1946-52), the oversized concrete structure is fully exposed to the elements on this extremely inclement afternoon. Fittingly, Neyland was also a brigadier general in World War II, overseeing the transportation of military supplies through the monsoons of Southeast Asia.

Settling into our seats, if one can actually "settle" on a dripping wet aluminum bench, we're approximately 30 rows from the Creamsicle-colored checkerboard in the south end zone, our backs to the Tennessee River. Unfortunately, the lone Jumbotron is also behind us. Having to look to the sky for video replays promises to be a challenge.

Seated to my immediate left is a fresh-faced woman in her twenties. We're exchanging pleasantries between raindrops when the stadium loudspeakers instruct us to direct our attention to midfield, where a small collection of raincoats is gathering around a microphone.

Fans of the home team erupt as Heath Shuler is introduced to recite General Neyland's "Seven Maxims of Football." Shuler, now a successful real estate professional in Knoxville, was a record-setting quarterback a decade ago when he led the Volunteers to a one-loss regular season and an appearance against Penn State in the Citrus Bowl. The Vols only loss that year (prior to their bowl game) was to the University of Florida on the same field being pelted by rain today.

The Seven Maxims of Football are the most well-known of 38 principles written by Neyland in the early 1930s. To instill confidence, he had his teams recite these seven tenets before every game, a tradition that survives to this day.

As the local real estate agent delivers the first of these maxims, we notice many fans saying the words in unison with the former front-man. "One: The team that makes the fewest mistakes will win," echoes across the field. The entire stadium stands, transfixed, as they recite the tenets together, ending in, "Seven: Carry the fight to our opponent and keep it there for 60 minutes." With the completion of this final principle, the fans scream at the top of their lungs, "GO VOLS!"

As the Tennessee Marching Band, proudly known as the Pride of the Southland, takes the field, the rain is falling at such a rate it's cascading down the bleachers, into the back of my running shoes, and out the mesh at the toe. My seatmate laughs out loud at the spectacle and introduces herself as Amy. At about the same time, the soggy strutting musicians assemble into a geometric formation on the field. The predominantly orange crowd (if not as orange as expected, due to multicolored rain gear and camouflage hunting jackets) goes wild as the band moves with precision.

In less than 20 seconds, all 330 band members transform into a gigantic T stretching from the goal line to midfield. The human walls create an open alley inside the oversized block letter. With a roar that can only come from a crowd this size, the orange team streaks directly toward us through the formation. An enormous Tennessee state flag and an equal-sized, single letter pastel flag race ahead of the procession as it makes a hard left to the sideline.

Following the "You can't spell Citrus without U-T" season, Phil Fulmer handed Steve Spurrier his first loss in the series. Tennessee finished that 1998 season with a perfect record. As impressive, the over-achieving Volunteers were crowned National Champions after their victory over the Florida State Seminoles in the Fiesta Bowl. Today, however, the opposing coaches from those years are not along the sodden sidelines.

At the end of the 2001 season, Spurrier resigned to eventually become head coach of the NFL Washington Redskins. His 12 years in Gainesville culminated with a stunning 32-to-34 loss to the Volunteers. Fulmer's last clash with the Florida head coach ended three decades of consecutive losses at The Swamp. Despite managing only 36 yards rushing, the Gators – led by second-year quarterback Rex Grossman – brought the score to within 2 points with a minute left. On the two-point-try, Grossman's hurried pass sailed out of reach of wide receiver Jabar Gaffney.

Today, the visitors' sideline is supervised by Spurrier's former associate head coach, Ron Zook. Hired after a stint as defensive coordinator for the NFL New Orleans Saints, Zook has just three games under his belt in Gainesville. The replacement to the Ol' Ball Coach vanquished the Blazers from Alabama-Birmingham and the Bobcats from Ohio University (both on his home field). However, in his second scrimmage at the helm, his Gators were shellacked (also at The Swamp) by the University of Miami. Suffice it to say, grumblings are already starting to swirl. (Florida's Athletic Director awkwardly acknowledged they settled on Zook after being snubbed by the top man at the University of Oklahoma, Bob Stoops.)

If Zook is ever to be embraced by the Gator Nation, his tenth-ranked team needs to find a way to upset the fourth-ranked, undefeated home squad this afternoon.

With rain streaming down the back of our ponchos, I notice our new acquaintance is wearing a Florida hat under the hood of her jacket. As happens in packed arenas, propinquity encourages kinship with strangers. With the home team kicking away from us, I lean into Amy and tell her that, given the swamp-like conditions, her aquatic reptiles should have the advantage today. She smiles.

"Let's hope so," she says. "For my family's sake!"

I'm not sure what this means.

I *am* sure that the soggy field looks to immediately be working against the Gators, as Arandric Kornell Carthon (nicknamed Ran), slips to the turf at the 9-yard-line. Rex Grossman opens the inaugural series of the game with an incomplete pass, the first of three during this drive. After nine plays, the visiting team is forced to punt.

The conditions aren't any more favorable for the home team. Their junior quarterback from Northridge, California, Casey Clausen, opens with a fumbled handoff in the backfield fortuitously recovered by Gibril Wilson. The orange jerseys proceed to splish-splash down the field for more than 9 minutes of game time. After 16 consecutive plays, the impact of Sun Tzu's critical component is not lost on the soaked crowd. Tennessee badly shanks their 27-yard field-goal-attempt.

The first quarter ends unforgivingly where it began: zero - zero. Four more punts and the score is unchanged halfway through the second quarter. Then, with only 5 minutes until halftime, and congruent with the skies over Knoxville, the floodgates open on the field. And, decisively in one direction.

After orchestrating a masterful drive featuring a 52-yard pass to wide receiver Taylor Jacobs, Rex Grossman has his Gators a couple yards away from the game's first score. Earlier this week, the 6'1" 215-pound signal-caller professed he was looking forward to avenging last season's stunning home loss to the Vols. During that sophomore season, he was the No. 1 passing efficiency quarterback in all of college football and earned first-team All-American honors, AP National Player of the Year, and runner-up in the tightest race to date for the Heisman Trophy, behind Eric Crouch from the University of Nebraska.

On first down, Grossman hands the ball to running back Ran Carthon. No gain. Quarterback-sneak on second down. Same result. Carthon's third-down dive up the middle falls 2 feet short of the goal. With 5:03 left on the clock, Zook calls a time-out. Then, in a moment of sheer boldness, and reminiscent of his predecessor, the former associate coach opts to attempt to pierce the plane of the plaid end zone rather than kick a seemingly automatic field goal.

The visitors peel away from the sideline to our left and move to the goal line directly in front of us. As we look into the faces of the offensive players standing at the orange and white checkboard, Valerie notices something.

"There's no way they're *not* going to score," she says. "Look at the linemen!"

Standing straight up, waiting for the referee to spot the ball, all six massive sled-movers are staring directly into the eyes of their defensive counterparts and pounding their chests with both hands. It's an audacious display of confidence.

As the rain continues, Grossman takes the fourth-down snap from center and hands it to running back Earnest Graham. The senior team captain is met by the entire middle of the defense and appears to be inches short of the goal. Just then, a collective gasp coincides with the raising of both arms by the line judge racing toward the pile of helmets and limbs.

Zook's bold decision was the right one, at least according to the call by the officials – and the scoreboard.

This unfavorable ruling for the home team, which continues to be loudly contested by the orange-clad fans in our section, appears to be a harbinger for the remaining minutes in the half. On the very first offensive play after the kickoff, Clausen fails to secure the slippery snap from center and turns the ball over on his 24-yard-line. Three plays later, with 3:40 on the game clock, Florida's seasoned quarterback fires a strike to Carlos Perez, his wide receiver from Hoboken, New Jersey. Their lead is now 14-to-0, causing my new pal Amy to jump out of her seat and shriek and high-five both Valerie and me. Now that's a fan!

As the ensuing kickoff sails toward us through the torrential skies, Tennessee's returner, Corey Larkins, unwisely attempts to field the ball on the bounce. Unable to handle the slick pigskin, a streaking Johnny Lamar recovers the fumble just inside the 20-yard-line. A massive groan swirls across the stadium. The surge by the Gators on the subsequent series is abruptly halted when Grossman's fade-pass is tipped and intercepted by free safety Rashad Baker.

On the first two plays after this fortuitous turnover, the home team exhibits how critical weather can be in battle. From just outside their goal line, Clausen fumbles the snap from center for a second – and then a third! – consecutive time. The Vols remarkably recover both. Nonetheless, with a little more than a minute-and-a-half till halftime, they're quickly forced to punt.

Grossman takes the snap and finds Perez open once again for a 22-yard gain. As if by will, the ensuing 8-yard pass from the 7-yard-line slips through the defender and into the arms of Taylor Jacobs, to put the visiting team ahead by 21 points. At the far end of the field, Tennessee's mascot, a 7-year-old bluetick coonhound named Smokey, lets out a soggy yelp that sounds more like a whine.

This second quarter deluge is not over yet.

After successfully fielding the kickoff with 30 seconds remaining in the half, the Volunteers incur an offsides penalty on first down. They follow this rain-induced mistake with a holding penalty. On second down, after a 14-yard run, the wet pigskin squirts from freshman running back Troy Fleming and into the arms of the swarming Gators. This almost unheard of *seventh* fumble – all in the first half – by the home team results in a first down just 24 yards from the end zone.

With 2 seconds left on the game clock, Zook races his field goal team onto the waterlogged grass field to tack 3 more unanswered points onto the scoreboard – and straight into the hearts of the dumbfounded Volunteer faithful. A smattering of boos rains down from rows above our heads.

As the teams head toward their locker rooms, Amy remarks that the downpour of precipitation, unlike the downpouring of points by her brother, is starting to lighten up.

"Wait," I say, "did you say, 'your brother?'"

Amy Grossman, one of two ash-blond sisters of this afternoon's visiting play-caller, reintroduces herself and informs us that she and her family have traveled from Rex's home state to cheer for his team; something she has done ever since he began playing organized football in grade school. Marveling at the 1-in-108,722 odds of sitting next to Rex Grossman's sibling, I take notice of her uncanny resemblance to the proficient quarterback currently trotting off the saturated field: same broad eyes, heavy eyebrows, and confident grin.

The rain *is* dissipating as the three of us strike up a halftime conversation about how Rex – having sat next to his sister now for two quarters, we consider ourselves on a first-name basis as well as close friends of the family – came to be the starting quarterback for the mighty Gators from Gainesville. Amy tells us she's from Bloomington, Indiana, and that her father, Rex Daniel Grossman, Jr., encouraged all three of his offspring to participate in year-round sports, "encouraged" being her polite word for "all but required."

At a very early age, Rex exhibited excellent skills, playing in a Bloomington youth football program started by his grandfather in the early 1960s. The first Rex Grossman was an outstanding college quarterback himself, playing four years for his home state Hoosiers from the University of Indiana, and continuing on to play for the NFL Baltimore Colts.

Rex III was coached by his father, also a linebacker for the Hoosiers in the 1970s, from second through sixth grade. However, it was his mother Maureen who suggested he be evaluated as a quarterback in seventh grade. Once in high school, Amy informs us, her brother started three years at Bloomingdale South. He capped off his senior year by commanding the Panthers to a dominating victory in the Indiana Class 5A State Championship game.

Following this state title, the third-generation Rex was recognized as "Mr. Football," the annual award presented to the top player in the state. He also earned the honors of 1998 Indiana Player of the Year by *USA Today*, high school All-American by *Parade* magazine, and top-15 high school players in the nation by *National Recruiting Advisor*.

Amy tells us her brother received letters from a myriad of major Division I schools following his senior season. With invitations arriving almost daily, Rex III heeded his father's advice to not form an opinion until visiting all top schools on his list.

According to his older sister, Rex wasn't heavily recruited by the University of Florida. However, during a visit to the campus in Gainesville, he fortuitously bumped into a white visor while wandering the halls of the offices alongside Ben Hill Griffin Stadium. Stunned yet composed, Amy said her brother introduced himself to the Ol' Ball Coach, and – taking a page from the same playbook I'd employed with Coach Johnson a couple of decades earlier – asked if the head coach would review a tape of his high school feats. Handing the highlights to Spurrier, Rex was pleased to receive a promise from the National Championship coach that he would personally watch at least some of his prep accomplishments.

Obviously, Spurrier liked what he saw in the former Panther.

With the sky over Knoxville concluding its crescendo of cloudbursts, both teams stream across the field to their respective benches. The response from the hometown faithful sounds more like an ultimatum than a cheer, and I'm thinking that Coach Fulmer better have recited *all* 38 of General Neyland's maxims at the top of his lungs to each of his players during halftime. Also, that he needs to find a way to stop the downpour by the visiting underdog team and its first-year coach, especially given this is the same team (and coach) that was humiliated two weeks ago when the Hurricanes rolled over the Gators, 41-16.

Unfortunately for the local constituency, the second half opens with yet another display of sheer ineptitude. Tennessee manages to gain a total of 11 yards after failing to bring the ball out of the end zone on the kickoff. This series features two incomplete passes by Clausen, another offsides penalty, and all of 1 minute of game clock before punting the ball. Valerie comments to Amy that it seems the vestige of the Ol' Ball Coach is rearing its visor-capped head, given the Gators' dominating 24-point shutout lead.

The Vols do finally catch a break when Rex fumbles during another bold fourth-down gamble on their side of the field. Tennessee recovers the wet ball on the 41-yard-line. Even though his team opens the drive with a personal foul penalty, Clausen proceeds to orchestrate the Vols down the field with 5 pass completions, the fifth caught by sophomore running back Derrick Tinsley from out of the backfield for a 15-yard touchdown.

Following a punt by the Gators, the Volunteers put together a masterful 14-play drive on their third possession of the third quarter (which includes an all-but-mandatory quarterback-sneak on fourth down and 1). The series takes more than 6 minutes off the game clock and culminates with a plunge by sophomore running back Jabari Davis. The crowd roars its approval, as the home team appears to be roaring back.

Turning to Amy, I see a look of consternation on her face as the scoreboard flashes 13-to-24, with the extra-point to come. No go: Tennessee shanks the attempt with only 20 seconds left in the third quarter.

Amy also has a look of concern over her brother's lower leg, which he appeared to have injured during the second series of this half. In this opening drive of the fourth quarter, Rex III not only puts his sister's fears to rest; he rises to a level of leadership typically exhibited by only the most elite play-callers of the game. Starting from his own 20-yard-line, with the rejuvenated crowd raining deafening jeers onto the still-sodden turf, Rex moves the ball with poise and precision.

His team's 12-play drive concludes with a 21-yard over-the-shoulder catch by wide receiver Taylor Jacobs in the orange-and-white checkerboard below. Neyland Stadium goes silent. Par for the afternoon, Florida also misses their ensuing extra-point. Nevertheless, they've moved ahead by 17 points with only a little more than 10 minutes left in the game.

The Volunteers' final two series are valiant efforts. Both, however, encapsulate the favored team's ineptitude on this inclement day. The 6 points added by Rex prior to the first drive put the Vols behind 13-to-30. Sensing the urgency, Clausen quickly maneuvers his desperate team to the 10-yard-line; only to give the ball back – after another offsides penalty on third down – when his over-the-middle pass falls incomplete at the goal line.

There's a glimmer of hope when, with 4:39 left on the game clock, cornerback Willie Miles intercepts a pass thrown by Amy's brother. After an arduous 16-play drive, this final push toward the goal ends in the same manner as their previous set of downs. With 17 seconds remaining, the Vols turn over the ball after another incomplete pass by their third-year quarterback from just 7 yards outside of the scoring zone.

Soaked to the core, our clothes are easily twice as heavy as they were when we made our way to the GameDay set early this morning. Still, the dampened spirits of the quickly dispersing crowd inside Neyland Stadium appear even heavier.

This weight, of course, is not felt by our new acquaintance from Bloomington or by the jubilant cluster cheering their victorious gladiators in the corner of the massive structure.

Waving to her brother – and beaming with Grossman pride – Amy wishes us well as we leave the now-cavernous concrete oval.

Driving back to our hotel, the car windows fog-over on the inside due to the moisture in our clothes. We tune the radio to the local sports station to catch up on scores across the nation.

"Do you theeenk," drawls a call-in fan, "that was a tch-down?"

This is the first of four consecutive calls from Tennessee fans with their opinion that the up-the-middle run on fourth down, giving Florida their first score of the game, failed to cross the goal line. Valerie gives credit to the local broadcasters for pointing out that whether it was a touchdown or not, today's 17-point loss was the largest deficit at the jaws of the Gators since 1995.

The timeworn adages from two celebrated military generals were in evidence today as these rival squads played their hearts out on the tempestuous banks of the Tennessee River. The art of war, as general Tzu Sun instructed, is governed by five constant factors, none, as we've just witnessed, more critical than weather. This is especially true considering its impact upon General Robert R. Neyland's primary maxim: "The team that makes the fewest mistakes will win."

CHAPTER FIVE
Welcome to the Terrordome
2003 Miami (FL) | *Virginia Tech*

Some things in sports *can't* be quantified. As experienced in Knoxville last year, the final score of many contests is often impacted by extemporaneous factors that no amount of preparation or skill can overcome. Some things in sports, however, *can* be. Understandably, their cause may be more difficult to isolate . . . or agree upon.

Teams playing at home win significantly more games than when traveling to opposing venues. It's proven they can have up to a 20% greater winning percentage in their own stadium. Co-authors Tobias J. Moskowitz and L. Jon Wertheim, in their book *Scorecasting: The Hidden Influences Behind How Sports Are Played and Games Are Won*, uncovered the following favorable home winning results: 53.9% in Major League Baseball, 55.7% in the National Hockey League, 57.3% in the National Football League, 60.5% in the National Basketball Association, and an astonishing 69.1% in Major League Soccer.

It's important to note that these figures were compiled through exceptionally large sets of data. The authors tallied all winning home games of every Major League Baseball team since 1903 and every NFL game since 1966.

This favorable advantage is just as prevalent in college sports. A study by *Bleacher Report* revealed, between 2001 through 2011, 62.8% of all Division I-A (a.k.a., Football Bowl Subdivision) games were won by the local team. *Sunshine Forecast Enterprises* also discovered home teams were victorious in 60.0% of all matchups played exclusively between FBS teams (i.e., not versus a lower division school) during these same ten years.

Through 2003, the following teams in this top division have the highest home-field winning percentages: 1. Boise State Broncos (97.2%), 2. Oklahoma Sooners (97.1%), 3. Texas Christian Horned Frogs (89.1%), 4. Ohio State Buckeyes (88.3%), 5. Louisiana State Tigers (85.9%), 6. Texas Longhorns (85.5%) and 7. Virginia Tech Hokies (85.1%).

The University of Miami *did* make it to the BCS National Championship Game last season. And, once again, they're a top-5 pre-season team in both national polls this year. Given my willingness to capitulate on our destination last season (and damn glad I did!), Valerie graciously extends this year's selection to me.

She does, however, convey she wouldn't mind a sunny destination.

"How about a team *from* a sunny locale?" I respond.

Aware of its raucous reputation, I suggest we attend the Hurricane's away game in the stadium with the nation's seventh-best winning percentage. My receptive bride eagerly jumps on board when she realizes which weekend this contest falls on.

Blacksburg, Virginia is home to Virginia Polytechnic Institute and State University. Surprising as it may seem, this institution with a very long and very academically focused name has a very good varsity football team. Known across the nation simply as Virginia Tech (or its even shorter nickname, Va Tech), their current gridiron squad is ranked as a top-10 team in both preseason polls. Coached by Frank Beamer in his tenth year, the Hokies finished their ten-win season last year with a victory over Air Force in the San Francisco Bowl.

The University of Miami, following its controversial double-overtime loss to The Ohio State University in the Fiesta Bowl, finished No. 2 in the nation last season. Stewarded by former Oklahoma State offensive coordinator Larry Coker (who was also at the helm of Miami's undefeated 2001 National Championship team), the Hurricanes are loaded with top NFL prospects, including junior quarterback Brock Berlin, second-year running back Frank Gore, junior defensive back Sean Taylor, and consensus All-American tight end Kellen Winslow. Each player, along with their seasoned coach, knows the path to their ultimate goal is through Blacksburg.

Two top-10 teams. Big-time players. Big-time coaches. Huge aspirations. All the makings of a spectacular show. But the most enticing aspect of this clash between the Hokies and the Hurricanes? It's scheduled to kick off at 7:45 in the evening. On Halloween weekend.

Home-field advantage is one thing. A night game in Lane Stadium takes it to a whole other level.

A hokie is a male turkey. Or so most college football fans think.

The word actually has nothing to do with a bird, of any kind. It's not even a word. In 1896, the Virginia Agricultural and Mechanical College and Polytechnic Institute (as Va Tech was then called) held a contest to create a new fight song. According to school archives, a student in that year's graduating class penned a rudimentary cheer that incorporated their abbreviated initials of "VPI" along with "Hoki." In subsequent years, an "e" was ingeniously tacked onto "Hoki." The senior, O.M. Stull, was awarded $5.00 for this winning spirit-song.

Founded as a land-grant military institute in 1872, Virginia Agricultural and Mechanical College primarily taught technical arts and applied sciences. With the evolution of its curriculum, the university changed its name to the mouthful truncated by O.M. Stull. Ostensibly since the school's name just wasn't long enough, they added, "and State University" in 1970.

Neither this full moniker nor its long-winded initials (VPI&SU) worked as a designation for their sports program. Thus, early in the same decade, the college adopted "Virginia Tech" as the official name of its athletic teams. Even among the most devoted Virginia Tech fans, however, the origin of their football team's name is disputed.

As one legend has it, the name "Gobblers" was used in the early 1900s to describe how the student-athletes devoured meals at their training tables. Another bit of folklore claims Branch Babcock, head coach of the 1909 varsity team, attempted to instill camaraderie amongst his players through an impromptu fellowship called the "Gobblers Club."

Whichever – if either – source is correct, 1913 is certainly when their mascot made its first appearance. That year, the student body elected Fred Meade to represent their team. Being an inventive young man, Meade harnessed a small cart to a very large turkey and rode the contraption up and down the field yelling "hokie, hokie, hokie, hy" throughout each home game. Local sportswriters and fellow students became enamored with these sideline antics, which included the ability of his oversized bird to gobble on command.

Virginia Agricultural and Mechanical College played its inaugural football game across a muddy crop field on October 21, 1892, against St. Albans Lutheran Boys School. The newly formed team handed the mighty prep school a 14-to-10 defeat that brisk autumn afternoon. One week later, the young men from the same Lutheran Boys School in Radford, Virginia, avenged this defeat with a 10-point shutout over the same gray-clad Virginia A&M students.

In addition to their original drab color, the A&M College uniform at the time included black-and-white-striped knee-high stockings, which inspired many spectators to comment that the players looked like escaped convicts. Thus, in the same year that the school changed its name for the first time, it adopted its highly recognizable – and unique for team colors – combination of Chicago Maroon and Burnt Orange. Love it or hate it, this uniform combination has remained unchanged since 1896.

One element that *did* change as the team entered the new century was their home field when games moved to a parade ground used for practicing military marches. Ironically, the inaugural scrimmage on this field resulted in a victory over another institution originally founded as a Lutheran male preparatory school. The maroon and orange-dressed athletes scored 49 points to shut out the (just as ironic) Maroons from

Roanoke College that year.

In 1965, the first scrimmage took place at the site commissioned to replace this original venue. The Hokies soundly beat the College of William & Mary from colonial Williamsburg, Virginia by a score of 9-to-7 in the unfinished structure that soon became Lane Stadium. Completed in 1968, the 35,000-seat arena was named after respected alumnus and cedar chest tycoon Edward Hudson Lane, who was responsible for financing the project.

With home-field advantage statistically proven, the obvious question becomes: What are its underlying causes? Most college football fans can come up with several seemingly logical answers. And most will be wrong.

College football incites passion from fans on any given game day. Invariably, this passion manifests into crowd noise that can reach physically dangerous thresholds. Decibel levels in modern football stadiums have been known to surpass those generated by a jet engine from 100 feet away. (The loudest stadium Valerie and I have experienced is the home field of the Oregon Ducks. This claim has nothing to do with local bragging rights and everything to do with topography. Even though it's relatively small, only seating up to 54,000 fans, the stadium is sunken into a hill alongside the Willamette River which causes the roar of the crowd to reverberate back toward the field, an effect dubbed the "Autzen bounce.")

In addition to crowd noise, another ostensible reason for higher winning percentages at home is familiarity with surroundings, including environmental conditions and playing surfaces. It's hard not to argue that players at Boise State University are better acclimated for home games than visiting teams in their conference, such as the Fresno State Bulldogs or the San Diego State Aztecs. Bronco Stadium sits at more than a half-mile above sea level. This, along with the only blue artificial turf in the nation and the home team wearing uniforms that perfectly match this playing surface, could explain their best-in-the-nation home winning percentage.

It's also reasonable to contend evolution has a lot to do it. For hundreds of thousands of years, we've been conditioned to protect our territory and our tribe. This habituation might logically imbue individuals to perform at heightened levels. To this point, British scientist Patrick J. Kiger discovered a player's hormonal system can become highly activated when performing in front of a domestic crowd. In his 2013 article titled *Why Does Home Field Advantage Matter?* Kiger theorizes this is "an evolutionary holdover, related to animal species' territoriality – that is, the tendency to vigorously defend their ranging area against intruders. Indeed, some studies have shown that animals defending their turf tend to have a home-field advantage, even if they are smaller than the intruders."

While these observations could be viable explanations, it turns out something hidden in plain sight has a much greater impact: referees.

In *Scorecasting: The Hidden Influences Behind How Sports Are Played and Games Are Won*, Moskowitz and Wertheim were able to verify that game officials exhibit a statistically favorable, albeit slight, bias for teams playing in their home stadium. This marginal preferential treatment reveals itself in the form of disputable judgments going in favor of local teams, such as a called third strike on the baseball diamond or a pass-interference penalty on the gridiron.

The authors' findings were summarized in the article *"Football Freakonomics": How Advantageous Is Home Field Advantage? And Why?*:

> [O]fficials don't consciously decide to give the home team an advantage – but rather, being social creatures (and human beings) like the rest of us, they assimilate the emotion of the home crowd and, once in a while, make a call that makes a whole lot of close-by, noisy people very happy.

The assimilation of emotions from a whole lot of nearby noisy people also *has* to have an effect on players and what's going on inside their helmets. And, even if one specific incident isn't obvious during a contest, the cumulative impact from the stands can really mess with the minds of 18- and 19-year-old combatants.

On this Halloween weekend in Blacksburg, a whole lot of nearby noisy people are about to definitively prove this theory.

It's the day before this year's game and we have set out along the historic corridor between our nation's capital and the city formerly known as Big Lick. We're staying in Roanoke, about an hour east of Blacksburg at the southern foot of Jefferson National Forest. This colonial town acquired its fantastic maiden name from vast outcroppings of salt near the Roanoke River, which has attracted herds of wildlife for eons.

With morning dew still on the car, we wind onto Interstate 81. A little over two hours later, we make a quick stop in Charlottesville; home to the University of Virginia.

Walking across an expansive commons, we pass a heralded monument at the north end of campus. The Rotunda is exactly half the height and half the width of the original Pantheon in Rome. A couple blocks later, we wander into a well-worn pub off University Avenue. Following our first-ever bison burgers (definitely better than alligator), we drive a few miles to the famed residence in low-rolling Southwest Mountains known as Monticello.

While residing at this 5,000-acre plantation, Thomas Jefferson commissioned Meriwether Lewis and William Clark to survey the land of our current residence. In deference to this expedition, a private liberal arts college in Portland, Oregon was christened in 1867 as Lewis & Clark. Today, that school's Division III football team is known as the Pioneers.

It's All Hallows' Eve in a rowdy Roanoke sports bar on the night before this showdown in Blacksburg. Ghouls and goblins carouse among soon-to-be-fellow stadium dwellers along with a life-sized electric plug holding hands with his girlfriend dressed as a same-sized wall socket. Even though we're enjoying the costumed revelry in this local haunt, our plan is to get a good night's rest so we can be fresh for campus festivities before kickoff tomorrow. Somewhat reluctantly, we'll leave the spirit-rousing tonight to the local souls.

The clear morning sky is a welcome sight as we approach the excessively long-worded polytechnic institute. If I were to choose one word is to describe Blacksburg, it would be "quaint." Driving along Main Street, the two-story, flat-faced storefronts look like a set for a Western movie. Or *The Andy Griffith Show*. Not much has changed over the years to blemish the aura of this being a close-knit, small-town community.

As we turn off Main Street, it's immediately evident Virginia Tech is more than just a member of the Association of Military Colleges and Schools of the United States (AMCSUS). It *looks* like a military fortress. Massive, all-stone buildings feature crenulated walls and concrete ramparts appear constructed as if to defend the institute from invading Mongols or Turks.

The campus also has an instantly identifiable architectural element unique to this New River Valley institution: Hokie Stone.

Formed by more than 450 million years of pressure, this predominantly light gray limestone is excavated from two local quarries owned by the university – one produces gray and multi-colored stones, the other supplies black stones. Most campus structures are constructed from these quarry rocks including the immense Burruss Hall (the main administration building) and the preponderance of residence halls. And most have the charm of a medieval castle.

In 1872, active military training was mandatory for all able-bodied male students at this Blacksburg college. During this founding year, however, its Corps of Cadets did not have a marching band. For the next two decades, except for a lone snare drum used to keep tempo during marching formations, the university hired local bands to perform at parades and commencements.

Recognizing an integral component of its military curriculum was missing, Colonel John Alexander Harman, Commandant of Cadets in 1892, strung together a six-piece drum and bugle group as the first semblance of an organized band. Since that inaugural year, the Regimental Band has become a distinct unit within the Corps of Cadets.

Expecting nothing less from this university with the wonderful team name, this now full complement of instruments is known as the Highty-Tighties. And, being Virginia Tech, the origin of its marvelous moniker is vehemently contested to this day.

Ask one Hokie fan and she'll tell you, much like the source of the team's name, the words "highty tighty" were originally embedded in a spirit cheer similar to "Hoki. Hoki. Hoki. Hy."

Query another supporter and he will attribute the name to an elaborate series of events in 1919, when the school's drum major dropped his baton during a ceremony for Field Marshal Ferdinand Foch, the supreme allied commander in World War I. The bandleader is said to have disguised his gaffe with a salute to the highly decorated French general. Members in the viewing stand supposedly cheered "hoity-toity." Following this display, it's claimed the saying was bastardized by local accents into the recognized name today.

Valerie and I are crossing a vast open green creatively known as the Drillfield. As we approach Virginia Tech Library, a six-story, convex-shaped edifice wrapped in light gray Hokie Stone, a solitary snare drum beats a methodical cadence into the midmorning air. Following in perfect precision are eight rows of 13 identical dark blue parade jackets with large white belts crisscrossed over their chests.

In preparation for tonight's showdown, the Highty-Tighties are practicing their intricate patterns on this historical training field. We stand captivated as the young cadets, male and female, maneuver across the field in matching white slacks and flat-topped white ceremony caps.

Virginia Tech has another officially recognized marching band known as The Marching Virginians. This 352-member assemblage (which, to no surprise, has Spirit of Tech as its second official name) consists of non-scholarship university students and was originally founded in 1974 following an impressive halftime presentation in Tuscaloosa, Alabama.

According to the Virginia Tech chapter of Tau Beta Sigma national honorary band sorority, this supplementary marching troupe sprung from an envious desire expressed by the school's administration after this contest:

> [M]any university officials – including the University President T. Marshall Hahn and his Vice President for Academic Affairs Leslie Malpass – attended the football game. The University of Alabama's marching band, known as the Million Dollar Band, was more than double the size of the Highty-Tighties and performed a show reflecting all of the pageantry, excitement, and musicianship . . . of the Southeast Football Conference. . . . On the plane back to Blacksburg, Malpass suggested, "if you want a big time football team, you're going to need a big time band." Hahn agreed, stating, "I want a band like that."

Big Al's Grill and Sports Bar is an iconic fixture in Blacksburg. Conceived by Al and Shirl Edwards in 1977, the street-level retail establishment was originally Big Al's Hair Salon.

Two decades later, the husband and wife opened this sports bar on the second floor. Ever since, innumerable students and alumni have reveled inside its memorabilia-lined walls, enjoying such colorful local concoctions as Trash Can, 3 Wise Men, and pitchers of Long Island Iced Tea. This Saturday afternoon is no different.

As expected on the day of the biggest home game in recent history, Big Al's is packed. And, foreshadowing what's to come this evening, loud. Really loud. As we squeeze our way to the top of its narrow stairs, patrons appear to be a single entity. The maroon-clad mass pulsates across the expanse of the tavern.

"We've Got Your Game!" is the motto of this bustling watering hole. With a multitude of screens, it's the perfect venue to watch the traditional rivalries held on this first weekend in November.

As we somehow appropriate barstools alongside two pool tables, Oklahoma State's cornerback, Darrent Williams, intercepts a pass by Jason White on the opening play of the third quarter to score a "pick-six." The Hokie faithful may not be watching, but I am as the large screen flashes 24-to-9 in favor of the current No. 1 team in the nation. I exuberantly circle the pool table for high-fives to celebrate this score by the underdog Cowboys.

Unfortunately, as we share several rounds of refreshments with four young pool players, the team from Stillwater fails to score another point in their 98th meeting with the crimson and cream puffs. Despite this disappointment, Valerie and I are having a blast as we share stories with the affable pool-playing students.

Even amid costumed holdovers from last night, our billiards buddies stand out.

A salacious form of derision on rivalry weekends across the nation is to wear school-colored apparel featuring the intentional misspelling of a significantly derogatory directive and the name of the opposing team. Examples include "Tuck Fexus," "FUCLA," and "Huck the Fuskies." They appear to take it a step further in Blacksburg. At least they do today.

With no attempt to obfuscate their contempt with cutesy

wordplay, each of our four acquaintances is wearing a dark maroon t-shirt featuring bold white block letters. Both the verb that begins with F and this weekend's adversary (MIAMI) are correctly spelled across their chests. Valerie chuckles at the sight of this candor. As we're about to take off she leans in and says, "I guess there's nothing hokey about this town's disgust for the dominant team in their conference!"

Throngs of hollering students hastily move from across the dark campus and into the glowing lights of Lane Stadium. Before we can find our entrance, Valerie and I are stunned by the noise coming from the packed arena. With wide eyes, we wonder what are we in for?

The entire arena is ablaze.

Though it officially holds only slightly more than 65,000 fans, the earsplitting music and cheers make the steeply-pitched stadium seem twice as large. Appropriate for tonight, a large black banner hanging from the center of the Virginia Tech student section reads: *Can You Handle the Terrordome?* On this Halloween weekend, I begin to wonder if there really is more to home-field advantage than just a crowd's marginal influence upon game officials. This place is scary!

In early 1990, the politically-charged rap group Public Enemy released its controversial single "Welcome to the Terrordome." This heavily-sampled song was their response to the Greekfest riots in Virginia Beach one year earlier. Ten years later, Virginia Tech's senior defensive end, Corey Moore, blurted the provocative song's title during a dismantling of the Clemson Tigers.

On that crisp Thursday night in 1999, due in large part to the pass-rushing performance by Moore, the No. 8-ranked home team pummeled the visiting squad from the state of South Carolina 31-to-11. The undersized lineman finished with two sacks, five quarterback hurry-ups, and one self-caused fumble he returned for a touchdown.

As ESPN reporter Jerry Punch interviewed the father of beleaguered Clemson quarterback Brandon Streeter along the sideline, Moore sauntered past the camera immediately after his scoop-and-score. Looking directly at the national television audience, No. 56 for the Hokies emphatically said, "Welcome to the Terrordome." From that moment, Lane Stadium became known by this song's disconcerting title.

It's also taken on the reputation of being a house of horrors for most visiting teams.

As we squeeze onto our aluminum bench at the 15-yard-line, the haunting opening chords of "Enter Sandman" detonate across the stands. The already chaotic crowd erupts into an even greater frenzy. Now it's getting really scary!

From the illuminated tunnel at the far end, in perfect timing with the exploding *one-two-three-four-five* guitar riff of this heavy metal anthem, the all-maroon-clad Hokies race through a corridor formed by the wildly ecstatic Highty-Tighties.

For the past three seasons, the Hokies have used this Metallica song for their dramatic stadium entrance. Just before the 2000 season, a high-tech video screen was installed at the north end of "The Terrordome." To introduce the appropriately dubbed "Hokie Vision," a video featuring this forceful track was played in the season-opening game that year versus the Yellow Jackets from Georgia Tech University. Eerily, that contest was canceled due to severe lightning.

The two parallel columns of Virginia Tech Regimental Band members frantically bound up and down as the Stars and Stripes, carried by sophomore offensive guard Will Montgomery, and the Virginia state flag, in the hands of junior running back Kevin Jones, lead the streaking parade across the field. The entire stadium is violently jumping and screaming as well. We can feel the stands begin to shake under our feet.

Now it's really, really getting scary!

Valerie screams something I can barely make out, something about this being reminiscent of the 1989 San Francisco earthquake. The purple-clad fans around us attempt to allay our fears by letting us know this happens every time the Hokies burst into the stadium.

Just when we think it can't get any scarier on this night after Halloween, Valerie shrieks for me to look behind the Hokies' bench. With his arms out in front, walking like Frankenstein's monster is the famed HokieBird wearing a sheet over his head with two ghostly eyeholes. The crowd roars with encouragement as the spooky poltergeist taunts the Miami cheerleaders at the back of the end zone.

The first officially-recognized costumed mascot for the then-named Gobblers appeared at the start of the 1962 season. That year, a young engineering student held a campus fund-raiser. With slightly more than $200, the industrious undergrad then constructed a full-body outfit featuring a head loosely resembling a cardinal. The costume, with genuine turkey feathers, made its debut along the sidelines of the then-annual (and very appropriate!) Thanksgiving Day scrimmage against fellow AMCSUS university, Virginia Military Institute.

Nine years later, the school modified the mascot's neck to over 7 feet tall. The towering burgundy bird became known as The Fighting Gobbler. Tonight's turkey-like mascot, haunting and taunting the sidelines with its smirking grin, first arrived at Lane Stadium – via a white stretched limousine – for the 1987 season-opening contest against Clemson.

Photo credited to Don Askers, Virginia Tech class of 1963

As frightening as the celebrated mascot's costumes are this evening, the night is about to get a whole lot scarier for the overwhelmingly favored team from the Sunshine State.

Virginia Tech first challenged the University of Miami in 1953; returning home with a demoralizing 26-point shutout. The Hurricanes continued dominance over this polytechnic institute for the next 11 successive meetings, including the 1966 Liberty Bowl and the 1981 Peach Bowl.

It wasn't until 1992, the year Virginia Tech joined the Big East Conference, that the schools began to play each other annually. And, amazingly, it wasn't until September 23, 1995, on their home turf, that the Hokies finally notched a win over the mighty Hurricanes. This 13-to-7 victory sparked a run of five straight victories.

Miami has steamrolled through the first half of this season. Their unblemished seven-game streak has been highlighted by a thrilling home victory over at the time No.18-ranked Gators from Gainesville and a defense-dominated win over undefeated No. 5 in the nation Florida State Seminoles.

Tonight, the visiting squad brings a three-game winning streak over the Hokies that began with a 41-to-21 dominant home-field victory in 2000, followed by a 26-to-24 slugfest in Blacksburg, and culminated with last season's 56-to-45 track meet in Miami. This is only the 21st time the teams have met on the gridiron. The Hokies have only been victorious in five of these past contests.

Suffice it to say, the fans surrounding us greatly desire to put this current stretch in a grave.

We both have our hands covering our ears as the teams spread across the field for the opening kickoff. The ball sails from the foot of Miami's kicker through the temperate sky and into the arms of Mike Imoh, standing on his own goal line. With an explosive display of speed, the nimble return-man appears to set the tone for what's to come, bursting 38-yards up the field.

Immediately, the Hokies maneuverer to the Hurricane's 25-yard-line via five consecutive rushing plays. On the seventh play of the drive, following an incomplete pass, junior quarterback

Bryan Randall throws an ill-advised ball into double coverage that's picked off by No. 19 in white. This first career interception for redshirt freshman Brandon Meriweather from Apopka, Florida sends a ripple of dismay through the crowd.

The team with the stylized orange and green U on the sides of its helmets trots onto the closely cropped Bermuda grass known as Worsham Field. Suddenly, the unmistakable sound of a turkey gobble blasts from its far end. The already chaotic crowd bursts forth a huge roar in response to this mating call of the male turkey.

Frank Beamer, who played for the Gobblers in the mid-1960s, was an advocate of this distinctive team name when he took over as head coach at Virginia Tech in 1987. However, by that time, the present name of the team was well ingrained in university lore. In honor of this original name, this unrivaled spirit-sound blares across the stadium at random times throughout all home games. And every time it does, Valerie and I gush with laughter.

Fred Meade and his turkey that gobbled on command would most certainly be proud.

Following the abrupt interception by their fledgling safety this evening, the Canes are only able to muster 3 yards and are forced to punt on their first series of the game. Forebodingly, two offsides penalties (caused by the crushing crowd noise) were called during this set of downs. The maroon-clad defense – and their out-of-their-minds fans – suffocated the stunned visitors from the swampland.

Both teams trade a couple hard-hitting series to no avail until Miami finally orchestrates their way to the 25-yard-line. After a short gain and two consecutive tackles behind the line of scrimmage, the Hurricanes settle for a field-goal-try just 22 yards away from the scoring zone.

Beginning in 1993, when Frank Beamer directed Virginia Tech to a respectable eight-win season in the Big East Conference, his teams have appeared in ten consecutive bowl games and have also won three conference titles. As many college football fans are also aware, Beamer is known as a master innovator of special teams. His reputation for taking risks on these plays has actually earned him a term in the lexicon of college football: "Beamer Ball."

As special teams coach, Beamer places extra emphasis on punt blocking, punt returning, kickoffs, and field goals during each and every practice. The result is Beamer Ball, a style of football characterized by game-changing plays that come at the most unexpected times. This chip-shot field goal is one of those times.

Sophomore placekicker Jon Peattie swings his leg into the ball as it's placed on the 29-yard-line. Virginia Tech's speedy cornerback, Eric Green, who is lined up as a defensive end, races from the left side. Fully extended, No. 1 in all-maroon swats the ball out of the air. The home crowd erupts to a new level in reaction to this 101st blocked kick since the 57-year-old coach took over Virginia Tech football.

Due to the ineffectiveness of Bryan Randall in the first few series, Beamer sends in promising freshman Marcus Vick following this blocked field goal. Most every booster in the stands knows Marcus is the younger brother of Michael Vick; arguably the most famous (and, for his involvement with illegal dogfighting, most infamous) graduate from this institute in Blacksburg.

Marcus's big brother was selected as the Big East Offensive Player of the Year in 1999. That year, Michael led the Hokies to a perfect eleven-win regular-season record, which featured a 43-to-10 blowout over the University of Miami and a No. 1 versus No. 2 national showdown against Florida State in the Nokia Sugar Bowl. Though No. 2 in the nation faltered against the overpowering Seminoles in this BCS National Championship Game, Michael Vick was chosen as the Best College Football Player in the nation at the 2000 ESPY Awards ceremony.

As the first quarter comes to an end, Michael's excitable younger sibling is able to navigate only 35 yards in his first series, which includes four penalties totaling 35 yards against the Hokies.

With both teams held scoreless, the Hurricanes begin the second quarter from their 10-yard-line. After four consecutive plays for positive yards, quarterback Berlin fakes up the middle and pitches the ball to his sweeping wide receiver, Roscoe Parrish, on an end-around. Impressively, the Hokies don't bite on this reverse. Parrish is rudely met by three maroon uniforms on the far side of the field. As the wide receiver struggles for an additional yard, the ball is stripped into the air. The flying pigskin falls into the arms of No. 4 on the home team. DeAngelo Hall, the speedy cornerback from Chesapeake, Virginia, races 30 yards into the end zone just across from us.

We are struck by the loudest outburst we have ever heard. Crazy. Scary. Loud.

The Hurricanes piece together a sporadic 12-play effort after this first score in the game. Following an incomplete pass by Brock Berlin, the drive stalls. (Miami's quarterback tonight was one of the most highly sought-after recruits in the country. If not for the proficiency of Rex Grossman, III, he more than likely would not have transferred from the University of Florida prior to this current season.)

Behind by only 7 points, head coach Coker decides to attempt a little Beamer Ball of his own. He sends his field goal team onto the field for seemingly another chip-shot field-goal-attempt. As the ball is snapped from the 27-yard-line, the defense crashes toward holder Matt Carter with the full intention of blocking their second kick. At the last second, Carter (who is also the Hurricanes' punter) pulls up from his holder position and fires a 30-yard strike to a wide-open white jersey standing on the goal line.

This perfectly thrown pass on this perfectly executed fake field goal hits Miami's tight end Kevin Everett perfectly in his hands. With no other player within 20 yards of the junior receiver from Port Arthur, Texas, the ball inexplicably falls to the turf. Welcome to the Terrordome.

In accord with this dropped sure-touchdown, the visiting team from south Florida is unable to mount any semblance of their national championship-caliber offense for the entire first 30 minutes. For the first time in five years, the Hurricanes fail to score a first-half point. After a 39-yard field goal by Carter Warley in the second quarter, the Hokies lead by 10 points. The teams head for their locker rooms.

With The Marching Virginians (and/or Spirit of Tech) taking

the field, Valerie points to the far end zone. Virginia Tech's costumed mascot has changed into yet another Halloween outfit. This time, the grinning HokieBird is carrying a hobo's knapsack on a stick while wearing oversized blue denim overalls and a red and white gingham shirt.

From the row behind us, a fan in an oversized maroon jersey explains this is the final year Virginia Tech will be a member of the Big East Conference. At the end of the 2003 season, the Hokies will join the Atlantic Coast Conference along with tonight's cross-field opponent. HokieBird is packing up and catching a train to the South.

All 65,000-plus screaming fans are on their feet as Devin Hester takes the opening kickoff of the second half from his 4-yard-line to almost the 40-yard-line. Much to the dismay of Miami fans, their team is once again forced to punt after possessing the ball for only a little more than 3 minutes of game time.

With unwavering support in the stands, Va Tech smashes ahead for 34 yards in the first three plays of their opening possession. Then, while attempting to scramble out of the pocket, Marcus Vick loses control of the football. Junior defensive tackle Thomas Carroll falls on the fumble to rip momentum away from the home team.

Sensing the importance of this sudden-change opportunity for the Hurricanes, the fans in our section raise their hands overhead and begin violently shaking their car keys. The metallic rattle from thousands of keys creates a piercing sound unlike anything we've ever experienced in any stadium. Our maroon-clad friend behind us hollers, "THIS IS A HO-KEY PLAY!"

Whether this innovative noise-making technique, a tradition here since the early 1980s, has an impact during this first play after the fumble by Vick, Miami's quarterback makes a poor decision. Faking the hand-off, Berlin is chased out of the pocket by senior defensive end Cols Colas, who streaks past a poorly attempted block by tight end, Winslow, Jr. Scrambling to his right, 15 yards behind the line of scrimmage, the former *Parade* magazine High School All-American and Gatorade National Player of the Year fires an errant pass directly into the chest of No. 1 . . . in maroon! Junior cornerback Eric Green catches the ball and zooms down the sidelines.

Ceremoniously dropping the ball at the base of the goalpost, Green jumps into the arms of his teammates up against the padded wall of the stadium. The sound is once again deafening.

Living up to its reputation, the Terrordome *is* becoming a nightmare for the visitors.

After both teams exchange three-and-outs, Miami starts its fourth drive of the third quarter from its 20-yard-line. Following four consecutive completions, Virginia Tech's frightening secondary once again picks off an eerily similar throw by Berlin. Chased out of the pocket after bobbling the shotgun snap, the quarterback from Shreveport, Louisiana rolls to his right and throws an ill-advised pass to the only player near the 50-yard-line. Safety Michael Crawford darts down the field with the intercepted ball to the 10-yard-line.

Two quick plays later, running back Kevin Jones dives over the goal to put the home team ahead by 24 points and, with 5 minutes still left in the third quarter, seemingly puts the game out of reach for the Hurricanes.

A minute-and-a-half of game time later, the Hokies drive the nail in the coffin.

After Miami fails to convert-on-downs following the Crawford touchdown, Marcus Vick, standing in the pocket on his own 45-yard-line, throws a perfect over-the-shoulder pass to his 6'4" tight end, Ernest Wilford. The home team stunningly puts their *fifth* unanswered score of the night on the board.

With a 31-to-nil lead, the temperament in the stands shifts from pent-up nervous energy to near-riotous celebrating. Students in purple face paint and orange wigs high-five fellow fans in alumni sweaters and blazers. Lane stadium has transformed from the Terrordome into a giant Halloween party.

With anxiety turning to exuberance in the stands, Valerie and I expect the acclaimed tradition during the break following this dominant third-quarter to be off the hook. Much like the celebrated "jump around" at Camp Randall Stadium in Madison, Wisconsin, fans in Blacksburg enthusiastically do the "hokey pokey" during this intermission before the fourth quarter.

Or so we've been told.

Perhaps our stadium-mates are worried their five-score lead might vanish like a ghost on this frightful evening. Nonetheless, whatever the reason, only the Virginia Tech cheerleaders, HokieBird, and Valerie(!) are putting their left foot in and their left foot out. Proving, maybe, that what it's all about is not the hokey pokey, but victory over their rival from down South.

The visiting team gains a smidge of respect by preventing a shutout on this night of horrors. In the waning minutes of the fourth quarter, Berlin throws a 9-yard touchdown to wide receiver Jason Geathers, after a time-consuming 12-play drive. Unfortunately for their mortified fans, this first score against the overshadowing defense is too-little-too-late. The team formerly known as the Gobblers has gobbled up the Miami offense on this weekend of trickery and treats.

The final seconds tick off the scoreboard that reads: VIRGINIA TECH 31. MIAMI 7.

Thousands of fans pour onto the field. Within what seems like less than a minute, the turf transforms from bright green to deep dark purple. There are so many fans on the field we could easily walk across the top of the crowd to the other side. HokieBird is lying flat on his back with his wings spread wide open above the fervent mob. Floating like a buoyant waterfowl on a turbulent lake, the spent mascot is passed from fan to fan across the playing field.

Being individuals who strive to base our lives on evidence, Valerie and I are aware of the reason why home-field advantage exists. At the same time, having been a part of the living, breathing beast called the Terrordome, it's easy to perceive that other extenuating factors contribute to an edge for teams playing in their own stadium.

Tonight's dominating performance by the Hokies put an end to the nation's best winning streak of 39 consecutive regular-season games. The Hurricanes are the highest-ranked opponent ever vanquished by a Virginia Tech varsity football team. And Beamer Ball, once again, shocked the college football world.

It's not possible to quantify the impact a single intimidating factor may have had upon this visiting team tonight. Nevertheless, we both acknowledge the combination of *all* threatening elements – from "Enter Sandman" to the relentless, thunderous mob in maroon – *has* to have gotten inside the heads of the young student-athletes now slinking into the dark corner of this aptly-nicknamed arena.

As witnessed during our trip to this small-town polytechnic institute, the battle on the field is many times won or lost in the space inside a player's helmet . . . regardless of the location of the game. And that's *really* a scary thought.

CHAPTER SIX

Fans and Formations

2004 Michigan | *Ohio State*

Selected in the first round of the 1983 Major League Baseball draft, Rob Dibble was an All-Star pitcher for the Cincinnati Reds in 1990 and 1991. The right-handed hurler was also voted Most Valuable Player in the National League Championship Series during his first year as an All-Star; the same year the Reds swept the Oakland A's to win the World Series.

As Valerie and I inch closer to the temporary stage along the back wall of an oversized banquet room inside the Buckeye Hall of Fame Café, the former All-Star is called out by the host of today's broadcast to reveal his new ink to the packed crowd. Jeers and cheers fly as the supporting cast member of the Dan Patrick Show, which airs across the nation on ESPN Radio, shamelessly walks across the stage draped with white and red 97.1 FM –The Fan banners.

The star of today's broadcast is a native of Mason, Ohio, less than two hours southwest of this famed Columbus eating establishment. Dan Patrick is also a proud graduate of the University of Dayton, whose sports teams are known as the Flyers. This outstanding team name pays homage to the original Wright Flyer I, fabricated by Orville and Wilbur Wright in their small bicycle shop on the outskirts of this small mid-western town.

The good-natured dignitary conveys how his fellow radio personality ended up with a new tattoo. Evidently, after several toasts to their return to the Buckeye State, the broadcasters challenged Dibble to new artwork following a dinner earlier this week.

Turning his back to the scarlet-hued crowd, the former Major Leaguer rolls up his pant leg. A dozen or so members from The Ohio State University Marching Band strike up a sultry strip-tease number in time for Dibble to reveal a bright red octagon, about the size of a baseball, etched into the middle of his left calf. As if on cue, the home team faithful who make up most of the crowd in the gold-paneled party room lets go a whoop of endorsement for the freshly carved Buckeye symbol.

Even though Rob Dibble never attended The Ohio State University (or, for that matter, any institution of advanced education), he did spend more than a decade playing Major League Baseball in a town just over 100 miles west of Columbus. Also, as evidenced by the tribal designs on his arms and the multitude of other random images surrounding this new blocked letter, Dibbs (as Dan likes to call him) has no qualms about adorning his body with tattoos.

According to our host, he doesn't even need a reason.

As Dibble makes his way back to the stage, Dan asks if anyone has a camera. Referencing a favorite catchphrase on his show, I shout, "Right here, En Fuego!" Dibbs stops. Following several quick shots, the big-league hurler hastily scribbles his e-mail address on a piece of scrap paper. With the intensity he was known for in the majors, the former All-Star instructs me to send these pictures to him in time for next Monday's show. Mr. En Fuego reaches over and thanks us for being such great sports.

On this third Friday in November, the day before the local university's biggest game of the year – the biggest game of *every* year – this nationally syndicated show is being broadcast locally by 97.1 FM, the sister station to 1460 AM here in Columbus, which produces a drive-time program featuring ESPN's Kirk Herbstreit. This weekend, however, the former Ohio State quarterback is *not* here for this contentious clash with the team from the "state that will not be mentioned by name." His absence is attributed to the overwhelming consensus that this year's game is not expected to be much of a contest.

The visiting team invades the state's capital tomorrow with an impressive 9-and-1 record (their only loss, a hard-fought 20-to-28 contest against the Fighting Irish in South Bend), while the home team limps in with only six wins and four disappointing losses. Because of this, ESPN College GameDay is in Salt Lake City, the site of this year's "Holy War" between Brigham Young University and the Fighting Utes from Utah. Tomorrow, the No. 5-ranked University of Utah is attempting to close-out their first-ever undefeated season and become the only non-BCS team to ever earn its way into a BCS bowl game.

When Valerie and I sat down in the summer to select this year's game, we (like the rest of the nation) had no idea the Utes would make this amazing run. The team from Salt Lake City was barely ranked in the top-20 entering this 2004 season.

Pre-season expectations, however, for both contestants in tomorrow's clash here in Columbus were off the charts. The Michigan Wolverines were ranked 8th; while the Buckeyes sat one position behind. This, along with our desire to attend a game within arguably the most venerated stadium in all of college football, cemented our choice.

Fans move in and out of the memorabilia-lined rooms in the Buckeye Hall of Fame Café, which is more of an Ohio State museum than a sports bar. Along a narrow hallway leading to the main banquet room, glass cabinets house a treasure trove of artifacts, including one of the five Heisman Trophies won by a Buckeye player. Another five or six vintage trophies from past conquests are displayed below life-size murals of players in a side room.

Returning to our high-top table, I hear D.P. (another of the host's nicknames) announce that they're going to take a short break. The rat-a-tat-tat from a single snare drum signals to the band to strike up their instruments. The youthful musicians, in full parade uniforms, maneuver to the middle of the teeming banquet hall as the well-lubricated crowd begins to sing a carnival-like melody called "Buckeye Battle Cry." The tempo increases toward the final stanza with the hometown fans screaming, "We cheer you as you go, our honor defend, so we will fight to the end . . . for O-HI-O!"

In harmony with these exaggerated final four letters of this bouncy song, the crowd engages in a ritual we expect to witness many times during our excursion to this Big Ten town. Surrounding the stage, fans in unison raise their arms overhead to form an O. Both hands straight into the air for the H. Clasp hands together over their heads for the I. Repeat the first letter as the surprisingly loud band carries the tune to its crescendo. Passing our table on the way to the stage, Mr. En Fuego shouts, "Man, it's great to be home!"

A squad of bright-faced cheerleaders launches into a well-choreographed routine. The crowd claps in synchronization as five burly spirit-leaders lift their diminutive female counterparts into a pointed pyramid. Descending to the scarlet carpet, each scarlet-skirted girl grabs several scarlet bundles from a bin at the side of the stage as the show host shouts, "Who wants a Buckeyes t-shirt?" The patrons in the packed banquet room, several hundred strong, react as if asked, "Who wants a million dollars?"

Rolled-up shirts fling into the raucous crowd. With one remaining in the hands of a petite young cheerleader, Dibbs points in our direction and hollers, "Make sure he gets that!"

On this weekend last season, The Ohio State University and the University of Michigan met for their centennial gridiron reunion. The home field proved to be advantageous that afternoon in Ann Arbor, as the young men in maize-and-blue soundly defeated their detested rivals 35-to-21. This conquest brought their number of victories in the series to 57. Ohio State has notched only 37 since they first faced each other on a muddy field in the budding college town, 35 miles west of Detroit. The two squads also played to a draw six times in the years since this first scrimmage in 1897.

Slightly less than 200 miles separate Ann Arbor from Columbus. A great deal more separates their inhabitants.

When the helmetless contenders assembled for their inaugural gridiron battle, the border dispute known as the Toledo War (also referred to as the Michigan-Ohio War) had been a real-life experience for some fans on the sidelines that day. Beginning in 1835, for almost two years, both states postured against each other on a narrow strip of land parallel to their contiguous border. Each state claimed this disputed territory situated between the St. Joseph River to the west and the Maumee River to the east as their sovereignty.

Though history books refer to this disagreement as a "war," the outcome was zero casualties, one injury, and the ceding of the land to Ohio in exchange for Michigan's statehood into the Union.

While very little (if any) blood was lost during the skirmish, its significance has never been lost on the citizens of both states. To this day, animosities generated during those two contentious years, and having been passed from generation to generation, are said to be the source of detestation between these major universities.

This year, this year's game truly is a *border war*.

Traveling along the Olentangy River on this game day morning, we catch our first glimpse of a genuine football cathedral.

Ohio Stadium, with its distinctive U-shape, was originally built at a cost of just under $1.5 million. Upon completion in 1922, The Horseshoe, as it's now almost always called, was the world's largest poured-concrete structure. With an original capacity of slightly more than 66,000 fans, many residents and university administrators at that time mocked it as an overbuilt monstrosity and predicted it would never be filled to capacity.

The doubting populace was feeling pretty smug when they saw the turnout for the first game inside the massive good-luck symbol. Slightly more than 25,000 fans cheered the home team to victory that day over the Battling Bishops, who traveled 30 miles from Ohio Wesleyan University. (This Delaware, Ohio school still fields a varsity football team today; it's now a Division III team in the North Coast Atlantic Conference. Since this inaugural scrimmage, The Bishops have challenged the Buckeyes twice. Not so stunningly, they've yet to notch a win over their foes to the south.)

Those who originally lampooned The Horseshoe were proven

wrong two weeks following this initial defeat of the schoolboys from Delaware. On October 21, 1922, an estimated 72,000 impassioned fans filled the monolithic venue to jeer the Wolverines from Ann Arbor. Although they may not have been overly chagrined by their incorrect derision of the arena, the local faithful surely had reddened cheeks following the 0-to-19 drubbing at the paws of the burrowing mammals that day.

Over the years, the stadium has undergone extensive renovations. The most recent facelift, in 2001, added 81 luxury suites along the west rim and increased its seats to 95,000.

One feature that this significant renovation did not affect however, is the awe-inspiring rotunda. Constructed to resemble the famed Pantheon of ancient Rome (but *not* at half its height and width like the Rotunda we visited last season), this architectural element is truly unique to Ohio Stadium.

Carved into the underside of the north-end stands, the concave half-dome stretches more than ten stories high. An arched pavilion showcases three splendid and immense stained-glass panels. The center rectangle features a vibrant red blocked O against a stylized blue and green background, while the panel to its left depicts offensive players in action, the one on its right players on defense.

Everything about The Horseshoe is grand.

Much of college football's pageantry comes from its myriad marching bands and their many traditions. Arguably, none more so than the one which humbly labels itself as "The Best Damn Band in the Land." This self-ascribed moniker isn't surprising given that it's from the institution that emphasizes "The" in its school name. Supporters of The Ohio State University Marching Band also annoyingly use the initials of its nickname in conversation.

Like many marching bands, "TBDBITL" traces its lineage to military assemblages. As combat strategies evolved, the need for marching bands to coordinate battlefield maneuvers abated. Regiments soon were relegated to ceremonial roles at parades, formal assemblies, and social events. In 1878, much like the

Highty-Tighties at Virginia Tech, this marching ensemble was formed to provide pomp and rhythm during the university's military exercises.

In these early years, many universities also assembled musicians along their sidelines. It wasn't until 1907, however, that a band in motion appeared at a college football game. During intermission at the University of Chicago versus University of Illinois scrimmage, students from the home team hastily met at midfield and marched in step as they played Fighting Illini fight songs.

Later that same year, Paul Spotts Emrick, director of the Purdue All-American Marching Band, orchestrated the first halftime show featuring configurations beyond basic military columns. Observing geese flying overhead, Emrick similarly visualized his band maneuvering across the Boilermaker field. The result: the first progressing letter formed by a marching band – a capitalized P.

Since this original maneuver, formations have evolved far beyond a single block letter. On this mid-November afternoon in Columbus, we're looking forward to perhaps the most celebrated of these animated arrangements.

After a stop at Varsity Club Restaurant & Bar just north of the rotunda, Valerie and I are walking on the outskirts of campus when we see, parked along the east side of the arena, a customized 18-wheeler used to transport equipment and field gear. Resting above the windshield is a massive replica of the famed helmet worn by the Michigan Wolverines, instantly recognizable by its "winged" design and accompanying three maize stripes.

Introduced in Ann Arbor after newly-christened head coach, Herbert "Fritz" Crisler, arrived from Princeton University, this iconoclastic design was originally fashioned from stitched cowhide. Crisler perceived that the pattern would enable his players to quickly identify teammates during the melee on the field. The "winged" portion also had the functional purpose of providing more padding at the front.

Whether worn for strategy or protection, the inimitable design became a permanent feature after it was first worn in the 14-to-0 victory over their cross-state rivals from East Lansing on opening day of the 1938 season. Valerie comments that the parking location of this rolling billboard with its creatively-painted cab is surely no accident.

From off in the distance comes the sound of approaching drums. Across the bustling parking lot, striding four abreast, the pride of Ann Arbor strikes up the opening chords of their fight song. Moving in unison through the campus corridors, row after row of maize and blue plumes cascade onto the crowded parking area. At the front, the high-stepping drum major, dressed in his all-white formal uniform and towering ivory hat with its bright yellow plume, ignores the smattering of boos from passing Ohio State fans.

The parade tune echoes across this institution of higher learning. Proclaimed by famed composer John Philip Sousa to be the "greatest college fight song ever written," the composition, titled "The Victors" (though commonly referred to as "Hail to The Victors"), was written in 1898 by University of Michigan student Louis Elbel. Originally, this song of triumph was not well received by many Wolverine faithful, as most considered "There'll be a Hot Time in the Old Town Tonight" to be their fight song.

"Listen to the band members!" Valerie says, as each marching musician lets out a succession of five wispy grunts.

Their "Go. Go . . . Let's-Go-Blue" elicits even louder boos outside the arena. Knowing their one-loss team awaits, the Michigan Marching Band ignores the jeering and boldly marches through the south end.

Most Big Ten fans expected this showdown today to decide the conference champion. Unfortunately for the home team, the season has not played out that way.

Signs of concern in Columbus came early. The Buckeyes struggled to victories in their first three games against the University of Cincinnati, Marshall University, and North Carolina State. The true harbinger, however, came on the road versus unranked Northwestern University, a team with only one win in four games. This overtime defeat in their fourth scrimmage was delivered by the same Wildcats that one week earlier experienced a humiliating 17-to-43 loss at the University of Minnesota. Just as deflating, Ohio State suffered their fourth loss last week to the Boilermakers in Lafayette, Indiana.

This unexpected trudge through this season is easily discernable across the stoic faces of red and white-cloaked fans as we enter the hazy sun-filled stadium today.

Expectations from Wolverine fans, however, continue to be as bright as their team's uniforms. Since their stunning loss in South Bend on the second week of this season, the team in blinding white jerseys and neon yellow pants has consistently improved from nineteenth in the nation to on the verge of cracking the top-5. In addition to an outright claim to the Big Ten title, the visiting squad can, with a win today, also secure an automatic berth to the Rose Bowl.

Favored by almost three touchdowns, the Wolverines are led by their head coach of ten years, Lloyd Carr – with two L's and two R's. The former star quarterback of the undefeated 1967 Wildcats from Northern Michigan University stands at midfield facing the curved end of the stadium. His battle-tested athletes strut across "OHIO STATE" in blocked letters at the far end like Lipizzaner stallions from the famed Spanish Riding School of Vienna, Austria.

Several fans acknowledge us as we settle onto our bright red bench, 20 rows above the turf just outside the letters spelling "BUCKEYES." A congenial woman with hair matching the color of the silvery helmets on the field asks if we're from out-of-town. In my gray sweatshirt emblazoned with "Oregon Football" across the chest, I ask, "Whatever gave you that impression?"

Valerie tells our section-mate about our annual gridiron pursuit, after which the seasoned silver-haired booster informs each new group of fans entering the stands about our mission. With less than an hour to kickoff, our section begins to hum in anticipation. As more and more people inquire about our quest, we surmise we're sitting on the home team's side of the stadium.

Having discovered that this is our first venture to the house that Woody built, four fans seated in front of us turn to tell some of their stories and traditions. They also convey their disdain for the contiguous state that shall remain unnamed.

The round-faced gentleman in the group with cheeks matching the color of the home team's jerseys drolly states, "When Buckeyes fans travel to Ann Arbor, we have to bring our own police force. When Wolverine fans travel to Columbus, they bring their own food!" Puzzled, I ask what he means. "To avoid making *any* contribution to our tax base, fans from the north won't spend money on anything during their trip," he says.

One of his grinning row-mates, also swathed in Buckeyes logos, conveys that they were wondering who'd be sitting behind them. Our seats, purchased from an online auction site, are apparently those of an Ohio resident whom they have known for many years. And, just like every season since he's had these seats, the missing season-ticket holder attends every home game. Sans one. Evidently, he gets so worked up over this annual showdown; he needs to watch it *alone* in his living room.

A husband and wife to my right insist Valerie and I need to learn a fight song to qualify as full-fledged Buckeyes fans.

Summonsing our row, the couple leads a colorful rendition of one of their favorites. "I don't give a damn for the whole state of Michigan. The whole state of Michigan. The whole state of Michigan. I don't give a damn for the whole state of Michigan . . . that cesspool to the north!" We gleefully chime in, once we realize the only variance is the last statement. "I don't give a damn for the whole state of Michigan . . . those Commies from the north!"

The ditty actually ends with "we're from O-HI-O!" in place of the salacious phrases exuded by our row-mates. Their derisive version of the visiting team's fight song originated from a play written in 1940 by Ohio State graduate, James Thurber. Much to our enjoyment, our silver-haired friend sings the irreverent song louder than any other fan in our section.

As the teams head to their respective locker room for pregame pep talks, Valerie comments that we've never seen a stadium so close to capacity this early before kickoff.

One of our section-mates lets us know that *true* fans do not miss opening ceremonies at The Horseshoe. Recognized by many as the greatest tradition in all of sports – not just college football – the floating script from a downtown Columbus theater is about to be unfurled on this pleasant late autumn afternoon.

Many a Buckeye fan might be surprised to learn that the first on-field formation of "Ohio" in script was presented by the marching band from Ann Arbor. During halftime in 1932, the visiting musicians formed their rival's four connected letters after spelling "Mich" at midfield.

Courtesy of The Ohio State University Archives.

Script Ohio, as we know it today, was introduced on October 24, 1936, at the scrimmage against Indiana on this field before us. According to then bandleader Eugene J. Weigel, his inspiration came from the vibrant marquee atop Loew's Ohio Theatre in Columbus.

Across the field, 200 or so band members position themselves into a blocked-letter O, three rows deep, as the resounding first chords of "Le Régiment de Sambre et Meuse" fill the stadium. Composed in 1879 by Robert Planquette, this proud French marching song, with its quick staccato pace and crashing cymbals, was arranged later that year by Joseph François Rauski into a military march. It's been the signature number to accompany Script Ohio since that early game against the Hoosiers.

Slightly askew from the 50-yard-line, the three concentric rows of charcoal pants and matching jackets begin marching in opposite directions. Scarlet plumes flutter above the brim of their parade hats. Leading the outer row of this rotating vowel is their striding drum major dressed in his scarlet and white frilled parade jacket and an absurdly oversized headpiece that looks like a fluffy white beehive. Strutting to the 25-yard-line, with a pied-piper line prancing closely behind, the leader abruptly executes a 90-degree left turn and begins his methodical march toward our section. Each band member thrusts their shiny instrument above their wavering plume as they snap toward the high-stepping leader.

Although the procession appears to be a simple follow-the-leader drill, a section-mate informs us each band member actually memorizes his or her path and its exact number of steps. Also, during annual auditions for the coveted troupe, all prospects perform the entire route solo to ensure they aren't just following their seasoned drum major.

The serpentine procession moves across the field forming the second and third letters. After signaling the location for the cursive "i," the high-striding leader peels away to await the start of the fourth letter. Folding back into the line, he seamlessly slides ahead of the musician playing a bright silver sousaphone.

When originally choreographed by Eugene Weigel, no extra emphasis was placed upon the unique vowel in this four-letter word. At the start of the 1937 season, the innovative director realized the sousaphone provided the perfect design for the lowercase letter and switched the position of the trumpet player with the tuba-like instrument. Unfortunately, due to this newly arranged order, the sousaphone player arrived several measures ahead of the scheduled punctuation. Realizing his mistimed error, Glen Johnson attempted to fill the seconds with the first thing that came to mind. With the packed stadium on its feet, he turned to the home crowd, removed his cap, and took an arcing bow with his oversized metal instrument. The roar from both local and visiting fans instantly convinced the quick-thinking bandleader that this was to be a permanent element of all game-day performances.

Since that fortuitous gaff, more than 800 sousaphone players and numerous honorary band members, including astronaut John Glenn, Bob Hope, Jack Nicklaus, and Woody Hayes have "dotted the 'i'."

This afternoon, as the winding line completes the spelling of their state's name from one 25-yard-line to the other, the high-spirited drum major leads this year's privileged tuba-man to the top of the third letter. Stabbing his gleaming silver baton into the turf, he ceremoniously marks the spot for the human dot. The packed stadium shrieks with glee, and we realize, this is the moment the faithful waits for each game. Still, it's the delivery at the end of this procession that visibly moves those around us.

Accompanied only by the rhythmic thumping of their sousaphones, each member of "The Best Damn Band in the Land" starts to sing the chorus of the "Buckeye Battle Cry." The rendition swells; it sweeps through The Horseshoe, culminating with a resounding "O-HI-O!" that brings most in our section, present company included, to tears.

No span during the 100 games played between these upper Midwest schools is arguably more symbolic of their mutual detestation than the "The Ten-Year War."

This bellicose title refers to the showdowns between 1969 and 1978. Each of these ten scrimmages had national championship implications. And, following an infamous quote, each saw a sage teacher square off against his former pupil.

The "teacher" was National Championship coach Woody Hayes. During almost three decades at the helm in Columbus, his teams finished No. 1 in the nation five times; captured 13 Big Ten titles and, amazingly, achieved an almost 77% overall winning percentage. Hayes had every right to be brash. Following the beatdown of the Wolverines in 1968, legend has it he was asked by a reporter why he went for a two-point-conversion up 48-to-20 with only 6-seconds left in the game. The defiant coach snarled, "Because I couldn't go for 3."

The proficient "pupil" was Bo Schembechler. As a college athlete, Schembechler was a starting offensive tackle at Miami University. (The RedHawks were coached at the time by Woody Hayes.) Hired as a graduate assistant by Hayes in 1952, Bo was promoted to offensive coordinator at Ohio State prior to accepting the top coaching position at his alma mater in 1963. Following 7 years in Miami, Ohio, the career coach took the reins at Michigan.

Schembechler also was no slouch when it came to notches in the win column. Over the 21 years as commander in Ann Arbor, his teams tallied an even higher winning percentage (78%) than his mentor at Ohio State. Only two major college head coaches, Joe Paterno at Penn State University and Tom Osborne at the University of Nebraska, surpassed 200 victories in a shorter period.

Unceremoniously, the fifth game of The Ten-Year War ended in a 10-10 tie at the "Big House," as Michigan Stadium is nicknamed. Following this stalemate, Schembechler was confident his 10-0-1 Wolverines would get the nod, over Woody's 9-0-1 Buckeyes, to play in the Rose Bowl. Even Hayes hinted Michigan deserved an invitation to this "Granddaddy of All Bowl Games." Nevertheless, the Big Ten powers-that-be decided, through a six-to-four telephone vote by their athletic directors, that Ohio State would represent the conference in Pasadena on New Year's Day. The pupil was livid.

He and his ardent fan base blew their collective top when the undefeated Wolverines weren't invited to *any* bowl game that year.

This decade-long battle ended when the team with the maize and blue headgear defeated their hated rivals, on their hated rivals' home field, by the score of 14-to-3. This final scrimmage nudged the Wolverines to one more win than the four recorded by Ohio State during this teacher-versus-pupil feud.

At the southeast field entrance, a smoky-haired gentleman restrains a pulsating wall of scarlet. Jim Tressel, in a white button-down, dark red tie, and signature light gray vest looks more like a financial planner than the home team's commander. His pedigree proves otherwise.

Hired as the 22nd head football coach in Columbus, he was lured from Youngstown State University following two years as an assistant coach at Ohio State. Under Tressel, the Penguins (another great moniker, especially for a team from America's heartland!) captured four national championships and the most wins of any Division I-AA team during the 1990s. They also earned him four Coach of the Year awards.

In 2001, the emperor of the Penguins was hired in Columbus to replace their abruptly terminated, 13-year head coach John Cooper. Many fans perceive Cooper's two victories over the Wolverines in 13 contests – even though he achieved a 111-43-4 record during his tenure – to be the motivating factor for his departure.

Tressel's counterpart, along with the glory of soundly defeating the Buckeyes last season, has triumphed in six of the past nine showdowns in this rivalry. Lloyd Carr began coaching in 1976 as an assistant coach at Eastern Michigan University. After stints in the same position at the University of Illinois and West Virginia University, he became secondary coach in Ann Arbor. At the end of seven seasons, Bo Schembechler promoted Carr to defensive coordinator. Following the departure of Gary Moeller in May 1995, he moved to interim head coach during a nationwide search for Moeller's replacement.

In his debut that season, the scoreless Wolverines trailed the University of Virginia by 17 in the fourth quarter. Somehow, the lifelong assistant coach rallied his team to the greatest Michigan comeback win *ever*. The maize and blue experienced only 2 defeats during that precarious season. As a reward, the 15-year home-town coach was promoted to head coach. By his own admission, he more than likely would not have been elevated to this position had he and his team not dug out of the never-before-experienced hole against the visiting Cavaliers.

As the massive edifice fills to more than 101,000 anxious fans, most of whom would like nothing more than to wash away the disappointment of this season with an unlikely victory over their smug rivals, Valerie turns to the alumnus on her left and asks, "What exactly is a buckeye?" The Columbus grad exclaims, "A lot of people think it's a nut, but actually, it's a nut-like seed!"

Perhaps off Valerie's blank reaction, or maybe to inject a bit of menace, her seatmate adds, "And they're poisonous!"

In 1953, the Ohio buckeye was designated as the official state tree. Three years earlier, the university selected the tree's dark brown kernels as its team nickname. With a light beige patch on their coffee-colored shells, the shiny seeds are said to resemble the eyes of whitetail deer, which thrive throughout Franklin County.

Complementing this somewhat silly name, the university introduced an equally silly costumed mascot, now affectionately known as Brutus, at their 1965 homecoming game versus the University of Minnesota. Several art students that year created a papier-mâché nut-like costume that covered the entire body of its wearer. Today, as Brutus leads the charging flecked helmeted players across the end zone immediately below our section, his costume is a much more accommodating foam headpiece in the shape of the seed.

Having won the coin toss and deferring to the second half, the Wolverines spread across the 35-yard-line. Throughout our section, the pent-up anticipation sounds more like a growl than a supportive cheer. The Ohio State players along the sideline closest to us raise their helmets – many speckled with silver-dollar-sized buckeye leaf stickers earned for outstanding plays and devastating hits – as they watch the ball cross over the white octagon letter at midfield and sail out of the end zone.

A palpable uneasiness emanates from the stands as sophomore Troy Smith leads the Buckeyes onto the field for just his fifth start. The promising young field general took over for season-starting quarterback Justin Zwick during the seventh game of the year. In that contest, after Zwick was forced to the sideline with an injury, Smith completed 8 of 12 passes for only 76 yards in a demoralizing 7-to-33 loss to the unranked Iowa Hawkeyes. Only

50 seconds into today's contest, however, the auspicious ballslinger brusquely ignites the spirit and hopes of all Buckeyes fans.

Standing tall in the pocket, the fledgling signal-caller throws a perfect strike on third down and 12 across the middle to Anthony Gonzalez. With defensive back Ernest Shao falling to the turf, the wide receiver snatches the superbly thrown ball and races across the entire field for a stunning 68-yard touchdown.

An explosion as loud as a jet engine blasts across the stadium. In one spontaneous motion, the rotund red sweater – jouncing like a fire hydrant on a spring in front of me – whips around in my direction and throws his arms around my waist. Violently hugging my midsection and screaming to the sky, I can't tell if the veteran fan is elated or stunned.

As their team lines up for the extra-point after this startling first foray into the end zone, fans in our section begin shouting "Nugent!" "Nugent!" "Nugent!" A hand-made sign asserting "Nugent for Heisman" waves wildly in the student section to our right. Tapping the shoulder of my new too-close-for-comfort friend, I ask if he can explain these cheers of endearment. He tells me they're for their diminutive placekicker.

Mike Nugent, a senior from Centerville High School located an hour west of Columbus, is currently on a record-breaking pace as a Division I-A kicker. No. 85 in scarlet and grey splits the uprights to continue his perfect season-long streak of extra-points.

Using the inertia from this opening explosion, freshman backup linebacker Chad Hoobler smashes through several striped helmets on the ensuing kickoff and violently tackles Steve Breaston on the 13-yard-line. Our section-mates wildly cheer their approval.

Jogging onto the field with his fellow warriors in bright white jerseys, true freshman quarterback Chad Henne is assailed with a barrage of derision from the far end of The Horseshoe. Most fans here today know, in the 100-year history of this contest, no true freshman quarterback (and there have only been three prior) has ever defeated the Buckeyes. Even so, a little berating is certainly warranted in a game of this magnitude.

It doesn't take long for the youthful leader to squelch the mania in the stands.

In less than 3 minutes of game time, Michigan ties the contest at 7 apiece. Henne, who one year ago was the three-year starting quarterback for the Bulldogs from Wilson Senior High School in West Lawn, Pennsylvania, masterfully orchestrates his offense down the field in nine plays, including a perfectly executed 38-yard screen-pass to freshman running back Mike Hart.

My too-close-for-comfort friend turns around with a "just what I expected" expression and grumbles something about a woman named Ann, whose last name rhymes with "harbor", being a lady of ill-repute.

After a flaccid three-and-out by the Buckeyes on the ensuing drive, culminating with a 21-yard shanked punt, the University of Michigan's varsity football team, in only 1 minute and 38 seconds, shows why they're a top-10 team in the nation. A collective groan rises from the stands as the Wolverines take the lead on another touchdown by Mike Hart. Behind a devastating block by his fifth-year senior fullback, Kevin Dudley, the stocky running back simply stutter-steps his way across the goal line.

With the visitors ahead, 14-to-7, the Buckeyes feed the fire of concern burning across our section. In three plays, the home team moves the ball only 2 yards. Fortunately, the Wolverines follow this futility with a similar series of their own and are forced to punt with a little more than 3 minutes left in the first quarter. This smidge of momentum in the direction of the home team is quickly extinguished as the punt is downed inside the 2-yard-line at our end of the field. Standing on the first blocked T of "OHIO STATE," fullback Branden Joe takes the handoff and rumbles out of the end zone to give his team room to breathe on the 7-yard-line.

With the first quarter coming to a close, after starting this 39-yard drive a few feet from their goal line, the undeterred Buckeyes offense heads to the sideline nearest us. During this break, our row-mates circle white towels in the air as the silver-helmeted warriors encircle their sweater-vested head coach.

With the violence of a volcano, the entire coliseum of scarlet and gray erupts on the first play of the second quarter.

From a perfect pocket, Smith sends a graceful arc over the head of senior cornerback Marlin Jackson and directly into the arms of Santonio Holmes. If not for a shoestring tackle by Jackson, the junior wide receiver would certainly have scored. A collective "so close!" washes over the stadium.

Nevertheless, a couple of plays after this 34-yard pass, Smith plunges over the goal line to bring the game within an extra-point of a tie. Less than 2 minutes of game time has transpired since the start of this second period. Once again, the ball splits the uprights after leaving the foot of Nugent. Ecstatic, and still somewhat in shock, our new companions extend us high-fives as they anticipate the ensuing kickoff.

Nugent again sends the ball into the end zone for a touchback. Expecting an immediate answer from the top-ranked offense in the Big Ten, every fan is on their feet as Henne drops back on first down. His senior wide receiver from Detroit, Braylon Edwards, catches the ball for a quick gain over the left side. Inexplicably on third down, the young signal-caller drops the ball on his 28-yard-line. Henne falls on the fumble as the crowd moans another "so close!" The Wolverines are forced to punt after only three plays.

The Buckeyes once again surprise the home crowd as Smith scrambles to his 39. This first down pales in comparison to the next play. From shotgun formation, No. 10 in scarlet delivers a 42-yard dart down the left side to his former high school teammate, Theodore "Ted" Ginn, Jr. Sensing momentum, Smith quickly fires another strike to another freshman teammate. Tight end Ryan Hamby rambles to the 2-yard-line. Receiving the shotgun snap, the former star quarterback at Glenville High School in Cleveland, Ohio (where he was coached by Ted Ginn, Sr., father of his current teammate) hands the ball to Brandon Joe, his fullback from Westerville, Ohio.

Unfortunately, not only is Joe stonewalled for no gain; on second down, Michigan does the same to his counterpart, Dionte Johnson. The visitors are also prepared for the quick jet-pass behind the line of scrimmage to Johnson and immediately tackle the stocky fullback less than a yard away from the goal. The

Buckeyes quickly line up with a little more than 8 minutes remaining in the half. Astutely, Lloyd Carr calls a timeout prior to the snap.

Having traversed two-thirds of the field, the offense trots back to the line to try to cover two-thirds of a yard.

Attempting to deceive the maize and blue, which has overloaded the middle in preparation for a quarterback-sneak, Smith fakes the handoff to Joe, who barrels headstrong into the back of his offensive guard. Taking two steps back, the adept quarterback lobs a fade pass to the right corner of the end zone. The Wolverines don't bite. With his receiver blanketed by their cornerback, the ball falls harmlessly to the turf.

If any solace can be taken from this failed field-long series, the visitors are now 99 yards away from the south end of The Horseshoe.

Impressively, the defense only surrenders 1 yard in the next three plays. Forced to punt, the team in neon gold pants sends the ball to Ted Ginn, Jr. With a quick side-step, he scoots to the Wolverines 33-yard-line. Four quick plays later, the Buckeyes find themselves once again first and goal on the 2-yard-line. And, once again, after three futile attempts, they face a fourth down inside the 5-yard-line. This time, the faux financial planner in the gray sweater vest chooses the safer route and sends his reliable kicker onto the field for a successful 21-yard chip shot.

Nugent puts the home team ahead, 17-to-14, with 2 minutes remaining in the second quarter. Valerie's seat-mate expresses that "he will be ever thankful" if the Buckeyes can only take this unexpected 3-point lead into the locker room at halftime.

His supplication doesn't play out.

On the ensuing series, after another kickoff into the end zone by Nugent, the Wolverines manage to gain only 14 yards while only taking 55 seconds off the game clock. Three consecutive incomplete passes force them to punt with 1:15 left until halftime.

Starting from the 30, Ohio State deftly maneuver across midfield as their QB scrambles out of a cratering pocket for a dazzling 18-yard gain. Following two incomplete passes, Smith, who has already connected on 10 of his 13 pass attempts (not to mention rushed for 75 yards on 11 carries, mostly on unplanned scrambles), fires another strike to Ginn. The catch carries the speedy wide receiver out-of-bounds at the 24-yard-line. Number 85 earns another buckeye sticker for his helmet by kicking a 41-yard field goal to give his team a 20-to-14 lead as time expires in the first half.

If the first 30 minutes on the field have been surprising, we're about to experience something as surprising in the stands.

A great deal of the pomp associated with this sport takes place during the break in the action between halves. Much of it, however, is often unseen by fans as the brief intermission usually means an opportunity to relieve the pressure of pregame libations or secure sustenance for the final two quarters.

Today, as the Michigan Marching Band strikes the first chord as they foray onto the field, Valerie points out that almost no one has left the stands; and those who have appear to be hustling back to their seats. Our row-mates, who have brought us into their fold, let us know that a significant number of fans secure tickets for home games just to enjoy the on-field formations and musical arrangements performed by TBDBITL. (Yes, our new friends use these irritating initials.)

As their rival's band launches into a late-70s pop song, our buddies in scarlet claim followers of the high-stepping students on the field also reduce their band's name to its initials. I try not to roll my eyes when I hear the fluffy plumes that look like dark blue candles lit by vibrant yellow flames are referred to as "MMB."

The visiting cavalcade, which a couple hours earlier was wispily grunting its way across campus to the derision of local fans, wraps up its quick set of over-the-top disco tunes. To our surprise, the scarlet-clad crowd cordially applauds the dark blue troupe as they retreat from the field.

Having shown their appreciation, the Ohio faithful then let out a gregarious roar as The Pride of the Buckeyes (the band's official name) strides across the north end zone. Led by their strutting drum major with his wedding-cake headpiece, 12 horizontal columns swiftly parade in front of our section and launch into their precisely choreographed halftime show.

To the dismay of the dark blue sliver in the northwest curve of The Horseshoe, the Wolverines open the third quarter with a sack from blitzing middle linebacker A.J. Hawk. The 6'1" 249-pound junior defender records his sixth tackle of the day so far. (Not only is Hawk a consensus All-Big Ten defensive specialist; he's also a fellow former Centerville High School teammate of Mike Nugent.) This sack sends a bolt of confidence through the scarlet and gray players and sets the tone for what's about to unfold.

Following three hasty plays, including another crushing sack by blitzing strong safety Donte Whitner, the Buckeyes take possession at midfield after a slashing 21-yard punt return by Ted Ginn, Jr. The home team is unable to capitalize on this run-back and, as quickly as their foes on their first series, punts the ball. The rapid back-and-forth exchange continues, as Michigan futilely executes seven plays for only 15 yards and punts after only a minute-and-twenty seconds of game time.

With less than 5 minutes gone in this third quarter, fifth-year punter Adam Finley sends a booming kick into the waiting arms of Ginn, Jr. Side-stepping at his 18-yard-line, No. 7 in scarlet circles toward the middle the field, stops on a dime as tacklers close in, and makes a 90-degree pivot. Racing past Finley, the freshman wide receiver streaks along the sideline at the speed of a whitetail stag.

Scoring his fourth punt return for a touchdown this season, and tying an NCAA record, Ginn defiantly stands atop the blocked letters of "BUCKEYES" as his teammates jump wildly onto his shoulders.

This spectacular runback, and the ensuing extra-point by Nugent, not only puts the home team ahead, 27-to-14, it puts the visiting team on their heels. One of the now-jubilant scarlet sweaters in front of us leans back and yells above the stadium roar, "Do either of you know why they replaced the turf at Michigan Stadium with cardboard?" Valerie shakes her head. "Because the Wolverines only look good on paper!" She screams with delight as the celebration around us continues to build.

On the next series, the boys in maize and blue once again fail to take more than 2 minutes off the clock after six plays. Adam Finley impressively punts the ball to just a few yards outside of the Buckeyes end zone. As the offense breaks from its huddle, fullback Brandon Joe positions himself 5 yards behind his goal line. With a burst, the 245-pound Buckeye plows for an 11-yard gain. Designed to create breathing room, this explosive play unexpectedly sets in motion another amazing 97-yard drive.

With the Goodyear blimp above the south end and less than 2 minutes left in the third quarter, Smith fires a strike from the 13-yard-line into the hands of his slanting wide receiver from Belle Glade, Florida. Diving into the end zone, Santonio Holmes adds 6 points to the already remarkable score.

Our screaming section-mates hug each other, seemingly more in disbelief, as Nugent increases the lead 34-to-14. They also high-five Valerie and me as if we're the season ticket holder of these seats – who, I imagine, at this very moment must be dancing alone in his living room.

The responding series from the Wolverines is as astonishing as this score at the start of this fourth quarter. After gaining 67 yards in two quick plays, Henne inexplicably throws his first interception of the day. This eleventh passing turnover of the season by the true freshman gives the ball back to the Buckeyes on their 21-yard-line.

Even so, following a quick three-and-out and a punt by senior walk-on Kyle Turano, Henne is back on the field. This time, with a palpable sense of urgency, his team scores their first points since halfway through the first quarter.

Like a world-class golfer, Henne arcs the ball over the left shoulder of wide receiver Braylon Edwards, who sprints into the southeast corner. The senior ball catcher, playing in his final scrimmage against his hated rivals, matter-of-factly hands the ball to the referee as he is congratulated by fellow Wolverines. For what seems like the first time today, "The Victors" song wafts across the stadium.

Reducing the home team's lead to 13 points, the No. 7 team in the nation needed just 56 seconds to score this third touchdown.

As if not enough to tighten the stomachs of the Ohio State fans, their team follows with three inert plays for 3 negative yards. On the following possession, sensing a critical juncture in the game, Lloyd Carr chooses to go for a first down deep in his own territory. Our section-mates once again jump into each other's arms as the fourth-down pass careens off the fingertips of Braylon Edwards.

Just 29 yards away from the goal, Ohio State gains zero yards. On fourth down, cheers which sound like boos pour onto the field. They turn out not to be boos, but the elongated first syllable of their kicker's last name.

Nugent, who currently holds 18 Ohio State records, trots out to attempt a 48-yard field goal. Even with 40 successful tries from this range over his collegiate career, our fellow fans hold their breath as the ball is snapped to his holder, tight end Rory Nicol. The ball sails precisely through the uprights. And the scoreboard rolls over to 37-to-21 in favor of the home team.

This is not the only thing to roll over after this field goal by No. 85.

Following another kick out of the end zone, the Wolverines attempt to muster a hurried attack. Fittingly, given how well the home team's previously much-maligned defense has played throughout this entire 101st meeting, Chad Henne throws a misfired pass over the head of Edwards on fourth down from the Buckeyes 32-yard-line.

After this turnover-on-downs, Troy Smith and his teammates run the game clock down to 1:31 before having to punt to their deflated adversaries. With the sky taking on the hue of the home team's jerseys, and after five plays of desperation, safety Nate Salley steps in front of another attempted pass to Edwards. The leaping interception causes the still-at-capacity stadium to erupt in pandemonium.

During the first three decades that these teams met on the gridiron, The Ohio State University only vanquished the striped mammals from The Great Lakes State six times. Just before their

31st meeting in 1934, first-year head coach Francis Schmidt conveyed that the Wolverines were no different – and no better – than the student-athletes from Columbus.

When asked by local reporters as to how well he expected his team to fare in his inaugural showdown, the former head coach at Texas Christian University replied with a common idiom from down South. In a defiant tone, he stated, "They put their pants on one leg at a time, just like the rest of us."

The Buckeyes scored 34 points in a stunning shutout against the vaunted team from the north on that Saturday afternoon in The Horseshoe.

From that victory forward, every year Ohio State defeats its rival, each team member and coach receives a gold lapel pin in the shape of football pants. Originally designed by two local businessmen, the pins feature the year of the game and its final score. At the end of that same season, the Gold Pants Club was proudly established in Columbus. To this day, it's responsible for awarding the gilded pins to all triumphant Buckeyes.

As the clock on the Jumbotron ticks to three zeroes, The Best Damn Band in the Land raucously blasts a rendition of "Hang on Sloopy" across the stadium. Fans pour over the concrete rim and race toward the mass of players celebrating atop the eight-sided letter at midfield. A lone bell gongs from the southeast tower across from our section.

One of our newfound friends, sounding a lot like Dan Patrick's exclamation yesterday inside the golden-paneled Buckeye Hall of Fame Café, turns around and shouts, "Damn, it's great to be in the Gold Pants Club again!" His face is as bright as his oversized sweater.

Amid the swelling crowd on the field, Lloyd Carr begrudgingly congratulates his counterpart dressed in office wear. The visiting players in now-not-so-bright pants hang their heads as they exit the corner of the stadium following this devastating second loss of the season. As if on cue, the seasoned fan with the helmet-colored hair leans into Valerie and whispers, "You can't spell 'Lloyd' without two 'Ls'!"

CHAPTER SEVEN
The Big Game
2005 California | Stanford

In 1982, the Stanford varsity football squad lined up for the 85th scuffle with their cross-bay rival in Memorial Stadium. The stands in Berkeley swelled to capacity on that hazy afternoon. Anticipation stirred in the hearts of all in attendance as it had every year since the inaugural clash on the east side of Golden Gate Park.

Even so, this showdown barely registered in the consciousness of fans throughout the rest of the country. Most were focused on the clash between second-ranked Southern Methodist University (led by the "Pony Express" duo of Eric Dickerson and Craig James) and the No. 9 team in the nation Arkansas Razorbacks, or on the Toledo War taking place in the Horseshoe. Even devoted fans of the Pac-10 were more interested in conference-leading No. 11 in the nation UCLA versus No. 15-ranked University of Southern California. However, by the time the dust – and band members – settled on the home field of the Golden Bears, the entire nation was fully aware of what is now simply called "The Play."

Proclaimed as "the greatest college football play of all time" by *The Best Damn Sports Show Period*, even the most casual fan would become aware of what many people consider the greatest ending in all of sports, period.

Driving into the City by the Bay, a flood of memories washes over Valerie and me. A decade earlier, with billowy fog rolling over its century-old landmarks, I proposed to my lovely bride-to-be atop the St. Francis Hotel in Union Square. Her answer set in motion our wonderful annual collegiate quest. Early in our marriage, we would routinely spend weekends in this romantic city taking in all its culture and beauty.

On this Thursday afternoon in mid-November, downtown San Francisco is bustling. Not because football fans are streaming into the city . . . but because it's a Thursday afternoon in San Francisco.

Contrary to our most recent pursuit of revelry and rivalry, there is zero indication that a significant showdown is about to be played between the two most prominent universities in this half of the state. No miniature flags atop cars scurrying down Market Street. No caricatures in school colors on windows of the upscale drinking establishments throughout the city's financial district. No ad-hoc radio shows. No derogatory sayings toward the visiting team on fast-food marquees.

As our sightseeing winds down the next day, it becomes clear we will not partake of any football revelry until we get to the prestigious south bay campus. Even though the Golden Gate city is ideal for our urban stroll, with its luxury retail shops and Mediterranean-like setting, we're somewhat disappointed by the dearth of any indication The Big Game is upon us. And then, just as we are about to pop into a pub for a pint, Valerie sees it.

Waving lethargically above the skyline is a massive deep red flag and an equally-sized dark blue and gold flag. The Stanford University flag atop the all-glass high-rise seems to be moving in tandem with its counterpart. "I guess there really isn't a visiting team as far as this city is concerned," I tell Valerie. The flags – the only portent of the annual showdown we've seen – finally ignite a sense of anticipation.

San Francisco is situated almost equidistant between the two schools – the public university in Berkeley is 15 miles across the Bay Bridge, and the private research institution in East Palo Alto a 30-mile drive down the San Mateo Peninsula. While the host campus this weekend, nestled among lush California live oaks, is gorgeous; it's also wont for lodging accommodation. Thus, we've chosen to stay at a boutique hotel in San Francisco, a few blocks from the iconic Transamerica Building.

Finishing our frosty Anchor Steams in the mahogany-lined pub, we return to Powell Street on this clear, cool evening in mid-November. Passing the hotel in Union Square where Valerie said "Okay!" in answer to me asking for her hand, we amble our way to a charming little Italian restaurant on the outskirts of Nob Hill.

The wine list is deep, the pasta handmade, and happy, happy we are. Over tiramisu, I proclaim that if the game tomorrow is half as good as the dinner, we are in for a great time. And then, football fanatics that we are, we talk about "The Play."

After the University of California – also known simply as "Cal" – is only able to gain 6 yards on its final possession of the 1982 slugfest with the Cardinal, the clock ticks down to 1:27. Unfortunately for Stanford, not only are they trailing 17-to-19 as the Golden Bear's punt travels out of their end zone; they used two of their time-outs during their rival's final offensive series.

Undaunted, John Elway deftly maneuvers his team to his 42-yard-line via a fourth-down pass over the middle. Following another perfectly thrown pass, the quarterback for the Cardinal pitches the ball to fellow senior teammate Mike Dotterer. The agile running back (who to this day remains the only Cardinal to earn four letters in both football and baseball) slashes his way to the 18-yard-line. With only 8 seconds left on the game clock, Elway calls his team's third and final time-out. The fourth-down field goal splits the uprights to put the visiting team ahead by 1 point. Only 4 seconds remain in the hard-fought scrimmage.

What unfolds during these seconds still resides in the hearts and minds of college football fans everywhere.

Rather than letting the clock run down to a just a second or two prior to this field goal, Stanford head coach Paul Wiggin chose to have Elway call their last time-out with enough time for a second attempt, just in case there was a defensive penalty during the try. This decision – and the 15-yard penalty for excessive celebration after their successful kick – will enable the home team to ridiculously rumble into the annals of sports.

As the players line up for the ensuing kickoff, with the raucous Stanford marching band assembling behind the home team's end zone, the University of California radio broadcaster Joe Starkey famously quips, "Only a miracle can save the Bears now!" In reality, all it took was ten well-conditioned 19- and 20-year-olds with the will to win.

Squib-kicking from their 25-yard-line rather than the 40 because of the unsportsmanlike foul, the Stanford players race toward Kevin Moen. Fielding the ball 5 yards short of midfield, the strong safety looks up to see several white jerseys bearing down on him. Remembering back to a favorite practice drill called "grab-ass," whereby one squad attempts to keep the ball away from the other, Moen quickly flips the ball to teammate Richard Rogers. This toss sets in motion the improbable series of five laterals, which ends with Moen regaining possession of the ball, crossing the goal – and running right into a throng of Stanford band members who've swarmed onto the field!

Moen jubilantly leaps with the ball held high overhead and crashes into an unsuspecting trombone player!

Like the rest of his Cardinal bandmates, Gary Tyrell was on the field – before literally being *on* the field – because he assumed the game was all but over after his team's successful field goal. And though it will remain controversial to this day, officials rule the play will stand.

As screaming fans swarm the field, Joe Starkey heralds the pitch-fest as "the most amazing, sensational, dramatic, heart-rending, exciting, thrilling finish in the history of college football!"

Most football fans are now familiar with "The Play." What some may not know about this highly improbable – and, by Stanford, just as highly contested – final touchdown is that it was accomplished with only ten Bears on the field: In the melee immediately following Stanford's go-ahead field goal, Cal inadvertently received the kickoff with one man missing from the field.

Following the inaugural meeting between these institutions, which saw the team from Palo Alto defeat the Golden Bears 14-

to-10, the venue for the game has been on the Berkeley campus during even-numbered years and at Stanford Stadium during odd-numbered years.

This first clash featured first-ever head coaches for both schools, Thomas Lee "Bum" McClung at Cal and Walter Camp at Stanford. Recognized by many as the "Father of American Football," Camp is credited with originating the sport's system of four downs and inventing the line of scrimmage. These innovations evolved the game beyond its rugby origins and into the orchestrated offense-versus-defense strategies we're familiar with today.

The now-annual showdown in the Bay Area was first designated "The Big Game" when the teams met at the turn of the last century, in the city then known as "the Paris of the West." On Thanksgiving Day 1900, after two years of consecutive shutouts by the Golden Bears, the Stanford team soundly blanked their in-state rival by the score of 5-to-0. Fittingly, three of their first nine meetings before that shutout in San Francisco ended in a tie.

Not so fittingly, football came to a screeching halt in 1906. And not just for these two budding programs, but for all collegiate teams across America.

Beginning in the mid-1890s, a vocal faction of the American public, purportedly led by then-president of Harvard University, Charles Eliot, began to call for an outright ban of the sport due to its violent nature and propensity for serious injury. Football tactics *had* in fact evolved to a lethal level at the time that The Big Game was entering its second decade of continuous scrimmages. Perfected by the Navy Midshipmen, the "flying wedge" formation very effectively – and very unfairly – overpowered defensive players. An 1892 article in *The New York Times* decried the formation: "Think of it – half-a-ton of bone and muscle coming into collision with a man weighing 160 or 170 pounds."

During the 1905 season, football had become so ferocious that the *Chicago Tribune* published a scathing article denouncing the sport as a "death harvest." This disparaging nomenclature was not far from the truth. By the end of play that year, according to this Mid-western publication, 18 young men had died on the field and more than 100 others were injured to the point of permanent disability.

An injury of a lesser extent also occurred on an Ivy League field. Lesser in severity, if not in prominence: Theodore Roosevelt, III, a starting offensive player for the Harvard Crimson freshman team and first son of our nation's Commander in Chief at the time, had his nose broken – some said deliberately – during the heated scrimmage against their rivals, the fighting Elis from Yale.

The U.S. President, being an avid fan of the game and a responsible parent (and sensing the escalating pressure from university administrators and national media outlets) decided to act.

In early October of that year, the elder Roosevelt organized a presidential council featuring several of college football's most prominent coaches, including Bill Reid from Harvard University, Art Hillebrand from Princeton University, and Walter Camp. This assemblage was to address the inherent danger of the current game and devise new rules to prevent it from being banned on campuses across the nation.

The committee took less than four months to create 19 new regulations, including the introduction of the forward pass to spread the field and abolishing the flying wedge by requiring six players on the line of scrimmage. Unfortunately, the regulations came too late for many major colleges which had already designated football an unsanctioned sport. The University of California at Berkeley and Stanford University were two of those schools.

For the next eight years, The Big Game reverted to the old game. During this forced hiatus, the two institutions from the republic on the west coast challenged each other to a rugby match each season. Fortuitously, the adoption of the new rules initiated by Roosevelt's council proved to dramatically reduce violence on the playing field. The Golden Bears resumed American football in the fall of 1915. Stanford followed suit three years later.

The hastily orchestrated collection of prominent coaches that came together under the direction of our 26th President went on to become the Intercollegiate Athletic Association. We know this

organization today as the National Collegiate Athletic Association
– NCAA for short.

During our early years in the Central Valley, Valerie and I became
friends with George and Irene Segale, an older but active couple
from Angels Camp, California. Though George was a graduate of
Valerie's soon-to-be second alma mater in Stockton, he'd always
been an avid fan of the Stanford varsity football team. Thus, when
the University of the Pacific elected to drop football as an officially
sanctioned sport in 1995, George became a season ticket holder of
the gridiron team from the San Mateo peninsula. Today, he and
his wife are hosting us at their tailgate party in Palo Alto.

Varsity football at the University of the Pacific played a
prominent role in advancing the sport to the game it is today. The
Tigers from Stockton first fielded a team in 1895. However, it
wasn't until the 1930s, when Amos Alonzo Stagg became head
coach at age 70 that the team made its mark in the annals of college
football. Stagg introduced several innovations, including an
offensive man-in-motion and the lateral pass. To this day, even
though it sits idle on the outskirts of campus, the former home
field of UOP football is known as Stagg Memorial Stadium.

During our years in Northern California, a former Pacific
Tiger was in charge of the sidelines in Stockton. Walt Harris, after
earning his master's degree at UOP, spent almost two decades as
an assistant coach at several prominent football programs
(including the Golden Bears from Berkeley). In 1989, he became
head coach of his alma mater. Although Harris left the University
of the Pacific after only two years, he did instill a sense of com-
petitiveness in the overachieving team from the Central Valley.

Driving south out of the city, a cool, dense fog hangs over the rows
and rows of narrow, wood-sided homes. The hint of light in the
east indicates the gray mist should burn off by late morning, as it
tends to do this time of year.

With the contest scheduled to kick off at 4:00 this afternoon,
we're well ahead of game-day traffic as we cruise alongside the
bay. We should roll into the rolling hills of Palo Alto with plenty

of time to take in the pageantry with our octogenarian friends.

Following the inaugural victory over their Northern California rivals, Stanford University adopted the shade of cardinal red as the official color of its varsity football team. (White was added as a secondary color several decades later.) It wasn't until the 1930s that the university adopted an official team name for its athletic program. By unanimous vote, the Executive Committee of the Associated Students approved both the "Indians" moniker and its feathered headdress logo. In 1972, however, the powers-that-be at the private university in Palo Alto decided to discontinue its current symbol and team name.

Citing pressure from 55 Native American students and following a vote by the Stanford Student Senate, then-president Richard Lyman christened "Cardinals" (yes, with an "s") as the replacement name for its athletic teams.

This new moniker was in reference to the bright red northern cardinal. And, since this avian species is found only in the eastern United States, numerous other nicknames were suggested: The Railroaders. The Spikes. The Sequoias. The Griffins. This last proposed label was so well received by the student body that two concrete griffins were moved from the Children's Hospital to the front of the school's athletic facilities.

Almost a decade after their original team name ceased offending the heritage of indigenous people, the next president of the school, Donald Kennedy, issued the following statement: "While various other mascots have been suggested and then allowed to wither, the color has continued to serve us well, as it has for 90 years. It is a rich and vivid metaphor for the very pulse of life." Thus, in 1981, Kennedy announced that Stanford athletics would be symbolized by this color. And their athletic teams would be identified simply as the "Cardinal."

It seems as though some fans didn't get the message.

As Valerie and I pull onto a field surrounded by towering eucalyptus trees, we see several "Go Indians" banners among the rows of glistening RVs and luxury SUVs. Looking more like a motorhome park than a tailgating lot, the expansive grounds along El Camino Real are already at capacity on this crisp sunny morning – mostly with well-mannered well-to-dos in red sweaters and pullovers.

Walking through the ad-hoc alleys, we're looking for a large, hand-woven blanket. Valerie spots it first, an off-white covering emblazoned with "Stanford Indians" and the logo of their chief. Sitting beneath the RV's awning are our friends and fellow college football enthusiasts. George greets Valerie the way he always does, with a, "Hello, little darlin'." I give Irene a generous hug. A dusty white poodle yips in excitement. She wears a hand-knit red sweater emblazoned with "Sweetheart."

As we enjoy a generous tailgating spread featuring tri-tip sandwiches with avocado, we learn from our hosts (who wear matching "Stanford Indians" sweaters) that today's game has significance beyond the meeting of unranked teams with four losses apiece. It's the final time these combatants will face each other inside the Northern California landmark known as "The Farm."

Originally constructed in 1921, the horseshoe-shaped structure was at the time the second-largest football venue in the nation. (Its 60,000 seats, however, paled in comparison to the Yale Bowl in New Haven, Connecticut, which held an additional 10,000 fans.) Located on the lush pastureland of this west peninsula, the wood and steel structure was expanded to almost a full bowl-shape with a capacity of 89,000 in 1927.

Officially known as Stanford Stadium, The Farm did not get its nickname because of crops grown on the grounds (there are none), or because of the school's agricultural curriculum (there isn't one). The pseudonym refers to the fact that the founder of the university, Leland Stanford, and his wife, Jane, owned a trotting horse farm on this land. To this day, the Stanford Equestrian In-tercollegiate Riding & Equestrian Center is housed in the original facility built by the charitable couple.

Affectionately known as The Red Barn, up to 45 students train inside the dark rouge facility each school year. The Cardinal Equestrian Team also competes annually at Intercollegiate Horse Show Association meets throughout the west coast.

The Farm was constructed as a multi-purpose stadium with an oval track of red clay surrounding its grass playing field. Unfortunately, the running surface makes for sub-par viewing at modern football games. This, coupled with its well-worn wood deck and benches, is why construction crews will begin demolishing the fabled stadium next week after the final regular-season game against the Fighting Irish from Notre Dame. In its place will be a 50,000-seat dual-deck octagon that promises to be significantly more intimate than The Farm's current capacity.

Unbeknownst to us as we set out across the pastoral campus on this late fall afternoon, the antiquated stadium with the rural name is not the only thing about to be demolished in the Bay Area.

Making our way toward the arena, we seem to have walked into what appears to be a traveling clown show. Frolicking musicians, wearing mismatched clothes and playing instruments of all shapes and sizes, swirl around us. I can't say what they're playing is music so much as a sort of metallic clang, a sound so discordant it makes my fillings hurt. I spot the source of my pain: a young undergrad in an oversized red blazer, untucked white button-down, and skinny black tie is carrying a stop sign and banging on it with a drumstick.

Somehow, we've timed our trek to The Farm at the exact moment the Leland Stanford Junior University Marching Band is parading through the temporary motorhome park.

Much in the same manner fans in Columbus pretentiously refer to The Ohio State University marching band by the initials of its unofficial nickname, this official marching band is also obnoxiously identified by the initials of its name. The LSJUMB, however, has absolutely nothing else in common with the traditional precision troupe from the Midwest.

Originally formed in 1893, the Stanford marching band supported the Indians for more than six decades, performing time-honored procession tunes at campus sporting events and civic parades. In the early 1960s, with social upheaval taking hold on campuses across the nation, both tradition and convention were replaced by mayhem and mockery, including on these pasturelands along the northern coast of California.

During the restructuring of its music department in the third year of that decade, the university's beloved band director, Jules Schucat, was unceremoniously relieved of his duties. This seemingly unwarranted discharge provoked the Stanford student band members to go on strike. To show their unification and indignation, the musicians refused to perform at the first two gridiron games of the season. Caving to pressure, the institution quickly hired a graduate student to fill the position.

Carrying the original title of Interim Band Director, Arthur P. Barnes realized he needed to gain the students' trust and, thus, quickly handed creative control to the band members. To this day, the university-sanctioned assemblage is almost entirely student-run – which is painfully obvious almost every time it performs in public.

On this hazy afternoon outside of The Farm, these students – with their bright costumes, shiny instruments, and painted faces – appear as if they're in a Mardi Gras parade as they tramp through the rows of expensive RVs and sumptuous food tables.

More like wandering medieval minstrels than an actual marching band, this carnival-like display has now become an expected exhibition on the former training grounds for trotting horses. Prancing like the fabled equine on the outskirts of campus, several saxophone players cross our path, irreverently holding their instruments upside down and playing an indiscernible tune high into the air.

Ever since this troupe discarded their military-style marching regalia, their official uniform has been a red blazer, black pants, and a white hat with red trim. Unofficially, according to a 1987 *Rolling Stone* article titled "Band on the Run" by James B. Meigs, it includes as many buttons and pins as can be affixed to a fishing hat and "the ugliest tie you can get your hands on."

Over the years, many halftime shows on The Farm have seen flamboyant outfits the likes of cartoon characters, pop-culture idols, and sometimes, not much at all. Today's pregame procession does not deviate from this now-customarily-deviant game-day attire.

Valerie abruptly stops two cute, young musicians dressed as identical Raggedy-Ann dolls with red-and-white-striped leggings, scarlet pigtails, and freckled cheekbones, and asks if they'll pose for a picture with me. Happy to oblige, the coeds position themselves akimbo as fellow band members scurry toward the oversized stadium. Following their brief photo shoot, the toy dolls scamper off to their fellow performers. A group of cardinal-red fraternity brothers high-five me and, as if orchestrated, shout in unison, "Beat the Commies!"

Coming into this season, the visiting team from the Left-leaning hills across the bay had much higher hopes than their current 6-and-4 record.

The Golden Bears opened with five consecutive victories, including two in-conference triumphs over the University of Washington and the Wildcats from Arizona. Ranked No. 10 in the nation as they prepared for their sixth game, whispers were heard about a possible "run for the roses," as the quest for the Pac-10 title is referred to, given that the conference champion traditionally plays in Pasadena on New Year's Day. Ironically, Rose Bowl Stadium is where these whispers were all but silenced.

In a thrilling contest for fans of both teams, Cal ended-up on the disappointing side of a 40-to-47 shootout against the other team in this state with a bear as its mascot. This upset by the Bruins from UCLA was followed by three more conference losses, culminating with a 10-to-35 trampling on their home field by the Trojans from Southern California, currently the top-ranked team in the nation. The team in all-white traveling uniforms, methodically running through pregame drills on the well-manicured grass, is no longer ranked in the top-25.

Valerie and I make our way toward the southwest curve of the stadium as members of the Stanford band, including six red Solo party cups and eight *Spy vs. Spy* characters (four in white cone hats and four in black), form two somewhat parallel lines at the entrance to the field. "Let's Get It Started" by The Black Eyed Peas blares across the sweeping arena.

Nonchalantly walking through the deep red facemask of an oversized white inflatable helmet, head coach Walt Harris leads a column of just-as-nonchalant red jerseys and white pants to the side of the end zone. A siren blares as the jaunty pop song is abruptly cut from the loudspeakers.

With the same demeanor as the home team players who are now casually jogging onto the field through the two columns of red-coated jesters and dancing tubas, the local fans in our section barely look up from their laptops and *Wired* magazines to watch this entrance by the underdog varsity football squad

In stark contrast to last year's game in The Horseshoe, and even though we've arrived at our seats an hour before kickoff, none of our section-mates have expressed any interest in welcoming us to The Farm. Most do not seem interested in being in the stadium at all.

Perhaps it's the sunny blue sky, the bucolic setting, or the fact that there are a lot of distractions in this epicenter of technology and entrepreneurship. Whatever the reasons, today feels more like being at a corporate retreat than a football rivalry.

A great deal separates Berkeley from Palo Alto.

The vestige of the radical 1960s, with its free speech, free love, and anti-establishment movements, still lingers through the halls of the liberal state school situated in the East Bay hills. Cal's official mascot, Oski the bear, has the appearance of an aging flower-power-era professor. Shuffling along the sidelines with his hands clasped behind his slouching back, the broadly-smiling costumed mascot with sleepy eyes and an oversized vintage yellow sweater looks more like a brooding school lecturer than a menacing California grizzly bear.

Stanford, on the other hand, is unequivocally recognized as the center of the digital revolution, both in terms of its location in the heart of Silicon Valley and its technology-based curriculum, free-market focus, and venture-capitalist connections. Also in true juxtaposition, the private school with the nobly-named athletic teams does not have an official mascot. Nevertheless, most fans can identify its unofficial costumed team character.

With oversized red and white eyes bulging from its branches, the Stanford Tree has informally assumed the role of team mascot ever since 1975. Originally constructed that year by then-student Christine Hutson, the dancing tree is said to represent the coastal redwood that appears on both the municipal seal of Palo Alto and the official seal of the university. The coed's original costume was nothing more than a large green dress.

In 1987, however, the dancing tree took on a life of its own. After the LSJUMB held inaugural tryouts for its mascot that year, Paul Kelly (who according to the story was the only student who showed up for the audition) spent the summer designing a comical, cone-shaped conifer with layers of dark green branches, surfing shorts, and a white jacket.

In his article for *Rolling Stone*, James B. Meigs described Kelly's costume as a "nine-foot pillar of bark and foliage – with legs and a maniacal smile – like a character from some low rent Disneyland. He ricochets around . . . with alarming abandon, rarely quite vertical but never entirely horizontal."

During halftime of The Big Game that season, the dancing Kelly was tackled to the turf by several Cal students. Immediately responding to this attack, the Stanford drum section pounced on the three golden hooligans and held them until security officers carted them off the field.

Since this first altercation, additional pranks have occurred between students from the state university and the sapling. During the Battle of the Bands at the University of California, Davis, Kelly's first-year tree costume was purloined from the Stanford bus by Berkeley students. The following week, the young student received a ransom note offering to exchange the infamous sprig costume in return for Cal's Oski costume, which had been pilfered earlier in the year. According to school archives, LSJUMB members did not perceive this be a fair offer. In their words, the Stanford Tree was "everything that the UCB mascot was not – new, fresh, and almost always sober."

Rather than accept the ransom note, the band chose to create a new costume. Every year since, a new carousing conifer is introduced as the Stanford Tree. And, every year, each costume wearer attempts to fashion a more outrageous shrub than the last. The audition process for the mascot – which features sensational stunts and daring performances – has turned into what's now called "Tree Week."

Across the field at about the 40-yard-line is four-year UC Berkeley head coach Jeff Tedford. Upon taking over for Tom Holmoe, who resigned after his 1-and-11 (worst-ever at Cal) season in 2001, Tedford immediately elevated the Golden Bears to heights not seen in more than half a century. During his first season, the 32nd head coach led his varsity football squad to its first winning season since 1993. He was justifiably recognized as Coach of the Year in the Pac-10 for his 7-and-5 record – the best turn-around record in the country that year.

In his second season, Tedford bested this record by one win. He also outlasted the visiting Trojans from Southern California in a thrilling triple-overtime victory. (The Associated Press crowned USC as 2003 National Champions even though Louisiana State University was victorious over the red and white team from Norman, Oklahoma in the BCS Title Game.)

At the end of his third year, the former University of Oregon offensive coordinator directed the Bears from Berkeley to their first ten-win season since 1949 – and only the fifth such season in the history of the program – to finish ninth in both national polls. That season, which was led by standout quarterback Aaron Rodgers, earned Tedford his second Pac-10 Coach of the Year trophy. Disappointingly, Cal missed out on the Rose Bowl last year due to Valerie's first alma mater in Austin receiving a few more points in the final poll of the convoluted BCS ranking system.

The deflated Bears closed out the 2004 season, in the Pacific Life Holiday Bowl, with a loss to the Texas Tech Red Raiders. Prior to this defeat, they did, however, vanquish their rivals from the east bay for the third consecutive year with a dominating 41-to-6 victory in California Memorial Stadium.

This year is going to be the year this humiliating three-loss streak gets turned around, according to our gray-haired friend and long-time booster of the Indians. Given that Cal's First-Team All-

Pac-10 quarterback, Aaron Rodgers, chose to forgo his senior year and enter the 2005 NFL draft, many more fans than just George harbor this hopeful sentiment.

Winning the coin toss, and choosing to defer to the second half, the kickoff squad for Stanford lines up on this unseasonable 80-degree afternoon. With the sound of luxury car keys rattling in the air from the Cardinal student section, the football sails into the waiting arms of Marshawn Lynch. The sophomore from Oakland Tech High School begrudgingly takes a knee for a touchback.

Leading his team onto the field and making his first-ever start at quarterback for the Golden Bears, Steve Levy was given the nod over Joe Ayoob earlier this week. This decision by Tedford did not come as a surprise, given that Cal has lost four of its last five games with Ayoob under center, including their most recent 10-to-35 home loss to Southern California. Levy, a junior from Cornwall, New York, has only played in four games before today. Also, as unorthodox as it seems, he earned his varsity letter as a hard-rushing fullback last year.

The visiting Bears fail to achieve a first down on this first series of the game, which features an end-around reverse by true freshman wide receiver DeSean Jackson, a run up the middle by running back Lynch (who only needs 71 yards to surpass 1,000 yards rushing this season), and an incomplete pass to Jackson by Levy on third down. The home team fans in our section, most of who appear to be more engaged with their laptops, politely applaud as their statistically worst defense in the Pac-10 shuffles off the field. Standing on his own 12-yard-line, David Lonie masterfully sends the ball to the Cardinal 28-yard-line, where it is fair-caught by T.J. Rushing.

From under center, second-year starting quarterback Trent Edwards hands the ball to his bruising senior running back, J.R. Lemon, who barrels through the line for a surprising 9-yard gain. Edwards, the 6'4" 220-pound senior gunslinger from Los Gatos High School (just 20 miles south of today's venue), quickly hands off to fullback Nick Frank for the inaugural first down of the game. Valerie points out that not only is this surge somewhat unexpected; it's also being executed against one of the most colorfully named defensive lines in the country: Phillip Mbakogu, Abu Ma'afala, Brandon Mebane, and Nu'u Tafisi.

These four mouthfuls stone the Cardinal on the first play, and Cal fans to our left let out an approving cheer. On the next play, the section to our right applauds as Edwards completes his first pass for 15 yards to wide receiver Mark Bradford. Even though the home team crosses into the Bears' territory, an errant pass on third down by Edwards forces Stanford to punt.

After a fair-catch by Tim Mixon, the Golden Bears quickly establish momentum with a 9-yard run by Marshawn Lynch. Not to be outdone in the colorful name for a defensive lineman department, starting nose guard for the Cardinal is senior Babatunde Oshinowo. The 320-pound lineman is also a junior. His full name: Babatunde Oluwasegun Temitope Oluwakorede Adisa Oshinowo, Jr.

After a slashing 5-yard run by sophomore tailback Justin Forsett for a first down, Cal's dodgy quarterback fires a long-bomb along the far sideline. The arcing projectile drops into the arms of DeSean Jackson at the 10-yard-line. With one move to the inside, the 6'0" 175-pound freshman from Long Beach, California leaves cornerback T.J. Rushing in his dust.

The dark blue and yellow-striped shirts in the north end stands screech in delight as their team celebrates the first points of the contest. Levy races across the white and red block letters in the far end zone to congratulate his young receiver. Abruptly however, following this initial piercing of the goal line, defensive end Julian Jenkins surges through the middle of the massive offensive line and blocks the extra-point. As is often true in rivalry games – every point has to be earned.

We are only 6 minutes of playing time into this 108th meeting between these Bay Area schools and already it feels as if the sun is setting on the home team.

Expecting consternation, Valerie comments on the looks from the fans in our section. Their seeming indifference is in stark contrast the California Gold and Yale Blue-clad students jumping up and down in unison in the northern curve of the stadium. (These official team colors are said to have represented the state's prospecting heritage and the vast Pacific Ocean ever since they were chosen in 1875.)

With the sun truly beginning to set behind us, the teams settle into a back-and-forth stalemate for the remainder of the first quarter. It's not until the Cardinal take possession after a 39-yard punt by Lonie with a little less than 14 minutes remaining in the second quarter that this stalemate is broken. And not by much.

Stanford's front-man, Edwards, orchestrates an 8-play drive featuring four completed passes and two dropped balls to the 20-yard-line. Facing 11 yards for a first down, Walt Harris chooses the safe route and sends his field goal team onto the field. With just under 10 minutes left on the undersized scoreboard above our heads, senior placekicker Michael Sgroi splits the uprights from the left hash-marks to bring the team from the private university within 3 points of the state school from the hills across the bay.

The 37-yard field goal elicits only a smattering of applause from our section-mates. Maybe they're used to more action? It's true that, other than the six sacks by the defensive linemen for both teams (four by Cal and two by Stanford) and four uneventful punts, this first half has seen very little scoring.

With 29 seconds on the game clock, the home team provides a smidge of excitement when they inexplicably incur the first penalty of the game by roughing Cal's punter. Rather than starting on their own 33-yard-line for the final series of the quarter, the illegal hit on Lonie by outside linebacker Timi Wusu gives the ball back to the visitors at just about midfield. In keeping with the tone of the contest, however, the Bears gain only a couple yards as the play clock rolls to zeros.

Prior to today's game, the former Indians led this in-state series by 12 games, winning 54 and playing to a tie 11 times. Fifty of these games have been decided by 7 points or less and 25 have been separated by no more than 3 points. As the teams all but laconically stream across the field to their respective locker rooms, and darkness overtakes the cool early evening sky, the Bears lead the home-team adversaries by the score of 6-to-3.

With the onset of halftime, the subdued fans in our section finally close their computers.

Parading onto the field from the north end is the University of California Marching Band (commonly known by its much simpler moniker, The Cal Band). I remark to Valerie that the 200-plus members, with their dark blue slacks, white vests featuring gold crossed sashes, and customary band hats with white plumes, are reminiscent of the visiting band in Columbus last year.

After several conventional parade songs, including "Fight for California," the band methodically exits the field in the same disciplined manner that they entered. Regimented, proper, and polished. I'm thinking what a refreshing change this is from our earlier run-in with the minstrel show from Palo Alto . . . Too soon!

Signaled by a blaring siren from the stadium speakers, all members of LSJUMB race from the south end zone across the field and begin dancing wildly to the cacophonous screech coming from their instruments. Scattered about the field, in no formation whatsoever, the costumed jesters and painted musicians seem to revel in the opportunity to be irreverent. This impertinence, it turns out, is what finally causes the local fans seated around us to react with delight.

With the stadium lights fully aglow, David Lonie kicks off to the home team to start the second half. After gaining only a yard on the first two downs, which includes another sack by the blitzing Bears, Trent Edwards completes an 11-yard pass to his diving senior tight end, Matt Traverso. Unfortunately, this completion is followed by another devastating sack, this time by right defensive tackle, Brandon Mebane.

Even more damning is the fact that Edwards is now crouching in serious pain on his own 20-yard-line. Clutching his left shoulder, the veteran leader of the Cardinal offense – and arguably of the team – is escorted to the sideline with his white helmet in his right hand by four trainers in deep red windbreakers.

After several quick practice snaps alongside the bench, Stanford's backup quarterback is thrust into a precarious second down and 20. Thomas Clinton Ostrander, the 6'3" 215-pound junior, is a hometown progeny who grew up less than 5 miles from here in Atherton, California. He's also seen very little action, throwing for only 180 yards, zero touchdowns, and one interception this season.

On his first play under the bright lights, Ostrander inadvertently turns the wrong direction after receiving the snap from his center, Alex Fletcher. Amazingly, he somehow stretches the ball to fullback Nick Frank, who scrambles for a 6-yard gain on the busted play. On the very next play, the back-up QB suffers the same fate as Edwards throughout the first half, the line is too porous and here come Phillip Mbakogu and Mickey Pimentel, resulting in a 5-yard sack.

With Stanford's inability to capitalize on the inkling of momentum at the end of the first half and sustaining what looks to be a game-ending injury to their starting quarterback, the visiting team quickly pounces.

After a 47-yard punt, Cal opens the second half with a powerful 11-yard burst by Lynch. From here, they never look back. Five plays later, including back-to-back scrambles out of the pocket by quarterback Levy, the Bears are at the 21-yard-line. On second down, head coach Tedford substitutes Justin Forsett in at running back. Under center, Levy quickly runs an option play to the right side. Just as he is about to be flattened by Stanford's crashing strong safety, the agile quarterback flicks the ball from 7 yards deep in the backfield to Forsett. One simple shimmy and the nimble tailback bursts past a sure tackle and drags three defenders into the end zone.

This spectacular read-option puts the visitors ahead, 13-to-3, with just under 10 minutes to play in the third quarter. Unfortunately for the home team, they will have to follow this demoralizing score with a callow quarterback and a sieve-like offensive line.

Over the next 15 minutes of game time – all the way to the 10-minute mark in the fourth quarter – Stanford is sacked 3 more times, forced to punt twice, and misses a 40-yard field goal to put no points on the scoreboard. Seizing momentum once again, Cal promptly marches down the field to score its third touchdown on a 3-yard plunge by Marshawn Lynch. With the score 20-to-3 and only 7 minutes left in the game, Oski broodily lumbers with his hands clasped behind his back alongside the far end zone.

As if to send a signal to the seemingly indifferent fans in our section that they can now leave early, Ostrander is once again sacked on the fifth play of the ensuing series. Even more devastating, the beleaguered backup has the ball punched from his hands during this tackle by Mickey Pimentel. The loose ball flies directly into the arms of Pimentel's fellow linebacker, Greg Van Hoesen.

Taking over on the 43-yard-line, the Golden Bears – behind a fabulous 22-yard scamper by Lynch – drive the figurative axe into the trunk of the Cardinal on the third play after this fumble.

With only three-and-a-half minutes left in the game, Tedford reaches into his golden bag of tricks. From the 14-yard-line, Levy pitches the ball out wide to his halfback, Terrell Williams, who in turn fires a pass to Craig Stevens. The lumbering tight end crashes across the goal line. Surprisingly, a faint but audible groan can be heard from several fans in our section as the scoreboard updates to 27-to-3 in favor of the visitors.

With the play-clock now under 3 minutes and Stanford feebly attempting one final drive against the stifling defense, I notice a small gathering on the clay track directly in front of our section.

I ask the cardinal-clad fan to my left what the commotion is behind the home team's bench. He informs us this tradition has taken place ever since the Stanford Axe was first presented to the winner of The Big Game in 1933. (Introduced as a prop in 1899, this woodsman's tool was used to decapitate a life-size straw man in a dark blue outfit at a pep rally before the cross-bay showdown.) Every day this past year, Cal has proudly displayed this trophy – engraved with the final scores from each annual scrimmage – on its campus.

With 2 minutes till the final gun, half a dozen or so undergrads from both schools form two parallel lines and face each other alongside the playing field as they've done at every scrimmage between these institutions for more than 70 years. Standing 2 feet from his counterpart, the tallest student in blue and gold holds the Stanford Axe to his chest.

As tradition has it, these two rows of school-colored human statues will stare unflinchingly into the faces of their adversaries for however long it takes the play-clock to expire. Blue-and-yellow-striped fans taunt the red row of unflustered undergrads. Both sides remain as composed as Buckingham Palace guards.

When the final gun sounds and the Cal student section erupts, the tallest Golden Bear turns his back to the line of stoic Cardinal students and slowly marches the axe toward the celebration at midfield.

In addition to scoring 24 more points, the state school from Berkeley thoroughly mauled the home team in this final intrastate scrimmage at The Farm.

As if playing dead, the Cardinal gained only 224 yards, including only 16 yards rushing against their grizzly opponent. Cal running back Marshawn Lynch rushed for 123 yards and one touchdown, surpassing 1,000 total yards for the season. His teammate in the backfield, Justin Forsett, also scored a touchdown; however, he fell 38 yards shy of enabling Cal to claim two 1,000-yard runners. Remaining unbeaten by his rival from across the bay since taking over four years earlier, Jeff Tedford and his Golden Bears have now outscored Stanford 126-to-32.

As we make our way across the unlit pasture to George and Irene's RV, most tailgate trappings have been packed away for next week's final game of the season. From behind us, led by an oversized rolling Japanese koi fish, comes the sound of the still-just-as-rowdy Leland Stanford Junior University Marching Band. Their papier-mâché carp is larger than a sedan and is being pulled by four red blazers topped with white fishing hats.

Valerie comments that it's difficult to discern from the roving pack of musicians that their team lost today. Congruent with the Cardinal's lackadaisical performance on the field, the costumed coeds seem indifferent to the final score.

Ever since the contentious final 4 seconds ran off the game clock in the most memorable contest between these varsity squads, Stanford University has refused to accept they lost in 1982. Claiming several infractions went uncalled – including an illegal forward pass and a player pitching the ball after being tackled to the ground – the school still will not acknowledge the outcome of "The Play."

It's a historical fact, however, after the implausible five laterals on the final kick-return inside Memorial Stadium that day, the scoreboard rolled to 25-to-20 in favor of the Golden Bears. It's also a fact that every year the Cardinal takes possession of the ceremonial axe, they remove this score and replace it with a brass inscription that reads: STANFORD 20 – CALIFORNIA 19.

Nevertheless, and as it has since the early 1930s, possession of the Stanford Axe will signify to fans of both schools – for the next 364 days – which team got chopped down today.

CHAPTER EIGHT
Fear the Thumb
2006 Auburn | Alabama

The thoroughfare at the south end of Bryant-Denny Stadium is closed to traffic on this sunny late-November afternoon. Walking under the massive, all-red scoreboard emblazoned with white letters, Valerie and I turn to see three hulking Prevost buses creeping toward the crowd at the corner of Paul W Bryant Drive and Wallace Wade Avenue. Flashing red and blue lights atop two police motorcycles lead the glass-enclosed vehicles which appear to be crawling on hands and knees through the fans milling in and out of the street.

With a loud hiss, the large transports come to rest alongside the boisterous horde gathered on the expansive concrete corner. Looking like General Douglas MacArthur returning to the shores of the Philippines, the eighth-year head coach of the Auburn University varsity football team, Tommy Tuberville, stands defiantly in the middle of the oversized windows of the lead bus. The door abruptly opens. A wave of cheers from the ever-swelling crowd of interlopers crashes against the massive vehicle.

Two years before today's arrival, Tuberville led the Tigers to their second unblemished season in the past 50 years – and their first thirteen-win season ever. Even so, these undefeated SEC champions did not play for the BCS Championship that year. To restate . . . an unbeaten, twelve-win varsity football team from the Southeastern Conference did not receive an invite to the National Championship Game. Even more repugnant than this snub was the team that *did*.

The unthinkable happened at the end of that 2004 season. To the horror of the illuminati who devised the convoluted BCS selection process, five teams from five conferences finished with perfect seasons: the Auburn Tigers from the SEC, the USC Trojans from the Pac-10, the University of Utah Utes from the Mountain West Conference, the Boise State Broncos from the Western Athletic Conference, and the dyslexic Sooners from the Big XII.

Much to the dismay of Auburn (and most SEC) fans, the BCS committee chose the two teams which entered the season at the top of the Associated Press poll for the National Championship game: the Trojans from Los Angeles and the Sooners from a town just south of Oklahoma City. The three others were evidently handicapped by not being ranked in top-15 positions before the start of the season.

Further exasperating both fans and representatives of the Southeastern Conference (if providing sheer delight for Valerie and me), Southern California obliterated the overwhelmed Sooners 55-to-19. The lopsided victory earned head coach Pete Carroll his second consecutive No. 1 ranking and his first BCS National Championship. To this day, we recall USC running back Reggie Bush stating he felt sorry for fans who, "paid hundreds or thousands of dollars for tickets and didn't see much of a game."

With this whipping of the crimson-and-cream in this Orange Bowl, the Trojans remained in the top position of both polls from the beginning of the season to the end for only the second time in the history of the program. Nonetheless, many fans perceived at the time – and to this day – the Tigers from Auburn would have put up more of a fight than the overmatched team from the Big XII Conference.

As a result of the controversy surrounding the selection process that season, the AP opted to disallow their national poll as a component of the BCS ranking formula. This, of course, provided no solace to the 2004 Auburn team and their fans. Even so, the Tigers finished their impeccable season with a hard-fought victory in the Sugar Bowl at the Louisiana Super Dome. The unblemished team prevailed in a 16-to-13 defensive struggle over the No. 8-ranked Hokies from Virginia Polytechnic Institute and

State University. Following this victory, three writers in the final AP poll voted Auburn University the No. 1 team in the nation.

Wearing a flame-orange pullover and an embroidered "AU" hat, Tuberville steps off the bus and directly into the mob at the south end of the coliseum. As high-pitched screams assail our ears, Valerie and I realize we're in the middle of the traveling version of one of college football's most storied rituals.

Proclaimed by Auburn University as "the most imitated tradition in all of college sports," this parade typically occurs two hours before every home kickoff. This afternoon, in the shadows of their cross-state rival's arena, the usually well-orchestrated procession feels more like a crowded train station than a much-emulated tradition.

Early before each game in the city of Auburn, thousands of fans line the streets to watch their team walk to Jordan-Hare Stadium. This tradition, known as Tiger Walk, began in the early 1960s when school kids gathered to watch the varsity players make this stroll from their dorms. Though a handful of other schools – including Stanford University and Williams College in Massachusetts – claim their parades originated well before this walk along Donahue Drive, no other pregame procession elicits the degree of passion and intimacy as Tiger Walk.

Avid boosters arrive on Friday evenings to stake a claim on prime parking spaces. Aubie the Tiger, the team's official costumed mascot, brazenly struts ahead of the procession in his dark blue No. 01 football jersey. Admirers clamor in the street, sometimes more than 20 rows deep, to cheer the squad as it passes by.

Today, the players in traveling-white jerseys and dark sweatpants follow Tuberville off the bus and into a screaming mass of fans. With barely room to move, the white line snakes its way under an oversized vinyl banner attached to white PVC pipes. This temporary billboard features "Tiger Walk – An AUBURN Tradition" in orange-and-blue letters bookended by menacing "Tiger Eyes" and the slogan "War Eagle."

Frenzied fans shake the hands and pat the backs of smiling

players as they slowly amble toward the stadium. Starting left tackle King Dunlap, at 6'8" and weighing 318-pounds, is the easiest to spot above the clamoring mob. Raising his arm, he gives high-fives to the second and third row of fans. Valerie quickly snaps a picture of me standing next to the imposing player with the fitting first name.

On February 22, 1893, a crowd of more than 5,000 fans witnessed the inaugural football game between the Tigers from the Agricultural and Mechanical College of Alabama and the University of Alabama Crimson Tide. When the final gun sounded on the field known then as Lakeview Park in Birmingham, the team from later-to-be-named Auburn University claimed a 32-to-22 victory. Oddly, the University of Alabama recognizes this gridiron clash as the *final* game of their 1892 season, while Auburn has it recorded in their archives as the *first* of its 1893 season.

Everything about this rivalry is contentious.

Bad blood flowed even prior to the existence of one of these institutions. In 1868, during the Civil War Reconstruction Era of the United States, the state legislature set out to build an agricultural and mechanical college using newly appropriated federal funds from the Morrill Land Grant Act. The ensuing political discourse surrounding the location for this new institution – and the dollars attached to it – went about as smoothly as General Robert E. Lee's occupation of Sharpsburg. (This Confederate invasion of northern Maryland in September of 1862 was brutally repulsed by the army from the North in the bloodiest single-day battle in the history of our country.)

At the time of this polemical tussle, a significant number of University of Alabama alumni resided in the state legislature. Many expressed an unabashed desire for the Land Grant funds to make their way into the coffers of their alma mater. Over the next four years, they petitioned the state to purchase land scripts for 240,000 acres in Tuscaloosa. To their great consternation, the funds were awarded to the city of Auburn.

One factor in this decision was the rural eastern Alabama town's willingness to donate, in addition to the land, all structures previously built for East Alabama Male College. Even with this selection by the legislators, many continued lobbying for the University of Alabama, to no avail.

Tensions also went beyond the governing halls. After their inaugural scrimmage in Birmingham on that early spring day, the varsity squads lined up against each other for three consecutive seasons. The soon-to-be-christened Auburn Tigers won three of these first four games. The schools did not meet again on the gridiron until 1900. Then, for 8 consecutive years, they battled in sweaters over leather shoulder pads and no helmets.

After the 1906 game, Auburn's head coach, Mike Donahue, protested that the Crimson Tide fielded an illegal player. He further threatened to never play the team again unless head coach Doc Pollard ceased using "unsportsmanlike tactics" such as complex formations and unorthodox shifts.

At the end of their 1907 contest, these threats collided with the political climate of the day and brought the series to a screeching halt. Two official reasons were given: the inability to agree upon the amount of travel expenses for players, and the insurmountable hurdle of where the game referees would be from. Arguably, the desire of many in the state's government to see the Agricultural and Mechanical College of Alabama wither on the vine contributed more to the stoppage.

For the next 41 years, the upstart Tigers and the team from Tuscaloosa didn't meet again on the gridiron.

Both Valerie and I acknowledge that the invective posturing between college football rivals and their fans significantly adds to our enjoyment of this wonderful pastime. Some may see this heartfelt passion as unsportsmanlike. We, on the other hand, know how enflamed *we* become every season as our respective alma maters are challenged by their worthy opponents (even if our adversary has a cheating past). And, that we want to win so badly!

Valerie also likes to point out that each game on our annual quest is so much fun because we get to experience it as if we are watching a motion picture thriller. We're not the ones hanging on the edge of a cliff – but, we get to watch those who are!

Football in the 22nd state of the Union is as pervasive as its humidity in August – and just as impossible to ignore.

In the mid-1940s, the re-named Alabama Polytechnic Institute in Auburn could also no longer be overlooked. The end of World War II saw the return of thousands of mechanically inclined men and women to rural towns and farms across the Southern state. Many of these veterans, having traveled halfway around the world, wanted more in terms of education and career opportunities than they could find in their hometowns. This, along with the newly introduced Servicemen's Readjustment Act, better known as the G.I. Bill, caused enrollment at the former Agricultural and Mechanical College of Alabama to more than quadruple from 1944 to 1948.

The dramatic surge legitimized the polytechnical institution in the minds of many state politicians and their constituents. With it came a yearning to renew the gridiron rivalry between the cross-state schools.

In 1947, the Alabama House of Representatives passed a resolution intended to do just that. Unfortunately, this act did not have the power of law. Both universities ignored the decree. At the end of the season that year, however, the State Legislature turned up their level of encouragement by threatening to withhold funding for both schools. This did the trick. Begrudgingly, the trustees at each institution voted unanimously to resume the long-deposed annual clash in the fall of the following year.

Four decades earlier, the closing game in the rudely interrupted series was fittingly played to a 6-to-6 tie. This stalemate in 1907 did not obscure the fact that during these inaugural 12 games, the newly established college dominated the acclaimed university, and brought the series to 7-4-1 in favor of the Tigers.

Evidently, citizens of Tuscaloosa have long memories.

At the restart of the series, the Crimson Tide handed the varsity team from renamed Auburn University a humiliating 55-to-0 shutout at Legion Field in Birmingham. This bludgeoning on December 4, 1948 stands as the greatest margin of victory in the history of the storied rivalry.

Evidently, regents in Tuscaloosa carry grudges for a long time as well.

Beginning with this rout, the Crimson Tide stubbornly refused to travel to Auburn, for the *next four decades*. During these 41 seasons, the annual game was hosted by the city of Birmingham. As unfathomable as it seems, it wasn't until 1989 that the contentious contest was held outside of Legion Field.

And, evidently, people on the rural plains can also carry a grudge for a long time.

On that warm December 2, 1989 afternoon, the No. 11-ranked underdogs stared across their home field into the eyes of Alabama football players. No Auburn player – or fan for that matter – had ever seen a Crimson Tide uniform inside Jordan-Hare stadium. Summoning the frustration of having to play four consecutive decades at what many considered to be Alabama's home-field-away-from-home (Birmingham being less than an hour east of Tuscaloosa), the Tigers beat the undefeated No. 2-ranked team in the nation 30-to-20. It was the largest-ever crowd at an Auburn game.

As the winding line of white jerseys disappears into the dark opening under the concrete buttresses of Bryant Denny Stadium, Valerie spots a rambunctious gathering outside of what looks to be an old-timey ice cream parlor.

On the corner of Wallace Wade Avenue is an unassuming single-story building with a room-sized addition on its roof. Red and white Coca-Cola signs adorn the bright walls of this turret-like afterthought. Above the single-door entrance is a dark red awning with the instantly recognizable white script *A*.

Careening along the sidewalk through boisterous crimson-clad fans, we stop at a temporary merchandise tent in the parking lot of this Tuscaloosa landmark. Everyone who knows us knows we always sport the local team's gear, preferably bought on location. This time, Valerie tries on a trilby-style hounds-tooth hat of the kind worn by legendary coach Bear Bryant. Several rowdy fans in red-striped golf shirts howl when they see it on her. Sold!

Recognized by locals as the "restaurant located in the shadows of Bryant-Denny," Rama Jama's opened its doors in September 1996. Formerly a vacated convenience store, the single-roomed eatery serves traditional "mom & pop" style Southern breakfasts and lunches every day of the year. On game days, however, it's the center of the universe for Crimson Tide fans.

Walking in, we see autographed photos, crimson jerseys, and even personalized license plates. Hundreds of other random knickknacks cover the walls from floor to ceiling – including the ceiling itself. Drenched in the aroma of fried onion rings and sizzling burgers, the bustling soda fountain-themed restaurant makes us feel as if we've stepped back an era or two.

With less than an hour to kickoff, we grab a couple "walking beverages" for the trek around the massive stadium. Scurrying along Paul W Bryant Drive, I point to what looks like a set from *Buffy The Vampire Slayer*. On the other side of this famed avenue is some of the most prime real estate in all of Tuscaloosa. There, however, sits Evergreen Cemetery.

Crossing the street, we see randomly placed newer graves of local residents interspersed between crumbling cement memorials and Civil War-era headstones. Century-old concrete blocks and the unmarked graves of soldiers and slaves lay at our feet. A small vertical slab marks the final resting place of the chief surgeon of the Army of Northern Virginia.

We marvel at the juxtaposition before us on this state's arguably most important day of the year: full-of-life fans on one side of the street, the eerie stillness of the historic graveyard on the other. As muffled sounds from a marching band emanate within the massive arena, we hastily join the living and continue toward its northeast side.

Bryant-Denny Stadium is huge.

Even though Neyland Stadium in Knoxville has the largest capacity, the oversized spiral concrete walkways in each corner make this arena seem bigger than any we've visited on our quest.

In 1929, the Crimson Tide christened this hulking home field by shutting out the (now-Division III) Choctaws from Mississippi College 55-to-0. Slightly more than 6,000 fans attended that opening game. Thanks to renovations completed just before this 2006 season, the imposing structure will hold more than 92,000 distinctly clad fans today.

Alabama opened the current season with a surprisingly evenly matched scuffle against the Warriors from the University of Hawaii. This inaugural victory in their newly enhanced home proved to be a harbinger.

Coming off an impressive ten-win season, expectations were tremendously high in Tuscaloosa. Unfortunately, the team preparing for their final regular-season game this afternoon brings an uninspiring 6-and-5 record into Bryant-Denny stadium. Even more disappointing, they've only notched two conference victories this entire season.

Shuttling through the turnstiles, I ask Valerie if she's noticed several white-and-orange t-shirts with the slogan "Fear the Thumb." Just then, several buoyant students raise their five fingers in the air and holler this peculiar catchphrase in unison.

Valerie stops the girls and asks them to explain the tagline. The troop of feline fans eagerly conveys that their team has been victorious in each of the past four scrimmages against its abhorred rival. A win today will enable the Tigers to add a thumb to their number of consecutive wins.

Coming into Bryant-Denny stadium as the favorite, this feat (and appendage!) certainly could happen this afternoon.

From 1951 to 1975, Ralph "Shug" Jordan commanded the Auburn sideline at their rival's "home field." During these years in Birmingham following the 41-year respite, coach Shug and his Tigers won slightly more than two-thirds of their clashes (not counting 7 ties) with the Tide. As their in-state showdown in 1964 approached, *The Washington Post* ran a story on Shug Jordan's slim chances of upsetting the undefeated and No. 1-ranked team from Tuscaloosa.

The Crimson Tide had given up an average of fewer than 6 points in each of their nine victories leading up to this contest. Thus, the Tigers' head coach was fully aware he needed to instill confidence in his players. When asked by the newspaper if he expected his team to be playing in a bowl game at the end of the season, coach Shug replied, "We've got our bowl game. We have it every year. It's the Iron Bowl in Birmingham."

This poignant statement was the first time the annual game was referred to by this title. Most residents at the time understood, and greatly valued, the economic impact the abundant iron deposits surrounding Birmingham had on the Southern steel industry and its communities. They also instantly connected with the newly bestowed nickname. It has stuck ever since.

Shouts of, "Fear the Thumb!" echo off the gray underside of the imposing arena.

In truth, if anyone this afternoon has a reason for fear, it's Alabama coach Mike Shula. During the past three years at the helm, his teams have yet to win an Iron Bowl. The Tigers won 28-to-23, 21-to-13, and, last year, 28-to-18.

As the former starting quarterback for the Crimson Tide from 1984 to 1986, many throughout the state had high expectations for the 38-year-old coach. And, following the ten-win season last year, most were pleased with his hire a year earlier. However, at the end of that impressive season, all ten wins were vacated due to NCAA violations surrounding improper benefits given to student-athletes.

Scandal has a lot to do with how Mike Shula got to where he is today. In 2002, the second year with Dennis Franchione in its top coaching seat, the Crimson Tide lost a 7-to-17 defensive struggle to the visiting underdogs from Auburn. At the end of that season, due in large part to sanctions for recruiting infractions in the late 1990s, Franchione resigned. Those NCAA penalties included forfeiture of 21 scholarships over three years, a two-year bowl ban, and five years of probation.

In May 2003, after the immediate hiring – and immediate firing – of former Washington State University head coach Mike Price for allegations involving strip clubs and a $1,000 room-service bill charged to the university, Shula was named head football coach of the Alabama varsity football team.

As Valerie and I enter Bryant-Denny, it's immediately clear our seats are surrounded by the victors of the last three Iron Bowls.

Squinting into the midafternoon sun, I see the very shiny head of a very large black man ascending the aisle. Wearing a dark blue pullover and an infectious grin and pausing at each row is one of the top three athletes to ever attend Auburn University. The "Round Mound of Rebound," as he was endearingly called during his days in Auburn Arena, Charles Barkley cheerfully shakes hands with doting fans of both teams.

Barkley referred to himself as "Sir Charles" when he was dominating the boards in a Tigers' uniform. However, due to his self-admitted struggle to keep weight off his hulking 6'5" frame, opposing players and fans were more apt to call him "Sir Cumference." Today, however, almost every fan in our section, regardless of which team apparel they're wearing, is eager to say hello to the former center, who led the SEC in rebounds each of his three years. Graciously accepting the attention, the good-natured Barkley continues through our section, a dozen rows from the field at about the 10-yard-line.

From the end zone to our right, the marching band known for its haughty name strides to the 30-yard-line.

Legend has it, their officially recognized moniker came from a response to a reporter's sarcastic question following a loss at the Georgia Institute of Technology (a.k.a. Georgia Tech). Early in 1922, fundraising efforts enabled the troupe to ride in luxury sleeper cars to and from this disappointing game. After asserting the university in Tuscaloosa didn't have much of a football team, the sportswriter asked William C. Pickens, "What *do* you have at Alabama?" To which the prominent alumnus shot back, "A million-dollar band."

As the expansive ensemble marches to a halt, I notice several cheerleaders making their way up the aisle. Not wanting to miss an opportunity, I stop the first approaching girl. She's adorable, in a blue-and-orange striped sweater and a bright orange ribbon in her auburn hair.

"Be quick!" I tell Valerie, who snaps a picture of me with my arm around the brave spirit-leader just as the Million Dollar Band snaps to attention.

At the opening in the east end zone, the musicians, in resplendent crimson, form a lengthwise corridor through the center of the field. The first chords of their fight song – imaginatively titled "Yea Alabama" – blare through the air as a male cheerleader, carrying a massive red flag emblazoned with the slanting first letter of the alphabet, dashes through the parted members.

On his heels is another well-built spirit-leader with a same-sized banner in reverse colors. Fans of the home team respond with unbridled enthusiasm, while the visiting fans jab five fingers in the air and rain boos upon the spectacle before us.

"Here they come!" Valerie shouts, as a stream of red helmets bursts through the tunnel.

With the force of a cannon, the Alabama varsity football team races into the bright stadium. The frenzied meeting of helmets on the large Crimson Tide logo at midfield has the appearance of boiling tomato soup. This same steamy adjective can be used to describe the sentiments of many of their fans in the stadium and across the nation today.

Wearing a black headset, Mike Shula paces along the sideline across the field from us. Hired as the youngest head coach in the nation, the son of legendary NFL coach Don Shula has every reason to be anxious. In this fourth year at the helm, his team has only notched two victories over Southeastern Conference foes; an uninspiring 13-to-10 win over cellar-dweller Vanderbilt University and a 3-point overtime victory at home against a sub-par Ole Miss team.

As the traveling all-white uniforms and gleaming white helmets spread across the far side of the field, the inglorious record of their home team rival appears to bestow confidence upon Tigers fans and team members alike. In addition to throngs of fingers being thrust into the air around us, the players from the university located on the former site of East Alabama Male College have a swagger that makes Bryant-Denny Stadium now feel small.

It's almost as if we're at an *Auburn* home game.

Coming into this season, the Tigers' roster was loaded with senior players who have never lost to their crimson foes. The veteran squad was also ranked No. 4 in the AP Poll and No. 6 in the Coaches Poll. By the fifth game of the season, Tuberville's team was ranked second in the county.

The following week, however, they suffered a 17-point home loss to the Razorbacks from the University of Arkansas. Their second loss came just as unexpectedly when they faced an unranked Georgia Bulldogs team in what is recognized as the "Deep South's Oldest Rivalry." Even with these setbacks, the raucous line of white uniforms exudes a cockiness that's expected from any nine-win SEC team.

As the ball sails from the foot of Alabama's kicker, the sharp cry of "War Eagle!" can be heard above the roar of the crowd.

Scrambling up the right side, sophomore running back Tristan Davis is rudely met by a red wave at the 33-yard-line. Perhaps forebodingly, the home team is flagged for an inadvertent facemask on this very first play of the game. Then, one of the two players with the most fitting name for this contest blasts up the middle for 9 yards on first down. Kenny Irons, who finished last season as the sixth most productive rusher in Tigers' history, follows this burst with three more bruising runs. Auburn's junior quarterback, Brandon Cox, however, fails to connect on third down.

Disappointing the fans in our section, the punting unit scurries onto the field. Just as dispiriting, the booming punt travels into the end zone for a touchback. There's a television time-out, during which the cries of "War Eagle!" start again.

Turning to the animated booster sitting to my immediate right, I ask the question Valerie and I have wondered about all day: what's up with this bewildering battle cry between schools whose mascots are an elephant and a tiger?

Before he has a chance to answer, two other fans start to talk over each other, each telling completely different stories. (As noted, a lot of things about the Iron Bowl are contentious – and evidently not just among opposing fans.)

According to the middle-aged fan on my right, the rally-cry stems from "a misperception." During a game in the early 1900s against the Indians from the now-defunct Carlisle Indian Industrial School, the team employed an unorthodox strategy designed to wear down the opposition's best player, named Bald Eagle. Rather than huddling after each play, Auburn simply lined up over the ball. The quarterback would yell "Bald Eagle!" and the team would run straight into the targeted linebacker. The tradition was born when spectators began to shout what they thought their quarterback was yelling on the field.

"Wait, wait, wait, that's a myth." This interruption comes from a recent grad with a large white thumb on his shirt. He insists the slogan started during the 1892 interstate contest with Georgia when a Civil War veteran brought a live eagle to the sidelines. As the Tigers marched down the field to score the game's only touchdown, the bird flew from the former soldier's arm and circled above the crowd. Without warning, it suddenly dove to its death at the end of that momentous drive. Even with its stunning demise, Auburn fans in attendance began yelling, "It's a war eagle! War eagle! War eagle!"

"Noooo . . . ya'aaall are both wrong!" says the coed standing arm-in-arm with this large white thumb. "It waaaaaas during a game with the Bulldaawgs, just not the same one." She then delivers a dubious story about some sort of eagle-shaped pin falling off some kind of military hat worn during a pep rally before some kind of game in the early 1920s. Somehow, her slightly slurred Southern drawl makes this version seem alluringly plausible.

Starting from his 20, Kenneth Darby gains only a yard on his team's initial offensive play. At the start of this season, the running back in red needed just over 1,000 rushing yards to surpass Alabama's career rushing leader, Shaun Alexander. Lining up for the second play of the day, he's gained only 788 yards (including this most recent 1) and zero rushing touchdowns in all eleven games this year. Following a 13-yard pass by John Parker Wilson, Darby gets his legs underneath him and rumbles for his second first-down.

On the ensuing third down, the quarterback from Hoover High School in the Alabama town with the same name scrambles for a roar-inducing 27 yards. This gain is immediately bolstered by another explosion from sophomore wide receiver, DJ Hall. It's first-down-and-goal at the 4-yard-line.

Valerie and I look at each other with genuine surprise. Perhaps the finger waving boosters have been a bit over-confident coming into this Iron Bowl. Our look of amazement fades as the Crimson Tide proceeds to muster only 2 yards on the next three downs and chooses to settle for a field goal with a little under 7 minutes to go in the first quarter.

Each team's opening possessions are followed by a back-and-forth defensive struggle. After three plays, Auburn punts. Four plays, Alabama punts. Three more plays, another punt. On the sixth play of the following drive, the Tigers' front four assail Alabama's sophomore quarterback, who seems to always be referred to by his three names. Flushed from the pocket, John Parker Wilson is violently sacked by defensive end, Quentin Groves. This staggering tackle by the 6'3" 253-pound senior from Greenville, Mississippi dislodges the ball to the turf. Pandemonium erupts around us as No. 40 in white, linebacker Kevin Sears raises the ball into the air just 27 yards from the goal line.

Brandon Cox leads his offense onto the field with 11 minutes remaining in the second quarter. The Auburn quarterback – who last weekend against unranked Georgia was sacked four times, intercepted four times, and only generated enough offense for four first downs in the entire game – proceeds to hand the ball to his running back four consecutive times. Brad Lester, the number-two running back in jersey No. 1, pierces the crimson end zone on the final rushing play of this pounding drive. The bruising 12-yard ramble for the score casts a pall over the home-field crowd.

Following a touchback, the pumped-up visiting defense races onto the field. Valerie points to both linebackers crowding the line of scrimmage, almost daring Wilson to pass after his fumble on the previous play. This aggressiveness immediately pays off. Running back Darby is sacked at the 14-yard-line. The second play of this stunted series is almost identical to the previous two.

So is the result.

For the second time in less than 2 minutes, defensive end Quentin Groves crushes Wilson as his pocket collapses on the 8-yard-line. Just like his first devastating sack, Groves shocks the ball out of the signal caller's hands. Our entire section screams in delight as this fumble gives the ball back to Auburn.

These cheers swiftly become squeals of glee just two plays and 20 seconds later as Kenny Irons rumbles 8 yards for his first touchdown of the game. Even a 15-yard unsportsmanlike penalty after the touchdown, applied to the extra-point, can't dampen the celebration in our section. Without flinching, the Tigers' placekicker splits the uprights on the extra-long extra-point. The scoreboard reads: Auburn 14. Alabama 3.

With 9 minutes left in the second quarter, and following the tenth consecutive Iron Bowl first quarter in which Alabama has failed to score a touchdown, Kenneth Darby opens with a 17-yard charge. The Crimson Tide encouragingly moves to third down and 1 at midfield via a swing-pass from Wilson to senior running back Le'Ron McClain. The heralded quarterback, however, fails to connect on his subsequent pass.

Displaying the same confidence he has all season; Shula sends the punt team onto the field. An outpouring of "boos!" slices across the arena.

This displeasure escalates to distress as the offense in all-white proceeds to methodically take more than 5 minutes off the game clock. The 14-play drive, which began just outside their end zone after the punt was downed inside the 1, includes a 31-yard pass from Cox to sophomore wide receiver Rodgeriqus Smith. Disappointingly for our section-mates, the 53-yard field-goal-attempt by John Vaughn at the end of this drive misses its mark. Even so, all the energy on the field – and on the sidelines – emanates from the guests to Bryant-Denny Stadium.

It's astonishing how quickly energy can reverse flow in college football.

With only 1:43 left until halftime and seemingly no sense of urgency, No. 14 in red completes a first-down pass to his true freshman receiver Nikita Stover. The crimson crowd senses the inevitable after two consecutive incomplete passes at the 47-yard-line. As home team fans head to the tunnels for halftime concessions, Wilson somehow finds the freshman from Hartselle, Alabama wide open on third down. Streaking 53 yards down the field, No. 9 scores Alabama's first touchdown of the game. Bryant-

Denny is deafening.

As teammates mob Stover in the end zone, Shula races across the sideline with two (not five) fingers in the air. Attempting to seize the first real momentum of the game and bring the 9-to-14 score within a field goal, the unwary head coach elects to leave his offense on the field. From just 3 yards outside the goal line, Wilson drops back in the pocket and throws a fade pass into the corner.

It truly *is* astonishing how quickly energy flows in this sport.

As the ball falls incomplete, the fans in our section erupt with cheers of mockery and relief. Wisely, after this stunning touchdown by the home team and with only 1:13 remaining in the half, the Tigers choose to run the ball up the middle a couple times and, when the halftime horn blares, run into the locker room leading their rivals by the same number of points as the number of digits on a human hand.

The Million Dollar Band doesn't seem as loud as it did during opening ceremonies. With the west side of the massive stadium casting an ominous shadow, their parade uniforms don't appear as vivid, either. Nonetheless, today's traditional tunes and precision maneuvers by the home team's myriad marching musicians would surely make William C. Pickens proud.

Much like halftime at The Horseshoe in Columbus, most of the more than 92,000 fans in attendance have remained in their seats throughout this intermission. My stocky seatmate in white grumbles something along the lines of, "I can think of a *million* reasons why I hate this part of the state!"

As the teams warm up along each sideline, Valerie shuffles back to our row with arms full of high-calorie concession stand treats. We're going to need added energy to make it through the final 30 minutes of this glorious grudge match! Defiant fans around us wave their fully extended fingers into the air as they await the second-half kickoff.

With the ball traveling out of the end zone, our new friend to my right informs us the home team has never scored more than 20 points during an Iron Bowl inside Bryant-Denny Stadium.

Two plays into this first drive, fortune does, however, swing in favor of Shula's squad. On third down, his starting quarterback completes a 10-yard pass to Nikita Stover once again. Wilson fires a second strike into the arms of his other freshman wide receiver, Will Oakley, for a gain of almost 34 yards. The sea of red surrounding our section rises like a tsunami.

Three rushing plays later, the Crimson Tide have the ball on the 14-yard-line. After a failed attempt up the middle, Wilson drops back and lofts a perfect pass to No. 83. The 6'2" tight end from the town of Prattville, just an hour-and-a-half south of this stadium, snatches the ball inside the boundaries.

Wilson races to join his teammates who are hugging Travis McCall in celebration of the sophomore's first career touchdown as an Alabama player. Waves of red roll across the stadium. Once again, however, Shula finds a way to turn back the tide.

Having just taken more than 6 minutes off the clock, the son of the all-time winningest NFL coach attempts to make up for his team's failed two-point-try in the first half. And, once again, the same pass as the first two-point-attempt results in the same outcome. The score remains 15-to-14 in his favor. Even with this second failed two-point-conversion, the fans in white surrounding us bemoan this unexpected lead change.

Just as troubling for the visitors, Auburn is forced to initiate their first possession of the second half from their 10-yard-line after a holding penalty on the kickoff. The Tigers impressively move to almost midfield on six plays, including a nifty 22-yard pass from Cox to junior running back Carl Stewart. The drive is stifled when their quarterback is sacked by 270-pound senior defensive tackle Wallace Gilberry. Forced to punt, the ball is fair-caught on the 11-yard-line after a booming kick by slip-of-paper, Kody Bliss, who could weigh maybe 170-pounds – but only after eating several armfuls of concession stand food.

Following a short run and two consecutive incomplete passes, the ball is punted back to the Tigers. Tre Smith waves his arm at midfield. Four plays later, in just over a minute in playing time, a wave crashes on the Tide. Wide receiver Prechae Rodriguez races 21 yards and leaps in the corner of the end zone with the ball in his hand. The 6'4" sophomore from Tampa, Florida taunts the home crowd by bringing his finger to his mouth gesturing silence.

With the score now 20-to-15, Tuberville's team cunningly accomplishes what the home team has failed at twice today.

Compounding the impact of this sudden score – and the derisive end zone shushing – Brandon Cox swiftly pitches the ball to Stewart following his pulling guards around the right side. At the last minute, the streaking running back lobs the ball forward to No. 25 in white, Lee Guess. The visiting team lurches ahead by 7 points.

With both teams huddling around their coaches, I comment during the break before the final quarter that no other play seems as deflating for the home team as this creative two-point-conversion.

Just then, the-instantly recognizable first chords of "Sweet Home Alabama" blare across the stadium. The crowd goes berserk. What Valerie and I initially perceive to be a spontaneous reaction to the Lynyrd Skynyrd anthem quickly shows itself to be an anticipated tradition for the fans in red: each time the first line of the iconic chorus of blares from the massive sound system, the stadium hollers in unison, "Roll, Tide, Roll!"

Another surprise awaits. As this Southern tradition reaches its crescendo, onto the field saunter two casually dressed men, one with blondish-white hair flowing to the middle of his back, the other wearing a dark fedora. Standing at the 20-yard-line directly in front of our section, both more-than-middle-aged individuals wave to the stands. The fans surrounding us murmur and don't appear to know who the somebodies are.

We don't either, and just when it's starting to feel a little awkward, the stadium announcer requests we, "Extend a warm Crimson Tide welcome to the lead singer and guitarist of Alabama's greatest rock-n-roll band!" The arena shouts their appreciation so loudly for these surviving members of Lynyrd Skynyrd, neither Valerie nor are I able to hear their names.

With the field lights flickering to life, we cannot know the final quarter will become a brutal defensive slugfest.

Following the 8 points scored at the end of the third quarter by the visiting team, Alabama is only able to eke out 11 yards on a 6-play drive. Forced to punt, Tre Smith once again calls for a fair-catch just 20 yards outside his own goal. After another bruising run for 18 yards by Irons, the home team finally catches a break. On the very next play, the burly running back is stoned at the line of scrimmage. This hit by their 6'6" 260-pound lineman, Chris Harris, rattles No. 23 so hard that the ball squirts to the turf and is scooped-up by Jeremy Clark. The 306-pound fellow lineman falls forward for an additional 4 yards.

Fortune is a fickle mistress. On the very next play, Alabama once again finds a way to take the air out of Bryant-Denny Stadium. Wide receiver Keith Brown catches an 8-yard pass at midfield from his quarterback, Cox. Failing to secure the ball, the swarming Tigers pounce on No. 81 in red – and on the loose ball – to take possession right back. A collective groan rumbles through the stands.

Auburn, however, fails to make a first down and is forced to punt. Unexpectedly, the home team marches on a 10-play, 70-yard drive. Unfortunately (yet not unexpectedly), Cox throws an incomplete pass on fourth down at the 19-yard-line.

With a little more than four-and-a-half minutes remaining in the game, we recognize the precarious situation both teams are in. Auburn needs to burn as much clock as possible. Shula's team desperately needs to get the ball back.

The Tigers gain 16 yards in five plays. They also take almost 3 minutes off the game clock. Alabama calls a time-out. The visitor's diminutive punter lets fly another tremendous boomer from his 35-yard-line. Catching the ball in stride at about the 20 yard-line, No. 28 in red, Javier Arenas (who, at 176-pounds, is not much bigger than Auburn's punter), zigzags up the middle of the field for 22 yards.

The game clock rests at 1:28.

The opposable thumb is a marvel of evolution. Millions of years of survival-of-the-fittest have resulted in its ability to enable humans to perform tasks far beyond those of all other creatures. These two digits, along with the ability to reason, are the defining characteristics of our species. All three, obviously, also enable us to perform the wonderful sport we cherish. Without them, even the most routine play could never be executed, let alone comprehended.

John Parker Wilson throws a quick out on first down to bring his passing performance to 252 yards on 18 receptions in this 71st Iron Bowl. With 1:26 left in the game, the sophomore quarterback stands over his center on his 43-yard-line.

Taking the snap, Wilson drops straight back without even attempting to feign a handoff to his running back, who crashes into the middle of the charging defense. Neglecting to look-off wide receiver Keith Brown, he thrusts the ball into double coverage. David Irons, the other all-white-clad player with the most fitting name for today's contest, races step for step along the far sideline with Brown. Stabbing his arm into the air, the 5'11" 190-pound sophomore instinctively activates his opposable thumb – along with the four other digits on his right hand – and snatches the ball out of the hands of No. 81 in crimson. The young defensive back quickly tucks the ball into his body and falls to the ground.

As several jubilant team members mob the instantly anointed hero of the game, I yell to Valerie to look at the head coach directly below us. With a Cheshire-smile, Tommy Tuberville unabashedly bearhugs his first-year defensive coordinator, Will Muschamp.

No time-outs remain for either team. All that's left for the Tigers to do is run a little more than a minute off the game clock.

Following a blatant act of frustration, the home team is flagged for an unsportsmanlike penalty on second down of this final series. With Auburn in "victory formation," senior outside linebacker Terrance Jones – who has never experienced a victory over the team from across the state – crashes into the back of the unsuspecting running back, Carl Stewart.

After accepting the egregious penalty, quarterback Cox takes-a-knee as time expires in the now fully lit stadium. Darkness has fallen on Tuscaloosa.

The defining feature of mankind is thrust high into the air by the fans in our section. To our right, the scoreboard glows: ALABAMA 15. AUBURN 22. Players in bright white jerseys race to join their teammates jumping up and down on the large script letter at midfield. All five fingers extend above each player. Fellow defensive tackles Chris Browder and Sen'Derrick Marks saunter side by side along the Tigers' sideline with their opposable digits pressed together high above their heads.

As we watch the swirling circle in the middle of the field sprint toward the blaring band in white at the curve of the stadium, fans across the nation are now unequivocally aware of the number of consecutive Iron Bowls won by Auburn in the past five years.

The number of disappointing plays by their opponent today can't be counted on just one hand.

Careening out of the cheerless arena, one of our former row-mates boasts, "Come to our house next year and y'all will see us start to work on gittin' the other thumb!"

Given the dominance exhibited this evening – and throughout the first half of this decade – this sounds like a distinct possibility. Not only has victory remained elusive for Mike Shula in this rivalry, once again the home team failed to score more than 20 points.

Valerie remarks how today's Tiger Walk across from Rama Jama's not only set the tone for this seventh game of our annual pursuit; it could be a metaphor for this Iron Bowl. Auburn certainly marched into Tuscaloosa today as if they owned the place.

Strolling into the dark neighborhood surrounding the just-as-dark stadium, the eerie silhouette of Evergreen Cemetery appears across Paul W Bryant Drive. I imagine the namesake of this street would roll over in his grave if he could be aware of the dismal performances that have led to the proud digits being waved in the air tonight.

This dark bone-yard is not the only place that's dead in the state of Alabama.

We poke our heads into a well-worn tavern that looks like it's seen many past nights of revelry. This evening, however, only a handful of dispirited Bama fans are sitting at the bar nursing their sorrows. After just one subdued round in this subdued haunt, Valerie gives me a big smile – and a big thumbs-up – on our decision to head back to the hotel.

CHAPTER NINE
Fiesta Time
2007 Oklahoma | West Virginia

Digging into this year's stack of preseason magazines at our kitchen table, it's apparent the Big XII Conference has a chance at a BCS bowl game this year, possibly two. Also, Valerie's alma mater looks to be the conference front-runner for one of these prestigious bowls.

The Longhorns have an average national ranking of No. 5 in our collection of periodicals. Nipping at their hooves, with an average position of No. 8, is their loathsome rival from across the Red River. Three other contenders, albeit long shots, are the No. 15 Nebraska Cornhuskers, No. 22 Texas A&M Aggies, and the University of Missouri. The Tigers from Columbia are outside the top-25 in all our magazines except *Phil Steele's College Football Preview*. This inch-thick tome from the self-professed preseason guru has Missouri ranked No. 19.

Even my alma mater, given their post-season performance last year, may have an outside shot at one of these five New Year's Day bowls. Oklahoma State capped off a six-win and six-loss season with a trip to the 2006 Independence Bowl. Both teams came into this mid-tier bowl with the same lackluster record. However, one did not arrive with the same coach it had during the regular season.

Immediately following the thumb-raising loss to the team from Auburn, the Crimson Tide's athletic director Mal Moore announced, "I have informed Mike Shula that he will not be retained as head football coach at the University of Alabama."

During this press conference after that emasculating 2006 Iron Bowl, he added, "Mike has been an excellent representative of our program. However, we did not make progress on the field this season and have not been able to maintain the positive momentum necessary to return Alabama football to a place among college football's elite programs."

The top brass at Alabama assigned head coaching responsibility for the Independence Bowl last year to defensive coordinator Joe Kines. Unfortunately for the interim coach, much like their substandard regular-season performance, the Tide ended up on the losing end of a hard-fought contest on that late December evening in Louisiana. The Cowboys from Stillwater defeated the now even more red-faced team from Tuscaloosa 34-to-31.

The controversial Bowl Championship Series was implemented at the start of the 1998 season. Prior to its formation, a "mythical" No. 1 team was chosen by the two nationally recognized polls at the end of each bowl season. It wasn't much of a secret that politics often played a significant role in this process.

Because of this, the NCAA came up with its convoluted BCS selection system, which designates five major bowl games as hosts of the ten top teams. Following these BCS Bowls, a final National Championship game is played between the teams with the highest number of BCS points based upon esoteric calculations from six computer programs combined with the national polls.

Glancing up from the pages of *Street & Smith's*, I mention to Valerie, herself immersed in one of the glossy publications, that the champion of the Big XII Conference has been contractually obligated to play in the Fiesta Bowl since the introduction of this newfangled BCS process. Given the real possibility one of our alma maters could finish in the top position of the conference, I have an idea.

"Let's go to the Fiesta Bowl for this year's game," I tell her. "I don't care which teams make it in. Let's have a party in the desert!"

The West Virginia University Mountaineers are ranked third in the 2007 pre-season AP poll. This highest-ever initial standing is due in large part to the return of two of the most dynamic players in the nation.

Pat White, prior to announcing his college choice, was a first-team all-state quarterback at Daphne High School in the eastern Alabama shoreline town of the same name. During his senior year, the multisport athlete threw for 1,488 yards and 15 touchdowns. He also rushed for more than 1,900 yards and 31 touchdowns. This dazzling performance earned him third place in the 2004 Alabama "Mr. Football" ranking, an honor awarded by sportswriters to the top high school player in the state.

Courted by the likes of Auburn, Mississippi State, and Kentucky, White originally committed to play receiver at Louisiana State University. However, when head coach Rich Rodriquez promised the opportunity to play quarterback, White signed his letter of intent to attend West Virginia University.

More than 1,000 miles north of Daphne, another standout athlete was being wooed by this same head coach.

Steve Slaton was the star running back at Conwell-Egan Catholic High School in Fairless Hills, Pennsylvania. He also excelled at track and field, recording the sixth-best long-jump in the nation. But the gridiron is where he truly shined.

Slaton, who started as a freshman, was an all-conference selection each of his four years. Rushing for more than 6,000 yards during his high school career, he set five school records and earned all-state honors at the end of both his junior and senior years.

Offers came from schools across the nation including the University of Maryland, Rutgers University, and the University of North Carolina. However, the speedy running back chose West Virginia also because of a promise by Rich Rodriquez. The head coach vowed he would have an opportunity to start right away as a defensive back.

While these high school phenoms came from very different parts of the country, they came together as a daunting one-two-punch during their first two seasons as Mountaineers.

The Mountaineers finished with a respectable 8-and-4 record the year before the arrival of White and Slaton. Even so, many fans in Morgantown (and beyond) had expected the 2004 season to be a breakout year.

Much to their chagrin, the team dropped their final two regular-season games, including their interstate rivalry game – appropriately known as the Backyard Brawl – against the University of Pittsburgh. Just as disheartening, they were soundly defeated by the No. 15-ranked Florida State Seminoles in the Gator Bowl. This was the third consecutive bowl appearance for the Rodriquez-led Mountaineers. It was the third consecutive double-digit loss in one as well.

Heading into his fifth season at the helm, the people from the hills were restless. And Coach Rich knew it.

This uneasiness, however, was emphatically put to rest on a crisp night in mid-October at the newly named Milan Puskar Stadium in Morgantown. Trailing the 19th-ranked University of Louisville by 17 points in the fourth quarter, the one-loss Mountaineers only had one score on the board. The possibility of a comeback dimmed during a bruising sack of their starting quarterback, Adam Bednarik. Slammed to the turf by linebacker Brandon Johnson, Bednarik was unable to get to his feet due to a painful injury to his right foot. Pat White, who had only experienced mop-up duty in the first six games of the season, was thrust into the spotlight for the remaining eleven-and-a-half minutes of the game.

From the moment he took the field, the demeanor of the offense changed. In less than 7 minutes of game time, White and his young running back Slaton had their team trailing by only 7 points. With exactly 1 minute on the game clock, Slaton plunged into the end zone to tie the score at 24-apiece and send the game into overtime.

The teams then scored 48-combined points. In three overtime periods.

In the final overtime, Slaton notched his fifth touchdown of the game on another 1-yard dive. The Mountaineers went ahead by 8 points after successfully executing their mandatory two-point-conversion. Four plays later, the Cardinals defiantly responded with a touchdown by junior running back Michael Bush. On the two-point-try, Louisville quarterback Brian Brohm boldly dropped back into his empty backfield. With no receivers open, the sophomore signal-caller tucked the ball and spurted through the collapsing pocket. He didn't make it.

At the end of this thrilling comeback, Rodriquez knew he had something special. The 46-to-44 defeat of the Cardinals solidified the reputation of Mountaineers' starting dynamic duo White and Slaton, who came to be known as "Nickel and Dime," given their respective jersey numbers of 5 and 10.

The win also ignited the team to finish the remainder of their season unblemished. With only one loss on their 2005 schedule, the men from Morgantown were invited to the Sugar Bowl. The underdog Mountaineers bested the SEC Champions, the Bulldogs from Athens, Georgia, in a back-and-forth track meet that ended 38-to-35. Pat White finished his freshman season with his blue and gold teammates ranked No. 5 in the AP poll.

The flight from Portland to Phoenix is a little less than 3 hours. And on this last week of the year, the two locations couldn't be further apart.

Settling onto the plane, we're very pleased with our decision back in August. It's a drizzly 42 degrees outside, as it has been since late September. The anticipation of 70 degrees and an abundance of sunshine, along with the excitement of our first BCS bowl game, lifts our spirits as the plane takes off.

Approaching Sky Harbor International Airport, we're aware this prestigious bowl game – much like the Army-Navy game at Veterans Stadium – is *not* nestled among historic grassy commons and antiquated academic buildings. Hosting this year's game is a civic arena that held its first event, a preseason NFL game between the Pittsburgh Steelers and Arizona Cardinals, less than 18 months ago. University of Phoenix Stadium also features a football field on wheels just outside its south end. The sun-grown turf is rolled into the stadium before each game.

If the massive silver-clad dome is recognized by *Business Week* as one of "the ten most impressive" sports facilities in the world, it's known to Phoenicians as the "Giant Toaster." As our plane banks on approach, I smile at the thought of the world's largest piece of bread popping up from the rectangular opening in its roof.

Following his senior year at Daphne High School, Pat White was selected by the Anaheim Angels in the fourth round of the Major League Baseball draft. He chose college football – much to the appreciation of the Mountaineer faithful. At the end of his sophomore season, the team from Morgantown finished with a second consecutive eleven-win record and their aforementioned second-ever win in the 2006 Gator Bowl. Coincidently, West Virginia defeated Georgia Tech by the exact score in this same illustrious bowl one year earlier against the other team from Georgia.

Eight games into last season, Pat White's undefeated Mountaineers ranked No. 3 in the nation. Whispers of Heisman Trophy consideration began to swirl around the country. Sometimes, however, they swirl down the drain. On the first Thursday in November, the Mountaineers were handed their first setback when the No. 5-ranked team in the country avenged their most degrading loss of the prior year. The Louisville Cardinals, in their home stadium, beat the team from Morgantown 44-to-34.

Even in this defeat, White displayed Heisman-worthy fortitude as he attempted another fourth-quarter comeback. Impressively, the young signal-caller finished the season with 18 rushing and 13 passing touchdowns. He also earned Big East Offensive Player of the Year and first-team all-conference honors.

Nonetheless, when the ballots were counted, it was his fellow offensive back who finished in the running for the Heisman. With 1,744 total rushing yards (third-best in the nation and best at his school), Steve Slaton received the fourth most votes behind Notre Dame quarterback Brady Quinn, runner-up Darren McFadden (sophomore running back from Arkansas), and winner Troy Smith (senior quarterback from The Ohio State University).

The top two teams in both divisions of the Big XII are battling it out for a spot in their conference title game this year. A possible trip to the Fiesta Bowl awaits the winner.

In the South Division, Valerie's alma mater got this 2007 season off to a resounding start. After winning their first four games, however, the Longhorns were mauled at home by the unranked Kansas State Wildcats. Her team followed this loss with a hard-fought defeat in their annual cross-river tussle at Cotton Bowl Stadium. Lamentably, this was their second conference loss. In their final regular-season game, the six-win and five-loss Texas A&M Aggies scored a touchdown on their first possession, a field goal on their second, and a cunning 3-yard fake field goal for a touchdown on their third. Even a valiant two-touchdown effort in the final minutes was not enough for the team from Austin to overcome these early scores.

The Horns finished their regular season with a disappointing 5-and-3 conference record. Because of this, and much to our dismay, the school with the little white wagon captured the South Division's spot in this year's Big XII Conference Championship.

In the North Division, head coach Mark Mangino was making history. Over the past 25 years, the University of Kansas has had only three seasons with more than five wins. This year, for the first time since the inception of football in Lawrence, the Jayhawks have won 11 games. With their final regular-season game remaining, the undefeated overachievers from this school known for its basketball program are averaging almost 46 points per game and are ranked No. 2 in the nation.

The University of Missouri is ranked third in the nation heading into this final week. The team from Columbia, which is also scoring more than 42 points per game, brings 10 wins into their final regular-season game for the first time since their "undefeated" 1960 season. (The Tigers *were* defeated that year; however, the visiting Jayhawks from Lawrence fielded an ineligible player and were forced to forfeit.) Missouri's twelfth game this season is the same contest as that vacated game.

Even though Kansas is considered by many to be the best team in the country, they're only a 1-point favorite in this much-anticipated Border War. Sometimes, the Vegas wise guys seem to know more than the public. Led by junior quarterback Chase Daniel, the Tigers scored 36 points and held off a 21-point fourth-quarter surge to win the slugfest by 8 points. The victory sealed a first-ever Big XII North Division title for the University of Missouri and a ticket to the Conference Championship Game.

From our downtown Phoenix hotel, it's difficult to feel any sense of revelry, let alone rivalry.

On this New Year's Day before the Fiesta Bowl, the Trojans from Southern California have just dismantled the University of Illinois. In this first BCS game of the season (and one of the most lopsided Rose Bowl games ever), the Men of Troy manhandled the boys from Champaign 49-to-17. USC scored 21 points in the first half. The Fighting Illini managed only a field goal before heading into the locker room at halftime. By game's end, with more than 630 total yards and 28 points in the second half, the No. 7 Trojans notched another dominating win in this "Granddaddy of All Bowl Games."

We have about an hour before the broadcast of the next BCS game and a tremendous desire for some semblance of collegiate merriment. Heading out, we hope to find plenty of flat-screens and not-so-flat frosty beverages. Once in Tempe, Valerie spots the sports bar recommended by the Arizona State University sophomore working behind the front desk at our hotel.

The Library Bar & Grill lives up to both parts of its name. The walls are lined in deep mahogany and floor-to-ceiling bookshelves, while our waitress is outfitted in a skimpy schoolgirl uniform straight out of a Britney Spears video. A logo stretching across the main bar reads, IN GOOD TIMES WE TRUST.

I tell Valerie I'm willing to bet this place has seen some pretty good times, and yet, right now does not seem like one of them: we pretty much have the place to ourselves, on this day after New Year's Eve. Lucky for us, the Library is designed for more than just reading. The lingering smell of spilled alcohol from last night confirms this.

A multitude of big-screens surrounds the dining area. While

nowhere near the manic environment of Big Al's in Blacksburg or Rama Jama's in Tuscaloosa, the unique campus bar instills a sense of collegiate spirit as we watch the kickoff to this year's Sugar Bowl.

In this highly anticipated contest, the No. 4 Georgia Bulldogs are pitted against the undefeated University of Hawaii Warriors. Formerly known as the Rainbows, the 12-and-0 team from the islands not only vanquished their perennial conference leader, Boise State, for the first time in history; they won the Western Athletic Conference for the first time since joining in 1979. Within a couple of pints, however, we get a sense of déjà vu.

The first 30 minutes of this bowl could easily be an instant replay of the first BCS game today. By halftime inside the Louisiana Superdome, the Bulldogs have scored 24 points. The former Rainbows have only kicked a field goal. Much like the overmatched Fighting Illini earlier, Hawaii is unable to muster any threat against the team from the mainland in the second half. As we settle our tab with Ms. Spears, it's 41-to-10 in favor of the Bulldogs. With this beatdown, no FBS team will finish the season undefeated.

West Virginia University set the stage for a golden 2007 season by unveiling dazzling yellow uniforms. The flashy new duds, along with the highest-ever preseason ranking, have the sleepy college town along the Monongahela River brimming with anticipation. Coming off their combined 49 touchdowns and almost 5,000 yards last season, Pat White and Steve Slaton are once again considered one of the most dynamic backfields in all of college football.

The duo lived up to this billing during the first four games of their junior season. The Mountaineers averaged slightly more than 47 points in these early contests, including in their in-state showdown with the wonderfully named Thundering Herd. (The team traveled 90 miles to the small town of Huntington for the first time in more than 90 years for this scrimmage with Marshall University.) Along with the electrifying attack of Nickel and Dime, a flash of future greatness revealed himself during this dominant victory: true freshman running back Noel Devine may have carried the ball only five times that day, but he gained an average of more than 15 yards and scored a touchdown.

The men from Morgantown traveled to Tampa for their fifth game to face the team that upset their BCS aspirations last season. The unranked University of South Florida stunned West Virginia on their home field last year, holding the second-ranked scoring offense to only 19 points and causing a fumble that was returned for a touchdown to win by 5 points. This season, on a warm late-September evening in Raymond James Stadium, the underdog Bulls once again trample the Mountaineer's not-so-farfetched dream of a perfect season.

Also reminiscent of last season, the Mountaineers regrouped and won their next 6 games, including victories over Mississippi State and three teams ranked in the AP Top-25. In addition to clinching their fifth Big East Conference title, Rich Rodriquez's squad secured a coveted spot in a BCS bowl game with this win – and the possibility of playing in this year's National Championship Game.

All that stood in their way was a gristly 4-and-7 team from the gritty steel mills of Pennsylvania.

The beleaguered Panthers from the University of Pittsburgh came into this 100th Backyard Brawl (which was first played in 1895 and has since seen little love lost across the 75 miles separating the schools) as four touchdown underdogs. The visiting team is starting a true freshman at quarterback for the first time since 1987. Pat Bostick and his fellow Panthers also haven't won a single game away from their home field all season. It's Senior Day in Morgantown. The home team has averaged 42 points and 310 rushing yards per game. And it's bitter cold on this bitter field.

College football has a funny way of reminding us no matter how shiny the brass ring may seem, many times it can easily rust away.

Head coach Dave Wannstedt and the rough boys from Pittsburgh shut down the high-powered machine from West Virginia. (In his third year at the helm, Wannstedt is a somewhat familiar face to me. Each time our practice squad lined up on

Lewis Field during my freshman year, his mustached face peered over the shoulder pads of Dexter Manley.)

Not only did the pesky Panthers shut down almost every drive by the Mountaineers; they knocked their Heisman-hopeful quarterback out of the game with a thumb injury. This pain must have paled in comparison to the agony of the final score. The 9-to-13 defeat removed West Virginia from any discussion about the BSC National Championship Game – and sent them to this Fiesta Bowl.

As we pull into the sprawling gray lot, Valerie notes that it feels more like arriving at a concert venue than a college football game.

All we see on this cool, clear Wednesday afternoon is the giant silver toaster surrounded by never-ending rows of parked cars. Except for a couple of small Tostitos Fiesta Bowl logos on the stylized silver panels, we are hard-pressed to even identify the specific event taking place today.

All of that changes as we walk toward the east entrance of the Arizona Cardinals' home stadium.

"Boomer!" . . . "Sooner!"

Ugh.

Fortunately, most municipal stadiums offer adult libations during college football games.

As this nauseating back-and-forth yell echoes across the terrace, we immediately head to the closest beer stand. Along with an oversized red No. 28 jersey with "Peterson" across the back, several rambunctious fans in our concession line are wearing 2008 Fiesta Bowl t-shirts.

"I notice they're not wearing 2007 Fiesta Bowl shirts," Valerie says. Is she smirking as she says it? A little.

The University of Oklahoma is making its second consecutive appearance inside this 2-year-old sports facility today. We're certain their fans expect a different outcome than their first.

The Sooners, led by their highly-touted junior running back Adrian Peterson, came into last year's Fiesta Bowl slightly more than a touchdown favorite over the undefeated Broncos from Boise State University. The theatrics on that New Year's Day cemented the David versus Goliath clash as arguably the greatest game in the history of the sport.

Or, if not the greatest, certainly one of the most entertaining.

The contest included a 50-yard hook-and-lateral on fourth down with only 18 seconds left in regulation, a half-back pass in overtime, a "Statue of Liberty" play for Boise State's victory AND the nationally televised marriage proposal by Bronco's running back Ian Johnson to cheerleader Chrissy Popadics.

Sports Illustrated in their article "Behind the Scenes with Boise," captured the inconceivable ending: "This was the ultimate underdog story of a team that believed from the start, refused to give up even when it looked bleak and pulled off the improbable. It's one thing for a Cinderella team to upset a heavily favored opponent, but c'mon, this was ridiculous . . . Boise State's mind-numbing 43-42 victory over Oklahoma in the Fiesta Bowl on Monday night had everything and will go down as one of [the] best games in college football history."

The boisterous fans in crimson swarming around us surely anticipate their beloved team to avenge this stupefying loss. And, just like last year, the Sooners arrive in Glendale as slightly more than 7-point favorites over their opponent.

The team with misaligned initials has already begun pregame warm-ups as we locate our seats about 20 rows from the field in the southwest curve of the stadium.

Picked by Big XII writers to finish second in their conference, the Sooners ended the regular season as one of the hottest teams in the nation. Ten games into their schedule, Oklahoma had only one blemish to an unranked Colorado team in their fifth game. Five consecutive wins later had them ranked third in the nation. And then, once again, they were defeated by an unranked team. This time, it was the Texas Tech Red Raiders in Arlington, Texas.

Heading into their final regular-season game, the Sooners needed a win in the Bedlam Series (as the scrimmage with their in-state rival is called) to take the division title and secure a spot in the Conference Championship Game. Unfortunately for my alma mater, the game at Oklahoma Memorial Stadium was a one-sided affair that firmly established red-shirt freshman Sam Bradford as quarterback-of-the-future for the Sooners.

In this 101ˢᵗ scrimmage with the Cowboys, Bradford threw four touchdowns. The home team's defense rivaled his performance, holding Oklahoma State to 299 total yards. Head coach Mike Gundy's team was averaging almost 500 yards per game until this disappointing effort in Norman.

Finishing with six wins and two losses in the Southern Division, the Sooners earned their spot in the Big XII Championship Game. Awaiting them were the victors of the epic Border War that took place a week earlier in Kansas City.

Entering the Alamodome on that first day in December; only eight FBS teams had scored more points per game this season than the undefeated Missouri Tigers. Once again, however, the wise guys in Vegas seemed to know something. The Sooners lined up as 3.5-point favorites against the No. 1 team in the nation.

At the end of the first two quarters, there was little indication of whether the casinos got the odds correct. The score was knotted 14-to-14 at halftime. The second half, however, was all Oklahoma. Three touchdowns and a field goal in the final 30 minutes sent head coach Gary Pinkel and his humiliated felines home to Columbia with a 17-to-38 loss – and propelled the team from Norman to today's bowl game here in Glendale.

Old Glory unfurls across 100 yards of sun-grown turf inside University of Phoenix Stadium. The stadium announcer asks us to stand for a tradition dear to our hearts. As the young woman at midfield belts out our National Anthem's final lines, Valerie gasps. She points to the upper deck, from which a solitary bald eagle has just taken flight.

Aptly named Challenger, the majestic raptor glides just below the closed roof as waves of fans react in wonderment.

Silently soaring towards the end zone in front of us, Challenger makes an arcing turn back toward the opposite side. Flying directly overhead, we see the bright white head and sharp amber beak of the noble bird. As if playing to the crowd, Challenger climbs back toward the roof. Valerie lets out a squeal as he again swoops across the middle of the oversized flag. After almost 2 minutes in flight, the national symbol circles a few feet above the red end zone and glides toward his handler.

Standing atop a bright yellow platform at the end of "OKLAHOMA," the trainer braces for the approaching bird of prey. The capacity crowd cheers as Challenger alights upon his arm.

Albeit much different than the flyover at the second rivalry of our quest in Philadelphia, this spectacle is just as moving, just as patriotic. Neither Valerie nor I attempt to conceal the tears rolling down our cheeks, and why would we?

The giant flag is hastily furled while a small group of bright yellow cheerleaders emerges from the stadium tunnel located diagonally across from our section. A deep, booming "BOOOO!" rolls across the manicured grass as the neon-colored troupe streaks ahead of the visiting team. Locked arm in arm, the Mountaineers confidently stride in rows of four toward our side of the field. Jogging amidst the streaming white jerseys and dark blue pants is head coach Bill Stewart.

The former assistant head coach, hired by Don Nehlen in 2000, has been elevated to interim head coach for this BCS bowl game. His unexpected promotion is due to a decision by the man who was at the helm for the past seven years. Two weeks following the stunning loss in the Backyard Brawl last month, Rich Rodriguez informed his team he was leaving Morgantown to take over for the retiring Lloyd Carr at the University of Michigan.

From the sea of red in the stands across the field comes the revolting ping-ponging cheer. Two diminutive white ponies poke their heads out of the stadium tunnel at the far end zone. With a blast from the University of Oklahoma band, the miniature equine spring to life. A large white flag with two intersecting red vowels follows closely behind the little covered wagon as it streaks across the crimson end zone. Valerie points out that at least this time – unlike the original gun-jumping settlers from the state – the comical farm-cart waited for the signal to enter the stadium.

As the all-crimson marching band struts across the tri-colored sun in the Tostitos Fiesta Bowl logo at midfield, the junior quarterback from Daphne High School casually throws warm-up passes to a fellow Mountaineer along the sideline directly in front of our section. Pat White looks relaxed and resolved. That he appears composed, just minutes before this most important game of his football life, is not lost on his teammates.

The coin toss at midfield is won by Oklahoma. Surprisingly, head coach Bob Stoops elects to receive.

This atypical decision by the indoor-visor-wearing coach appears to be an attempt to set the tone with his high-scoring offense. (The Sooners come into this bowl averaging 42.3 points per game, sixth-best in the nation.) It may also be to exploit a porous defense that gave up more than 430 yards per game and ranked only 77th nationally this past season.

Whichever it is, it's obvious the team in crimson helmets and matching jerseys wants to send a message right out of the gate in their fourth visit to the Fiesta Bowl. This attempt is immediately tempered as kick-returner Juaquin Iglesias slips at the 20-yard-line. The junior wide receiver slams the ball on the turf in frustration after bringing it out of the deep red end zone to start the game.

As Sam Bradford trots onto the field, most fans today are keenly aware of his accomplishments. The 20-year-old from Putnam City North High School in Oklahoma City not only led the nation with his 180.5 pass efficiency rating this season; he set an all-time team record.

Instead of opening with his explosive passing attack, Stoops chooses to test the undersized defensive line with three up-the-middle running plays. Even though the Sooners gain a first down, the linemen in dark blue helmets – whose counterparts in crimson each outweigh them by almost 40 pounds – do a great job containing senior tailback Allen Patrick. It's their aggressively blitzing linebackers, however, who truly rise to the occasion.

After a quick out-pass to the 36-yard-line, Bradford fakes the hand-off and drops straight back in the pocket. Slicing through the left side of the massive sled movers, inside linebacker Reed Williams swats the football out of No. 14's throwing hand. The

Mountaineers faithful in our section erupt in excitement, only to be immediately disappointed as Bradford fortuitously falls on the loose ball. Even so, the speed of the 228-pound junior linebacker is not lost on the typically untouched quarterback in the shiny red helmet.

On the very next play, Bradford drops back 10 yards and is rudely slammed to the groomed turf by No. 93 in blue and white. Johnny Dingle, the undersized 6'3" 270-pound right tackle who, despite being blatantly held by 6'8" 337-pound left tackle Phil Loadholt, records his team-high ninth sack of the season – and only the eleventh sack allowed by the team from Norman all year.

After a fair-catch on their own 29-yard-line, the unanimous Big East Offensive Player of the Year sets his own tone for the evening with a 6-yard keeper. Pat White dramatically adds to this tenor on second down. Breaking out of the well-developed pocket, he scrambles untouched across midfield and out-of-bounds at the 45-yard-line. Unfortunately for our section-mates, following two more slashing runs, the drive stalls after two incomplete passes. Just as frustrating, the 50-yard field-goal-attempt misses its mark to the right.

Valerie comments that this inability to convert on their first series seems to have handed momentum to the team originally called the Rough Riders. Her prognostication is quickly proved wrong after the scrappy defense from Morgantown forces Bradford to throw two incomplete passes and a third-down completion for negative 3 yards. The Sooners punt from their 35-yard-line.

Our entire section explodes as the Big East-leading punt-returner, Vaughn Rivers, blasts up the middle from his 28-yard-line. Leaving three red jerseys in his wake, No. 19 splits the remaining Sooners at the midfield and is dragged down from behind at the 22-yard-line by senior linebacker Demarrio Pleasant. If not for having to cut back into the middle of the field, Rivers would have easily made it to the end zone.

After three futile plays, the Mountaineers settle for a 38-yard field goal. Even with these first points of the game, our row-mates groan about not being able to move into the "red zone" against the stout OU defense. Their consternation ramps up when they survey the sideline. All-American running back Steve Slaton has left the field with an apparent hamstring injury.

With slightly less than 6 minutes left in the first quarter, the Sooners answer the Mountaineers' explosive punt return. Allan Patrick scoops up the bouncing kickoff and runs directly into the back of his blocker Joe Jon Finley. He appears to be stopped at the 30-yard-line. And yet! The junior running back scrambles out of the scrum and scampers all the way to 9 yards away from the goal line. As the four-syllable fight-song booms across the field, we see a look of "this is what we thought might happen!" on the faces of Mountaineer fans.

Following this electric 73-yard return, the WVU defense squelches the crowd's anxiety on third down and goal. Dropping back untouched in the pocket, Bradford hurls an ill-advised spiral into the end zone and directly into the arms of safety Quinton Andrews. No. 8 in white flails wildly into his fellow teammates as he celebrates along the sideline.

The underdog team from Morgantown follows this momentum-changing turnover with a methodical 10-play drive featuring the passing and rushing combination of quarterback White and replacement running back Noel Devine. Our expectation turns to disappointment when White's third-down pass from the 25-yard-line slips through the hands of Devine and sails out-of-bounds. Settling for a second consecutive field goal, the Mountaineers take a 6-point lead with only 2 seconds left in the first quarter.

After back-to-back punts by both teams, the Sooners complete a first-down pass along their sideline at the 46-yard-line. Fans across the field immediately erupt following this routine pass to tight end Jermaine Gresham. Then, a yellow flag flies over the heads of the red-clad players. Seconds later, another flag soars into the air. At the end of this seemingly innocuous play, a 15-yard personal foul penalty is called on senior defensive back Ryan Mundy for evidently hitting Gresham out-of-bounds. As the officials were sorting out the details, Vaughn Rivers inexplicably charged into the face of one of the referees.

Whatever the 5'9" 170-pound defensive back said during this fleeting encounter results in another unsportsmanlike penalty. These combined 30 penalty yards equal more yards than Oklahoma has in pass receptions. With a little more than 9 minutes remaining in the first half, the vaunted offense in red (which averages almost 200 rushing yards per game) has not rushed for a single yard!

Following these two vexing penalties, the Mountaineers once again shut down the Sooners.

From the 23-yard-line, Bradford is only able to navigate 3 yards in three plays. Stoops unwittingly adds to the growing confidence on the sideline across the field as he elects to kick a field goal. The first 3 points for the No. 3 team in the nation illuminate the scoreboard.

At about this time, Valerie notices a large African-American fan several rows in front of us. The oversized young man is wearing an oversized dark blue sweatshirt and is energetically encouraging our section to applaud this surprising effort by the undersized defense.

Moments later, the entire eastern half of the municipal stadium explodes. From under center, White hands the ball to his 6'3" 260-pound fullback, Owen Schmitt, for a quick-hitter through the right side. Rumbling behind a crushing block by his massive 360-pound freshman tackle, Stephen Maw, the fireplug-of-a-fullback breaks into open field along the Mountaineers' sideline.

To my amazement, the beefy former walk-on accelerates to speed even D.J. Wolfe, the swift 196-pound defensive back, is unable to match. Crossing the goal, No. 35 in white not only thunders for the longest run of his college career; he puts himself in the record books with the second-longest run in West Virginia University bowl history. With the successful point-after-kick, the Mountaineers lead 13-to-3.

Less than six-and-a-half minutes remain in the second quarter. On the first play of their next series, after the (maddening) squibbed kick-off is returned to the 42-yard-line, Bradford expertly launches a long bomb into the arms of Quentin Chaney. Somehow, the 6'5" junior wide receiver from Tulsa gets behind both the cornerback and the safety. This perfect pass sets up a first and 10 on the 13-yard-line.

Once again, the undersized defense rises to the sudden assault and forces another field goal. Even though OU-not-UO answered in less than 90 seconds, the fact that they are unable to pierce the goal line is not lost on the fans of both teams.

Our mountain-sized young man in blue, whom we assume to be a recent WVU grad, again implores our section to cheer this resilient muster.

Up by 7 points, White confidently ambles onto the field following the kick return to the 22-yard-line. On second down, the 6'1" 192-pound signal-caller slips a quick swing-pass behind the line of scrimmage to his running back. Though slight in stature, the 5'8" 180-pound sprinter displays a flash of what might be coming ahead as he (dare I say "divinely") slashes his way past four Sooners along the near sideline for 34 yards.

A little more than 2 minutes after Oklahoma's second field goal, White shows why he's a bona fide contender for the

Courtesy of Andrea Joilet

Heisman.

From the 21-yard-line, No. 5 fakes a hand-off and scrambles horizontally to the left side. The entire secondary collapses forward to prevent another big rushing gain by the nimble quarterback. This mistake leaves wide receiver Darius Reynaud wide open in the slot. White casually lofts the ball to his teammate for another touchdown.

Down 6-to-20, with two-and-a-half minutes till halftime, Bradford throws three consecutive 3-yard passes. Facing fourth down and less than a foot on their 45-yard-line, Stoops opts to put trust in his superior-sized line. Bradford hands the ball to sophomore running back Chris Brown. He slams into a stone wall. This stunning turnover-on-downs causes our favorite mountain-sized fan to again explode out of his seat.

Only 1:09 remains on the game clock. After a nifty QB scramble to the 27-yard-line on third down, interim head coach Stewart chooses to attempt a 44-yard field goal with 2 seconds remaining in the half. A low trajectory enables the leaping Sooners to block the three-point try.

Even so, heading into the locker room, Stewart *has* to be pleased. His attacking defense has harassed Bradford on almost every series. The nation's sixth-ranked offense has been held to two field goals. Just as stunning, they have gained 11 rushing yards.

Halftime at University of Phoenix Stadium means shuffling in and out of overcrowded restrooms, standing in slow-moving lines for overpriced beverages, and listening to marching-band renditions of 80s pop songs. Tonight, it also poses a greater challenge: enduring these undertakings surrounded by crimson and cream – and random bursts of "Boomer!" every few seconds.

We are, however, able to satisfy the hole in our stomachs with delicious street tacos and cold Kilt Lifter amber ales from a local craft brewery. Say what you want about municipal arenas, they typically do have scrumptious food.

With starting running back Steve Slaton standing along the

sideline in sweatpants, our oversized favorite fan swirls his dark blue jersey over his head like a lasso.

Slaton's young replacement, Noel Devine, receives the second half's opening kick and races to the 23-yard-line, where he is tackled by swarming red jerseys. Capitalizing on the momentum of the blocked field goal at the end of the first half, the energized Sooners hold West Virginia to a three-and-out on this first series. A grumble rises from our section.

On their first offensive play, OU's tailback, Patrick, breaks free off the left side and streaks 38 yards to the 50-yard-line. Immediately following, Bradford scrambles away from the blitzing defense and fires a dart to junior wide receiver Juaquin Iglesias. The invigorated QB from Putnam City North throws another quick strike for another first down. This frenetic drive is abruptly stalled when first-team All-American offensive tackle Duke Robinson is called for a holding penalty. Two plays later, the befuddled Sooners settle, once again, for a 42-yard field goal. These 3 points bring the Oklahoma deficit to only 11.

Even so, the Sooners have been kept out of the end zone. And, once again, this is not lost on the 70,000 fans surrounding us.

After another disappointing three-and-out, Pat McAfee in blue and white booms the ball more than 60-yards to Dominique Franks. The soaring punt slips through the hands of No. 15 in red at the 5-yard-line. Players from both teams chase it across the goal line. The Sooners' Nic Harris scoops the loose ball as his momentum takes him out of the end zone. The stadium erupts as we expect 2 points to be added to the Mountaineers' side of the scoreboard. Much to our bewilderment – and that of the entire east side stands – the officials somehow rule the play a touchback. Our favorite fan leads a chorus of boos as the Oklahoma offense trots to the 20-yard-line.

Taking advantage of this disputatious call, Bradford orchestrates a 7-play scoring drive sparked by a perfect strike to wide receiver Quentin Chaney. With the score now 15-to-20 after the touchdown plunge by running back Chris Brown, the Sooners defiantly line up for a two-point-try. Standing deep in his empty backfield, Oklahoma's front-man lobs a poorly thrown ball over the head of wide receiver Iglesias. Fans surrounding us breathe sighs of relief as the ball sails out of reach. Nevertheless, they know momentum has been seized from their team.

The Sooners immediately attempt to accelerate this momentum.

On the ensuing kickoff, their visor-wearing coach catches everyone off guard. Everyone, that is, *except* Ridwan Malik. The senior defensive back races from the middle of the field and snatches the sneaky onside kick as it wobbles from the kicker's foot.

With a little more than 6 minutes remaining in the third quarter, the Mountaineers start their drive after the failed two-point-conversion and this botched onside kick just 39 yards away from the end zone. White quickly navigates the short field. On the sixth play, following a spectacular block by his fireplug-of-a-fullback, reserve running back Devine scoots 17 yards untouched. And, just like that, after only 2 minutes on the field, West Virginia increases its lead to 27-to-15.

Following another three-and-out forced by the relentless harassment of Bradford, Pat White takes the direct snap on a planned quarterback-sweep on second down and 7. The agile signal-caller shreds the vaunted No. 8-ranked rushing defense for 42 yards. On the very next play, he rolls to the right and flips the ball to Darius Reynaud on a reverse. Thirty yards later, the 200-pound junior wide receiver lunges from the 5-yard-line to put the Mountaineers up 34-to-15.

The jaunty fight-song from the marching band in the curve to our right echoes throughout the domed arena. The remaining time on the scoreboard in this BCS game will echo across the entire collegiate landscape.

After another maddening squib kick, Juaquin Iglesias sprints all the way to midfield before being tackled by Ridwan Malik. From this fortuitous field position, Bradford navigates to a fourth down and 1 on the 19-yard-line. With less than 14 minutes left in the game – and, given the size of his seasoned offensive line – Stoops chooses to again forgo the seemingly automatic field goal.

Faking the hand-off, Bradford drops back in the pocket. With the entire defense biting on the play-action fake, No. 14 in red finds No. 84 in the end zone. This 6-point bullet to Quentin Chaney takes the score to 21-to-34.

The Sooners line up for their second two-point-try to make up for their first failed attempt. Our favorite fan again lunges his oversized body into the air as middle-linebacker, Marc Magro, perfectly anticipates the hand-off to running back Chris Brown. The 240-pound senior from Morgantown stuffs the hole and tackles Brown a yard shy of the goal line.

With 337 yards of total offense thus far, White receives the shotgun snap after the kickoff following this failed conversion by the Sooners. Standing tall in the pocket, he sails the ball across midfield and into the arms of his sophomore wide receiver Tito Gonzales. Shrugging off defensive back Marcus Walker, Gonzales scampers the entire remaining length of the field. He crosses the goal line without another player within 20 yards. Our side of the field goes out of its collective mind. The extra-point extends the margin by 20 points for West Virginia. Nineteen seconds have ticked-off the game clock.

The following series, however, causes our side of the stadium to come unglued. On third down, Bradford hands the ball to running back Brown, who is tackled out-of-bounds by his facemask. The 15-yard penalty moves the ball to OU's 48. On the ensuing play, defensive back Vaughn Rivers is called for pass-interference on Quentin Chaney. Inexplicably, as the ball sails out-of-bounds, senior defensive back Ryan Mundy lowers his helmet into the backside of the wide receiver. For the second time tonight, Rivers is involved in a 30-yard gain on penalties against the Mountaineers.

Following these 45 unearned yards, Bradford once again finds Iglesias wide open in the back of the end zone. With 10:20 left in the game, the score is back to within two touchdowns.

On the ensuing kick-off, Noel Devine spurts the ball to the 30-yard-line. The pintsized-but-explosive running back proves his worthiness as a replacement for Heisman contender Slaton on second down. From the 35-yard-line, Devine follows Owen

Schmitt on a sweep to the left. With one shimmy, he puts junior linebacker Curtis Lofton, the Big XII Defensive Player of the Year, on his heels. Breaking away from another crushing block by his fireplug-of-a-fullback, speedy No. 7 glides 65 yards into the end zone. The roar is deafening.

Devine unknowingly just bested Schmitt's second-quarter touchdown to record the longest rushing touchdown in his team's bowl history. The band members at our end of the field yell "W – V – U" in unison. It's 48-to-28 as the extra-point kick flies through the uprights. There's still 9:21 left in regulation time.

West Virginia has scored on *seven* of their last eight possessions. They now look to their scrappy defense to shut down the high-powered Sooner offense. Valerie gleefully cheers-on our favorite fan who, incongruent to his size, squeals in a high-pitched voice, "Git after heeum! He's scared. Git after heeum!"

Sacked three times so far, the red-shirt signal-caller *does* appear rattled as he throws back-to-back incomplete passes. A blow to the helmet by linebacker Reed Williams adds to his frustration even with the 15-yard penalty. Two plays later, our favorite fan again squeaks, "Git after heeeum!" as Bradford is chased on fourth down and 19. His last-gasp pass to Iglesias is knocked down in the end zone.

Taking control of the ball, and taking the game clock down to under 2 minutes on three running plays, West Virginia boots the ball to Iglesias who runs to his own 15-yard-line. Appropriately, the return-man is slammed to the turf-on-wheels by the fireplug-of-a-fullback.

Just then, directly in front of our section, several players raise an orange Gatorade bucket over their heads and douse their interim head coach with icy blue sports-drink. No. 19, Vaughn Rivers, bear-hugs the drenched 54-year-old substitute commander.

Bob Stoops' team runs four consecutive rushing plays as time runs out on the scoreboard clock. His counterpart tonight becomes the only interim head coach this season to win a bowl game.

"Stew!" "Stew!" "Stew!"

Lifting their head coach onto the shoulders of two offensive linemen, the entire Mountaineers team chants in unison as Jonny Dingle violently waves a massive bright yellow flag in the crimson end zone.

Even given all their adversity – losing the Backyard Brawl to their unranked rival, dropping out of contention for the National Championship, losing their 7-year head coach just days before this biggest game in school history, as well as their All-American running back in the first 9 minutes – the resilient team from the school on the banks of the Monongahela River made its mark in the annals of college football this evening. Against one of the most storied teams in the nation.

Pat White threw 176 yards and two touchdowns. He ran for 150 yards. He and his fellow mountain men from Morgantown rushed for 349 yards in this prestigious bowl game, the most *ever* against a Bob Stoops' team from Norman.

As we stand with jubilant fans in our now-partially vacated section, Valerie mentions how the badgering defense was just as instrumental in this victory, how the top-tier Oklahoma offense gained only 49 more *total* yards than West Virginia had in *rushing* yards, how they converted only 4 of 16 third-down attempts, and how the scoreboard reads 48-to-28. The same scoreboard which, 12

Courtesy of Andrea Joilet

months ago to the day, glowed 43-to-42 in favor of the Boise State Broncos.

After rattling off these stats that obviously make us giddy, Valerie races down to our favorite fan. Beaming with pride, the oversized booster gives her a hug as big as this win for West Virginia.

CHAPTER TEN
World's Largest Cocktail Party
2008 Florida | Georgia

Two months before Pat White and his Mountaineers will stun the Sooners in University of Phoenix Stadium, one of the most unexpected displays of disrespect ever to take place on a football field happened between the University of Florida Gators and the Bulldogs from Georgia.

On that Saturday in late October, Valerie and I settled into our TV room eagerly awaiting the 85th (or 86th, depending on which fan base you listen to) meeting between these storied Southern squads. The ensuing drama that spilled across the screen convinced us that following our trip to the 2007 Fiesta Bowl, our next destination would be Jacksonville, Florida.

Eight weeks into last season, both SEC rivals entered that contest – defiantly known as the "World's Largest Cocktail Party" – with five wins and two losses. Even though its star quarterback was nursing a sore shoulder on his throwing arm side, the team from the Everglades was favored by 7.5 points. This injury to Tim Tebow occurred a week earlier in the thrilling 47-to-35 victory over the University of Kentucky, which featured the now renowned Tebow "jump pass" to tight end Aaron Hernandez.

As expected, emotions were running hot on both sides of the field, especially along the sideline of the underdogs. The team across the field had treated them like a pound puppy over the past two decades, winning 15 of the 17 most-recent meetings and 8 of the past 9. In six clashes with the reptiles from Gainesville, the current head of the Bulldogs has only been triumphant once.

Lately, it has not been much of a party for the team with the proud canine mascot.

Then it happened.

Following a fumble on Florida's first series, the Bulldogs marched down the field on eight consecutive rushing plays, seven of which were by freshman Knowshon Moreno.

I quickly mentioned that many in the college football world predict this kid from New Jersey is going to be Georgia's third Heisman winner by the time he graduates. (He was the all-time leading scorer and second-leading rusher in the state as a Middleton South Eagle.) On their ninth play of this drive, the 207-pound running back plowed across the goal for the first points of the contest. Pandemonium flowed across our screen.

Before Valerie had time to ask if I thought Moreno had pierced the plane, the entire Georgia team raced onto the field.

Vern Lundquist, calling the game for CBS Sports, started shouting, "Here comes the entire team! How's this for excessive celebration . . . we may have 15 hankies in the air on this one!"

With mouths agape, Tim Tebow and his fellow Gators watched from the sideline as all 85 players in red swarmed around their young tailback in the end zone. It took several minutes to break up this obviously premeditated display of defiance. Two personal fouls, including a taunting penalty for a flamboyant dance (which Valerie chuckles about to this day) on freshman tackle Trinton Sturdivant, were charged to the Bulldogs once the melee was cleared from the field.

This brazen decision to trample on college football's well-established rules of conduct was certainly meant to send a message to the Gators and their head coach.

Even though Florida scored in three quick plays following this rebellious celebration, Mark Richt's team overpowered their outraged rival to win the game 42-to-30. Moreno ran for 188 total yards. Tebow was sacked 6 times. The planned bench-clearing exhibition became infamously known as the "Gator Stomp." Richt got his second Cocktail Party victory. And none of it was ever to be forgotten by Gators' coach Urban Meyer.

Much like other border wars on our quest, everything associated with this party is prickly, to the point that (once again!) neither school is willing to accept an agreed-upon number of times they've met on the gridiron. The University of Georgia contends its first organized football game versus the team from America's swampland took place in 1904 – and that they shut out the Gators by 52 points. Their interstate rival asserts they didn't even *have* a football team until the year its name changed from Florida Agricultural College, in 1906.

Both colleges *do* agree that 11 years after this game (which may or may not have happened), their teams lined up against each other in Jacksonville. Just like the alleged result of the perhaps mythical game of 1904, Georgia routed the Gators during this agreed-upon happening in 1915.

This abasing outcome quickly led to a trend in the early years of this cross-border scrimmage. During the first quarter-century of play, not only did the Bulldogs lose just four games to their neighbor to the south; Florida was held scoreless 11 times. Worse, the Gators averaged only slightly more than five-and-a-half points in these inaugural 25 games between the two schools.

The most recent quarter-century flipped the outcome of the early decades. Florida has swamped the Bulldogs, winning 18 games during this span. In addition, the university from Gainesville has won two National Championships, one in 1996 under Steve Spurrier and one in 2006 under the head coach who experienced "Gator Stomp" first-hand. They also earned seven SEC Championships and produced two Heisman Trophy winners.

Over the same 25 years, Georgia won the Conference Championship only three times, twice with teams led by Mark Richt, in 2002 and 2005. The school's second Heisman Trophy was also awarded, in 1982, to their three-year starting running back, Herschel Walker.

Early in the 1950s, a reporter for *The Florida Times-Union* is said to have coined the bibulous nickname associated with this annual showdown between Southern rivals.

As the story goes, a young sportswriter said he saw a well-lubricated fan attempting to offer a potent potable to a police officer outside of Gator Bowl Stadium (the name, at the time, of the arena in Jacksonville). Whether this actually happened, the nickname in his column stuck. Until 1988. That's when, in an attempt to project a more refined image, city officials announced they would no longer refer to the weekend festivities as "The World's Largest Cocktail Party."

The SEC followed suit when the tagline was dropped from all promotional materials in 2006. Despite these injunctions, most fans from this part of the country (and beyond) still refer to the festivities on Jacksonville Landing by its non-sober sobriquet.

This year's Cocktail Party has all the ingredients – a contentious history, conjoined states, confident players, and chagrined coaches – to be a spectacular show.

With our travel plans booked for this trip in a couple weeks, the Red River Rivalry is getting ready to kick off in our TV room. And, not just your run-of-the-mill shootout: the No. 5 nationally-ranked team from Valerie's alma mater is suiting up against the unanimous No. 1 team in the nation. Did I mention, this year's cross-border quarrel also happens to fall on her birthday?

From the kitchen, I smell fresh coffee as the team in traveling all-white uniforms enters through the lone tunnel on the outskirts of the Texas State Fair. Over the next 3 hours, the Longhorns proceed to deliver Valerie a wonderful birthday present.

Eighty combined points – the most-ever in its 103-year history – are amassed during this Shootout/Rivalry. The scoreboard glows 45-to-35 as the game clock rolls to triple zeros. Valerie looks like she's floating on air. I give her a huge hug of congratulations and, knowing she will savor the pleasure of the win for at least an hour, head out for a quick ride. (As an avid mountain biker, I usually enjoy several exhilarating rides a week on the ridgeline carved by the Columbia River behind our house.)

Racing up the trail, my mind is on celebrating Valerie's birthday and toasting the victory over the contemptible team in crimson. I reach top speed on my descent as a gentle rain hits the logging trail. Before I realize it, I also hit the logging trail, just not gently.

Following a walk out of the forest and a drive to the emergency clinic, I phone Valerie to let her know I'm waiting for results of the X-rays on my left forearm. Sitting in the waiting room with an ice pack, I realize it must be well past halftime in the SEC game-of-the-week. The eleventh-ranked Gators are hosting the fourth-ranked Tigers from LSU.

Valerie, who arrived a few minutes earlier, receives a call from her mother with birthday wishes. Immediately, she asks for the score in this Southeastern showdown. Hey, priorities! Plus, with tickets to Orlando already purchased, we *really* want Florida to win this weighty contest today.

Emerging from the X-ray room, the doctor-on-call informs us that I've split my radius.

With the wonders of modern medicine coursing through my veins, my alma mater kicks off to the undefeated Tigers from the University of Missouri in our TV room at home. Resting my arm above my head, Valerie crosses in front of the screen with a bowl of leftover chili. I remind her that the other undefeated striped felines from Baton Rouge were surprisingly man-handled by the Gators from Gainesville this afternoon, that this year's Cocktail Party will be a matchup of two top-5 teams, her alma mater crushed Norman Junior College, and that I do love her on this birthday evening.

The earliest opening for surgery is two days before our flight. My orthopedic surgeon, who happens to be a college football fan with an even greater passion for the team from his undergraduate school in Ann Arbor (not to be mentioned by name), is not so keen on me traveling across the United States so soon after his repair to my radius.

Following a cautionary lecture, Dr. Jason Kurian asks me if I desire a specific color for my fiberglass cast.

"Gator orange!" I tell him.

"How about we go with Wolverine blue instead?" he says.

Blue it is.

Arriving in Orlando on Thursday of this same week, we rise early the next morning for much-anticipated festivities on the campus of the Gators. Picturing this state in our heads, we saw palm trees, sun-drenched beaches, and bright bikinis. Traveling north on Interstate 75, we cannot be further from this state of mind. If not for roadside citrus stands and souvenir alligator shops alongside every off-ramp, we'd swear we're traveling from Valerie's alma mater to mine (sans the oil wells). Small farms, trailer parks, and weathered houses blur into a familiar rural landscape from our college days.

As we enter the southern end of the Southern college town, we become distinctly aware something is missing. Apart from a few flags hanging on front porches in its tree-lined neighborhoods, this doesn't seem much like the day before the biggest showdown of the year for the nationally ranked home team. Cruising toward the heart of campus on this Friday morning, we get a sense the school may even be on break.

Turning onto aptly named Stadium Road, we drive past aptly named Gator Pond on our way to Ben Hill Griffin Stadium. Though a handful of coeds amble along the sidewalk, it quickly becomes obvious most students have already departed for the annual SEC showdown. The "Party" tomorrow takes place an hour-and-a-half north of Gainesville, as it has almost every year for the past three-quarters of a century.

A virtually empty college town. We should be pretty good at this by now; let's see what we can find.

In 1992, head coach Steve Spurrier made the following proclamation: "A swamp is where Gators live. We feel comfortable there, but we hope our opponents feel tentative. A swamp is hot and sticky and can be dangerous. We feel like it's an appropriate nickname for our stadium."

Walking through an open gate, Valerie and I are aware of the historical games seen by hundreds of thousands of fans in this iconic venue with the fitting nickname bestowed by the former head coach. Today, however, except for three or four students jogging up and down its steep stairs, there's no sign of life within the vast orange and blue arena. The desolate stands reveal no indication of the excitement witnessed within its angular walls. Even the notorious "This is . . . THE SWAMP" slogan in the south end zone seems lackluster on this balmy afternoon in late October.

Four short weeks ago, this was not the case.

On that slightly overcast morning, the fourth-ranked team in the nation hosted the unranked Rebels from the University of Mississippi. This fourth game of the season on the fourth Saturday in September featured the front-runner for the Heisman on one side, and a sophomore quarterback (who'd missed all of the previous season due to an NCAA transfer rule after sitting on the bench for a year behind Colt McCoy in Austin, Texas) on the other. Tim Tebow had all the confidence in the world. Jevan Sneed had a two-win team, which lost a week earlier on their home field to the Vanderbilt Commodores.

The Gators had chomped through their first three opponents (the University of Hawaii, the Hurricanes from Miami, and the Tennessee Volunteers) by a combined score of 112 to 19. Ole Miss had home victories over University of Memphis and Division I-AA foe Samford University. It was also the first time the Gators faced Ole Miss at The Swamp since they were unceremoniously defeated by Eli Manning and his fellow Rebels in 2003. Oddsmakers had Urban Meyer's fourth-year team favored by 22 points.

In this rematch, the visiting underdogs scored the only points during the first quarter. The home team answered with two touchdowns and a field goal to go into halftime with a somewhat comfortable 10-point lead. Their confidence may have led to complacency. After two uncharacteristic fumbles, the first by wide receiver Percy Harvin and the second by his Heisman-contending quarterback, Florida quickly saw its lead evaporate as Ole Miss put 17 unanswered points on the board in the third quarter.

With five-and-a-half minutes left in the game, Harvin scampered across the goal to put Florida within an extra point of tying the game. The home crowd sank in their seats as the try was blocked by sophomore defensive end Kentrell Lockett. The scrappy Rebels, who had only 10 first downs compared to 24 by the Gators, held on to upset the stunned home team 31-to-30.

At the press conference after this upset by Ole Miss, a teary-eyed Tebow delivered the following now-famous pledge:

> "I'm sorry. I'm extremely sorry. We were hoping for an undefeated season. That was my goal, something Florida's never done here. But I promise you one thing: a lot of good will come out of this. You have never seen any player in the entire country play as hard as I will play the rest of this season and you'll never see someone push the rest of the team as hard as I will push everybody the rest of this season, and you'll never see a team play harder than we will the rest of this season."

Leading into tomorrow's Cocktail Party, his team has made good on this promise. They ripped through their three most recent opponents by a combined score of 152-to-33. This streak featured a 31-point win at Razorback Stadium in Fayetteville, a 51-to-21 slamming of then-No. 4 Louisiana State on the day I slammed onto the logging trail, followed by a 63-to-5 shellacking of the surging Wildcats from the University of Kentucky.

Leaving the desolate stadium, we stop at the training facility built into its southwest corner. Completed just three months ago, Heavener Football Complex greets visitors with a 15-foot bronze alligator perched menacingly atop a massive granite block. Engraved on this shiny slab are the words "BULL GATOR" and a dedication to the 2006 National Championship team led by senior quarterback Chris Leak, who was backed up by a freshman named Tim Tebow.

With my blue cast draped across the neck of this fearsome frozen reptile, Valerie snaps a quick picture and suggests we make our way to a local watering hole for the world's smallest cocktail party.

Timothy Richard Tebow was destined to be a star college football player. Homeschooled all his life, he took advantage of Florida legislation granting parent-taught students the right to compete in high school sports. As a junior at Allen D. Nease High School in Ponte Vedra, he was awarded Player of the Year in the state, an award he won again his senior year.

In addition to leading the Panthers to victory in the Class 4A State Championship game in his final season, the heralded teen quarterback was selected as an All-American by *Parade* magazine and was awarded "Mr. Football" by the Florida Athletic Coaches Association as the top player in the state. Coming out of high school, Tebow was courted by most major schools including the University of Alabama and Florida State University. Much to the delight of Gator fans everywhere, "Mr. Football" chose to play for Mr. Meyer in Gainesville.

After serving mop-up duty his first year, the precocious signal-caller (who seems to always be called by both his first and last names) became the first sophomore ever to win the Heisman Trophy.

Tim Tebow finished his second season under Urban Meyer with the second-highest passing efficiency rating behind Colt Brennan from the University of Hawaii. The 6'3" 235-pound local boy from Jacksonville also broke the record for most yards on the ground (166) by a Florida quarterback when he accounted for all four touchdowns (and 427 yards of his team's 507 total yards) in their game at Ole Miss. Also by season's end, Tebow shattered the Southeastern Conference records for most touchdowns in a season (55), most rushing touchdowns in a season (20), and most rushing touchdowns in a single game when he single-handedly scored five in the 51-to-31 blowout over the Gamecocks in Columbia, South Carolina.

With less than 24 hours until the highly decorated signal-caller faces the team that delivered last year's in-your-face defeat in Jacksonville, it's evident Tim Tebow is more than "Mr. Football," he's *Mr. Florida*. Banners featuring his likeness hang from light poles along the tree-lined sidewalks. Heisman Trophy posters adorn windows of small retail stores on University Avenue. Tucked among these pizza joints and donut shops are several obligatory college bars and campus clothing stores.

Strolling past a sign on this quaint boulevard that simply reads BALLS above two neon beer signs, we step into a small apparel shop. After perusing the shelves, I turn to see Valerie holding a bright blue t-shirt emblazoned with "I LOVE TIMMY" across the front in orange letters and a red heart.

With our purchase in hand, we stroll past several glass doors along the two-story, red-brick facade. Just past a two-chaired barbershop, a small white sign dangling above another single glass door lets us know the Salty Dog Saloon was established in 1982. Valerie says it looks more like a hair salon than a saloon. Aside from hastily hung neon signs on each side of the unadorned entrance, there's little indication this is one of the most popular campus bars at the University of Florida.

Adjusting our eyes on this bright afternoon, we're immediately greeted by a very large elk watching over a smattering of patrons along the left wall of this very narrow corridor.

The Dog, as it's known to students and alumni, is nothing more than a long hallway pinched between several other linear spaces in this half-century-old brick strip mall. Over these decades, however, this corridor has managed to collect more Gator memorabilia and outmoded beer signs than a Saturday flea market. Even Elvis, the massive mounted elk, gets lost among the floor-to-ceiling malt beverage merchandising.

Framed newspaper headlines of past national championships and conference victories hang on the back wall alongside several flat-screens. Adding to the cornucopia of cheap promotional items and random sports trophies are hundreds of bottles of every kind of liquor we'd expect to find in a campus bar of this stripe. Even the ceiling is covered with oversized beer posters and Salty Dog shirts on hangers. It's a tossup which aroma is stronger: the pungent, yeasty smell of decades of spilled beer or that of sizzling burgers and fries. Our kind of place! We belly up to the tap handles.

According to our barkeep, Friday happy hours at The Dog are typically rowdy, standing-room-only affairs. On this day before the World's Largest Cocktail Party, however, apart from a handful of patrons who appear to be locals (but not necessarily local students), we pretty much have the narrow bar to ourselves. Two post-graduate-age guys in cargo shorts stand next to the jukebox that's blaring some late 90s post-grunge song. Their buddy sinks the eight ball into the center pocket of the lone pool table.

Our bartender – appropriately clad in a white No. 15 jersey and a short black skirt – informs us that the entire town pretty much shuts down the week before the showdown with the revered Bulldogs from up north. Most of the revelry associated with the Cocktail Party, we learn to our dismay, has already left for Jacksonville.

On game day morning, we meet up with a friend from home for breakfast before the hour-and-a-half drive north. Alex, whose family lives in Orlando, grew up in Izhevsk, Russia, a former Soviet military city located approximately 750 miles east of Moscow, and home to the factory which has manufactured AK-47s since the end of World War II. He's a business associate who shares office space with us in downtown Portland.

He also has never been to a college football game.

Traffic starts to slow as the landscape transitions from lush green to the suburban neighborhoods of Jacksonville. Passing through sprawling subdivisions, we soon approach the east side of downtown. Home to three naval bases and a submarine base, Jacksonville is less than an hour from the Atlantic Ocean. It's also home to Alltel Stadium, which sits along the St. John's River on the former site of Gator Bowl Stadium.

This massively unattractive structure, with its web of angular concrete walkways and insect-like stadium lights reaching over its outer rim, was built in 1995 to be the home field for the NFL Jacksonville Jaguars. It has also hosted every Cocktail Party ever since.

During our subdued party at Salty Dog Saloon yesterday, we asked several locals why this annual rivalry is not played at each university's home field. The theory seemed to be that the neutral site provides an even playing field for both teams. Factually, however, fairness on the field takes a backseat to finances. According to the *Jacksonville Business Journal*, both schools receive 50% more revenue with this game in Jacksonville than if it were to alternate between home fields each year.

Turning off Arlington Expressway, we park north of the stadium alongside Gator Bowl Boulevard. Kickoff is scheduled for 3:30 this afternoon. Plenty of time left to experience the largest adult beverage festival on the planet. Surveying our surroundings, this description may be a bit exaggerated. Except for bumper-to-bumper traffic inching around the cloverleaf, there's little activity. Alex notices a trickling of fans walking in the direction of what appears to be a beige and teal ranch-style house with a giant white slab jutting from its roof.

In lemming-like fashion, we follow our fellow soon-to-be partiers toward the small crowd milling around this unassuming establishment.

Approaching its large metal awning, we discern from the oversized white slab and turquoise lettering that the Tailgate Bar & Grill is housed inside. If not for this bizarre monolith on its roof, the corner-lot building could easily be mistaken for any of the half-century-old homes scattered along the north side of the NFL stadium.

Once under the converted doublewide carport, we each grab a cold 16-ounce can from the makeshift bar along the outside wall of the seemingly makeshift brick tavern. Small clusters of fans, in either all-blue or all-red apparel, mingle under the gray awning. A jovial fraternity brother, wearing a plastic alligator hat, stops to ask if the cast on my arm is real, or did I just wear it because I am a Gators fan? Nice! After a couple more refreshing cans, we work our way onto barstools next to the lone pool table.

The converted *Leave It to Beaver*-style home is crowded. Still, as Valerie points out, the atmosphere seems somewhat restrained for a cocktail party supposedly larger than any other in the entire world. Missing are vendor booths, inflatable displays, onstage bands, and sponsored promotions. The "cocktail" in its nickname most certainly is not.

Adult libations of all types flow freely inside Tailgate Bar & Grill, under its carport, and at every parking space in the adjacent field. Taking on the appearance of a giant red and blue quilt, small tents with Georgia logos are scattered alongside the same type of canopies with blue and orange reptile logos. It's a patchwork held together by tension. Very few partygoers, if any, mix with their adversaries.

Many of these primary color encampments have been here since early morning; refreshments appear to have started just as early. As we walk past a particularly rowdy group of "tail-gators," I comment to a girl dressed in blue we expected the World's Largest Cocktail Party to be much more extravagant.

"Oh," she replies, "the actual 'Cocktail Party' is along the waterfront on the other side of the stadium."

Once again, most of the revelry has eluded us.

With less than 45 minutes until kickoff, we decide to forgo the merriment along the riverbank. Call us party-poopers, but the opportunity to experience pregame activities inside Alltel Stadium on this hazy afternoon seems more enticing than playing "corn-hole" with undergrads. Crossing Gator Bowl Boulevard, we're joined by throngs of distinctly clad fans making beelines toward the unsightly structure with the bug-like appendages.

As we enter at the northwest end, we quickly surmise our seats are on the Georgia side of the teal-colored stadium. Today, as it is every year on this weekend, the pro-football venue will be bifurcated from goalpost to goalpost by a sea of blue on the east side and an equal-sized sea of red on the west.

We briefly stop at a merchandise booth just outside of our section. Along with the tradition of buying a ball cap at each of our annual games, I'm hoping a Georgia logo atop my head will endear us to our seatmates. Alex and Valerie skip the merchandise stand and head to a concession booth.

Emerging from under the stands, we locate our seats in the curve behind Georgia's end zone. The stadium looks like a teal glazed donut rolled in blue and red sprinkles as both teams go through pregame warm-ups. Without meaning to, we walk directly into the unofficial biggest fan of Bulldogs football.

A common fixture at all Georgia games for several decades, the oversized middle-aged man in black overalls and a red t-shirt is surrounded by several similarly clad fans. Mike "Big Dawg" Woods is also proudly sporting – as he's done at every Georgia home game since 1990 – a full-color rendition of the team's mascot on his bald head.

The affable booster, who has missed only one Cocktail Party in his life, tells us the scowling canine atop his head is in honor of his late father, who started this tradition ten years earlier. As we

turn to walk up the aisle to our seats, Valerie snaps a quick picture of Big Dawg and me. Of course, he's looking down at his feet. The painted mascot is the star of the shot.

The No. 8-ranked Bulldogs come into this party with seven wins and only one loss. In their fourth game, Alabama's second-year coach, Nick Saban, handed Mark Richt his worst defeat in eight years at the helm in Athens. The then-No. 8 team in the nation scored on each of their first five drives during this humbling 30-to-41 setback at Sanford Stadium.

Nevertheless, the ensuing three Saturdays saw the Bulldogs reel off three impressive wins, including a hammering of No. 11 LSU. Matthew Stafford, during this 52-to-38 beatdown in Baton Rouge last week, threw two touchdowns and ran for one more.

Georgia's third-year quarterback out of Highland Park High School in Dallas was one of the most highly touted players – ranked even higher than Tim Tebow by Rivals.com – during his senior year in high school. A *Parade* All-American in 2005, he led the Highland Park Scots to a perfect fifteen-win season and a victory in the 4A Division I Texas State Championship game. The gifted quarterback (a five-star recruit) graduated early with a scholarship to the University of Georgia.

Before he ever played a down in college, ESPN Radio football analyst Mel Kiper, Jr. stated, "Stafford eventually will be the No. 1 pick in the NFL Draft. Write that down."

As a true freshman, the 18-year-old was thrust into the starting quarterback position before Georgia's third game of the 2006 season. Due to an ankle injury to fifth-year senior Joe Tereshinski, III sustained a week earlier against the South Carolina Gamecocks, Richt was forced to start Stafford in this non-conference game versus the University of Alabama at Birmingham. The Bulldogs blanked the out-classed Blazers 34-to-nothing in this debut. They went on to finish the season with a 9-and-4 record after a remarkable 31-to-24 victory in the Chick-fil-A Bowl over the fighting gobblers from Virginia Polytechnic Institute and State University. The Stafford-led team trailed Virginia Tech 3-to-21 at halftime in this thrilling bowl game.

Coming into this season, Georgia was the unanimous No. 1 team in the nation. This lofty designation was justifiable, given the number of high-profile starters returning from 2007.

Last year's squad not only shocked their rivals in the infamous "Gator Stomp" game; they finished with an overall 11-and-2 record after humiliating the previously undefeated Warriors (not Rainbows) in the Allstate Sugar Bowl that we watched at the Library Bar & Grill in Tempe. Georgia's defensive end, Marcus Howard, was awarded MVP of that bowl game. Finishing with three sacks and two forced fumbles, he was the first defensive player ever to earn this honor.

Stafford ended his sophomore year with more than 2,500 passing yards, 19 passing touchdowns, and two rushing scores. Several preseason magazines this year have Stafford as a Heisman Trophy contender. A dominant performance today by the 6'3" 237-pound gunslinger will go a long way toward confirming this designation.

No longer looking like a sprinkled pastry, a royal blue hue now covers the entire half of the stadium across from us. On our side, a blanket of red ripples from goal line to goal line. Patchy clouds cast shadows on this 70-degrees autumn afternoon. As the Redcoat Marching Band forms ten evenly spaced lines parallel to the Bulldogs bench across half the field, the three of us notice an uneasiness surrounding our rows.

Only a few minutes ago the fans in this curve of the stadium were high-spirited and rowdy. Now, their mood seems to have turned somewhat hostile. With the blue cast on my forearm and a blue shirt peeking through Valerie's light jacket, several fans in red and black cast suspicious glances our way.

Fortunately, I am wearing my black Georgia cap and Valerie's windbreaker is effectively covering "I (heart) TIMMY." Feeling like an interloper, Alex slips away from our row as a deafening blast of boos travels over the heads of the marching band.

Alltel Stadium's tunnels open onto the field at each 20-yard-line from under the west stands. Outfitted in shiny red helmets, matching jerseys, and white pants with red stripes, the University of Georgia varsity football team bursts from the tunnel closest to us. Led by spirit-squad members carrying black flags with single red letters unfurling into G-E-O-R-G-I-A, the players make a sharp right turn in front of the marching band and head toward their bench.

As the slightly favored team from Florida shoots from the other tunnel, our side of the stadium sends a round of boos across the field. Several Georgia players taunt the Gators alongside the Bulldogs' bench. A red-clad male cheerleader carries a massive black flag with a giant G into the oncoming stream of all-white uniforms. The Florida players, in their orange helmets with the blue script on each side, to my amazement, ignore the heckling as they run past the SEC logo at the midfield to their bench on the far side.

I tell Valerie, "Florida appears to be taking this first rematch since the 'Gator Stomp' very seriously."

Today is the first-ever meeting in the history of this 86-year (or 87-year) rivalry in which both schools are ranked nationally in the top-10 by both polls. Georgia leads the overall series 47-37-2. The winner today moves into first place in the SEC East. Both have several Heisman-contending players. And none of this matters to Urban Meyer.

The desire to erase last year's embarrassment in this stadium is all that concerns Florida's head coach.

In his autobiography written after the Gator's National Championship season last year, he stated, "It wasn't right. It was a bad deal. And, it will forever be in the mind of Urban Meyer and in the mind of our football team."

As Georgia trots to the south end to receive the opening kickoff, several opposing fans in front of us begin shouting at each other. The booze-fueled argument quickly escalates into a pushing match. Surrounding fans step in to stop the quarrel as the two scrappers wearing two distinct colors wrestle to the ground. Even Mike with his painted bulldog angrily barks at the combatants to stop. Several stadium security officers finally arrive and escort the somewhat bloodied rivals out of the stadium.

Alex is walking up the aisle as the two men are being led down and hastily makes his way back to his seat. Wearing a newly purchased blood-red shirt with the Georgia mascot on its front, our Russian friend figures, given the tension in the stands, it's best to blend in with the pack.

Opening kickoff sets the tone for Urban Meyer's squad.

With a roar from our side of the stadium, Ramarcus Brown receives the kick from freshman Caleb Sturgis at the far end of the field. In less than what seems like a second, the 170-pound senior is smothered by a congregation of gators on his own 17-yard-line ("congregation" being the proper name for a group of alligators). Half of the more than 84,000 fans in Alltel Stadium scream with delight and immediately break into their notorious "gator chomp." Almost every fan in the east stands is clapping both hands together with arms extended to mimic the menacing mouth of their mascot.

After a screen-pass into the middle of the defense for no gain on the first play of the day, Florida really gives the blue side of the stadium something to chomp about.

Matthew Stafford hands the ball to sophomore running back Knowshon Moreno. Running off the right side, the tailback from New Jersey crosses his 15-yard-line. Just then, as if shot from a cannon, No. 51 in white slams into Moreno so hard he sends him flying backward. Florida's middle linebacker, Brandon Spikes, knocks the highly touted running back literally off his feet.

The "ooh!" from the stands is more like a reaction to fireworks than to a football play.

Following a false start penalty and another rush for only 2 yards, the Bulldogs are forced to punt. Several fans behind us shout a litany of slurred curse words as Florida's return man, Brandon James, calls for a fair-catch on the Gator's 42-yard-line.

The bellowing from our side of the stands has an immediate impact on the Gators' first play. Florida's offensive line bursts out of their stance prior to the snap. This battle-tested unit is led by the Pouncey twins; No. 56 Maurkice at center and No. 55 Mike at left guard. Both stand 6'3" and weigh 312-pounds. They were both four-star recruits from Lakeland High School in the Florida city with the same name. Coming out of Lakeland at the end of 2006, Rivals.com listed Maurkice and Mike as the fifteenth and sixteenth best offensive guards in the nation. Since the start of this season, the identical twins have lined up next to each other in the middle of their offensive line.

After a quick slant to Percy Harvin on first and 15, Tebow runs up the middle to pick up the initial first down of the game. On the following third down, Florida jumps offsides again. Coach Meyer, in his blue windbreaker and khaki pants, folds his arms in disgust. Losing 3 yards on a failed screen-pass to the right, the Gators are forced to punt after their first drive. I comment to Alex that the high-scoring prediction by the talking heads this past week appears to be in doubt.

Following these two tightly wound series, the Georgia coaching staff opens up the offense.

On first down from the 19-yard-line, Stafford fakes the ball to his running back and hits wide receiver Mohamed Massaquoi in stride for 32 yards. The unruly fans in our section holler when Florida is called for a roughing-the-passer penalty following this perfect pass to the highly-sought recruit from Independence High School in Charlotte, North Carolina. (During the four years Massaquoi played at Independence, the Patriots never lost a game and won four straight state championships.) A quick sideways pass to Moreno out of the backfield has our section screaming even louder. Scrambling along the Florida sideline, the stout running back picks up the third first down in three plays.

This impressive 70-yard drive to the 10-yard-line has taken less than 2 minutes and has the fans in our section convinced their Bulldogs are going to strike first in this slugfest. Back-to-back sacks by the Gators erase this conviction and forces Richt to send his field goal team onto the field. With the ball placed at the 20-yard-line, freshman kicker Blair Walsh from Boca Raton, Florida sends the ball sailing wide to the left of the left upright. Our section sinks to their chairs in disbelief.

With 5:16 remaining in this scoreless first quarter, Tebow takes the shotgun snap to begin his second series. The events that unfold on this drive once again have Alex fearing for our safety.

On third down and 2, Tebow rolls to his left on a designed quarterback-keeper. No. 35 in red shoots from his linebacker position and wraps up the decorated quarterback. Even from our vantage point, it's obvious Rennie Curran stopped Tebow short of the first down. Our seatmates react in violent disgust as the head linesman signals otherwise.

After a few seconds, Mark Richt calls a time-out to challenge the result of this play. The head coach responds in the same manner as the fans in our section when the official declares the ruling on the field "stands."

On the fifth play following this questionable call, the entire west side of the stadium erupts in anger once again. Breaking on the ball as it leaves Tebow's hand, No. 23 in red intercepts the pass intended for Harvin alongside the Florida sideline. As Prince Miller, the 5'8" 196-pound cornerback from Duncan, South Carolina, raises the purloined ball over his head, Valerie shouts. She's pointing at a yellow flag at the line of scrimmage.

After a couple moments of discussion, the officials charge defensive tackle Jarius Wynn with a personal foul for ripping the helmet from Carl Johnson's head. The penalty results in a first down for the Gators on the 13-yard-line.

With patches of sunlight rolling across the east side of the stadium, after what would have been only his third interception all year, Tebow rolls to the left on an option play and pitches the ball to his tailback. There's not a single red jersey within 5 yards as Harvin strolls into the end zone. He's immediately mobbed by his teammates in the corner diagonally across the field.

A communal expletive spews from all rows in our section. For the first time in the game today – and for the first time at any spectator sport we've attended – I am a little fearful for our safety.

With this opening touchdown, Harvin has scored in each of the past 10 consecutive games. Coming into this Cocktail Party, the Gators, under Urban Meyer, have also lost only once in 28 games when scoring first.

At the start of the second quarter, however, a glimmer of hope appears across the red faces in our section. Following nine consecutive plays, including a 26-yard pass on third down from Stafford to Massaquoi, the drive stalls at the 17-yard-line. Richt elects to attempt another field goal on this fourth down. This time, his first-year kicker, Walsh, makes amends for his first try and sends the ball 35 yards through the center of the uprights. Even with this successful field goal, the drive feels like a win for the Gators.

On the ensuing kickoff, 3 minutes into the second quarter, Mark Richt tries to squelch this feeling. It's an audacious move. Lining up in typical formation, the Bulldogs attempt an onside kick. Walsh short-hops the line drive directly into the arms of No. 37 in white. Butch Rowley (also the holder on field goals and extra-points) falls with the ball cradled in his arms on Georgia's 40-yard-line. The reaction throughout our section feels like a shudder.

After 5 quick plays, Tebow takes the shotgun-snap on third down and plows 2 feet for what looks like Florida's second score of the game. From our seats, we're not able to see the ball as the pile of bodies unfurls at the goal line. To our amazement, not only does the replay booth overturn the called touchdown; they rule Tebow fell short of the first down. Trotting back onto the field, Tim Tebow waves his arms to fire up his side of the stadium.

On this fourth down and a foot, the former "Mr. Football" follows a great block by his 5'8" 176-pound freshman tailback, Jeff Demps, into the end zone.

Racing from the red block letters at the end of the field, Tebow enthusiastically does the "gator chomp" toward the blue half of the stadium. With this 37th rushing touchdown of his collegiate career, No. 15 now holds the record for most rushing touchdowns at the university.

Sometimes you have to roll the dice. And, as the fans in our section are realizing, the dice don't always roll your way.

Not only has the failed onside kick resulted in 7 points for Urban Meyer's team; it seems to firmly establish momentum on the other side of the field.

Starting the next drive on their 40-yard-line, due to an erratic kick out-of-bounds, the Bulldogs appear determined to bite this momentum in the bud. Knowshon Moreno opens the series with an impressive 7-yard burst through the middle of his offensive line. The preseason Heisman Trophy favorite proceeds to rip off three more runs for 12 yards, 9 yards, and 6 yards to the Florida 21-yard-line. After a punishing sack by sophomore defensive end Duke Lemmens, Stafford throws a strike on third down and 19 to Massaquoi for a first-and-goal on the 6-yard-line.

Sometimes the dice *really* don't roll your way.

On the next play, Stafford executes a play-fake to Moreno and slips to the right side of the pocket. Tripp Chandler, the 6'6" 260-pound tight end from Woodstock, Georgia, sprints uncovered toward the end zone. Failing to set his feet, the overly anxious quarterback throws the ball 2 yards behind the junior receiver. Richt, on the Jumbotron to our left, rolls his eyes in disgust. On third down, rather than throwing to one of his very tall and very proficient wide receivers, Stafford lobs a pass to Moreno at the back of the end zone. No. 35 in white, Ahmad Black from Lakeland, Florida, bats the overthrown pass out of the field of play.

And sometimes the dice come up "snake eyes."

On fourth down, Richt sends his kicking team onto the field for another chip-shot field goal. Freshman Blair Walsh stands stunned as the ball ricochets off the left goalpost. Biting expletives once again swirl all around us.

Content to go into halftime with the lead, Florida runs the ball up the middle three times and then punts with only 10 seconds left on the game clock. Stafford takes a knee. The half comes to an end with the Gators ahead, 14-to-3. Their lead feels much greater.

With the sun shining through the high haze behind the west side of the stadium, a cool shadow covers the entire red half of the stands. The fans across the field from us are sitting in much brighter seats.

As the Florida players take the field to receive the second-half kickoff, Alex points to a gray plastic box with red letters next to the visiting spirit squad.

Just then, our seatmates begin howling "Ugg-uh!" "Ugg-uh!" "Ugg-uh!" With encouragement from his handler, the 56-pound bulldog trots out of his travel carrier.

Dressed in a small red jersey with an oversized black G on his chest is the seventh member in a line of all-white English bulldogs to don the custom-made outfit. Introduced eight weeks ago at the opening game of this 2008 season, Uga VII is owned by the Frank W. "Sonny" Seiler family in Savannah, Georgia.

In 1956, the Southern trial lawyer with the bright nickname and his wife, Cecelia, took the soon-to-be Uga I to the opening game of the season versus Florida State University. Ever since that 3-to-0 victory over the Seminoles, Uga I and his descendants have roamed the sidelines as the official mascot of the school. And each wrinkle-faced canine has received a varsity letter upon assuming this role.

Florida's first series of the second half stalls at their 38-yard-line when the normally sure-handed Brandon James drops a 10-yard roll-out pass from Tebow. The derailed drive takes a favorable turn for the Gators as second-year punter Chas Henry sends the ball 49 yards to the far end of the field. His long-snapper, James Smith from F. W. Buchholz High School in Gainesville, emphatically slams the ball to the turf several inches outside the goal line.

A couple of surly fans, returning from halftime, grumble as they force their way through the row behind us. Cocktails, it becomes clear, are not just a pregame pastime in Jacksonville.

From what looks like dire circumstances, the Bulldogs swiftly gain spectacular momentum. Standing on the R in the white blocked letters of "FLORIDA," Stafford hands the ball to Moreno. Three plays after the fazing punt by Henry, Stafford connects with his freshman wide receiver, A.J. Green, for a first down just 30-yards outside of Florida's end zone. Highlighting this surging drive is a sensational 18-yard run by Moreno that features his signature high-hurdle over a lunging defensive back. For the first time today, positive energy exudes from the lubricated fans in our section.

Then it happens.

Dropping straight back in the pocket after a fake hand-off to Moreno, No. 7 in red fires an ill-advised pass over the right side directly into the arms of Joe Haden. Catching the ball in mid-stride, the cornerback streaks along the Florida sideline at full-speed, cuts back toward the middle of the field and crashes out-of-bounds at the exact spot where Georgia began its 70-yard drive. The tackle by Mohamed Massaquoi at the 1-yard-line thwarts the seemingly destined "pick-six" by the 5'11" 185-pound former high school quarterback.

One play after this 88-yard interception, Tebow strolls untouched over the left side. The University of Florida's fight song, "Orange and Blue," blares from the white and blue-draped Gator band at our end of the field. The scoreboard rolls to 21-to-3.

After a touchback, Georgia gains 1 yard in three plays and is forced to punt. Tebow and his fellow reptiles take over at their own 44-yard-line. In less than 1 minute of game time, the Gators strike again. On the fourth play of the drive, Mr. Football lofts a perfectly thrown 44-yard pass to Louis Murphey, who never breaks step as he crosses into the far scoring zone. Sunshine bathes the fans across from us. Our section, in the shade of this now blue-sky late afternoon, seems a little cooler – and a little darker. The score is 28-to-3.

Richard Samuel is rudely met by another congregation at the 24-yard-line on the succeeding kickoff. Following a diving 17-yard reception by A.J. Green, Stafford pitches the ball to Moreno. The ball flies from the running back's hands as Florida's defensive end crashes through the block of his pulling guard. Sophomore defensive tackle Terron Sanders scoops up the fumble. With the grace of a ballerina (I'm not kidding!), the 300-pound lineman in all-white performs a perfect pirouette to avoid the lunging Matthew Stafford and ambles all the way to the 10-yard-line.

Sixth-year defensive coordinator Charlie Strong jumps into the arms of the sophomore tackle from Bradenton, Florida as he is mobbed along the sidelines.

Two plays later, Tebow takes the shotgun snap and waltzes 8 yards between two crushing blocks by his offensive line and crosses onto the white and blue letters for his third rushing touchdown of the game. Two minutes have run off the game clock since the last Gators' score. With the sun setting behind the Georgia side of the stadium, it's now 35-to-3.

Following five successful plays to midfield, Stafford once again drops back in the pocket and fires a pass in the direction of his wide receiver, A.J. Green. The heralded quarterback hurries his throw to avoid the tenacious rush. Making an acrobatic leap, No. 32 in white bats the poorly thrown ball into the air. With a quick spin, Dustin Doe catches the ball he tipped and falls to the turf on his 40-yard-line.

The middle linebacker from Jasper, Florida races into the arms of his teammates along the sideline. Stafford hobbles to his bench with a noticeable limp to his right leg.

As the third quarter comes to an end, so does the party for many of the fans in our section. Several groups of spectators in red and black pack up their belongings and head toward the exits.

Even though Florida is forced to punt following this spectacular interception by Doe, they do take 2 more minutes off the game clock.

Since coming through the far tunnel at the start of the second half, the Bulldogs have had four offensive possessions: an interception, a three-and-out punt, a fumble, and another interception. Following an illegal-motion penalty, a batted-down pass in the backfield, and a delay-of-game foul, Stafford stands on his 8-yard-line awaiting the shotgun snap. On this daunting third down, he successfully fires a 40-yard pass into double-coverage to A.J. Green. All these yards are immediately erased on the very next play.

Breaking over the middle, wide receiver Kris Durham leaps for the ball, only to have it tipped into the air by Dustin Doe (again!) and into the waiting arms of No. 35 in white. Ahmad Black races with the intercepted ball along the Georgia sideline until he is tripped-up by Stafford and finally tackled by Massaquoi (his second touchdown-saving tackle of the game).

On the very next play, from the 25-yard-line, Tebow finds Harvin all alone in the middle of the end zone.

With more than 11 minutes left in the game and the punishing score now 42-to-3, the west side of the stadium has turned teal.

The empty blue-green rows become even more pronounced as the stadium lights illuminate the early-evening field. So many fans have left our side that we decide to "upgrade" our seats. We pretty much have the entire center section of the stadium to ourselves as the deflated Bulldogs trot back onto the field.

Even after an impressive 60-yard return by Richard Samuel, the team from Athens is only able to gain 1 yard in four plays.

At this late stage in the fourth quarter, John Brantley steps in for Mr. Heisman and swiftly moves the Gators to within 10 yards of the goal line. On third down, the redshirt freshman from Ocala, Florida fires a strike into the hands of freshman wide receiver Deonte Thompson to put the *seventh* touchdown on the scoreboard for the team from the Sunshine State.

The few red-clad fans around us don't even react to this demoralizing score.

A little more than 7 agonizing minutes remain in the game. With second-string players on the field for both teams, Stafford's replacement, Joe Cox, orchestrates a nice drive down the field. On third down from the 19, the junior quarterback finds freshman tight end Aron White open in the end zone at the opposite end of the field. A surreal absence of cheering greets this touchdown.

The west half of the stands are almost completely devoid of fans with 3 minutes left on the game clock. Alex, Valerie, and I mockingly perform "the wave" from our 50-yard-line seats.

Then it *really* happens.

The Gators start their final series of the game. They open with five positive plays. Then, on first down --- on their 40-yard-line --- up by 39 points --- with only 44 seconds left on the game clock --- Urban Meyer calls the first of his two remaining time-outs.

With a Cheshire cat smile, Tim Tebow flails his arm wildly along the sidelines toward the blue (not teal) side of the stadium. Taking the handoff from Brantley following this emasculating time-out, Emmanuel Moody rambles 16 yards for another first down.

Immediately after this demoralizing moving of the sticks --- on first down --- on Georgia's 45-yard-line --- with only 30 seconds remaining in the contest --- Meyer calls his third time-out.

The entire half of the stadium across the field is emphatically slamming their extended arms together. CHOMP! CHOMP! CHOMP!

A referee races towards Mr. Football who is waving a white towel over his head while prancing on the sideline between the 5 and 10-yard-lines. Threatening to call an unsportsmanlike penalty, the official instructs the signal-caller to return to his bench. The three of us stand in awe of this audacious display.

Having no more time-outs left to call, Meyer watches the game clock roll to triple zeros. The scoreboard glows 49-to-10.

With his arm draped around Charlie Strong and a devilish look in his eyes, Urban Meyer briskly makes his way to the center of the field. Surrounded by blissful fans and jubilant players, he cursorily shakes hands with Mark Richt. At this point, every fan in the stadium tonight – and across the entire college football world – realizes last season's "Gator Stomp" really *will* "forever be in the mind of Urban Meyer and in the mind of our football team."

Within minutes, most players have left the field and our side of the Alltel Stadium is empty. Not a single fan that I can see has left the Florida side.

Tim Tebow, following a hug-fest with offensive coordinator Dan Mullen, hands his helmet to a trainer. With the Gator band playing "Orange and Blue" in the still fully-occupied west side of the stands, he's made good on the promise he tearfully delivered after the Ole Miss loss just four short weeks ago.

Realizing he's more to the Florida faithful than just the winning quarterback, the triumphant field general embarks on a lone victory lap around the outside of the illuminated field. Valerie awaits the MVP of the game in the curve of the end zone. Hanging over the railing, she receives a high-five from "Mr. Florida" as he jogs past the three of us.

Elation does not begin to describe the look on my beautiful bride's face. Alex looks relieved. He's survived his first collegiate football game. And what a game at that! One with so much drama and excitement, I forgot all about my blue-casted arm.

CHAPTER ELEVEN
Midnight Yell
2009 Texas | Texas A&M

It's a little past 7:00 in the evening.

Valerie and I are seated on a long plank running parallel to the serving counter of the open kitchen inside the oldest bar in the Northgate district of College Station. We've been relegated to this side-bench due to the number of patrons packed inside Dixie Chicken on this night before the local team's annual showdown with its despised in-state rival.

Across from us in a glass-enclosed display under the counter are various over-sized plastic food containers, Velveeta cheese blocks, and sleeves of saltine crackers.

It's not surprising this old-timey saloon is bursting at the seams, given that it's within spitting distance of the Texas A&M University campus. As we enjoy a little Aggie revelry in this quintessential college town, our intent is to be near the stadium around midnight.

Much like Barley's Taproom in Knoxville, Big Al's in Blacksburg, and last season's Salty Dog Saloon, we've discovered The Chicken (as it's known around campus) by chance. Situated next to several brick-walled taverns along University Drive, this celebrated locale appears to be constructed from old barn siding. With its faux back porch and split-rail fence, it also looks like the set of a low-budget 1950s cowboy movie.

A campy, Old-Western theme permeates its interior as well: rusted cattle ranch signs, antique feed-store billboards, and random taxidermied mammals adorn its rustic wood walls. All that's missing are the animatronic characters from Disney's "Country Bear Jamboree."

A steady stream of wrapped cheeseburgers and paper plates loaded with various fried foods, many drenched in some sort of white sauce, flows across the rolled-tin serving counter. In addition to cheese-smothered Tijuana Fries (which are in high demand), the hand-painted menu above the counter lets us know we can order Dixie Tacos, Texas Toothpicks (which look like fried worms), Pickle Chips, Texas Toast, Frito Pie, and something simply called Stuff.

For $32.00, we can also enjoy a *pound* of beef jerky.

Most intriguing, however, is the Sausage, Cheese and Crackers Platter. This "specialty of the house" consists of a dozen or so slices of dry pastrami on a bed of square Velveeta slices, served alongside an unopened sleeve of saltines. Yep, an entire brick of waxed paper-enclosed dry crackers. I chortle and say to Valerie; it has all the charm of a prison meal.

Ordering directly from the kitchen staff, we choose more standard fare.

Working through our amazing meals on a bun, we notice the crowd at the center of the elongated saloon beginning to thin out. We move to one of the chunky wooden tables along the wooden wall across from the wooden bar. Hoary deer antlers poke down from the wooden ceiling. Almost every inch of the table and benches is covered with carved graffiti and etched initials. It's obvious this tradition has been going for decades, probably since the place opened.

Founded in 1974 by two local business partners, the converted pool hall got its name from an album title by the Southern rock band Little Feat. It's said Lyle Lovett and several other country music legends got their start playing impromptu sessions on it's back porch. From an initial investment of $7,000, Dixie Chicken has now grown into one of the most popular establishments in College Station.

Three years ago, *Playboy On-Campus* claimed the tavern sells more beer per square foot than any other bar in the United States. Whether or not this is verifiable, The Chicken certainly ranks as one of the top purveyors of malt beverages that we've seen on our quest – now in its 10th year! Checking our watches, we have several more hours to enjoy the campiness that is Dixie Chicken before we leave for one of the most memorialized rituals in all of college football.

Midnight Yell Practice takes place inside the stadium across campus on the night before each home game. This community-wide pep rally got its humble beginning early in the 20th century when specialized regiments at the all-male military college came together to learn each other's battle hymns and fight songs.

In the early 1930s, as the legend goes, several first-year cadets approached their upperclassmen with the idea of teaching their pep songs to all students at the school. They suggested a campus-wide rally at midnight on the evening before the varsity football game with their arch-rivals from Austin. The senior cadets said it wouldn't be possible to schedule an event in the military dormitories that late in the evening. However, they *did* say they might be able to stop by the off-campus YMCA around that time. The next day, the Aggies beat the University of Texas 7-to-6; and, thus, the tradition was born.

Since its earliest days, students leading cheers has been a part of college football.

In the mid-1880s, an all-male pep squad at Princeton became the first officially recognized cheering group in the nation. Thomas Peebles, a former member of that squad, brought organized cheerleading to the University of Minnesota. A fellow medical student petitioned the school to sanction a group of students to rally their fans at sporting events. Jonny Campbell, following his successful appeal, is credited with the sport's first organized cheer, which he trumpeted through a large golden megaphone: "Rah, Rah, Rah! Ski-U-Mah! Hoo-Rah! Hoo-Rah! Varsity! Varsity! Minn-e-so-tah!"

In 1923, at the same university, women joined organized cheerleading. With the introduction of synchronized routines and acrobatic tumbling in the 1940s, they became a common fixture along the sidelines.

During this era, Lawrence "Herkie" Herkimer, while enrolled at Southern Methodist University, organized the nation's first cheerleading camp. Credited with introducing pom-poms and the spirit stick, his ostentatious "herkie-jerk" routines became a staple on sidelines across the country. As the popularity of cheerleading grew, so did his summer camps. In 1961, Herkimer formalized his organization as the National Cheerleading Association, which continues to host camps to this day.

There are no cheerleaders at the university formerly known as the Agricultural and Mechanical College of Texas.

Instead, the school – which officially changed its name to Texas A&M University in 1963 – has "Yell Leaders." Each year, the all-male troupe of three seniors and two juniors is chosen via a campus-wide vote.

This tradition of masculine Yell Leaders began more than a century ago when, according to Aggie lore, senior members in the Corps of Cadets instructed a group of first-year cadets to do what they could to entice students from Texas Women's University to stay on campus after an intrastate sporting event. The freshmen reportedly snuck into a maintenance closet, donned white coveralls, and paraded alongside the tracks at the railway station while yelling A&M-themed chants. Ever since, Aggie Yell Leaders – dressed in white button-downs and white military parade pants – have been fixtures at all varsity football games.

They are also master of ceremonies at the midnight pep rally which takes place before the annual clash with that sprawling university just a little more than 100 miles to the west.

Sharing our country-style table, Valerie strikes up a conversation with several A&M alums. Being deep in the heart of Aggieland, we both chose *not* to wear burnt orange (or bright orange, or any orange) this evening. This decision is serving us well as we listen to a convoluted story about one of many traditions here in College Station.

According to its menus, Dixie Chicken is "The original home of the Ring Dunk." Our tablemates inform us this refers to a ritual involving Aggie Rings, which any student can purchase, but *only* if he or she has at least a 2.0 grade-point average. Valerie whispers to me, "I guess they don't sell many, do they?"

One of our fellow patrons proudly shows the intricate eagle and shield design on his ring as we order another pitcher.

Aggie Rings, we are told, are given out three times a year during ceremonies on campus. On these Ring Days, students flock to this fowl-named establishment for a rite that began in the late 1970s. Allegedly, a cadet at the time dropped his newly purchased Aggie Ring into a pitcher of beer. Challenged by his friends, he proceeded to chug the entire pitcher and catch the shiny metal band with his teeth. (As of four years ago, the state of Texas no longer allows pitchers to be sold on Ring Days. Valerie rolls her eyes as our acquaintances tell us that The Chicken can sell 32-ounce mugs.)

How well-known is Ring Dunk around here? Let's just say that it has been recognized by the President of the United States we met several years ago in the aisle at Veterans Memorial Stadium.

During his commencement speech at last year's graduation ceremony, George W. Bush proclaimed, "I'll say this for A&M, you've got some mighty fine traditions. Back in my day, I think I would have enjoyed 'dunk my ring.'" The 43rd Commander in Chief even made apologies for Bob Gates, the former president of the university and current Secretary of Defense, who was unable to attend the ceremony by stating, "He's got an excused absence. It's not like he's over at the Dixie Chicken."

At the end of this jewelry-soaking story, Valerie mentions she expected this popular campus eatery to be much busier, given it's only eight o'clock before the biggest game of the year. Our ring-wearing friend casually mentions that most students have probably already left to get good seats at Midnight Yell, which starts in a half-hour.

"WHAT?"

This would be Valerie and me, shouting in unison.

Yep. MIDNIGHT Yell Practice – one of A&M's most time-honored traditions – takes place at 8:30 p.m.

Throwing-back our final gulps, we say good-bye to our Aggie

buddies and head out the back door.

Finding our bearings, we enter a narrow alleyway between the wood siding of Dixie Chicken and the brick wall of Dry Bean Saloon. Hastily advancing toward University Drive, we notice the entire length of this dark corridor is covered in old bottle caps. The thousands and thousands of rusted metal caps, which must have been tossed from these adjacent taverns for decades, make a soft grinding sound with each step. It's a little past eight.

Winding through the dark campus, Valerie spots a small green pamphlet on the ground. Its cover reads *Fish Camp 2009 – Discover the Aggie Spirit*. We have no idea what the booklet is referring to. From its back cover, we do know it belonged to Allisen Jones, in cabin Windham B07, at camp Thorpe, on bus 18.

Flipping through the dozen or so pages, we surmise Fish Camp is some type of retreat for first-year A&M students. This handbook contains its rules of behavior and scheduled events. On its inside back cover is a hand-drawn map which looks like a setting from the Bill Murray summer camp comedy *Meatballs*, complete with color-coded cabins, counselor lodges, and a lake. (Our guidebook informs that we are *not* to go into the lake.) It also contains several wonderful pages detailing the lyrics and hand signals of the Fightin' Texas Aggie Yells & Songs.

Started in 1954 by a student activity director as a simple camping trip for a few incoming freshmen, Fish Camp is now an officially recognized, four-day orientation attended each year by three out of every four first-year students. Last year, almost 6,000 high school graduates traveled two hours north of College Station to Lakeview Campground in Palestine, Texas, for what our booklet claims to be "A Freshman's First Tradition."

As printed on the inside cover, the mission of Fish Camp is to "welcome freshmen into the Aggie family by sharing the traditions and values of Texas A&M University and creating a universally accepting support system that allows them to build relationships and embody the Aggie spirit." We're just glad fish-cadet Allisen Jones dropped it on her way to Kyle Field this evening.

Crossing a dark drill field, we meet other soon-to-be yellers heading along Houston Street toward the massive rectangular stadium. As we round a corner, Valerie spots a welcoming sight.

This enormous tractor-trailer used to transport the Longhorns' team equipment is parked directly across from their rivals' home field. The 40-foot rolling billboard touts her alma mater's gridiron accomplishments over the years. Pictures of former coaches and famous players, Big XII Championship trophies, National Championship trophies, and the Heisman Trophy surround the Longhorns logo and the words "Unity" "Family" and "Strength."

Without hesitation, Valerie jumps on the running board for a quick photo. Holding onto the mirror, she flashes a surreptitious "Hook-em" hand-sign as Aggie fans scurry toward the Bernard C. Richardson Zone of the dimly lit stadium.

As we approach the gate, we notice a maroon banner hanging from a streetlight. Listed in white block letters is the following itinerary:

3:30 Hours Prior to Kick-Off
Aggie Fan Zone Opens

2:45 Hours Prior to Kick-Off
Kids Yell Practice

2:30 Hours Prior to Kick-Off
Team Spirit Walk

2:00 Hours Prior to Kick-Off
Kyle Field Gates Open

90 Minutes Prior to Kick-Off
Corps Steps Off from Quad

70 Minutes Prior to Kick-Off
Calvary Enters Kyle Field

60 Minutes Prior to Kick-Off
Corps March-In

30 Minutes Prior to Kick-Off
Aggie Fan Zone Closes

22 Minutes Prior to Kick-Off
"Spirit of Aggieland"

12 Minutes Prior to Kick-Off
National Anthem

Everything about Texas A&M is regimented. (Which is not surprising given its proud military heritage and it being one of only six universities in the nation with a standing cadet corps.)

We don't have time to read the final few minutes on this vinyl banner as we scuttle into the dark football arena.

It's 8:45. Midnight Yell Practice has been in full swing for 15 minutes.

With field lights illuminating only the east stands, we squeeze into its lower section at about the 30-yard-line. Valerie is in a blue pullover fleece; I'm wearing a black, discreetly-logoed Oklahoma State sweatshirt. We present no concern for the Aggie faithful standing in our row. In fact, we're welcomed with open arms. Literally.

Within minutes, our arms are locked around the waists of our seatmates as each row rocks back and forth like chains swinging in the wind. Following instruction from five cadets dressed in maroon t-shirts and blue overalls, featuring their hand-painted name across each bib, our entire section breaks into a song about sawing the horns off some guy named Rusty.

As former President Bush remarked last year, they sure do have some mighty fine traditions at A&M. They also have searing disdain for their burnt orange rivals.

According to our Fish Camp manual, we're currently swaying to A&M's official fight song titled "The Aggie War Hymn." Our cheat sheet informs us that the 20,000 or so students, alumni, and local citizens crooning at the top of their lungs are not calling for the dismemberment of "Rusty." Arm in arm, they're singing about severing the horns from Bevo.

For some reason, this melodic battle hymn refers to the live longhorn mascot as "Varsity" – which sounded a lot to us like "Rusty." Also, for a fight song at Texas A&M University, it sure has a *lot* of emphasis on the school in Austin.

As printed in Allisen's pamphlet, the lyrics echoing across the vacant field tonight are:

> Hullabaloo, Caneck! Caneck!
> Hullabaloo, Caneck! Caneck!
>
> Good-bye to texas university
> So long to the Orange and the White
> Good luck to dear old Texas Aggies
> They are the boys who show the real old fight
> "The eyes of texas are upon you . . ."
> That is the song they sing so well
> (Sounds like hell)
> So good-bye to texas university
> We're gonna beat you all to
> Chig-gar-roo-gar-rem
> Chig-gar-roo-gar-rem
> Rough! Tough! Real Stuff! Texas A&M
> Saw Varsity's horns off!
> Saw Varsity's horns off!
> Saw Varsity's horns off!
> Short!

Valerie can't stop snickering as the faithful lean forward, with arms still locked around each other's waists, to listen to the Yell Leader named Weston (according to his overalls). The ruddy-faced cadet in his broad-brimmed white cowboy hat is reciting a folk fable of some sort about farmers revolting against something.

As the four other overall-clad cadets begin rotating one arm over the other in alternating directions, the entire east section of the stadium immediately shouts, "Farmers fight! Farmers fight! Farmers fight! Farmers, farmers fight!"

This startling cheer is followed by another fight song with *another* nod to their in-state rivals:

> Late one night, when the t-sips were in bed
> Old Sul Ross put a lantern in the shed
> An Aggie kicked it over and winked his eye
> and said
> It'll be a hot time in Austin tonight!

Adding to our bewilderment, three cadets in maroon t-shirts and overalls kneel over two cadets in white t-shirts and overalls at midfield. Facing each other, the two male students in white are performing what appears to be half push-ups. (At least that's what we *hope* they're doing.)

The five cadets are the only ones on the half-lit field. And no one is paying any attention to them, let alone acknowledging their purpose. Finding no explanation in our campground handbook, Valerie turns to the middle-aged Aggie next to her for insight into this bizarre activity transpiring atop the A&M field logo.

According to the drawn-out yarn from our fellow 8:30-Yeller, each yearly class has its own "wildcat," which we ascertain to be a combination of hand-signals and some sort of loud noise at the end of each yell. Fish-cadets flail their hands over their heads and let out an exaggerated "A!" sound. Sophomores chant the letter "A" five times while waving their hands in the shape of a pistol. Juniors yell "Whoop!" as they point their pistol-shaped fingers to the ground. And seniors convey their alleged expertise in marksmanship by pointing their make-believe pistols to the sky and letting out an "A-Whoop!"

If an underclassman is caught performing the wildcat of a higher class, push-ups are the punishment.

The ritual at midfield this evening pays homage to the hierarchical importance of each wildcat. The two junior Yell Leaders have been performing these exercises – non-stop – during all three battle hymns tonight. And each song is several minutes long.

Following the final ballad, the orderly clapping ends. It's now that the two white-shirted cadets cease their push-ups and make a half-hearted attempt to run to our side of the field. What happens next is something Valerie and I laugh about to this day. The five Yell Leaders in painted overalls proceed to enact a faux football game complete with fake attempted blocks, exaggerated missed tackles, and goofy facial expressions.

The Aggie alum next to us gleefully explains that the senior cadets in maroon shirts, who were kneeling over the exercising underclassmen, represent the A&M team attempting to prevent their opponents from moving down the field. This hackneyed exhibition clearly lacks the realism that's expected to take place between these same hash marks tomorrow.

Nevertheless, it's sort of delightful.

With the multitude of stories, silly gesticulations, and songs-of-envy coming to a close, the Yell Leader, named Casey, directs our attention to the north end of the stadium.

From behind the goalpost, a group of coaches, trainers, and players saunters onto the dark gray track. The casually dressed athletes, in matching light gray tracksuits, maroon shirts, and gray tennis shoes, assemble, somewhat reluctantly, along the sideline facing the Aggie faithful. As they stand with hands in pockets, it feels more like a mandatory class assembly than the pep rally before the biggest game of the year.

The not-so-late-night crowd parrots back a loud "howdy" to Casey. Reverently, the Yell-Leader hands the microphone to head coach Mike Sherman, who is in his first full year after taking over for the disgraced Dennis Franchione last November. The former head coach unceremoniously resigned immediately after the victorious 38-to-30 scrimmage with the "tea-sippers" (his second consecutive win over the Longhorns) following an inquiry into a newsletter subscription scheme that evidently violated NCAA rules.

The 54-year-old Sherman proceeds to deliver a matter-of-fact speech about unity, camaraderie, and the importance of support from Aggie Nation. As a hush falls over the stands, we're aware the "practice" part of Midnight-Yell-Practice-at-8:30 has come to an end.

As every yeller tonight knows, their adversary tomorrow is one of six teams with a perfect eleven-win record this season. Currently ranked third, Texas is a fraction of a percentage point behind top-ranked Florida and the University of Alabama. They have arguably the top Heisman Trophy contender at quarterback and a defense ranked first in rushing yards allowed and second in total defense nationally.

The Longhorns also lead this in-state series with 74 wins. The Aggies have only been victorious 36 times. Last year, they suffered a 40-point beatdown to Colt McCoy's team at Darrel K Royal Stadium. This season, their defense ranks among the bottom 20 teams in all categories. There's not much to "whoop" about on this cool evening before Thanksgiving.

Coach Sherman hands the microphone to one of his senior players. The collected Aggie in gray sweats emboldens his teammates and their devotees by proclaiming: "They say we can't beat 'em. They say they have a Heisman Trophy quarterback. They say they're better than us. That they're gonna beat us by three touchdowns." After each of these punctuated statements, the crowd lets out a long "hissssssssss."

Evidently, booing is discouraged at A&M. Instead, when an opposing team executes a good play, or a referee makes an objectionable call, Yell Leaders let out a "horse laugh yell" which is followed by an extended hiss from the fans.

A roar rips across the vacant field as the poised player at the microphone exclaims, "Let's see what they're saying this time tomorrow night!" Equally as loud, a cannon – manned by cadets in full military parade uniforms – blasts from the south end zone. The enlivened crowd chants four times in unison, "Beat the hell outta TU, hey!"

Midnight Yell Practice ends with the players huddling on the A&M logo at midfield. It's a little past 10:00 p.m.

The Agricultural and Mechanical College of Texas was founded in 1876. However, it wasn't until 1904, when a professor of horticulture named Edwin Jackson Kyle was appointed president of the school's General Athletics Association, that consideration was given to a dedicated football field on campus. Much to the frustration of the school lecturer, the college was unwilling to contribute the necessary funds.

Kyle, an 1899 graduate and ardent promoter of Aggie athletics, took matters into his own hands – and his own pocketbook – and roped off a section of land set aside for his cultivation classes. Using $650 of his own money (equivalent to about $20,000 today), the science teacher purchased a covered grandstand from the local fairgrounds and placed it alongside the newly marked field. Seating capacity on the wooden benches topped out at 500.

Finally acknowledging his foresight, the Board of Directors officially designated the sporting area that same year. The Corps of Cadets christened it two seasons later as Kyle Field. This same piece of land is now emblazoned with a large maroon and white Texas A&M logo, with a distinctive white ribbon wrapped around its T, for this weekend's showdown.

Ten years before this evening, one of the nation's worst on-campus tragedies befell Texas A&M University.

Early in the morning of November 18th, students and alumni were constructing a 60-foot-tall tower of logs on the school's equestrian fields. As had been a tradition for more than 90 years, it was to be the centerpiece for the college-sponsored bonfire and pep rally on the night before the upcoming scrimmage with their in-state rival. At 2:42 a.m., the unthinkable happened.

More than 5,000 tree-sized logs, stacked in a 3-tier wedding cake design, collapsed as their massive weight caused the containment wires to break. Eleven students and one former graduate were killed; 27 others were injured. Rescue operations took more than 24 hours due to the inability to use heavy equipment for fear of crushing survivors. Along with the Corps of Cadets and hundreds of students, the entire A&M football team rushed to the polo field to assist in the rescue efforts.

Five years ago, a circular memorial featuring 12 doorways and 27 polished stones was dedicated at the spot of the catastrophe.

Walking along the north side of Kyle Field a few hours before kickoff to this 116th meeting between in-state rivals, we spot several white promotional tents across the street from the University Bookstore. A smattering of burnt orange is peppered throughout the hordes of maroon-clad fans meandering around the temporary pavilions on this pleasant Turkey Day afternoon.

Approaching the canvas encampment, we're met by a spunky dark-haired girl with black Heisman Trophy stickers under each eye and an oversized camera in her hand. Wearing a black baseball cap with the image of the Heisman Trophy emblazoned across the front and the *Sports Illustrated* logo on its side, she asks if we'd like an autograph from John David Crow.

On Thanksgiving Day in 1956, the Texas A&M varsity football team accomplished a feat no other team had in the history of the program. In a 34-to-21 slugfest, the tough-as-nails team was the first squad to vanquish its in-state rivals inside Darrell K Royal-Texas Memorial Stadium. The team's bruising running backs, sophomores Loyd Taylor (with only one L) and John David Crow, combined for almost 200 of the 336 total rushing yards in the game. After this first-ever victory in the Austin arena, the Aggies warbled "Poor Tea-Sips!" in the locker room under its stands.

With this historic win, A&M finished the season ranked No. 5 in the nation. Led by third-year head coach Paul "Bear" Bryant, they were also the first to go undefeated in the Southwest Conference since the 1947 Mustangs from Southern Methodist University.

Eight games into the following season, thanks to the hard-nosed rushing by their fullback, the Aggies had yet to lose a game. Ranked No. 1 in the country, coach Bryant proclaimed, "If John David Crow doesn't win the Heisman Trophy, they ought to stop giving it."

During his senior year, even though he was only able to play in 7 games due to an injury in the season opener against the University of Maryland, No. 44 in maroon ran for 562 yards and scored six touchdowns. Playing both offense and defense in every game, he also intercepted five passes, including a game-preserving pick to seal the 7-to-6 victory over the Arkansas Razorbacks.

At the end of the 1957 season, the crew-cut-topped running back from Springhill, Louisiana was named a unanimous All-American and *Sporting News* Player of the Year. On December 3rd of that same year, he became the first Aggie ever to win the Heisman Trophy.

Unbeknownst to us, this 2009 season is the 75th year the stiff-armed trophy will be awarded to the sport's most outstanding player. This white Quonset hut we've entered is part of a traveling celebration for this diamond anniversary. The cute photographer in the Heisman hat lets us know that in addition to honoring Crow, this promotional tour is here because the quarterback of his former cross-state rival is a front-runner in this year's race.

To the disgust of half the citizens in the Lone Star State, Colt McCoy is having a fantastic season, one certainly worthy of the illustrious statue. A big game today could propel him atop the other contenders, including senior running back Toby Gerhart at Stanford, sophomore tailback Mark Ingram at Alabama, Ndamukong Suh (a rare defensive candidate) at Nebraska, and the former "Mr. Football" at the University of Florida.

Persuaded by the young photo-journalist with the face stickers (it didn't take much!), we join the long line slowly inching toward a table at the back wall. A large Heisman Trophy banner hangs immediately behind a silvered-haired gentleman sitting next to a stack of magazines. These commemorative programs are the "Texas A&M Aggies Heisman Winning Edition" of the *Sports Illustrated* tribute series featuring a profile of John David Crow.

Wearing a maroon V-neck sweater and a mocha-colored jacket, the 23rd recipient of the famed statue patiently signs the gold-colored editions for fans of both universities. The actual trophy presented 52 years ago, at the Downtown Athletic Club in New York City, sits on a shiny black block to the right of its distinguished now-73-year-old recipient.

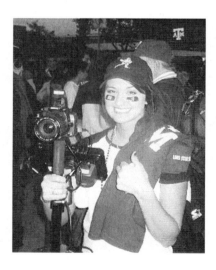

College football's traditions are many times started by the most obscure occurrences. Its fans can be just as obscure.

Exiting the Heisman tent, we see several coeds standing alongside a life-sized bronze statue of A&M's famed "12th Man." In the middle of this small cluster is a fellow student dressed in blue overalls with "Colt McCoy" painted across his bib. He also has white kitty ears and fuzzy white paws.

"What are you supposed to be?" Valerie asks, at which the

male tabby strokes his painted whiskers and whines, "I'm a whittle pussycat. A whit-ohhh pussy." Valerie extends best wishes to the students but gives me an eye-roll before we head to the north end of Kyle Field.

According to its brass plaque, the bronzed "12th Man" sculpture of E. King Gill was a gift from the class of 1980. In 1921, this second-year student became the source of arguably the most renowned tradition of this university's many, many, many renowned traditions.

After quitting the varsity football team, Gill moved to the press box to be a spotter for the game announcers. At the end of that season, the five-win, one-loss, two-tie Aggies earned a trip to the Dixie Classic (now the Cotton Bowl Game) to face the No. 1 team in the nation.

During this post-season scrimmage, the undefeated Praying Colonels (real name) from Centre College (real school) located in Danville, Kentucky roughed up the team from College Station so badly they only had 11 players left standing. (The Praying Colonels, led by former A&M head coach Charley Moran, earlier in their perfect ten-win season also handed Harvard University their first loss in three years.) With no one left on the bench, Aggie head coach Dana X. Bible (real name) spotted the former back-up running back in the press box and waved him down to the field.

The rest is history.

The underdogs upended the Praying Colonels 22-to-14 in what the local newspaper described as "the most spectacular, most nerve-tingling football game ever staged in the history of the game in the southwest." E. King Gill, however, never left the bench.

After the game, the reserve player stated to the Post, "I wish I could say that I went in and ran for the winning touchdown. But I did not. I simply stood by in case my team needed me." Ever since, the entire student body has adopted the "12th Man" moniker. They also stand for the entire length of each football game, symbolically waiting to be called onto the field if needed.

In 1983, head coach Jackie Sherrill added a novel twist to this legacy. At the beginning of that season, tryouts were held to select players to fill one position on kickoffs at each home game. The tradition still exists today. Each non-scholarship special-teams player wears the No. 12 maroon jersey.

Ask any Aggie and they will tell you: Texas A&M is the "Home of the 12th Man." Walking into the same section we were in less than 24 hours ago practicing whoops and yells, this proud slogan is mounted on the terrace above our heads.

Argue as they may – and they may – this military school in College Station however, was not the first organized sports team to adopt this catchphrase.

Almost a decade before the former third-string running back stood on the Aggies sidelines for an entire game, a former captain of the University of Iowa football team used the nickname to describe the bolstering support from fans in 1903 during the surprising 12-to-0 shutout over the University of Illinois. E.A. McGowan, in a 1912 edition of *The Iowa Alumnus*, wrote, "The eleven men had done their best; but the twelfth man on the team (the loyal spirited Iowa rooter) had won the game for old S.U.I."

The stadium clock reads 75:00 and is counting lower. If the banner we saw on the lamppost is correct, the Calvary should be entering Kyle Field in 5 minutes, the operative word being "if," given the start-time of last night's Midnight Yell Practice.

Much like the polytechnic institute in Blacksburg, the cadets at College Station attend classes alongside civilian students and wear parade regalia to all home games. From the open end of the horseshoe-shaped stadium, the first corpsmen in these ceremonial uniforms saunter onto the gray track atop dark brown horses. Two abreast, the dozen or so cadets with brown flat-brimmed Cavalry Stetsons and shiny battle sabers ride past our section.

Following slowly behind is "Spirit of '02," a 1902 artillery gun used to celebrate touchdowns at Kyle Field. The olive-green cannon has been fired by the Parsons Mounted Calvary after every score since 1984. This four-wheeled field piece is preceded by an old-fashioned wooden cart, complete with spoked wheels and a white schooner-shaped canvas cover. Two brown mules pull the covered wagon along the rim of the track.

A total of 68 equine – 61 horses and 7 mules – make up the

Parsons Mounted Cavalry. As the squeaky schooner passes our section, these well-behaved mounts plod onto the track.

Immediately following the beasts of burden is a band of cadets dressed in gray t-shirts with a yellow Cavalry shield across the chest, Wrangler jeans tucked into brown cowboy boots, and oversized silver belt buckles. Six are carrying brooms and large snow shovels – only not for snow! The seventh is pushing a burnt orange wheelbarrow with the letters "TU" on each side.

Close behind this cleanup crew, a cavalcade of cadets flows into the stadium like a scene from an old-time Western movie.

A color guard consisting of four cadets struts ahead of the approaching parade. The lead cadet in shiny knee-high brown boots carries a saber, the two on each side are flag bearers, and the fourth is holding a leash to a medium-to-small size dog. A maroon cape with "Tex Aggies" on each side drapes across the well-behaved brown and white pup.

The Fightin' Texas Aggie Band sitting to our immediate right strikes up a stirring marching song as the collie and her escort slowly prance by. Recognized as the "First Lady of Aggie Land," the dog (who looks a lot like the television star *Lassie*) also happens to be the highest-ranking member in the Corps of Cadets, outranking their four-star commander by one star.

And she knows it.

Reveille VII, wearing a replica of the cape worn by the school's first mascot, is the fifth full-blooded rough collie to serve in this capacity. Fondly known as Miss Rev, the sporting hound was introduced last season following the death of her predecessor, who reigned from 2001 to 2008.

Prior to 1960, each mascot roamed freely across campus. Since that year, a sophomore in Company E-2 has been chosen by fellow Cadets each spring to be Mascot Corporal. During their 12-month tenure, each privileged cadet will have Reveille by his side at all times, including social functions, formal events, and home for holidays.

As tradition has it, if the coddled canine barks while in class with her handler, the professor is to acknowledge this as an indication of boredom and therefore must cancel the remainder of the session. Also, if Miss Rev falls asleep on a Cadet's bunk, the outranked student must find somewhere else to sleep.

With only a few minutes before the teams take the field, the current Mascot Corporal rounds the north end zone to our right. Valerie says it's surprising, with all the pomp and pageantry, there isn't a second pooper-scooper crew in the procession. I tell her that on all our annual pursuits, we've seen rivalry, but this is the first time we have experienced Reveille!

This evening's Lone Star Showdown (as the contest is known throughout this state) is the second University of Texas game on our annual quest. It's also the second attended by a President of the United States with the last name of Bush.

Sitting across the field with Texas Governor Rick Perry is George H.W. Bush, the 84-year-old father of the President who joined us at the Army-Navy game in 2001. The former first baseman at Yale University and 41st President of this great country is wearing a full-length khaki jacket – and a maroon baseball cap. (Ten years ago, an imposing presidential library was christened in his name across an expansive 90-acre plaza on the west side of this campus.)

A massive burnt-orange flag with the distinguished white-horned logo streaks ahead of the team from Austin. Even though we're on the Longhorns' side of the stadium, all we can hear is high-pitched hissing from the Fightin' Aggie Band next to us. While the casually-dressed player in the gray jogging suit last night correctly noted that the visiting team is favored by a little more than three touchdowns, you wouldn't know it from the energy surrounding us.

The enormous Jumbotron – the largest we've ever seen – at the south end shows a close-up of Valerie's favorite player. Wearing No. 8 in all-white, Jordan Shipley, the star receiver from Burnet, Texas, casually catches warm-up passes along the sideline.

To my dismay, the giant screen also reveals an abhorrent modification to my favorite uniform in all of college football: Each player's number has been affixed above the orange longhorn logo on their white helmets. The supplementary stickers are difficult to read. They're also unnecessary clutter on the iconic headgear.

"Why mess with perfection?" I say to Valerie.

"Yeah!" she half-yells. "Don't mess with Texas!"

Each maroon helmet on the opposite side of the field features logos matching the design at the center of Kyle Field. The dates "1999 – 2009" are printed across the commemorative ribbon of each emblem.

On this solemn anniversary, the university has impressively constrained its memorializing of the tragic construction project. The logo and a pregame moment of silence convey sincere respect. Entering the stadium tonight, we also noticed several dark-maroon "Bonfire Remembrance" t-shirts.

It's a perfect evening for football, and yet the tension surrounding us can be cut with a slaughterhouse knife.

Sophomore Justin Tucker from Austin effortlessly sends the ball through the clear sky into the arms of Justin Swope. The Aggies' freshman return-man (also from Austin) ambles to his own 30-yard-line. After two plays for negative 2 yards, the Aggies 6'5" 235-pound quarterback stares across the line at the best third-down defense in the nation. Jerrod Johnson wears jersey No. 1, appropriate since he's thrown more touchdown passes and fewer interceptions this season than his notable rival standing on the near sidelines.

From the shotgun formation, the junior quarterback drops back in the pocket and – to the audible amazement of the almost 83,000 fans inside Kyle Field – finds a wide-open Jeff Fuller streaking down the field. Racing alongside the white line of Longhorn players standing stupefied on our side of the field, the sophomore wide receiver high-steps into the far end zone.

One minute and 16 seconds into the game and the packed maroon stadium is going berserk.

No one in the arena is prepared for this 70-yard touchdown. Not the Parsons Mounted Cavalry, who are late firing the Spirit of '02. Not the Aggie couples in the crowd, who are cheering so wildly they've forgotten to kiss each other. And certainly not the team in white.

As the son of the President in the stands tonight stated, they sure *do* have a lot of traditions at A&M. One is each time an Aggie player crosses the goal line; cadets kiss their girlfriends. The adage behind this being, "When the team scores; Aggies score!"

When young men are so shocked they forget to kiss their girlfriends, you know there's trouble brewing.

Another tradition is waving white towels. In 1985, the Student Aggie Club erected kiosks outside the stadium to sell "12th Man" spirit towels for $2.00 at the first home game that year against the Indians (now Warhawks) from Northeast Louisiana University (now the University of Louisiana at Monroe). Within 30 minutes, the student group was completely sold out. Much to Valerie's consternation, the stands at this moment look like a dark purple sea covered in wispy whitecaps.

Just as troubling, Colt McCoy and his Longhorns turn the ball over-on-downs at the 32-yard-line after marching down the field on their first drive.

The Aggies come out firing on the very next play. But, an illegal block negates this 15-yard pass from Johnson to sophomore Ryan Tannehill. The setback stalls momentum and forces them to punt. The roar from the fans with the little white towels across from us is genuinely deafening, as loud as any stadium we have visited on our quest.

The decibels have little impact as the visitors methodically move once again down the field. After a bone-jarring hit on wide receiver Jordan Shipley by defensive back Trent Hunter, McCoy scampers on a designed quarterback-draw to the 9-yard-line. On the twelfth play of this second drive, No. 12 in all-white finds a finalist for the Biletnikoff Award open in the northwest corner. Shipley leaps into the arms of his senior offensive guard, Charlie Tanner. This first touchdown for Texas is the jubilant receiver's tenth this season.

After the Aggies' ensuing 6-play drive bogs down, McCoy shows why he is a front-runner for the Heisman. Following an 8-yard pass to Malcolm Williams, a 10-yard quarterback scramble, and a 7-yard pass to Shipley, the senior quarterback from Tuscola, Texas tucks the ball under his arm on another planned draw up the middle. Sprung by a wonderful block from Charlie Tanner, McCoy sprints 65 yards for his team's second touchdown.

There's a lot of hissing – and not a lot kissing – in our surrounding rows.

With 10 minutes remaining in the second quarter, Jerrod Johnson and his maroon-clad teammates defiantly move down the field against the nation's No. 1-ranked rushing defense on the ensuing series. (Opposing teams have gained less than 2 yards-per-carry versus the Longhorns coming into this game.) After a piercing 36-yard pass from Johnson to backup quarterback Tannehill, who is playing wide receiver, the Aggies execute back-to-back 8-yard running plays to the 14-yard-line. On first down, the confident quarterback delivers a strike to Jeff Fuller to stunningly tie the slugfest at 14-apiece.

Defensive coordinator Will Muschamp rips the gray headset from his head. In less than 3 minutes, A&M traversed 92 yards in eight plays. "Beat the hell outta TU, whoop!" resounds throughout the stadium.

Two-and-a-half minutes later, the Longhorns take the whoop out of the air and score their third touchdown. Following what should have been an easy interception by junior defensive end Von Miller on the fourth play of this 8-play drive, McCoy once again found his childhood best friend open in the end zone. Jordan Shipley again jumps in celebration with his offensive guard Tanner after catching this 15-yard bullet that puts the Longhorns up by 7.

Mack Brown, in his burnt orange pullover and khaki pants, congratulates his players as they reach the sidelines. The confident band in the far end blares "The Eyes of Texas" fight song across the stadium.

Thousands of swirling towels attempt to rally the underdog team with exactly 5 minutes left in the first half. To the dismay of those doing the swirling, after moving the ball to the midfield, Jerrod Johnson is sacked all the way back at the 39-yard-line by defensive end Sam Acho. As their punt-return team trots onto the field, the explosive Longhorns have an opportunity to blow this game wide-open before the close of the half.

Racing through several converging Aggies, Valerie's favorite player signals for a fair-catch. With a shock felt through the stands, the ball hits one of Shipley's teammates and rolls into the arms of cover-man Lewis Anthony.

Slightly more than one minute of game time later, No. 1 in maroon stands tall in the pocket on the 25-yard-line and rifles the ball between two defenders into the diving arms of Howard Morrow, to tie the game at 21 apiece.

Both defensive backs, Nolan Brewster and Emmanuel Acho, stand in disbelief as the senior wide receiver from Keller, Texas tosses the ball to the referee. Whoops and hollers emanate from the Fightin' Aggie Band assembling behind the end zone as the extra-point sails over their heads.

The thrill of their 3-touchdown underdog possibly going into halftime tied with the No. 3 team in the nation can be seen on the faces of the Aggie faithful around us. This elation is very short-lived.

With 1:03 left on the clock and three time-outs at his disposal, No. 12 in all-white surgically maneuvers the Longhorns toward the massive Jumbotron at the far end. After two scrambles for first downs, McCoy hits junior wide receiver James Kirkendoll on a quick-out inside the orange pylon. The visitors to Aggieland go up 28-to-21 with only 4 seconds till the Corps of Cadets take the field. The oversized burnt orange flag again flutters across the south end zone.

Following 20 minutes of maneuvers and a solemn tribute to the lives lost in the tragedy ten years ago, the team which has already punched its ticket to the Big XII Championship Game versus Nebraska next week starts the second half from their 22-yard-line. McCoy once again quickly escorts the Longhorns across midfield. On fourth down and 1, Mack Brown rolls the dice. Surging under the offensive line, Von Miller and his fellow Aggies stone the sneaking quarterback for no gain.

Taking over-on-downs, A&M opens the third quarter with a 15-yard pass to Jeff Fuller. Disaster strikes on the very next play.

Quarterback Johnson fails to secure the ball into the belly of his tailback on a quick dive off the right side. Christine Michael loses control of the ball. Senior defensive end Sergio Kindle instantly smothers the errant pigskin.

Eight rushing plays after this third turnover in the game, the Longhorns score their fifth touchdown on a barreling 7-yard run by running back Tre' Newton. Six-and-a-half minutes remain in the third quarter. The scoreboard reads 35-to-21 in favor of the team from Austin.

The seemingly insurmountable task of outscoring one of the nation's most high-powered offenses – along with arguably the best defense in all of college football – gets a lot more challenging at the end of the Aggies' second drive of the second half.

After hastily navigating to the 13-yard-line in seven plays, including a 43-yard scramble by Johnson, A&M lines up for third down and 5. Devastatingly for most fans in the stands, the junior signal-caller lofts the ball into the end zone . . . and into the hands of No. 12 in all-white. Earl Thomas, the safety from (dare I say "burnt") Orange, Texas, falls to the ground with the ball for a touchback. The cadets in our section deflate with a loud "hisssssssss."

After a quick three-and-out and another devastating sack by Miller, the Longhorns punt the ball to midfield. On the first play of the following series, Jerrod Johnson (whose father was a standout receiver at A&M in the late 1970s) makes amends for the touch-back interception on the previous drive. From the 50-yard-line, No. 1 in maroon takes the shotgun snap on a designed quarterback-draw and rambles untouched for 38 yards. Only a shoestring tackle by safety Earl Thomas prevents Johnson from scoring.

The Aggies begrudgingly settle for a field goal following this explosive run, closing the gap in the score to 24-to-35. A little more than 1 minute is left in the third quarter. Half-hearted kisses are exchanged throughout our section.

These 3 points are followed by three incomplete passes from the visiting team after a holding penalty on the kickoff. The third quarter comes to an end with a fumble by Aggie punt-returner

Ryan Swopes – and an immediate recovery by teammate Bradley Stephens – at midfield.

Throughout the entire break between these quarters, almost every fan inside Kyle Field is locked arm in arm, swaying back and forth, and singing about sawing Varsity's – not Rusty's – horns off. (We later learned that during the ten seasons leading up to 1903, the team name of the visitors from Austin was simply "Varsity.")

Each row moves in the opposite direction of the other to simulate a giant saw blade. From across the field, the stands themselves appear to be moving from side to side.

At the start of this fourth quarter, with only half the field in front of them, the Aggies deftly move to the 16-yard-line. On the sixth play of the series, the stadium feels as if it really *is* moving.

Taking the ball off the right side, tailback Christine Michael executes a perfect spin-move and high steps into the end zone to bring the Aggies within 5 points of the stunned team from Austin. Newly-christened head coach Mike Sherman brazenly elects to go for a two-point-try to bring the score within a field goal. Johnson lobs a perfectly thrown pass over the shoulder of wide receiver Tannehill. The scoreboard now reads 32-to-35 in favor of the visitors with 13:38 left in the game.

Five Yell Leaders – dressed in what Valerie refers to as "milkman outfits" – perform baffling choreographed gyrations on the track in front of our section. The noise is ear-splitting as the Longhorns prepare to receive the kickoff.

I yell to Valerie this is easily the most exciting game of our quest so far. She socks me on the shoulder and nervously turns to watch her highly favored team spread across the field. One-minute-and-30 seconds later, she's hitting my shoulder for a different reason.

Following another scramble up the middle for 43 yards by her quarterback, who now has over 160 yards rushing in the game, the Longhorns surge ahead again by 10 points. McCoy, on third down and 12, hits wide receiver James Kirkendoll on a quick-out. The speedy junior from Round Rock, Texas makes a nifty move toward the middle of the field and scampers 47 yards to the end zone. The giant Jumbotron shows No. 11 in white taunting the Aggie faithful behind the goalpost. The scoreboard taunts the home crowd with 32-to-42.

Slightly more than 12 minutes remain in this Big XII brawl. A&M is not about to back down.

Coming into this evening, Texas has only allowed an average of 50.1 yards rushing and 239 total yards per game. At the start of this drive, the Aggies have 172 yards and 447 yards, respectively. To our amazement, after ten explosive plays, Jerrod Johnson again connects with Jeff Fuller on a 20-yard fade route for the wide receiver's third touchdown of the night.

The Aggies are back within 3. Seven minutes remain on the game clock. Yards are racking up against the Longhorns – and so are points. The Texas-size scoreboard now reads 39-to-42.

Every fan of the home team, just like their celebrated substitute player from long ago, has not sat down once tonight. All the momentum is along the far side of the field. The swirling towels and insane yelling project even more confidence.

There are moments in every sporting contest however, when one play seemingly crushes the will of an opponent, makes a mockery of traditions, demoralizes their fans, and leaves little doubt as to the outcome. That moment is now.

First-year return-man Marquise Goodwin snatches the ensuing kickoff out of the air five yards from his goal line and darts straight up the middle of the field. A deafening gasp engulfs the stands. Last year, as a senior at Rowlett High School in the Texas town with the same name, Goodwin was state champion in the long-jump and triple-jump, a member of the 4x100 meter state championship relay team and ran the second-fastest 100-meter dash in the entire state. Crossing the 50-yard-line at full stride, No. 84 leaves the rest of the field in his wake. Valerie screams as the 5'9" 170-pound track star zooms untouched into the end zone directly in front of our section. No other player is within 15 yards.

A hush falls over Kyle Field. "The Eyes of Texas" can be heard from the far end of the stunned stadium. Colt McCoy congratulates his fellow Longhorns as they buoyantly return to their sideline. The scoreboard glows 49-to-39 in favor of his team, with a little under 7 minutes left to play.

The Aggies are unable to regain momentum – or composure – after this 95-yard dash, the eleventh non-offensive touchdown this season by the Longhorns. Even with a spark of hope from a 40-yard return on the ensuing kickoff and an added 15 yards for a personal foul penalty, they are forced to settle for a field-goal-attempt from 6 yards outside the end zone. The 10-play drive comes to a dispiriting halt as sophomore placekicker Randy Bullock pushes the 23-yard try to the right of the goalpost.

Only 3 minutes remain in the game. "Texas fight! Texas fight! And it's goodbye to A&M!" blares from the Showband of the Southwest in the southeast corner.

Tonight's shootout is the highest-scoring game in the 116-year history of this series.

Not only did the home team triple the average points allowed this season by the top-rated defense in the nation; they finished with a near unfathomable 532 total yards of offense. Jerrod Johnson threw for 342 yards (38 more yards than his counterpart). He also averaged more than 10 yards per completion. Despite these facts, when the game clock rolled to triple-zeros, it was Colt McCoy who rolled into the record books.

The former all-time passing leader in Division 2A Texas high school football is now the winningest quarterback in all college football, surpassing David Green from the University of Georgia, with 44 career wins as a starter. He averaged 7.6 yards per completion, had four passing touchdowns, and didn't throw a single interception. He also completed the game with a career-high 175 yards rushing.

With this win tonight, the Longhorns finished the regular season with a perfect 12-and-0 record for the first time in the storied history of organized football at the University of Texas.

As with most stories passed from generation to generation, the origin of how the Texas mascot got its name is both factual and fantasized.

It *is* true that early in the morning on February 12, 1917, several Aggie students snuck into the corral that held the longhorn steer and branded the score of their 1915 rivalry game on the side of the tamed beast. The final score of that contest in College Station was 13-to-0 in favor of the home team.

Storytellers from A&M like to embellish this tale.

To obscure this burning reminder of the two-year-old defeat, the student handlers of the mascot altered the branded score to read BEVO by connecting the 1 and 3, changing the dash to an E, and adding a V before the zero. This, the Aggies faithful claim, is how the bovine got its name.

Nonetheless, two months *before* this nefarious searing by the cadets, an article in *Alcalde* (the official publication of the Texas Exes alumni association) revealed this moniker was actually bestowed by the magazine's editor. In his recap of the rivalry game, Ben Dyer wrote, "His name is Bevo. Long may he reign!"

The white-blazed mascot was officially introduced that year after an alumnus, Stephen Pinckney, suggested a steer would better symbolize the school than its current (and original) mascot – an American Pit Bull Terrier named "Pig."

Bevo XIV, whose predecessor was at the Red River blowout

Courtesy of The Dolph Briscoe Center for American History, The University of Texas at Austin

we witnessed a decade ago (and who attended George W. Bush's inauguration that same year), has horns that measure 72 inches from tip to tip. As the Texas Longhorn Band blasts their fight song over the top of these very long spikes, the equable mascot watches the midfield celebration from the southeast corner of Kyle Field.

In his third year representing the university, the 1,800-pound steer has no cognition of the thrilling clash that just transpired across the turf in front of him.

He did, however, stand for the entire contest.

A jubilant male cheerleader waves the oversized burnt orange and white flag directly in front of Bevo as Mack Brown shakes hands with his defeated adversary at midfield. The fans of both schools know they've witnessed a hard-fought battle between equally talented teams. They also know, if not for an explosive runback by a diminutive former track star, it could have gone either way.

Congratulations are extended to us by the woman in a maroon sweater standing next to Valerie. Exiting the stadium, the elderly fan turns to us and says, "Y'all drive careful, now."

Even with her polite Southern drawl – and kindness we've enjoyed throughout our visit to College Station – this well-wishing sounds a lot like, "Don't let the barn door hit you on your way out of town!"

CHAPTER TWELVE
The Fight in the Dog
2010 Yale | Harvard

Neyland Stadium in Knoxville. The Horseshoe in Columbus. Bryant-Denny Stadium in Tuscaloosa. Each bulged with more than 90,000 fans on the weekends of our pursuit over the past decade. Even on a morning so inclement the Volunteer Navy (and the Volunteers!) refused to show up, we were still surrounded by more than 108,000 soggy SEC devotees.

These massive structures also command acres and acres of real estate. At many universities, it's not unusual for the varsity football complex to usurp a lion's share of its overall campus grounds. Throw in multiple practice fields (both indoor and outdoor), coaching facilities, maintenance departments, equipment structures, and acres of parking and RV lots, and these programs can easily envelop half of all property at a university.

This year's venue does not fall into that category.

Harvard Stadium does rank near the top, however, in the annals of American football. Built in 1903, the horseshoe-shaped arena is the first free-standing concrete stadium in the nation and was designed to be a monument to the permanence of the game. Two years after its construction, however, Theodore Roosevelt's son broke his nose during a scrimmage inside this stadium against the fighting Elis from Yale University, followed by the *Chicago Tribune* publishing its "death harvest" article.

To address the savagery of the game, the presidential council assembled by young Roosevelt's father proposed its initial solution: increase the width of the field by 40 yards. Damningly for

Harvard, the dimensions of the field had already been set in stone. Literally. More than 37 million pounds of concrete had been poured to create 37 cascading rows of cement seats.

To avoid having to rebuild the hulking stadium, head coach Bill Reid suggested a novel change to the game: the forward pass. Not only did this adopted innovation diminish the importance of injury-prone wedge plays; it changed the game forever and enabled the fabled arena in Cambridge to remain intact.

This venue along the Charles River is the smallest on our quest. It's also the only one we've visited to have shrunk.

In 1923, the prestigious university expanded the arena to accommodate more than 57,000 fans. However, due to reduced attendance over the ensuing decades, the added seats in the north end were removed after the 1951 season. This deconstruction returned Harvard Stadium to its original seating capacity of just over 30,000 fans and enabled it to reclaim its classic horseshoe design.

Even with its size, the Romanesque structure is one of only four athletic venues in America designated as a National Historic Landmark. (The others: the Rose Bowl, the Los Angeles Memorial Coliseum, and the Yale Bowl.) Nestled alongside famed Harvard Business School, the stadium was a gift from the Class of 1879 on their 25th graduation reunion.

Approaching from North Harvard Street, I quip to Valerie that the stone-gray structure, with its four-story rectangular turret and double rows of repeating arches, looks like an antediluvian prison. It's not until we reach the south end that we recognize what *The New York Times* described in 1903 as "an athletic field surrounded by permanent banks of seats – the like of which is to be found only in a few of the ancient cities of Greece and Italy."

The curved end of the stadium really *does* have the appearance of a coliseum from antiquity. Three stories of poured concrete wrap 180 degrees from east to west. The bottom level features dome-shaped openings every 6 feet or so which support the second level of identical arches and the third level of square openings.

Crossing the slightly muddy field at this south end, we find ourselves in the midst of the most cultured tailgate party we've ever experienced. Several rows of luxury SUVs stretch across the relatively small piece of land, no larger than a football field itself, on this somewhat chilly, clear November afternoon. In stark contrast to the super-sized festivities at previous destinations, this pregame gathering feels like a picnic at a polo field.

There are no living-room-sized canopies in team colors. No RVs with flat-screens and retractable awnings. No barbecues the size of pickups. No multi-table spreads of game-day food. There *are* two sprinter vans on the brick-red oval at the north end of the school's track and field complex, letting us know that Crimson Catering is supplying today's tailgating event.

Subdued fans from both schools meander in and out of a simple white tent. A small picnic table draped with a red tablecloth and a red "Harvard" banner sits at the back of a shiny Range Rover. White mums in a glass vase, champagne in a silver bucket, soft cheeses and fancy crackers on a ceramic platter, a half-a-dozen uncorked wine bottles, a mound of maroon grapes, and a carryout box of Dunkin Donuts coffee are casually displayed across this impromptu fold-out.

"Sausage, cheese, and crackers" clearly has a different presentation in Cambridge than it does in College Station, Texas.

College football in America has three divisions: Division I, Division II, and Division III. Each is roughly based on enrollment size. The larger schools across the country compete at the Division I level. In 1978, this highest stratum was divided into subdivisions originally called Division I-A and Division I-AA. With the launch of the Bowl Championship Series in 2006, both of these monikers were changed to the mouthfuls they are today.

Along with consideration given to enrollment, a program needs to average 15,000 or more spectators at its home games to be eligible to compete in the Football Bowl Subdivision. The "big boy" schools in the FBS are also able to offer up to 85 scholarships, while Football Championship Subdivision schools are only allowed up to 63.

FCS teams do not participate in bowl games at season's end. Rather, the subdivision hosts a 16-team playoff featuring eight conference champions and eight at-large teams from across the nation. Winning teams proceed through Round One, Round Two, and the Quarterfinals of the three-week tournament, culminating with a National Champion crowned in the Division I Football Championship Game.

Of the 13 FCS conferences in the nation, three choose to forgo the privilege to participate in this month-long playoff tournament. The Ivy League (where both of today's contestants reside) is one of these three. Also, the eight schools within this northeastern conference each play a slate of only 10 games every season. Ostensibly, these self-imposed restrictions are to ensure academics do not suffer at the cleats of athletics.

Many historians claim the name of this conference stems from the ivy-lined walls found throughout the old New England universities. Planting ivy was an annual tradition (known as "Ivy Days") for soon-to-be graduating seniors at several original conference schools in the early 1800s. Others, however, claim the moniker is a nod to the oldest dining establishment at Princeton University. Memorialized by F. Scott Fitzgerald in his 1920 novel *This Side of Paradise*, The Ivy Club opened in 1879 and still serves lavish dishes to this day.

Though the origin of this botanical term is highly disputed, it's been used in this part of the country for well over a century. On October 14, 1933, sportswriter Stanley Woodward proclaimed his eagerness for the college football season by penning, "A proportion of our eastern ivy colleges are meeting little fellows [i.e., out of conference teams] another Saturday before plunging into the strife and the turmoil [of conference play]." However, it wasn't until the formation of Division I athletics in 1954 that the elite institutions formally adopted "Ivy League" as their official conference name.

Prior to the start of the 1981 season, teams in this conference, which include Brown, Columbia, Cornell, Dartmouth, Harvard, Penn, Princeton, and Yale, competed in the top level of college football. Although eligible, no team from any one of the "elite eight" schools ever played in a bowl game during these years. (Columbia University is the last Ivy League college to play in a national bowl game. In 1934, traveling by train to Pasadena, the Lions from New York City scored 7 points to shutout the highly favored Stanford Indians in the Rose Bowl.)

Since moving to Division I-AA at the start of the 1980s, the conference has qualified every year for an automatic bid into the championship tournament. Not a single Ivy League team has ever competed in this post-season quest for a national title. In addition to this self-imposed ban, scholarships in *any* athletic activity are not offered by Ivy League schools.

Even so, the spirit of past glories and heated rivalries is alive and well on this slightly windy early afternoon outside of Harvard Stadium.

Harvard and Yale are squaring off on the gridiron this afternoon for the 127th time. They first met on November 13, 1875.

A tad more than 2,000 fans lined the field at Hamilton Park just outside of New Haven, Connecticut to witness the inaugural clash of the upper-crust schools. The visiting team won the rugby-style scrimmage by the obscure score of 2 touchdowns and 4 kicks to zero. (During the seven seasons the teams played ahead of 1883, touchdowns and field goals were tracked separately.)

On November 12, 1881, the fighting Elis from Yale University won the sixth game in this early series by an even more abstruse score. At Hamilton Park once again, the boys in blue and white sacked the Harvard ball-carrier four times in the end zone that day. The rules at the time stated a loss was immediately given to a team that incurs four safeties in a game.

The Bulldogs – who are also called the "fighting Elis" (a nickname derived from the first name of the well-to-do Welsh merchant with the last name of "Yale" who gifted a substantial sum to the university in 1718) – were the dominant team in the early decades of American football. During the first 40 years of the sport, the team from New Haven won 26 National Championships.

One season in these nascent years truly stands out.

In 1888, the mostly-mustached team resoundingly finished undefeated in all 13 games. Coached by Walter Camp, the Bulldogs scored an average of more than 53 points per game, finished No. 1 in the nation (ahead of USC, Notre Dame, Harvard, and Princeton), and even scored 105 points in their second-to-last game against Wesleyan University. The Methodists from Wesleyan – and all of Yale's opponents that season – scored *zero* points.

During the same four initial decades, Harvard University made it to the top of college football in America seven times. The school's first National Championship on the gridiron came in 1890 when the boys in crimson vanquished all 11 of their opponents by a combined margin of 155-to-12.

From its inception through 1920, the football program with a color as its team name shared or won the National Championship title twelve times. The undefeated season of 1920, albeit with a 14-to-14 tie against Princeton, produced the last National Championship football team in Cambridge. Co-champions that year with Notre Dame, Georgia, California, and Princeton, only two teams on its nine-game schedule crossed the goal line.

Even though their inaugural clash wasn't the first college football game (or the longest-running rivalry), Harvard and Yale were the first institutions of higher learning in America to meet in athletic competition.

In May 1843, the Elis established the nation's first university-sanctioned crew team. Originally a recreational sport, the rowing team entered the lore of collegiate athletics when it challenged the crew from Harvard to "test the superiority of the oarsmen of the two colleges." This first-ever intercollegiate sporting event in the country took place at New Hampshire's Lake Winnipesaukee on August 3, 1852, pre-dating the country's first college football game and the inaugural gridiron scrimmage between these schools by 17 and 23 years, respectively. Harvard won the two-mile race by two lengths.

Legend has it the official team name at the school was first bestowed when crimson-colored scarves were given to the boat mates at a regatta in 1858 so fans could readily identify their crew from shore.

Arriving at Harvard Square on the Red Line of Boston's subway, known locally as "the T," Valerie and I see a crowd dressed in either red or blue apparel surrounding a small domed turret. The Cambridge Visitors Information Center at the convergence of Harvard Street and John F. Kennedy Street appears to be a popular staging point for today's showdown.

Yesterday afternoon, we began our exploration of this exclusive campus from this same spot.

Our casual expedition included a visit to the imposing Widener Library, the pretentious Harvard Book Store, and a relaxing stroll across Harvard Yard, where a large dark bronze statue of John Harvard sits on a tan granite pedestal overlooking the college he helped establish nearly four centuries ago. Visitors mistakenly thinking it a university tradition to touch the founder's left foot for luck have rubbed its boot to a high golden sheen.

Today, walking south along tree-lined John F. Kennedy Street toward the Harvard Street Bridge, we pass centuries-old brick buildings interspersed among upscale apparel shops, modern fast-food restaurants, and numerous predictably cutesy cafés. A steady flow of fans from both northeastern seaboard universities saunter with us along the red brick sidewalk.

As we approach the north side of the Charles River, a group of red stocking-capped coeds chants a cheer of some sort across the intersection and toward another group of crimson-clad fans. Valerie snaps a quick picture of me with my arm around a fresh-faced student in a long-sleeve red t-shirt. Across the front of his shirt is a turned-down thumb (Facebook's icon for "dislike") next to "Yale" in bright white. Even the taunting at Harvard (which Facebook founder and CEO Mark Zuckerberg attended for several years) has an air of cultural currency and sophistication.

Pregame activities outside the south end of the Panathenaic stadium also exude pomp and circumstance.

A small crowd of fans from both schools respectfully listens to a group of four mop-haired undergrads in blue sweatshirts, mismatched jackets, and plaid scarves singing spirit-songs. (The young men may or may not be part of the legendary Yale a-cappella group The Whiffenpoofs, founded in 1909 and counting Cole Porter among its noted members.) Following each hymn, the leader of this group delivers a brief soliloquy about the composition and its importance to this storied rivalry.

Wearing an oversized fur vest made from some long-dead mammal, the underclassman waxes eloquently about the disputed source of the official fight song of Yale University. Evidently, the spirited ballad, titled "Boola," is credited to a 1901 grad named Allan M. Hirsh who, along with several fellow students, set out to create a rally song for their varsity football games. The undergraduate songwriters originally claimed that "boola" was Hawaiian for an exclamation of joy.

Several years after it became recognized as the university's fight song, an astute student pointed out that there is no B in the Hawaiian language. Hirsh admitted, in a 1930 letter, that the obscure word was simply chosen because it was easy to say and had a pleasant sound.

The quartet at the south end of Harvard Stadium today adds a heartfelt enthusiasm to the final stanza:

> Now isn't it a shame, now, isn't it a shame,
> To do those fellows up so bad?
> We've done it before; we can do it once more,
> Though they'll feel very sad.
>
> We'll roll up the score so very high.
> That you will hear them sigh,
> "Boola, Boola, Boo, Boola, Boola, Boo,
> Boola, Boo, Boola, 'oola, Boola, Boo!"

Valerie and I stare pie-eyed at each other. We both recognize the nauseatingly familiar melody of this song. The fur-draped orator explains it's been adopted by several other colleges across the nation, including the public university located in Norman, Oklahoma. Ugh.

A brisk wind blows from the curved end of the stadium. The plot of land it occupies, now called Soldiers Field, was donated to the university in 1890 by the founder of the Boston Symphony Orchestra, as a memorial to soldiers who lost their lives in the Civil War. From our visitors' side, Valerie observes that, while the stadium might have been created in the Gilded Age, it retains few ornate comforts.

Cement gray pillars create a band of square openings around the top section of the austere four-story arena. Passageways through the stands are dank tunnels. There are no luxury skyboxes. No Jumbotron screens. No padded seats. Just weathered slabs of cold concrete. Even the aisles between sections are nothing more than blocks of cement at the base of each row.

Our section at the 40-yard-line begins to swell with homogeneous fans dressed in rustic New England catalog wear. We're surrounded by tartan pants and Fair Isle sweaters and two-tone rubber boots I'm pretty sure are meant for duck hunting. Valerie points to a tall, gray-haired gentleman in a full-length raccoon coat (boola!) several rows in front of us.

Painted across the green artificial turf to our far left is the word "CRIMSON" in block letters. In the north scoring zone at the open end of the stadium is "HARVARD." A large red and white H stretches from hash mark to hash mark at the center of the field. At each 30-yard-line is a white shield-shaped logo with a red H and a light blue Y. Above the two distinct letters is "The Game" and below is "127th" in script.

Not to be confused with the nickname of the Stanford-Cal rivalry, this annual scrimmage is recognized around the country as simply The Game. While the origin of this title is disputed, many maintain it pays homage to the inaugural athletic contest between the schools. Following the heralded victory by the crew in red scarves, the annual rowing event became known as The Race.

Facing toward the home team's sideline, the marching bands from both institutions demonstrate one of the most remarkable displays of cooperation we've seen on our pursuit.

The white and blue musicians from New Haven have maneuvered into the large red H created by the Harvard University Band to form the intertwined Y depicted in the shield-shaped logos on the field. Following an indiscernible marching tune played in unison, the co-mingled formation quickly disperses into a mad scramble to opposite sidelines as the countdown clock at the north end approaches triple zeros.

An animated column of crimson jerseys, matching helmets, and light gold pants streams from a solitary arched opening to our left. Amassing behind the "CRIMSON" end zone, the home team players wait for the signal from their 17-year head coach, Tim Murphy.

Led by three male spirit-leaders, the varsity squad rumbles through two parallel lines of crimson-skirted cheerleaders. Enthusiastic applause greets the large red flag with a bold white H fluttering at the front of the pack. Due perhaps to the relatively small size of the stadium or its horseshoe shape, the cheering is less of a roar and more of the sound of an ovation at a tennis match.

Immediately following this procession, the visiting Bulldogs in all-white uniforms with dark blue numbers and matching helmets appear at the opposite corner of the stadium. A few subtle boos emanate from the well-mannered crowd as the challengers trot across the end zone toward our side of the field.

Harvard comes into this interstate rivalry with six wins and three losses, including a deflating 14-to-34 loss last Saturday to the University of Pennsylvania. The one-loss Quakers sit atop the conference on this final weekend of Ivy League football. The Crimson's only other conference loss came on the road at Brown University in the second game of this 2010 season. Even though we're at Harvard's home field, the fighting Elis are slight favorites today.

The Yale squad has won 7 games and lost only 2 this season. Their only conference defeat was also to the Quakers in a hard-fought home game that ended 20-to-27. Thus, the winner of today's meeting on Soldiers Field will finish second in the conference.

At midfield, after winning the coin toss and choosing to defer to the second half, Harvard's captain, senior defensive back Collin Zych, shakes hands with the captain of his white-uniformed opponents, senior defensive tackle Tom McCarthy. The solid cement stadium is only about half full as the teams line up for the opening kickoff.

Waddling along the sideline 15 rows below us is a droopy-faced white and brown bulldog wearing a tight-fitting blue sweater with a bold white Y on its back. Comically, the sleeves of the sweater reach all the way to his front paws. As the energetic row of white-clad players eagerly awaits kickoff, the smartly dressed canine pays little attention to the reserved cheering emanating from the grandstand.

Handsome Dan XVII is the latest in a long line of bulldog mascots at Yale University and is the third consecutive live canine mascot on our annual quest.

Born in Johnson City, Tennessee and originally named Sherman (after the World War II armored tank), the 50-pound bulldog assumed his coveted role in winter 2006 following the two-year reign of Handsome Dan XVI. Each canine mascot at the Ivy League school typically holds the position for life.

Nonetheless, Sherman's predecessor evidently preferred retirement in Hamden, Connecticut to a life of raucous sporting events.

The original Handsome Dan was spotted by Yale's starting offensive tackle, Andrew G. Graves, outside a blacksmith's shop in 1892. Graves was so drawn to the young bulldog that he offered $5.00 to the shop owner for the brown-faced puppy.

The companionable pooch followed Graves everywhere, including football practice and campus sporting events. Yale students quickly adopted Handsome Dan (so named by Graves because of his stocky chest and distinctive face) as their mascot. The local paper questioned the appropriateness of his name, however, with the following: "In personal appearance, he seemed like a cross between an alligator and a horned frog, and he was called handsome by the metaphysicians under the law of compensation." Factually, he was one of the finest representatives of his breed at the time, winning more than 30 first-place ribbons at prestigious dog shows across the United States and Canada, including Best in Show at Westminster Kennel Club.

The Bulldogs from New Haven, following the opening return to their 29-yard-line, quickly ramble for 18 yards on the first series of the game. Unfortunately for the visiting team, starting tailback Alex Thomas from Ansonia, Connecticut is stopped short of the line to gain on third down by a crushing hit from junior middle linebacker Alex Gedeon.

From the vantage point on our concrete slab, the speed and ferocity of these initial plays appear no less than what we've witnessed at FBS rivalry games. The only difference, as pointed out by Valerie after this drive-stopping tackle, is the size of the players. Starting linebacker Gedeon is 6'1" 230-pounds. Even so, I comment we shouldn't underestimate the size of the fight in the dog.

My quaint canine adage is quickly validated following the 40-yard punt by the Crimson after only 3 yards on their opening series. Yale's junior running back from Ansonia is a generous 5'9" 190-pounds. Nonetheless, he and his teammates maneuver 52 yards in 10 methodical plays to put the first points on the scoreboard. On first and goal from the 2-yard-line, much to the dismay of the home crowd, the diminutive tailback barrels his way into the end zone to put Yale ahead by 7 points.

Handsome Dan reacts to the jubilation along the sideline with a half-hearted yelp and gets a pat on the head from his blue-clad handler.

This first bite by the Bulldogs also awakens the home team.

On the ensuing series, Harvard capitalizes on a brilliant 46-yard pass by quarterback Collier Winters to move within striking distance of the goal. On the third play of this 6-play drive, the 5'11" 190-pound signal-caller from Claremore, Oklahoma laterals the ball to wide receiver Adam Chrissis, who immediately pitches it back on a flea-flicker play. Winters fires a perfect pass between three white uniforms to senior wide receiver Marco Iannuzzi at the 5-yard-line. Four plays later, No. 22 in crimson and gold plunges into the end zone to tie the game for Harvard.

Senior running back Gino Gordon, whose height and weight happen to be the same as Yale's running back, celebrates with his teammates in the rectangle to our left as the scoreboard shows 7-to-7.

On the third series of the game, the Elis once again deftly move down the field. Seven plays into the drive, the visiting team faces a third down from the 12-yard-line. But a 15-yard personal foul penalty, followed by a 2-yard sack, forces the Bulldogs to attempt a long field goal. More disappointing for second-year coach Tom Williams, the 46-yard kick sails wide of the goalpost on this windy afternoon. Williams, who was a four-year starting linebacker and team captain at Stanford University, is the first African-American head coach at Yale, and only the second ever in the Ivy League.

After an impressive three-and-out forced by his defense, the head coach and former two-time Academic All-Pac-10 player watches his punt returner, Gio Christodoulou, call for a fair-catch on the Bulldog's 40-yard-line. Eight plays later, including a 36-yard screen-pass by quarterback Patrick Witt to running back Mordecai

Cargill, the head coach elects to go for a first down on fourth and 1 just 10 yards from the goal line.

With a little less than 6 minutes left in the second quarter, this crucial decision backfires as the running back is immediately stuffed in the backfield on a gutsy double blitz by crimson-clad linebackers, Nick Hasselberg and Alexander Norman. The choice to not kick a field goal may have been an attempt to send a message to the crimson and gold team across the field from us. It also may have been because of the stiff wind now swirling throughout Harvard Stadium.

Fortunately for the dejected fans of the visiting squad, the Bulldog defense once again stands tall following this turnover-on-downs by their offense. After six plays, the Crimson muster only 13 yards and are forced to punt. Just as fortunate, the blustery conditions cause the kick by Jacob Dombrowski to sail out-of-bounds at the 50-yard-line with just under two-and-a-half minutes remaining in the half.

Quarterback Witt wastes no time moving the Bulldogs deep into Harvard territory by throwing a 30-yard strike to sophomore receiver Chris Smith. Six plays later, on a third and goal from the 6-yard-line, the 190-pound wide receiver gets hit prior to touching the pass. This pass-interference results in a first down with 13 seconds left till halftime. Witt quickly hands the ball to tailback Thomas on first and goal from the 2. Following an impressive kick-out block on the defensive end by freshman fullback Keith Coty and a crushing lead block by pulling left guard Colin Kruger, Thomas rambles into the north end zone.

Witt jumps with elation in the backfield as his teammates celebrate atop the D in "HARVARD." With only 7 seconds remaining in the half, Yale leads 14-to-7. The dismayed home team takes a knee on the ensuing first down and heads towards the dark tunnel.

Every year, this showdown showcases some of the best gridiron performances in the Ivy League. It's also been home to some of the most infamous pranks in all of sports. These practical jokes, known as "hacks," have been a part of The Game for decades and are more than just typical in-stadium satirizing.

In 1934, staff members from *The Harvard Lampoon* (the school's undergraduate humor magazine) kidnapped Handsome Dan II on the day of the game at Soldiers Field. Although the white bulldog was returned minutes before kickoff, a photograph of the mascot licking the feet of John Harvard in Harvard Square appeared the following week in the student publication. (The young canine was coaxed by smearing raw meat on the bronze sculpture.)

Prior to the 1961 scrimmage, *The Harvard Crimson* (the official campus newspaper) printed fake copies of *The Yale Daily News* announcing Harvard graduate and current Commander in Chief, John F. Kennedy, would be in attendance. Standing at midfield during halftime, the president of the campus publication – accompanied by faux Secret Service agents – received a warm welcome from the unsuspecting fans as "Hail to the Chief" emanated from the Harvard University Band.

One year later, at 3:00 in the morning on the same weekend, the same marching band paraded through the streets of New Haven blaring Crimson fight songs. Much to the displeasure of the sleepy coastal town on Long Island Sound, the interloping band finished their noisy procession without any action from local law enforcement.

The most audacious hack between these advanced universities – and perhaps in all of college sports – was pulled off by a band of brazen Yale undergraduates in 2004.

The seemingly simple prank required more than a year of planning by two senior roommates. After months of reconnaissance, stadium schematics, and sophisticated calculations, the pair of upperclassmen recruited a dozen or so fellow students to hand out large red and white paper squares at that 121st edition of The Game. The hurdle was how exactly to distribute the 1,800 pieces of construction paper– weighing more than 150 pounds – to unwary fans inside Harvard Stadium.

The clever duo came up with the non-existent Harvard Pep Squad, complete with silk-screened red t-shirts, fake student IDs, and crimson face paint.

As halftime approached, each member of the newly formed faux spirit-squad handed a stack of posters to the first person in each row of the center section. On each square were the instructions to take the top card and pass the rest down the row.

Once distributed, the imposters in red and white rallied the unsuspecting fans into raising the boards over their heads. Thinking the design spelled "GO HARVARD," the Crimson boosters screamed with delight as the bogus Pep Squad signaled their approval.

Across the field, the Yale faithful squealed with delight, seeing the red block letters stretching across the section-wide white canvas that trumpeted, "WE SUCK."

There have been no discernable hacks today. Halftime is filled instead with all the campiness of dueling high school drama teams. And plenty of cardboard.

Stretched across the sunny field are four columns of musicians dressed in loosely matching dark blue blazers and casual white pants. Facing our side of the field, the Yale Precision Marching Band appears more sloppy than precise. Random untucked t-shirts, various styles of winter caps, mismatched scarves, and haphazard buttons and ribbons adorn its roughly 80 members. Three blazer-clad students unfurl a 20-foot white cardboard sign which reads "Y-H: AVATAR." The stadium announcer mumbles something about an exoplanetary moon called Pandora as a block-faced red cardboard character with stiff cardboard arms ambles onto the field.

Imbued with all the sophistication of an elementary school costume constructed from kitchen-appliance boxes, the rectangular performer wears a large black top hat and carries a cardboard axe in one hand and a blue pop-gun in the other.

From across the field, a dozen or so blazer-wearing students carry a blue pterodactyl-looking contraption through the ranks of the musicians in loose-fitting business attire. Riding on the back of the cardboard creature are two students adorned in oversized bright blue scarves and matching face-paint. Both are waving clear acrylic scepters. A female student carries the elongated head of the

beast while two other coeds attempt to hold its 10-foot wings off the green turf. Above its toothy blue face juts a blue shark fin with a large white Y.

At the conclusion of this bewildering cardboard confrontation between the red refrigerator box and the blue-winged lizard, the crimson-clad band members take the field. Facing away from us, the marching musicians in dark sports jackets and black slacks maneuver into position across the home team's side of the field.

The stadium announcer brings our attention to a fair-haired girl in a bright red dress traipsing behind a large four-wheeled drum pulled by two band members in all-white uniforms. On both sides of the 8-foot-tall rolling percussion instrument is "Harvard University Band" in bold red letters.

As the young lady scurries through the musicians, a large white papier-mâché dog's head enters the field from the Harvard sideline. Supported by two students representing its front legs, the oversized canine with a big black nose chases after the girl in red. A light brown wicker basket hangs from her arm.

In the same manner that the blue-faced Avatar characters vanquished the block-headed villain, the crimson-clad Little Red Riding Hood is able to escape the pursuit of the laughable Handsome Dan dog's head.

I comment that today's halftime presentations are by no means comparable to the polished formations of the Million Dollar Band, or Dotting the "i" in Columbus. Even so, there's something charming about both school's on-field skits. Much like the good-natured pranks between the prominent schools over the years, today's rudimentary props, simple formations, and casual attire harken back to the earliest days of football in America.

From the far-right corner of the stadium, the all-white visiting team enters the field for the start of the second half. With long shadows now draping Soldiers Field, the home team prepares to receive the kickoff. Even following the light-hearted halftime presentations, many Crimson fans have a look of concern given the momentum swing on the final drive of the first half.

Their disconcerting looks are short-lived, however. Very short-lived.

Standing to our left in the curved end of the stadium, senior wide receiver Marco Iannuzzi awaits the sailing kick from Yale placekicker Philippe Panico. The 195-pound return-man from Calgary, Alberta, who was cleared to play just one day ago after sitting on the bench for most of this season with a broken collarbone, catches the ball on the 16-yard-line, makes a slashing move to his left and scurries along the far sideline. His teammates across the field go wild as he crosses the goal to instantly tie the game at 14-to-14 on this opening return.

The cheer from the stands seems muted due to the stiff southern wind blowing over the shallow curve of the stadium.

This streaking run-back appears to swing momentum to the team from Cambridge after their opponent's dominating performance in the first half. The Bulldogs ran twice as many plays and held Harvard to only three first downs and 15 rushing yards in those first two quarters.

On their opening series in this third quarter, they're only able to gain 4 yards and are forced to punt. After the ensuing 7-play drive by Harvard stalls, the Elis start their next drive on their 18-yard-line after a fair-catch by Christodoulou.

Following six promising plays, including a 16-yard run by 5'8" 175-pound freshman running back Deon Randall, Yale's offense takes a step backward. On second down and 9 at midfield, quarterback Witt attempts to scramble out of the pocket and is sacked for a 12-yard loss by senior defensive tackle Josue Ortiz.

Forced to punt, the Elis feel the full force of the (dare I say "Crimson") tide.

Slashing through the middle of the line, Ortiz follows this spectacular sack with the defensive play of the game. The 6'4" 260-pound lineman from Avon Park, Florida blocks the attempted punt and recovers the ball on the Bulldog's 23-yard-line.

Exactly two-and-a-half minutes of game time later, the home team takes its first lead. Running back Gino Gordon, following a bruising block by his fullback, rambles into the open end of Soldiers Field to put his team up 21-to-14. Three minutes are left in the third quarter.

As the wind continues to swirl, the home team continues to take the wind out of the Bulldogs' sails.

Following an 8-play series that manages only 22 yards, Yale punts once again. Harvard, starting from their own 20-yard-line, only picks up 5 yards in three plays and quickly punts the ball back to the visiting team. Due to another sack on third down, the struggling Elis fail to convert a first down. With the punt team back on the field, disaster once again blows through the team from New Haven.

Though not blocked, the ball – after traveling just 15 yards – is stricken to the turf by the strong wind. Harvard defensive back Dan Minamide snatches the loose ball and runs out-of-bounds at Yale's 36-yard-line.

In less than 3 minutes of game time, after six grinding plays, Crimson quarterback Collier Winters hits junior wide receiver Alex Sarkisian with a 12-yard strike. Sarkisian (whose grandfather was captain of the 1949 Rose Bowl champions Northwestern Wildcats) raises his arms as he is surrounded by jouncing teammates. The small scoreboard at the open end of the stadium glows 28-to-14 in favor of the home team with just under seven-and-a-half minutes to play.

With strong headwinds in his face – both literally and figuratively – Yale's quarterback attempts to breathe some life back into his struggling offense following this fourth touchdown by his rivals.

An oversized dark red flag with a large white H flaps several stories above the rectangular turret at the northwest end of Harvard Stadium.

Witt opens with a 13-yard swing-pass to wide receiver Chris Smith. On the following first down, backup quarterback Brook Hart, a gangly 6'5" 210-pound senior from State College, Pennsylvania, is flushed out of the pocket. The second-string signal-caller scrambles for his life along the Harvard sideline on this attempted flea-flicker and runs out-of-bounds after making it all the way to the 21-yard-line.

With starting quarterback Witt back on the field, the Bulldogs are unable to move into the "red zone" on the following three plays. On fourth down and 9, their head coach chooses to gamble with just under 6 minutes remaining in the game. Rather than secure 3 points with a field goal, Williams has Witt throw a screen-pass to Chris Smith. He only picks up 7 yards before being tackled by swarming linebackers.

Taking over on their 13-yard-line, the confident team in crimson appears to have the game well in hand. But not so fast!

On the first play of this ensuing drive, sophomore running back Treavor Scales has the ball stripped by defensive tackle Tom McCarthy. The senior lineman wraps up the fumble at the 19-yard-line. Blue and white-clad fans in our section leap from the cold slab with a renewed sense of vigor.

Witt gives them something more to cheer about on first down by connecting on a pass over the middle to the 7-yard-line. The visiting fans sink back onto the hard cement seating when Witt is sacked on the 18-yard-line by blitzing linebacker Ryan Burkhead. They're really chilled on the next play as their junior QB fires a pass directly to linebacker Alex Gedeon, who falls to his knees just outside of the goal line. But wait! Harvard is called for an inexplicable roughing-the-passer penalty, which negates this seemingly game-ending interception.

Four plays later, running back Thomas crashes into the end zone on fourth-and-goal. With slightly more than 3 minutes left in the contest, the Bulldogs bring the score to within a touchdown.

The crowd may be smaller, and they may not be able to

tailgate worth a fig, but Valerie insists today's clash is easily as exciting as any "big boy" rivalry we've experienced over the years. And it *is* exciting!

The Bulldogs' defense stiffens following the return by Marco Iannuzzi to the 34-yard-line. The Crimson muster only 4 yards in three plays and take only 1 minute off the game clock. With 2:09 remaining, the punt team trots onto the turf. The Elis appear to be in an excellent position to mount a drive to tie the game as a cool dark shadow now covers the entire field.

Trailing only by a touchdown, return-man Gio Christodoulou cheats up to midfield as he awaits the punt at the south end of Soldiers Field. A stout gale blows directly into the face of Harvard's punter.

Receiving the snap, Jacob Dombrowski astonishingly booms the ball through the driving wind more than 50 yards. The ball lands out-of-bounds at Yale's 17-yard-line. This improbable flipping of the field by the sophomore kicker from Gaylord, Michigan sends a pall over the visiting team and its fans.

With no time-outs in their arsenal, the Bulldogs are unable to generate a final push against the bend-don't-break Crimson defense. After three plays, they're only able to navigate to their 35-yard-line. A final desperation pass ends with an offensive pass-interference penalty called on wide receiver Chris Smith. Fans of the local team cheer as the penalty is declined and the players in crimson and gold rush onto the field. The small red and white scoreboard above the Harvard Varsity Club at the open end of the stadium reads: FINAL SCORE. HARVARD 28. YALE 21.

The blustery cold wind swirls around us, picking up discarded wrappers and other debris as fewer and fewer fans remain in the ashen stadium. At midfield, surrounded by several hundred celebratory (and yet somehow still reserved) schoolmates and alumni, the team pays little attention to the nippy gusts on this late November afternoon. They also give no notice to the small white banner on the brick wall of the Varsity Club in the far endzone touting the lone bowl game appearance by a team from this prestigious institution.

It's true that in 1920, the Crimson traveled by train to Pasadena to take on the fighting Webfoots from the University of Oregon. The defensive slugfest ended in a 7-to-6 victory and a Rose Bowl Champion trophy for the squad from the Ivy League. But, for the remaining fans in the stadium this afternoon – and fans of Harvard Athletics everywhere – today's victory is all that matters. As is the case every year on this weekend.

Returning north across the Charles River toward Harvard Square, we notice an energetic group of fellow fans congregating alongside a stand of large trees in full fall color on the left-hand side of John F Kennedy Street.

Known as Winthrop Square, this grove of indigenous flora is nestled next to what appears to be a sidewalk café. Cordial fans in blue and white intermingle with triumphant fans in red and white below a small round sign featuring some sort of troll-like creature holding a salad bowl in one hand and a giant Dagwood in the other.

As we approach the spirited gathering, we realize the entrance to this small pub is down a flight of stairs and below street level. Once again, we've stumbled upon a wonderful campus eating and drinking establishment with an extraordinary following – and legacy.

According to the circular sign with the simian-looking character, Grendel's Den was established in 1971. The basement-level saloon feels more to us like a cozy neighborhood coffee shop than a tavern. There are no flat-screen televisions adorning its brick walls. No neon beer signs. No local sports memorabilia of any kind. Just warm cherry-wood tables and a warm fireplace, both welcome amenities on this chilly autumn evening.

There's also a large rectangular bar, at which patrons bend elbows and swap animated stories. I tell Valerie it's like we've entered the set from the television show *Cheers*, only with a lot more patrons.

Grendel's Restaurant was named after one of the three antagonists in the fabled Anglo-Saxon poem *Beowulf*. (Evidently, everything associated with Cambridge is in some way fabled.) The eatery is also well known locally for successfully challenging a state law that allowed churches to veto the approval of liquor licenses.

In 1982, the United States Supreme Court ruled in favor of the restaurant; and in doing so, altered numerous antiquated "blue laws" across the nation. It also enabled Grendel's Restaurant to open a tavern in the basement of this unassuming row house. Students, locals, and professors soon began to frequent the pub. Upstart craft breweries, such as Boston Beer Company (brewer of the then-newfangled Sam Adams Lager) and Cambridge Brewing Company often introduced their newest style beers here.

Shuffling up to the highly-lacquered bar surrounded by fellow attendees of today's scrimmage, a familiar color catches Valerie's eye. Seated on barstools is a sunburnt couple smartly dressed in burnt-orange apparel. The middle-aged gentleman is wearing a gray pullover emblazoned with the Longhorns logo and "2006 National Champions" across the chest. Valerie leans in and flashes a "Hook 'em" hand sign as we commandeer barstools next to her fellow alumni. After our first round of frosty New England ales, we learn the former University of Texas graduate received his master's degree from the distinguished Business School here in Cambridge.

Earlier this afternoon, the varsity football team from Valerie and his alma mater in Austin vanquished the four-win Florida Atlantic Owls 51-to-17. Almost 100,000 fans witnessed the home team achieve that fifth win in 11 games at Darrell K Royal Stadium. Slightly more than 30,000 genteel spectators were a part of the 127th meeting between the undersized teams in Harvard Stadium today.

The Ivy League is well known for excellence in academics. And, we can attest, their sports teams are just as excellent. The athleticism displayed on Soldiers Field this blustery afternoon was as impressive as any we've witnessed on our quest.

When the final gun sounded inside the stadium, the Crimson notched their fourth consecutive win over the illustrious institution to the south. The red and gold-clad senior players on the field earlier today are the first graduating class to go undefeated against Yale, Princeton, and Dartmouth during all *four* of their school years.

Though outgained 337 total yards to 178 and only notching 10 first downs compared to the Bulldogs' 19, Harvard was excellent when it mattered most. The fighting Elis, even with equal-sized players, lacked the bite to vanquish their rival. Yale crossed the home team's 20-yard-line seven times and only scored on three of these drives. Harvard scored on all trips into the red-zone.

No hacks were needed.

CHAPTER THIRTEEN
Flight and Fight
2011 Texas Christian | Air Force

It's six months before Colt McCoy and his fellow steers will vanquish their tradition-laden traditional rival during our first-ever excursion to College Station, and we're standing at the outskirts of an expansive exhibition field in the southern-most region of New York's Catskill Mountains; the same piece of terra firma converted by Cadet Dennis Michie and his fellow underclassmen in 1890 for their inaugural gridiron clash against the Midshipmen. A massive block of gneiss – a steely gray stone quarried in the Appalachian Mountains – known as Washington Hall looms over a life-size pale green statue of George Washington sitting atop a prancing steed.

At the far end of this manicured parade ground stands a solitary band-member in full parade dress. A shiny silver trombone rests in his right hand.

Over the next 30 minutes, more than 4,000 fresh-faced men and women in presentation uniforms will stride through two tunnels on each side of Washington Hall commissary and past the effigy of the founder of our country. Lining up in precise columns, today is the last time this year's seniors – "Firsties," as they are called – will march across this hallowed field as members of the Corps of Cadets.

Recognized simply as The Plain, this former pastureland above the western bank of the Hudson River is the annual site of Graduation Review at the United States Military Academy. Valerie and I are here to applaud a specific cadet on becoming a commissioned Second Lieutenant in the United States Army, and to celebrate the commitment and effort put forth by these soon-to-be soldiers in dark jackets, chin-strapped "tar bucket" hats, and starched white trousers.

"Auld Lang Syne" emanates from the Corps Band as the underclassmen execute well-rehearsed formations across this lush green field. One by one, the Firsties step away from their companies and march toward the grandstands at its opposite end. Standing before family and friends, the newly formed "long gray line" executes an about-face.

For the first time since this group of a thousand or so students stood on this same field four years ago during their Acceptance Day ceremony, the Firsties are *facing* the barracks of West Point. Two-foot high plumes of shiny black feathers flutter atop their black and silver spring parade hats.

The three undergraduate classes, all facing toward the aluminum bleachers, extend a salute as they march past the senior cadets. Tomorrow, on the storied gridiron inside Michie Stadium, these Firsties will become officers in the United States Army.

As the West Point Band strides into the stone-walled passageways of the commissary, we make our way through throngs of beaming parents and proud relatives and toward the line of soon-to-be-christened military leaders in their splendiferous headwear. We've been invited to this inspiring ceremony by a Firstie named Zach Enlow, who was on the varsity football squad four years ago at the same high school Valerie attended in Tulsa.

A former classmate of Valerie's who coached Zach introduced her to the young cadet early last year. Ever since, the two have forged a remarkable online friendship based on shared values surrounding individual liberty and individual responsibility. We are both eager to meet the sagacious undergraduate for the first time on this early afternoon in May.

Zach, whose nickname here at West Point is "Sweet," instantly recognizes Valerie. He gives her a big hug and introduces us to his very proud family and several fellow Firsties.

After changing into street clothes, he leads us on a guided tour of the classrooms, facilities, and monuments that make up the United States Military Academy. Following a hands-on inspection of the wood and leather apparatus in the antiquated gymnasium, and several arm-in-arm photographs at Trophy Point with its "million-dollar view" of the Hudson River, we convey congratulations and appreciation to our genial young friend. Valerie also lets him know that his fellow cadets gave him a truly appropriate nickname.

Bidding us farewell, cadet "Sweet" Enlow tells us he'll be fulfilling his upcoming obligation to the United States Army at Fort Carson military base just outside of Colorado Springs.

Following our personalized tour of this fortified campus, Valerie states that we need to be at the Academy entrance by 2:30 p.m.

Hastily walking alongside the murky Hudson toward Thayer Gate, I grin as we pass the campus home of the Superintendent of the Academy, Lieutenant General Franklin L. Hagenbeck. Four gold and black planter boxes filled with bright red geraniums sit atop a wrought-iron railing surrounding the front porch of the broad-faced house. A single word adorns the face of each flower box: "GO" "ARMY" "BEAT" "NAVY."

As we approach Buffalo Soldiers Field, an expansive piece of land dedicated to the segregated U.S. Cavalry regiments from 1907 to 1946, Valerie directs me toward a non-descript sedan with government plates parked outside the gray stone entrance. Unbeknownst to me, another tour is on tap for this already remarkable day. This one, I will soon discover, features instantly recognizable artifacts from the two other main branches of our Armed Forces.

We drive north along the river. Paul is behind the wheel. The husband of Valerie's former roommate at the University of Texas, he turns onto the far end of the tarmac at what appears to be an Air Force base. Two massive all-gray C-5 Galaxy transport planes are parked alongside several large unmarked aircraft hangers.

Paul informs us that each four-engine giant can carry up to six Apache helicopters or five Bradley armored fighting vehicles at a time. Today, they've been used to transport less menacing– albeit still lethal – cargo to this obscure airport just outside of Newburgh, New York.

We park in front of a small office attached to the oversized beige hangers. A simple wood sign lets us know we've arrived at Stewart Air National Guard Base. I still have no indication of the surprise Valerie has arranged for us. Following a 15-minute wait for what I surmise will be formal background checks, Paul leads us into the capacious hangers. Turning the corner, about a dozen or so heavily armed soldiers in combat fatigues and black Velcro vests purposely come to their feet near a cluster of cargo bins.

One of the guardsmen, holding an M16 rifle across his chest, furtively unlatches the wire door of a small cage. The words "Caution – Military Working Dog" are emblazoned in bright red letters on each side of the wheeled metal box. I stare across the vast expanse of the hangers. Sunlight gleams off the desolate runway.

My mouth drops.

Visibly pleased with my reaction, Valerie informs me that Paul is the coordinator of the Executive Flight Detachment known as "Whiteside." Across the polished floor sit four polished rotary-wing aircraft. Facing toward the opening of this five-story shelter, each glistening olive-green transport helicopter is emblazoned with "United States Marine Corps." Several soldiers in olive drab flight suits meticulously inspect these identical Boeing CH-46 Sea Knights.

As Paul walks us over to the main group of Marines, he explains these long, narrow-body, tandem-rotor helicopters provide escort and support for the flight squadron that has "Marine One" as its call signal. Valerie and I stop in our tracks.

Just past the four shining Sea Knights are two instantly recognizable symbols of this great country of ours.

Directed by the White House Military Office, Marine Helicopter Squadron One is responsible for transporting the President of the United States to and from official ceremonies and national events. Tomorrow morning, one of these matching dark green SH-3 Sea Kings, originally built by Sikorsky Aircraft as anti-submarine helicopters, will fly our 44th President from this base to graduation ceremonies at West Point. (The other white-capped aircraft will be used as a decoy.)

Both Marine One, the handle given to the specific helicopter carrying the President, and its veil were transported here by the two hulking C-5 Galaxy planes we passed as we arrived at the airport. The words "United States of America" in bright white letters run along the back half of each bulbous-nosed Sea King.

Stepping onto its pullout set of metal steps, Valerie ducks her head under the American flag painted above the entryway of the imposing aircraft.

Given its overall size, the inside is rather cramped. A bench runs along one wall of the monochromatic-gray passenger area. Directly across from this elongated seat is a small square table between two identical chairs. A dark blue presidential seal hangs above the rear-facing chair. The only object on the table is a small rectangular case, no bigger than an iPhone.

In this box are red, white and blue packets of chewing gum, each standing on its end, forming the design of our nation's flag. According to Paul, President Obama likes to have gum available to squelch his cravings for cigarettes. Previous presidents, including Ronald Reagan (who candidly loved jellybeans), had this box stocked with snacks of their choice.

Following our inspection of Marine One, we stroll to the rear of one of the glossy green transport helicopters. Paul informs us that the Marines we've met today – including the Malinois (not named Kevin, so far as we know) stealthily following behind us – arrived with these four Sea Knights in the Galaxies at the end of the runway.

Entering under the retracted rear blades, the tubular-shaped aircraft doesn't offer much in the way of creature comforts. Two rows of black foam seats face each other on each side of the tunnel-like interior. Every inch of the walls and ceiling is covered in shiny green padded vinyl.

Exiting the spartan helicopter, and with our spirits soaring, we extend profound appreciation to our host for what the Executive Flight Detachment calls a "cage tour." As we bid farewell to the amiable soldiers, Valerie encourages them all to stay safe.

West Point stands in stark contrast to the United States Air Force Academy.

The former Continental Army quarters in upstate New York was originally established in 1802 and is the oldest continuously operating Army post in the country. With its massive gray and black crenulated walls and stone turrets, the military institution appears to have been built for the Knights of the Round Table rather than the Black Knights of the Hudson.

The central complex of the campus, including its spired, 10-story Cadet Chapel, was constructed in the early 1900s in a gothic-revival style. Half a century later, architects commissioned by the Department of Defense designed the heavily fortified Cadet Barracks in the same speckled gray gneiss. In addition to Washington on his pale-green stallion, numerous other Civil-War-style statues dot the landscape of this historic military school, including monuments to the "Father of the Academy" Sylvanus Thayer, General Douglas MacArthur with arms akimbo, and General Tadeusz Kościuszko, the original designer of this garrison during the Revolutionary War. Nestled in the thick hardwood trees and rolling hills of one of America's most picturesque valleys, the Medieval-looking fortress conveys the brute strength of America's military might.

The Air Force Academy, on the other hand, conjures up images more of George Jetson than George Washington. The early 1960s cartoon character would be right at home in the austere expanses and mid-century-modern buildings of this prestigious officer training school, located a few miles north of Colorado Springs.

On this Friday afternoon before the gridiron showdown with Texas Christian University, our tour of *this* academy is a self-guided one. Walking past Harmon Hall, the main administrative building on the campus, it's evident the meticulously planned academy is much more than just a group of buildings set at the foot of the Rampart Range of the Rocky Mountains. The entire campus itself is a work of art.

James Joyce stated that for an object to be considered art, it must possess *wholeness, harmony,* and *radiance. Wholeness* is the characteristic that enables an object to be perceived as a complete entity in and of itself. *Harmony* is the ability of all components of the object to combine in unison to create that wholeness. And *radiance* is the quality that enables a perceiver to ascertain the original inspiration for creating the object. Based on this erudite definition from the renowned 20th-century Irish novelist, the United States Air Force Academy is a masterpiece.

Standing across from a five-story rectangle made of white marble and shining blue glass, we easily see that the campus is a complete entity designed from a single clear vision. Each unadorned silvery building is an essential element. No other structures are necessary. And none can be taken away. The entire complex radiates mid-century modernism, with its sharp angles, wide concrete walkways, and low flat-roofed buildings.

Even the name on this ascetic rectangular recreational facility known as Arnold Hall looks like chrome lettering on a 1950s Lincoln Continental.

Following an assessment by President Eisenhower early in the decade, the Air Force Academy was commissioned in 1954 to meet the air-defense demands of the accelerating Cold War. The new officer school saw its first class of cadets graduate in 1959.

During its four-year construction, these 306 students were housed in renovated World War II barracks at Lowry Air Force Base in Denver. Instructed by Air Training Officers, most of whom were junior U.S. Army officers from West Point, the Class of 1959 established many traditions still recognized today, including its Cadet Honor Code. Upon completion, the stylized campus of 19 concordant structures covered 29 square miles across this low-lying valley at the foot of the southern end of the Rocky Mountains.

Wandering into Arnold Hall on this day before the Falcons clash with the top team in their conference, we see several glass-enclosed displays dedicated to the design and construction of this military institution. One silvery photograph depicts cadets from the early years of this Academy standing in parade dress uniforms. (It's said these bluish-gray waistcoats and white-topped hats were designed by the illustrious Hollywood director Cecil B. Demille.) The inscription on the display captures the principles behind the architectural intention of the campus:

Modernism Molds Individuals & Society
One of the most important tenets of modernism was a belief that architecture could not just influence its inhabitants, but could play a major role in molding individuals and society. This coincided perfectly with the idea of a military academy.

Every structure across this valley exudes this precept. Arnold Hall, the center of social life for cadets, has all the warmth of a downtown post office, its purposeful design obviously meant to convey precision, order, and obedience. Like most buildings on these expansive grounds, this recreation center makes extensive use of reflective glass and aluminum cladding.

In addition to embodying mid-century aesthetics, the gleaming exteriors are a nod to the jet planes and spacecraft of the era. The most visible example of this is the triangular-shaped, 17-spired Cadet Chapel that rises above the flat parade grounds at the far end of this sand-colored courtyard outside of Arnold Hall. Originally controversial, this modern-day cathedral looks like a row of fighter planes set vertically on the tips of their diamond-shaped wings.

Everything about the campus is also an exercise in right angles.

Standing at the edge of the wide-open rectangular plaza outside of this rectangular activity hall, we look down upon the center feature of the military institution. The Terrazzo is a sprawling, square piece of land about the size of four football fields. At each corner of this geometrically precise lawn is a retired jet airplane pointing outward toward the square tiles of the surrounding walkways.

The aircraft closest to us, in the northwest corner, is an F16 Fighting Falcon from the 57th Fighter Weapons Wing at Nellis Air

Force Base in Nevada. Across from this single-tailed jet is a much larger F-105 Thunderchief in the northeast corner of the grassy square. Painted in camouflage olive green and tan, this fighter has been on permanent display here since 1968 and is an amalgamation of at least ten sister planes that flew combat missions in Southeast Asia.

In the farthest corner, at the southeast end of a maze of water features known as the Air Gardens, sits an F-4D Phantom II. This black-nosed attack jet is the only United States aircraft credited with shooting down six enemy MiG fighters since the Korean War. Captain Richard S. Ritchie, a 1964 Academy graduate, recorded his first and fifth aerial combat victory in this plane. It was decommissioned to this lawn in 1986.

Completing the quadrant, a 1976 twin-tailed, dark gray F-15A Eagle is on display in the corner to our right. This newest addition to the Terrazzo was flown on intercept missions by the 48th Fighter Squadron for the Southeast Air Defense Sector and arrived from Virginia's Langley Air Force Base in the spring of 1993.

The checkerboard of broad tiles surrounding this square exhibition field is mimicked across the plaza between Arnold Hall and the Cadet Chapel.

Known as Honor Court, this upper plaza was designed for public interaction with the monuments and statues at the Academy. Valerie does just that with the kneeling statue of America's first jet ace, Jimmy Jabara, as she hams it up for a photo op. Shooting down 15 Russian-built MiG fighters, Jabara became a "triple ace" in his F-86 Saber jet and was the second-highest scoring pilot during the Korean War.

This bronze monument of the helmeted pilot sits alongside a railing overlooking the wide-open parade grounds. From this vantage point, we see several cadets casually loading gray plastic chairs onto dollies next to the grassy square below. A gray stone monument, incongruent with the sleek aircraft on this exhibition field, rests at the northwest corner of the Terrazzo.

Several hours earlier on this September 9th morning, the entire student body marched in silence across this checkered plaza to honor the innocent lives lost ten years ago in New York City, at the Pentagon, and in Shanksville, Pennsylvania. Resting on an easel at the base of a gray stone monument is a small green wreath with red and white flowers. Between the 10-foot-tall twin columns hangs a portion of a rusted girder. This twisted beam from the wreckage of the World Trade Center rests permanently above a pentagon-shaped slab of polished granite.

As the last rows of plastic chairs are rolled away, a woman standing at the railing, whose daughter is a current cadet, informs us this monument was a gift from the graduating class of 1976. The words, "We will never forget" stretch across a small silk banner on the green wreath at its base.

We're walking across a dusty parking lot about an hour before kickoff. Flags of various squadrons and cadet groups hang from makeshift flagpoles strewn throughout the crowded field. Making our way alongside Falcon Stadium, Valerie lets me know Zach is waiting at a large bronze statue next to the oversized tent on Falcon Alley.

I spot the solid soaring raptor swooping in-flight about 10 feet above several brown boulders. The coppery mascot of the United States Air Force Academy appears to be descending upon human prey milling about the sidewalk outside this unassuming arena. Standing on the lawn in front of the monument is a stocky young man with tightly cropped black hair, gold-rimmed Ray-Bans, and a smile as wide as the falcon's frozen wings.

Our friend and recently commissioned Army officer, former cadet Zach Enlow, has made the 30-minute drive from Fort Carson to join our pursuit of revelry. Over the past year, he's settled into this Army garrison that sits at the foot of Cheyenne Mountain.

Home to the 4th Infantry Division and the 10th Special Forces Group, Fort Carson acts as a sentinel to the North American Aerospace Defense Command Center. The famed NORAD aerospace surveillance and warning installation operates deep underground in the mountain range that towers above the site of today's Mountain West Conference matchup.

It's a gorgeous early fall morning. Billowy white clouds float above the team flags of the eight schools that make up the Mountain West Conference.

Valerie, in jeans and a white Air Force Academy t-shirt, and I in shorts and a new white AFA hat, stop for an arm-in-arm photo with the home team's costumed mascot. Creatively named The Bird, the furry yellow-beaked falcon with oversized white and blue sneakers and a matching jersey numbered double-zero, is happy to oblige.

As we enter the stadium, Zach has us veer to the right. Walking around the north end of the field, he directs our attention to an obvious attempt at intimidation by the home team. Above the players' tunnel is a sign with the ominous message, "WARNING: LACK OF OXYGEN. ELEVATION 6,621 FT ABOVE SEA LEVEL."

Falcon Stadium sits in a hole carved into these rolling foothills about 3 miles from the Academy campus. Constructed three years after the Academy was opened, the asymmetrical stadium runs parallel in a north-south direction to US Interstate 25. The west side of the arena rests on the upper slope of the foothills and includes a rectangular press box designed in the same mid-50s architecture as Arnold Hall.

This side also features an additional third section above two bowl-shaped sections that encircle the artificial turf below. The words "AIR FORCE" in massive white block letters are written across this top section just below the reflective teal windows of the bi-level press box.

Making our way to this west side, we locate our exceptional seats at the 45-yard-line, just 9 rows from the shiny green field. Both teams are running through pregame drills as the trainers for the home team set up their equipment alongside the aluminum team benches directly in front of us.

Ranked 25th in the nation, Texas Christian University, almost universally known by their initials, comes into this second game of the season as double-digit favorites, according to Vegas oddsmakers.

Even though Air Force won their opening game this season, while TCU was defeated in theirs, the level of competition was not the same. Then ranked 14th in the nation, as well as holding an FBS-best 25 consecutive regular-season wins, the team from Fort Worth lost a thrilling 48-to-50 shootout on the road against quarterback Robert Griffin III and his Baylor Bears.

The Falcons, on the other hand, bested the FCS Coyotes from the University of South Dakota by the score of 37-to-20 on their home field. If the "flyboys" are going to win today, they'll need a bit more firepower than their opening cakewalk, and a lot more than they brought to their 31-point loss to the Horned Frogs last year in Fort Worth.

One year after this Academy was commissioned, Air Force fielded its first football team. Dubbed the Falcons by this inaugural squad, they played eight other freshman squads from schools across the nation, including the University of Colorado Buffalos, the Colorado State University Rams, and the OU-not-UO Sooners. All "home games" that season were held at the University of Denver.

In their first-ever scrimmage, the cadets vanquished the freshman team from this private university 34-to-18 and went on to finish with a four-win and four-loss record. The following year, they competed as an independent team in Division I-A against a slate of nine varsity squads.

With the completion of Falcon Stadium in 1962, the team hosted their first game at the Academy, an impressive 34-to-0 shutout of their rivals from down the road at Colorado State University. The Falcons transitioned into the Western Athletic Conference in 1980. Nineteen seasons later, they became a charter member of the Mountain West Conference, where they've remained through our game today.

TCU's nickname is the Horned Frogs. Their mascot, however, is a horned lizard. (*Horned frogs* are wide-mouthed amphibians native to South America, while *horned lizards* are spiked-back reptiles indigenous to the Southwest that shoot blood from their eyes as a means of defense.)

Ever since its earliest days, this private university west of Dallas has used the aquatic Ceratophrys (also called PacMan frogs because of their round shape) as the official name of its athletic teams. In 1896, the inaugural football squad from then-named AddRan Male & Female College vanquished Toby's Business College in their maiden scrimmage (8-to-6); and, finished the season with one win, one loss, and one tie. A couple years before the institution became known by its current name in 1902, the purple-clad team embraced their abstruse amphibian label.

Heading into today's game, these teams have only faced each other as regular-season opponents nine times. Fittingly, their one postseason meeting, the 1959 Cotton Bowl Classic, ended in a 0-to-0 tie. This first bowl game for the Falcons, just three years from playing freshman teams in their inaugural season, came after nine wins and one tie (a 13-to-13 stalemate against the University of Iowa, who went on to win the Big Ten Conference and the Rose Bowl).

In their scoreless postseason matchup, the Falcons and Frogs combined for 13 fumbles and five missed field goals. Not counting this mistake-laden bowl game, the overall record between the squads stands at 7 victories for TCU and only 2 for Air Force.

Since their opening season in the Mountain West Conference in 2005, the purple frogs/lizards from the Lone Star State have dominated the conference. In the six years leading up to this matchup today, TCU has finished at the top three times and in second place twice. The only season they did not win 11 or more games was 2007 when they went 8-and-5. Commanded by head coach Gary Patterson since 2001 (and throughout their entire tenure in the Mountain West), TCU finished with an unblemished record last season.

The 13-and-0 Horned Frogs, behind both an aerial attack led by conference-leading quarterback Andy Dalton and the No. 1-ranked defense in the nation in terms of total yards, capped off that season with a thrilling victory over the University of Wisconsin in the Rose Bowl. The outcome of that granddaddy of a bowl game however, was not solidified until 2 minutes remained to be played.

Following a grinding 10-play, 77-yard drive, running back Montee Ball plunged into the end zone to pull the Badgers within 2 points of the team from Fort Worth. Wisconsin chose to go for a two-point-try. Unfortunately for the Badgers, the purple-clad linebacker with a tremendous football name, Tank Carder, batted down the pass at the line of scrimmage to seal the victory 21-to-19.

TCU finished last season No. 3 in the final BCS rankings and No. 2 in both national polls behind the National Champions from Auburn, Alabama.

With 30 minutes until kickoff, the sound of precision drumming echoes from the tunnel to our left.

Entering the field across the north end zone is the U.S. Air Force Academy Cadet Drum and Bugle Corps. Known rather airily as Flight of Sound, the 135-member marching band's mission is to support the Cadet Wing at military ceremonies, official parades, and varsity athletic competitions. The troupe also competes against the U.S. Naval Academy and the U.S. Coast Guard Academy in the annual Interservice Academy Drum &

Bugle Corps Competition, a brass and percussion contest held in conjunction with each year's scrimmage against Navy.

Sunshine glistens off the dual rows of chrome buttons on their light blue parade jackets and the forged silver eagle on their white-capped exhibition hats.

Zach informs us this procession is usually followed by the "March On." Heading into the start of each home game and unfolding before us now, the entire Cadet Wing – all 40 squadrons – march onto Falcon Field in slow-moving rectangular columns. The stream of dark trousers, matching field caps, and light blue short-sleeved button-downs fill the bright rectangle with a patchwork of equal-sized blue squares.

After standing at attention for what seems like an eternity, the cadets join the Falcon cheerleaders in yelling "A-I-R-F-O-R-C-E" followed by "FIGHT! FIGHT! FIGHT!" Suddenly, each quadrangle explodes like a New Year's Eve confetti popper.

The cadets race from their geometric formations to the stands at the opposite side of the field. An amazing aspect of this tradition, as pointed out by Zach, is the immediate squelching of their frenetic antics upon reaching the stands. Our newly-commissioned Army officer friend explains the cadets are instructed to show "civility and respect" as they quickly and orderly move to their seats.

Soaring high overhead is a "flyover" which is truly unique to this institution. During their third year at the Academy, approximately half the student body participates in its USAFA Soaring Program.

With two years of aviation and airmanship courses under their belts, each of these cadets pilots one of 19 German-made DG Flugzeugbau sailplanes maintained by the Academy. These lightweight gliders are towed into the sky by bright yellow Piper Super Cubs that take off from Academy Airfield just a mile south of Falcon Field. The three of us count a half-dozen of these unpowered planes as the pregame countdown clock approaches 5 minutes.

With our eyes to the sky, Valerie spots a group of very small rectangles circling high above the now-full stadium. As the blocks grow larger, Zach mockingly conveys this precision parachute team has a nickname just as haughty as the name of the marching band making its way into the stands across from us.

Since 1967, the Wings of Blue have competed – and, as to be expected, excelled – in the USPA National Collegiate Parachuting Championships. This annual skydiving event regularly pits the distinguished parachuting team against more than 40 other collegiate teams, including the Black Knights from West Point.

On this early afternoon, against the backdrop of the rugged Rocky Mountains, even our former Firstie begrudgingly admits the cadets descending upon the field are "pretty cool."

Having exited a DeHavilland UV-18B Otter just moments earlier, the first of seven black-helmeted skydivers swirls across the north end of Falcon Stadium. Yellow smoke trails behind as he lands to the left of the large blue and white "AF" logo at midfield. Above the rim to the north, the second daring diver circles into the stadium. Trailing 20 feet in his wake are several red, white, and blue streamers. Flags from all branches of the military and a black Prisoner of War flag, each stacked one on top of the other, dangle below the fourth gliding cadet. The fifth and sixth skydivers, both with trailing streamers similar to those of the second jumper, execute perfect landings onto the 50-yard-line. Lastly, with the Stars and Stripes fluttering beneath his left foot, the final Wings of Blue member enters the perimeter of the sunken arena. A cadre of fellow cadets quickly snatches the American flag before it touches the ground.

Scrambling to gather his deflating chute, the black-suited skydiver hands the game ball to the official standing at midfield. The stadium announcer informs us each jumper today flew a special flag in honor of the victims of the September 11th attacks, ten years ago this weekend. A wave of cheers rolls across the stadium as the seven skydivers scurry into the tunnel at the north end zone. Another successful jump, of the more than 600 per year, for each cadet on this esteemed squad.

From the north end zone, blue-clad cadets unfurl a massive American flag across the glossy turf. Senior members of the Cadet Wing hold the outer edge as their fellow undergrads run underneath. As the 300-foot banner is stretched to the four corners of the field, the Flight of Sound prepares for the National Anthem along the sideline of the home team. Valerie leans over to Zach and says this is the second 10th anniversary of tragic events we've experienced in the past two seasons.

Much like the reserved yet tasteful tribute to the victims of the bonfire collapse at Texas A&M, today's remembrance is succinct and respectful. Other than the field-sized Stars and Stripes undulating across the field, no over-the-top ceremonial exploits are needed.

As "land of the free, and home of the brave" reverberates across the sun-filled stadium, four Air Force F-15C Eagle fighter jets streak over the relatively small scoreboard at the south end and, almost instantly, become nothing more than white dots in the skies to the north.

This angled formation of attack aircraft, led by Major David Johnson, an Academy graduate from the class of 1997 (according to the stadium loudspeakers), leaves behind a resounding roar as they hit their after-burners and disappear from view. Valerie gives a soft hug to both Zach and me as the crowd cheers in salute.

Entering beneath the blue altitude-warning sign, the home team flows through the field tunnel into the back of a large white inflatable helmet just outside of the end zone to our left. As the crowd lets out a cheer, the blue facemask of the balloon spreads apart. Led by fifth-year head coach Troy Calhoun, the Air Force varsity football team races through two parallel lines of cadets along the sideline in front of us.

The former Air Force quarterback took his alma mater's top coaching position at the end of the 2006 season when legendary coach Fisher DeBerry retired after 23 years at the helm.

Directing the Falcons to a nine-win season during his first year, Calhoun was named 2007 Mountain West Conference Coach of the Year. Unfortunately for the AFA faithful, his team lost in a thrilling 36-to-42 seesaw battle that year to Jeff Tedford's University of California Golden Bears in the Armed Forces Bowl. This highly entertaining post-season contest was played at Amon

G. Carter Stadium in Fort Worth, Texas – home of the TCU Horned Frogs.

With his return-team on the field for opening kickoff, the head coach paces in front of the long line of players stretching across the field before us. Our seats are close enough for us to hear Calhoun, who is dressed in a sky-blue polo shirt with a strange white bar across the chest and a black baseball cap, shout orders to his assistant coaches. A television cameraman on a motorized platform, two stories off the ground, passes across our view as we anticipate the flight of the ball from the foot of the Horned Frogs' kicker.

On the front of Calhoun's cap is the blue and white lightning bolt logo that matches the logos on his players' helmets. Legend has it this logo was selected during the fledgling years of the Academy because fighter pilots "dive like falcons and strike like lightning."

Our friend Zach boasts that an eagle grasping lightning bolts also adorned many Army Air Corp planes during World War II.

Senior kicker Ross Evans sends the ball deep into the north end zone to start this rematch of the 1959 Cotton Bowl. The Falcons, smartly attired in their sky-blue jerseys and matching white helmets and pants, start from their 20-yard-line. Senior quarterback Tim Jefferson quickly scrambles for 4 yards. On his right shoulder, a patch signifies he's in Cadet Squadron 27, a unit known as the Thunderbirds. Disappointingly, this first set of downs abruptly ends after 10 grinding plays, when Jefferson is tackled for only 3 yards on fourth down and 4 from his own 45-yard-line.

TCU wastes little time setting the tone in these early moments of the first quarter. Three minutes after gaining possession, the visiting team in traveling all-white uniforms and dark purple helmets scores the first touchdown of the game on a 3-yard pass from their sophomore quarterback to senior fullback Nick Shivers. Casey Pachall, the successor to record-setting Andy Dalton (who graduated at the end of last year's unblemished season), jumps into the arms of his fullback in the end zone.

Air Force's next possession is even less successful than their first. After only three plays and a total of 6 yards, the Falcons are forced to punt the ball back to the Horned Frogs.

The visitors, on the other hand, quickly match the success of their first drive. Following six plays for positive yards, including a pounding 22-yard run by 6'1" 225-pound junior running back Mathew Tucker, the team scores its second touchdown on a 1-yard plunge by Tucker.

With 1:09 left in the first quarter and two offensive possessions for both teams, the scoreboard at the south end reads 14-to-0 in favor of the purple invaders.

Valerie points out that the logos surrounding the screen on this smallish scoreboard aren't the usual ubiquitous soft drink and fast food brands found in other arenas on our quest. As could be expected, this in-stadium screen is sponsored by Lockheed Martin, FLIR Thermal Imaging, and Boeing Defense.

I reply that it looks like the home team could use a little more than just advertising support from these sponsors.

In the stands across from us, a raucous patch of bright blue begins yelling some sort of military-sounding sequence at about the 10-yard-line to our left. Surrounded by a sea of fellow cadets, the rowdy section hollers encouragement onto the field as the Falcons begin their third drive after the ensuing kick sails out of the end zone.

Known as the Cadets in Section 8, most of these future airmen and women are wearing pale blue t-shirts with a white fist holding a lightning bolt across the front. Scattered among them are shirtless cadets with painted chests and faces, an occasional white and blue wig, and even a white-helmeted corpsman with mirrored aviator glasses and belts of fake machine gun bullets draped across his blue tank top.

Disappointingly for this animated section and their fellow enlists, the Falcons' advancement comes to an abrupt halt after 42 yards. On the ninth play of this drive, quarterback Jefferson has the ball stripped from his grasp on the 37-yard-line by sophomore safety Trent Thomas.

After trading series, both of which result in punts, the Horned

Frogs take over on their 20-yard-line with a little under 9 minutes left in the half. Eight plays later, the visitors bring the enthusiasm emanating from Section 8 to a reticent standstill.

After completing passes of 18, 21, 13, and 8 yards, Casey Pachall hands the ball to tailback Tucker who dives over the top of his 300-pound center, Eric Tausch. There is 5:35 left on the clock. Pachall has completed his first 11 passes, including an amazing one-handed grab by wide receiver Antoine Hicks on this last drive. And there are now 21 points on the TCU side of the scoreboard.

Ever since its formation in the late 1950s, the Air Force varsity football team has relied on one of the oldest offensive schemes in college football: the triple-option. By the end of last season, this traditional formation resulted in a rushing attack that averaged slightly more than 306 yards per game. Only Georgia Tech – with its own triple-option offense – averaged more. Today, it's evident that TCU has prepared exceptionally well for the flyboys' ground game.

On the Falcon's next series, the Horned Frogs give up only 8 rushing yards. Air Force is forced to punt with a little under 3 minutes left in the half. David Baska sends the ball all the way to the 16-yard-line. No. 11 in all-white catches the booming kick over his shoulder and quickly turns to face a cast of Falcons ("cast" being the proper term for a group of falcons). Skye Dawson (who with this first name should be playing for the home team) attempts to make a move past the first defender. Inexplicably, the ball squirts from his grasp. Fortunately for the speedy sophomore from Mesquite, Texas, his teammate, Greg Burks, recovers the loose ball on the 26-yard-line.

Only two-and-half minutes remain in the second quarter as Pachall brings his offense back onto the field. I mention to Valerie that, with two time-outs in his pocket, there's more than enough time for the star quarterback from Brownwood High School in the central Texas town with the same name to put this game out-of-reach. In five quick plays, the visiting team moves the ball 59 yards. With only 20 seconds on the clock, Pachall takes the snap and drops back in the pocket.

Like a bolt out of the blue, blitzing sophomore linebacker Jamil Cooks blasts into the blindside of the unsuspecting quarterback. The jolting tackle by the 6'4" 210-pound linebacker from Colorado Springs causes the ball to fly out of the young quarterback's hands. With amazing agility, Cooks scoops it off the glistening turf and rumbles to the TCU 44-yard-line, where he is tackled from behind by a lounge of lizards ("lounge" being the proper term for a group of lizards – even though the tackle was made by an army of frogs!).

As unexpectedly, the triple-option-based offense – with only 15 seconds remaining on the clock – completes three consecutive forward passes and quickly calls a time-out. From 19 yards out, as time runs out in the half, freshman placekicker Baska sends the ball through the uprights to give the home team their first points of the afternoon.

There's no evidence supporting the rumor that the NCAA banned live falcons from playing fields during the early days of the Academy.

Storytellers claim cadets trained the speedy raptors to dive-bomb mules and thus, the governing body prohibited them at football scrimmages, especially when the Black Knights were in town. In truth, the only aerial attacks endured by Army's live mascots over the years are verbal bombardments during their annual inter-branch contest. Cadets at these showdowns are known to chant, "Let's see the mule fly! Let's see the mule fly!"

Live falcons *do* perform a series of bombing runs during halftime shows at all home games inside Falcon Stadium. Only, instead of brown mules, they strike a brown lure tethered to their handler.

Falconry at the Academy, an extracurricular activity offered to select cadets, got its start after the inaugural Cadet Wing selected the bird of prey as its official mascot. In October 1955, this first student body presented a peregrine falcon named Mach 1 to senior officers at the military college. Today, a dozen or so flying predators are housed in state-of-the-art enclosures, called mews, at the north end of the sprawling campus. Each 12'x12' mew features open-air windows, sterilized flooring with built-in drainage, and automated feeding chutes.

A team of 12 falconers maintains the modern aviary facility. Four freshmen cadets are chosen at the end of each school year to replace the four graduating seniors from this highly revered team. Several breeds of raptors native to North America, including the peregrine falcon, prairie falcon, and the largest of the species, the gyrfalcon, make up the roost at the Academy. Each bird requires more than 300 hours of training before it's ready to make an appearance at sporting events and ceremonial festivities.

As the Flight of Sound stands at attention facing our side of the stadium, a lone female cadet swirls a rectangular-shaped leather pouch attached to a 30-foot tether in a circular motion across the slick green turf. The only sound in the stadium is a series of high-pitched whistles emanating from the twirling cadet.

Without warning, Zach points to the south end of the stadium. Diving at more than 100 mph, a white streak zeroes-in on the bait-filled satchel.

A roar erupts as the female white-phase gyrfalcon named Aurora (after the Roman goddess of the dawn) swoops like a dive-bombing jet. Just as the 15-year-old mascot attempts to strike the small brown sack, the fresh-faced cadet in a dark blue jumpsuit jerks the long cord aside. Aurora instantly flies toward the sky to make another pass at its prey. After four attempts, the large female falcon strikes the lure in midair and knocks it to ground. Valerie and I quickly wipe away tears as the majestic bird pecks at raw meat inside the pouch.

Aurora is one of only two performing live mascots in all of college football. Earlier today, a golden eagle known as War Eagle VII soared high above Jordan-Hare Stadium to signal the start to Auburn's thrilling victory over visiting Mississippi State. The 12-year-old eagle, whose actual name is Nova, has been performing pregame fly-overs since November 2006. Aurora, on the other hand, has been on duty since 1996.

As the young falconer extends her arm to the white speckled mascot in the far corner, Zach lets us know that, just in case the female falcon should fail to return to the lure during exhibitions, a small battery-powered transmitter is attached to her leg. Leave it to the flyboys to keep advancing flight technology.

With the sun high overhead, both teams take the field to start the second half.

Trailing 3-to-21, the Falcons look to capitalize on their momentum following the field goal heading into intermission. It appears they may be able to do so, after holding TCU to a quick three-and-out on their first series. Momentum looks to really swing their way as junior return-man Mikel Hunter from Conyers, Georgia catches the punt at midfield.

Instead, the ball is instantly punched from his arms by Travaras Battle (who should also be playing for the Falcons given his fabulous military name). Fellow Horned Frog Kris Gardner knocks the undersized cadet aside as No. 40 in purple and white, linebacker Greg Burks, falls on the loose ball.

Eight agonizing plays later, including a 5-yard run on fourth and 1 from the 25-yard-line, Casey Pachall throws his second touchdown of the game. The 21-yard strike to freshman wide receiver David Porter III puts the visiting squad ahead, 28-to-3.

With slightly less than 9 minutes in the third quarter, not a lot of calamity is coming from across the field in Cadet Section 8.

Jonathan Warzeka, the Falcon's 180-pound return-man, snags the ensuing kickoff and scampers 22 yards. After three triple-option rushing attempts, his team faces fourth down and 4 on their 34. Evidently sensing this desperate time in this one-sided contest calls for desperate measures, coach Calhoun rolls the dice in a big way. Receiving the ball from his long-snapper, Calhoun's punter takes off running. The 182-pound freshman kicker, David Baska, scurries 32 yards before being run out-of-bounds by the duped amphibians from Fort Worth.

Directly across the field, members of Flight of Sound and the rowdy cadets in Section 8 perform a quirky gyration with their hands-on-hips, followed by an animated first-down signal. Zach rolls his eyes and conveys this ritual and its accompanying drum cadence has been performed after each Falcon first down today.

Calhoun hasn't put his dice away just yet. On the next play following this fake punt, Jefferson fakes the dive to his fullback and races along the left side of the line in what looks like another typical triple-option play. At the last minute, he pitches the ball to wide receiver Jonathan Warzeka, who comes racing from the opposite direction. The reverse catches TCU completely off guard as Warzeka abruptly launches the ball 32 yards downfield into the waiting arms of wide-open Zack Kauth. The junior wide receiver from Dayton, Ohio races for the home team's first touchdown of the day.

Much like the ritual of goofy gyrations after each first down, Air Force cheerleaders, known as Cadet Wing Spirit, perform push-ups after every Falcon touchdown.

In the back of the end zone to our left, male cheerleaders in white V-neck shirts and long pants and female cheerleaders in matching short skirts, await the ensuing extra-point to perform 10 push-ups. Even though these calisthenics can be grueling, we're confident Cadet Wing Spirit hopes to do many more in the remaining quarter-and-a-half. (Two seasons ago, during the lopsided 72-to-0 victory over FCS Nicholls State University, each member of this squad performed 409 push-ups in this same stadium.)

With the score 28-to-9 in favor of the visitors, Calhoun refuses to put the gambling cubes away. Rather than kick the extra-point, he keeps his offense on the field for a two-point-try. Unfortunately, his third trick-play in a row, a pass attempt by 260-pound defensive lineman Harry Kehs, is one roll too many. Cadet Spirit Wing performs only 9 push-ups.

Even so, momentum appears to have shifted in favor of their fellow cadets.

Exactly 7:00 remains in the third quarter. Plenty of time for the home team to get back into this suddenly interesting game. All Calhoun and his Falcons need is a quick stop on the upcoming possession. The Horned Frogs are thinking otherwise, of course. And, just like the dominance exhibited throughout the first half, they methodically make good on this line of thought.

Ten plays and five-and-a-half minutes following this trick-laden scoring drive by Air Force, Casey Pachall hands the ball to tailback Waymon James, who barrels 4 yards up the middle and across the goal. This fifth touchdown for the Horned Frogs takes the score to 35-to-9. It also takes most of the air out of the oxygen-deficient stadium.

The air doesn't get any richer for the Falcons as they're only able to muster one first down on the ensuing drive that takes the game into the fourth quarter.

Following their punt, the Air Force defense impressively holds their opponents to only 2 yards on a quick three-and-out series. Taking possession at midfield, the Falcons new quarterback, Conner Dietz, who replaced Jefferson at the start of their last series, manages to navigate the Zoomies (yet another creative nickname for the cadets) all the way to the 4-yard-line.

In what feels like the waving of a white flag, Calhoun sends in his field goal team on the final down of this 9-play drive. With a little more than 8 minutes to play, Cadet Wing Spirit performs 12 push-ups.

Following three consecutive punts, two by TCU and one by the cadets, Air Force takes possession on their own 22-yard-line with only 2:12 left on the game clock. The Horned Frogs, up 35-to-12, have substituted many of their second and third-team players onto the defensive side of the ball.

In a valiant yet much too late effort by their second-string quarterback, the Falcons manage to put their second touchdown of the game on the scoreboard after moving the ball 77 yards in 6 quick plays. On the seventh play of this final drive of the afternoon, Dietz sneaks the ball for a 1-yard score. After the successful extra-point, the scoreboard to our right reads: AFA 19 – TCU 35.

The game clock shows only 4 seconds remaining in the contest.

Today's victory, the eighteenth consecutive Mountain West win for TCU, ties a conference record set by Brigham Young University in 2008. The Horned Frogs, who out-played the cadet varsity team in all phases of the game this afternoon, have not lost a conference contest since that same year.

Even with this one-sided scrimmage today, most of the nearly 40,000 fans are still inside the stadium as the game clock rolls to triple-zero. Our former Firstie friend leans over and informs us that, though he considers this academy to be a rival of *his* academy, the spectacle about to unfold on this hazy afternoon is truly one of the most wonderful traditions in all of sports.

Originally titled "Army Air Corps" when it was written in 1939, the official song of this avant-garde institution at the foothills of the Rampart Range is now known simply as "The U.S. Air Force." The resounding parade-like tune has a feeling of glory, of proud pilots soaring into the bright blue yonder.

Its third verse, however, has a much different melody.

Recognized by *all* military branches as the "Toast to the Host," this verse is conducted as a separate piece after every varsity Air Force sporting event. Delivered as a tribute to those who have fallen in service to the United States, its tone is one of reverence.

Former cadet Sweet Enlow conveys that the song is sung whether the Falcons win or lose, to remind the student body, and all of us, of what really matters in life.

Standing in the northeast corner of the field, facing their fellow students in the steel gray stands, the team which represented the United States Air Force on the gridiron today prepares to recite this third verse. Each player holds the hand of a fellow cadet as the slow, solemn notes ease from the brass section of the Flight of Sound.

With the sun setting over the edge of Falcon Stadium, the now helmetless players along with the entire Cadet Wing softly sing:

> Here's a toast to the host
> Of those who love the vastness of the sky,
> To a friend,
> We send a message of his brother men who fly.
> We drink to those who gave their all of old,
> down we roar to score the rainbow's pot of gold.
> A toast to the host of men we boast, the U.S. Air Force!

CHAPTER FOURTEEN
A Sobering Affair
2012 South Carolina | Clemson

As far as we know, there are two types of people in South Carolina: the individual who identifies with the Gamecocks from the University of South Carolina, and the one whose allegiance is to the Tigers from Clemson University.

Standing in the middle of a packed poolroom – if two coin-operated tables can be considered a poolroom – inside one of the most recognized establishments on College Avenue, these are the only kinds of people we've met on this mild Friday evening before the intrastate rivalry between the Southeastern Conference school and this Atlantic Coast Conference (ACC) school.

They are also individuals who don't like each other, as we are about to find out.

Above the entrance to this rowdy tavern is a sloshed orange and white tiger sitting in an oversized beer mug. This locally prominent image lets us know we're in Tiger Town Tavern, situated inside Clemson's oldest still-standing building. It also pays homage to the official mascot of the local university.

Ingeniously named The Tiger, this mascot's likeness adorns many bright orange t-shirts surrounding the rectangular bar in this very rambunctious public house. Several dark blue t-shirts also feature the beer-soaked grinning feline atop the number "21" and the words "I'm Legal." Evidently, patrons can receive one of these coveted complimentary shirts on their 7,665th day of existence. A stained-glass rendition of the striped moggy in his mug and the inscription "Est. 1977," shines from a curved wall of glass blocks at the entryway.

Known as "Triple T's" by locals, Tiger Town Tavern is a few blocks from the campus of this second-largest university in the Palmetto State, and a couple hours northwest of the largest. Valerie and I quickly surmise that a considerable number of fans have made the short drive this evening from Columbia. A boisterous tension permeates the crowded bar.

It doesn't take long for two very large men in dark polo shirts to be drawn into a verbal altercation between an animated garnet-clad undergrad and an orange-capped Southern gentleman. The bouncers, both of whom look like former Clemson linemen, quickly quarantine the hot-headed combatants and politely inform them that they've both had enough.

Clemson is a small town. A quintessential college town, one that feels a lot like Stillwater, Oklahoma. It's not *really* in the middle of nowhere, but there sure is a lot of nothing around it. It's also, as the saying goes, a drinking town with a football problem.

This year especially, the source of that problem is just a short drive down Interstate 26. For three consecutive years now, the football team from this state's capital has beaten the school that shares its name with this charming town. In these most recent meetings, Clemson has scored a total of four touchdowns.

This year's game, they confidently say, will be different.

The home team comes into this final contest of the regular season with ten wins and only one loss. That heart-breaking defeat took place at Florida State University. (The No.4-ranked Seminoles went on a 35-point run in the second half to beat Clemson by the breathtaking score of 49-to-37.) The Tigers quickly put the loss behind them and emphatically ran through all remaining ACC foes. Because of this, there's a slight air of arrogance in this small college town. Their team is ranked No. 11 in the nation. It's a night game inside the stadium they call "Death Valley." They've won 13 home games in a row. And Dabo is going to get his due.

William Christopher Swinney got his nickname as an infant. His elder brother, before the age of two, always referred to the family's newest addition as "that boy." Ever since, his younger sibling has been known as Dabo.

The former walk-on and Academic All-SEC wide receiver on Alabama's 1992 National Championship team took over at Clemson halfway through the 2008 season. That year was the tenth consecutive season of head coaching duties for Tommy Bowden. It was also one of the most anticipated seasons in Clemson since the Tigers' only National Championship in 1981. Bowden's team was coming off a nine-win season and was ranked ninth in the nation in both preseason polls. Most summertime annuals had Clemson picked as favorites to win the ACC.

Following three humbling defeats in the first six games of the season, including an inexplicable loss on their home field to the unranked Terrapins from Maryland, Bowden stunned the football community by resigning and handing the reigns to his 38-year-old wide receivers coach. Swinney won four of the remaining six regular-season games and earned the privilege to play the Nebraska Cornhuskers in that year's Gator Bowl. In their final home game of the season, his Tigers also soundly defeated their intrastate rival 31-to-14.

Since that interim year, fans of the orange-clad team have had a "love-hate-love-hate" opinion of their young head coach.

Many long-time boosters questioned the decision to promote the underdeveloped assistant. He had never held a coordinator position, let alone had any head coaching experience. That view changed to "love" after his first full year.

In 2009, the Tigers surprisingly won the ACC Atlantic Division title. Not only did they win nine games, including a marquee victory over then No. 8-ranked University of Miami; Clemson triumphed over the University of Kentucky in the Music City Bowl. Dabo also excelled as a recruiter that year, securing several blue-chip recruits. This signing class was punctuated by a high school phenom (and co-MVP of the U.S. Army All-American Bowl) named Tajh Boyd.

The faithful's view turned to "hate" the following year. Clemson lost half their regular-season games in 2010, including a devastating 3-point overtime defeat to Cam Newton's Tigers from the University of Auburn, and another 3-point heartbreak on a last-second 55-yard field goal at Doak Campbell Stadium in Tallahassee. To make matters worse, the team was thoroughly out-classed during their home-field loss in the final game of the regular season. The Gamecocks humbled the nascent coach and his squad by the score of 7-to-29.

Many fans, along with members of the regional press, began calling for both Swinney and athletic director Terry Don Phillips to be immediately fired following the team's demoralizing defeat in the Meineke Car Care Bowl. That loss to the Bulls from South Florida University, a perceived inferior team from the perceived inferior Big East Conference, resulted in Clemson's first losing season since 1988.

The natives were restless. And Dabo knew it.

Fortuitously, his sophomore protégé quarterback quickly changed their opinion back to "love" during the 2011 season. Tajh Boyd led the Tigers to nine regular-season wins, including victories over the returning National Champions from Auburn and No. 21-ranked Florida State. They earned their tenth win of the season in the ACC Championship Game against the No. 5-ranked Hokies from the school with a mouthful of a name in Blacksburg.

Even though Swinney was honored with the 2011 Bobby Dodd Coach of the Year Award (presented to the FBS coach whose team excels on the field, in the classroom, and in the community), this "love" switched back to searing "hate" following the Tigers' appearance in the Orange Bowl that year.

Heading into this prestigious post-season game against the West Virginia Mountaineers from the perceived inferior Big East Conference, Swinney boasted during a pregame interview on ESPN, "Hopefully when this thing is over, people are going to be talking about the Clemson defense." Unfortunately, Dabo got his wish in spades!

The mountain men from Morgantown not only crushed the team wearing the same color as the title of this bowl; they shattered the scoring records of all bowl games ever played in the 109-year history of post-season play. West Virginia scored the most ever points in a quarter (35), the most ever in a half (49), and the most ever in a game (70). The Tigers scored 33.

Valerie and I exit the tiger sports shop, an apparel store at the south end of College Avenue which spells its name on their theater-style marquee in all small letters (not sure why). While I purchase a new tiger paw baseball cap, Valerie totally scores with a wonderfully comical knit cap that mimics Clemson's creatively named costumed mascot.

The googly-eyed orange-and-white face of The Tiger grins above her head as we saunter along the tree-lined avenue toward the corner of Old Greenville Highway and Oak Street.

Halfway through our stroll, we pass an open field with a bright paw at its center and small brick-lined stands along each sideline. Home to Clemson's soccer teams, historic Riggs Field is also the fifth-oldest collegiate athletic facility in the United States. The namesake of this first home football field, Walter Merritt Riggs, is recognized as the "founding father of Clemson football" and was the Tigers' first head coach in 1896. Riggs was also president of Clemson University from 1910 to 1924, and earlier, in 1900, had hired John Heisman to succeed him as head football coach.

Heisman, whose innovations and successes inspired the sport's illustrious trophy, commanded the Tigers for four consecutive years. At the end of his first season, the team vanquished all six of their opponents.

After thumping Davidson College 61-to-0 in their opening game, they shut out the Terriers from Wofford College. (Early in this second game, both squads agreed that after three touchdowns, all subsequent scores would not be recorded.) Clemson also beat the teams from Virginia Agricultural and Mechanical College and Polytechnic Institute, the University of Alabama, and the University of Georgia. Most importantly, his Tigers pounded their in-state rival from Columbia. The 51-to-nil final score remains the largest margin of victory in the history of this contentious rivalry.

Heisman won the conference title three of these four years and still holds the highest overall winning percentage at this Southern university. Fittingly, his memorial at the College Football Hall of

Fame proclaims that he "stands only behind Amos Alonzo Stagg, Pop Warner, and Walter Camp as a master innovator of the brand of football of his day."

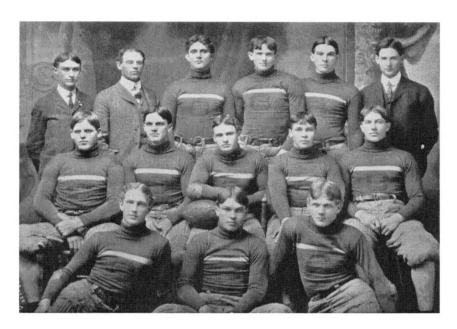

Walking past the purple arch at the entrance to the Clemson Tigers Tennis Complex, we spot our destination.

It's 7 hours before kickoff to this 110th meeting between these prominent schools and already The Esso Club parking lot is packed. Throngs of orange-clad students, alumni, and families are standing on the corner of what looks like a dilapidated roadside gas station. Two large white ovals, one hanging from a rusted pole and the other on the wall next to a small patio, announce that this former fueling station sold Esso gasoline. Evidently, Gulf gasoline was also available. Four dull-orange metal letters spell out this brand above the flat roof of the weathered building.

Back in the 30s and 40s, when this highway was the main thoroughfare between Greenville, South Carolina and Atlanta, Georgia, these three signs, each more than 7 feet long, encouraged motorists to fill their tanks in advance of the 3-hour trip to the capital of the Peach State. On this slightly cool and hazy Saturday in November, they act as beacons for fans of both teams.

In 1933, James A. Stevenson opened his service station just outside the main campus of this quaint college town. In addition to gasoline, Stevenson provided maintenance and repair work. Ever the profiteer, the young owner from Arkansas secured a beer license so patrons could find refreshment while their cars were attended to in the garage. For the next 50 years, rough-edged locals and cash-strapped students made their way to this homely roadside station for cheap beer.

During the late 1950s, Stevenson's station was the only place in all of town where you could sit down and enjoy a cold brew.

In the early 1970s, Standard Oil Company changed its name and its gasoline to Exxon. The people of Clemson, as they did with most cultural advancements of the time, paid little attention to this change. The small station on the corner of Oak Street continued to offer Esso as its featured fuel brand until it ceased selling gasoline altogether in 1985.

Varsity sports at Clemson University garnered national attention, once again, around the time Esso Service Station became The Esso Club.

This notoriety came in large part courtesy of the stunning victory by their football team over the powerhouse University of Nebraska Cornhuskers in the 1981 National Championship game. The unranked team from this rural university opened that season with a 45-to-10 victory over the first team they ever played back in 1896, the Wofford Terriers. They finished their season undefeated, thanks to the passing arm of junior quarterback Homer Jordan and the defensive talents of freshman tackle William Perry.

After this unforeseen championship season, more and more campus sporting events came to be covered by national television networks. Following his first visit to Stevenson's former fueling station, CBS's play-by-play announcer Brent Musburger also began shining light upon the school.

Valerie and I snake our way into the crowded single-story tavern. A rusted gas pump from decades ago sits next to a massive flagpole proudly flying both the Stars and Stripes and an orange paw. The main section runs perpendicular to the patio attached on its west side.

Above the heads of fans from both schools, I spot a tarnished wooden plaque. The small sign behind the bar reads, "Brent Musburger Is An Honorary Member Of The Esso Club" in dark orange letters. The announcer's signature is scribbled across the bill of a dingy white Esso hat hanging to the side of this sign. Even more autographed hats from former players and random down-South celebrities, including basketball sportscaster Dick Vital and comedian Tim Allen, hang above the bar. According to the jovial patron on the barstool next to me, any time Musburger is covering a Clemson game, he mentions The Esso Club.

Enjoying one of the largest (not to mention least expensive) Oktoberfest lagers I have ever had; we look around the crowded former filling station for familiar faces. Joining us today will be two fellow Oregonians. They, of course, let us know they'll be wearing orange.

Without warning, a shrieking voice yells out "Valerie!" from the far side of the bar. Gina throws a big hug around my lovely bride as her fiancé also hollers with delight.

"If not for Valerie's ultra-amazing stocking cap, we never would have seen you guys!" Gina shouts as I signal to the bartender to get a round of oversized beverages for our Pacific Northwest pals.

Committed to marrying Gina in the coming summer, Boyd Pearson is a Clemson grad and one of the most passionate Tigers fans we've ever met. As he and I discovered soon into knowing each other, we share more than just a love of frosty refreshments in flimsy plastic cups. From age six through high school, he attended almost every football game across the street from this well-worn tavern. As a high school senior in the late 1990s, Boyd was a standout tight end for the Porter-Gaud Cyclones.

Upon graduating from the prep school in Charleston, South Carolina, Boyd attempted to walk-on the varsity football team here in Clemson. With a naïve sense of invincibility, the vigor of youth, and a raw passion for the game, the lanky receiver performed well enough to make it through the cut-off period for walk-on hopefuls. And, much like me, he quickly surmised there's only room for the best of the best at this level.

Boyd's walk-on experience was dauntingly similar to mine. Early morning practices in the dark, another practice in the evening, repetitive drills against the starting defense, a continuous state of exhaustion, plus the ridiculous time requirements of trying to excel in the classroom. Every day, I lined up as a blocking dummy against Dexter Manley. Every day, Boyd witnessed the pure raw talent of Rahim Abdullah. And, just as my daily adversary went on to star on the biggest stage of the sport, the 6'5" 245-pound Abdullah was selected in the second round of the NFL Draft at the end of Boyd's sophomore year.

To this day, he and I marvel at the speed and agility we witnessed on our respective practice fields. And not surprisingly, my fellow reserve player still proclaims he's never been in the presence of a greater physical specimen than No. 53 in orange and purple.

Our quest for success at a major college football program ended in the exact same manner and for the exact same reasons. Nevertheless, we wouldn't have changed a minute of it.

The Esso Club bills itself as being "In the Shadow of the Valley."

Suspending the impossibility of this description, it's meant to convey the watering hole's proximity to the school's football stadium. Officially christened as Clemson Memorial Stadium in 1942, the massive open-air arena is known throughout college football, and more so locally, as "Death Valley." The nickname apparently came from the town's first cemetery, which sat on a hill overlooking the newly constructed stadium.

Former head coach of Presbyterian College Lonnie McMillian is said to have stated just before their 1948 scrimmage that he wasn't very eager "to take his team up to Clemson and play in Death Valley." (Presbyterian College in Clinton, South Carolina still has a varsity football program. It also has one of the most amusing team names in all of sports. Every fall, fans of this team from the Big South Conference proudly root for The Blue Hose.)

As we settle our tab – about the size of tips at other establishments on our excursions – Boyd lets us know the bar we're resting our elbows on is made from the original bleacher seats inside Memorial Stadium. During its 1972 renovation, aluminum benches replaced these very same timeworn cedar planks.

Exiting the converted fueling station, I notice an oversized black and white team photo in the hallway. A plaque on this 4-foot rectangle reads: 9 and 7 in the Atlantic Coast Conference. I chortle and say to Boyd it's evident his alma mater is a *football* school, given this basketball record is worthy of a wall-sized memorial.

Crossing Old Greenville Highway, we veer south on Centennial Boulevard to the west side of the stadium. On this comfortably cool early afternoon, the four of us approach a bright orange tent in a crowded parking lot. This open-sided canopy is about the size of the professional catering tent outside Harvard Stadium during our quest two years ago.

Boyd introduces us to his best buddy from high school. Known to his friends as Stevie, Boyd's former dorm-mate has been hosting this tailgate party at all home games for many years. Southern rock blasts from oversized speakers in the back corners. A bright orange Christmas tree, complete with blinking lights, sits at the far end of four folding tables holding an uncountable variety and number of beverages. Above our heads hangs a full-size chandelier.

It's a little before 5:00 in the evening. Kickoff is in about two hours. And this party (and the hundreds of similar encampments surrounding it) has been here since midmorning. That's a long time to be exposed to adult libations. And Southern rock. The effects of both are showing. Small streaks ("streak" being the proper term for a group of tigers) of slightly staggering orange and purple-clad fans shout "Go Taagers!" on their way toward the orange brick and gray concrete stadium.

Stevie, ever the consummate host, has positioned a large screen connected to a small satellite dish in the middle of our tent. Several new acquaintances inform us they're watching the *ABC*

Game of the Week, which started a couple hours earlier.

With the sun setting outside Death Valley, a historic Bedlam Series game is unfolding inside this vibrant orange canopy. For the first time in the 107-year history of the rivalry, Oklahoma State and the team with the miniature ponies are heading into overtime.

With a little more than 6 minutes in regulation time, the visiting Cowboys have never trailed throughout the game. The Sooners, lamentably, grind out an excruciating 17-play drive that leaves 4 seconds on the game clock. OU then scores on a direct-snap, student-body-right. The following extra-point knots the score at 45-to-45.

The real pain, however, comes when Boyd informs us that, if we want to be inside Memorial Stadium for what Brent Musburger described as the "twenty-five most exciting seconds in college football," we need to leave *now.* One of the most exciting finishes to Bedlam ever – and hopefully one of the most epic victories for my alma mater – is about to play out on the screen. Nevertheless, the reality that time-waits-for-no-fan forces us to hastily exit the suddenly empty tent. We grab a couple traveling beverages from an orange cooler and race to catch up to our entourage.

Atlas Shrugged.

The adage of this being a drinking town becomes even more evident as we scurry past quickly dispersing tailgate parties. Half-empty bottles of very hard liquor and piles of empty very light beer cans litter the impromptu encampments.

We make our way along Avenue of Champions behind Memorial Stadium. Funneling toward the west end of this thoroughfare, we sense both anticipation and tension racing through the raucous crowd. Throngs of well-lubricated alumni and students shout indiscernible chants above our heads.

Shoulder to shoulder, we slowly compress into a dozen or so swaying parallel lines. Verbal jeers are hurled at fans wearing garnet and black. Two slightly tottering fans, bellies bursting from large dark red jerseys with "Cocky" across their backs, burble something about making it four in a row. After one adds that it's taken three games for the home team to score as many points as the Gamecocks did three years ago, Boyd turns me and says, "We'll see who's laughing three hours from now."

Valerie and I are on the visitors' side of the field, at about the 30-yard-line and halfway up the lower section on the north side of the brightly lit stadium. Our former pregame revelers are sitting across from us behind their home team's bench. The ubiquitous tiger paw, with its consistent 30-degree slant to the right signifying the traditional 1:00 p.m. kickoff time for home games, faces away from us at midfield.

In the back of the end zone to our left are two large nets filled with vivid orange party balloons. Both nets, each about the size of a semi-trailer, slowly sway in the breeze.

A grassy corridor bisects the crowd in this east end from the top of the arena to the orange and white "CLEMSON" in the end zone. At its zenith stands Dabo Swinney in an orange pullover sweatshirt and khakis, surrounded by several assistant coaches in matching pants. Behind them, rocking back and forth in time, stands the No. 11-ranked team in the nation.

Twenty minutes ago, following pregame warm-ups, the players in orange jerseys and matching helmets lined up across the 20-yard-line to our right. Standing shoulder to shoulder with their arms linked, they stretched from one sideline to the other.

With a command from their head coach, the solid line slowly plodded toward the west goal line. Upon reaching the back of the end zone, the tightly-bound row exploded in a frenzy and raced into the northwest tunnel of the standing-room-only stadium. Immediately following this procession, the Clemson marching band took the field.

The strutting musicians in white jackets with the famed paw on the back have now formed two parallel columns beginning at the grassy opening in the back of the end zone to our left. The human corridor runs all the way to midfield. Behind us, a more than slightly inebriated fan in an orange No. 10 jersey shouts for us to look at the Jumbotron.

"It's a good thing he's here tonight," Valerie teases. The massive video screen above this eastern curve of Memorial Stadium is so bright it's like being in an IMAX Theater.

As the home team exits the far end of the stadium, a cameraman follows the procession.

What began as a simple suggestion before the final game of the 1972 season to head coach Hootie Ingram by senior defensive back Ben Anderson has evolved into one of the most recognized – and most convoluted – entrances in all of college football. That year, following four quarters of play in the battle against their cross-state rivals, the scoreboard read 7-to-6 in favor of Anderson's team.

Up until this victory in Death Valley, the team had only averaged slightly more than 13 points during their 10 games. The not-so-ferocious felines lost to the Owls from Rice University by 19 points in the second game of the season and followed with a 3-to-52 drubbing at the hands of the team with the misplaced initials from Norman, Oklahoma. A total of 19 points was scored in their shutout over the Division I-AA team from down the road at The Citadel. Immediately after this unexpected 1-point defeat of the reviled Gamecocks, Coach Ingram decided to make Anderson's suggestion a permanent fixture at every home game.

Trotting alongside the players in the northwest tunnel, the Jumbotron cameraman captures the first peculiar part of this elaborate procession. After their arm-in-arm trudge to the end zone, each player receives several poker chips as they leave the field. Approaching three massive buses at the top of the stadium tunnel, the orange-clad players drop their chips into an orange bucket held in the air by an assistant coach. The words "ALL IN" adorn the outside of this plastic pail.

From here, the players, in game-ready uniforms with helmets on, make their way onto the large transports.

At the door of the first bus, Dabo Swinney enthusiastically greets each offensive member of his team. The second bus is for his defensive players, while the third hauls reserve players. Hordes of fans high-five team members as they hasten aboard each vehicle.

Led by flashing blue and red lights above two highway patrol motorcycles and a state trooper sedan, the three shiny carriages creep along the west end of Memorial Stadium before making a right turn onto the Avenue of Champions. It's as if the crowd surrounding us is watching a funeral procession on the screen rather than the one traveling behind us.

Perhaps *this* is actually how the stadium got its nickname.

Easing to a halt at the east end, the oversized vehicles release their air-brakes at the top of the grassy strip leading onto the field. The motorcade traveled less than 1,500 feet.

Both costumed mascots – The Tiger in his No. 0 orange jersey and his companion The Cub in a matching No. ½ jersey – stand with their backs to us at the top of this jam-packed knoll. Suddenly, the entire stadium erupts as the tiger paw cap of Swinney appears from under the glaring Jumbotron.

Each mascot cautiously trots down the semi-steep, ad-hoc aisle. Stopping halfway, the fuzzy felines stand on each side of an orange-clad student holding a small two-wheeled dolly typically used for deliveries at convenience stores. A dull-orange carpet with the word "CLEMSON" runs lengthwise to mid-point of this grassy path. Glistening helmets and flashes of white paws jounce in the semidarkness of the brick entrance.

The players, swaying back and forth with their arms linked, begin to bunch together like wildebeests attempting to cross a crocodile-infested river. The entire stadium is on its feet in anticipation. "Tiger Rag," the school's official fight song, blasts forth from the two parallel lines of marching band members.

Dabo reaches out and touches a small pedestal in the center of the swaying row of orange jerseys.

In the early 1960s, a large piece of white flint was given to then-head coach Frank Howard. This unassuming rock, about the size of a basketball, was found by an avid fan in California's Mohave Desert. Up until the 1966 season, the cantankerous coach used the muddy-brown stone as a doorstop. During a meeting with a well-to-do booster named Gene Willimon, Howard declared he wanted the unadorned piece of earth out of his office. Recognizing its novelty, Willimon had it mounted on a small plinth at the top of the grassy end of Memorial Stadium.

To this day, just before the start of each home game, each coach and player touches "Howard's Rock."

With the massive scoreboard showing exactly 3 minutes before kickoff, the undergrad standing midway down the sloping passageway abruptly fires a small cannon on his convenience-store conveyance. He and the furry mascots scurry as fast as they can down to the field. The onslaught of streaking orange uniforms is right on their hocks. As each player prepares to leap across the muted orange carpet, they rub the dull rock on the black granite pedestal that reads: "From Death Valley, CA to Death Valley, SC."

A steady stream of orange jerseys and white pants flows over the edge of the precipitous pathway. Most bound down the hill using an aggressive skipping motion, Valerie and I speculate to avoid an unplanned tumble on their somewhat harrowing descent. Thousands of bright balloons release from the nets into the night sky. As the last few players race through the corridor formed by The Tiger Band, the entire stadium yells out a staccato chant that ends with: "C-L-E-M-S-O-N."

Entering from the same tunnel used to start this preposterous circumnavigation is the twelfth-ranked team in the nation.

Wearing all-white uniforms with matching white helmets, the Gamecocks from the University of South Carolina are met with a cacophony of boos as they jog toward our side of the field. The fans surrounding us appear fully aware that, coming into this in-state scrimmage tonight, the team from Columbia has won nine games and has only one more loss than their opponent on the opposite side.

Trotting alongside this peloton of white is the head coach

we've always wanted to see on our annual excursions. We expected to watch him lead the Gators in Neyland Stadium a decade ago. However, his abrupt decision just before that season changed all that.

After 12 years of orchestrating the "Fun 'n' Gun" in Gainesville, Steve Spurrier announced he was leaving for the NFL. His brief tenure as head coach of the Washington Redskins did not play out as he (or the professional franchise) had expected, however. Following just two disappointing seasons, including his first losing season as a head coach at any level, the former Heisman Trophy winner at the University of Florida resigned in 2002.

The allure of once again coaching in the SEC was evidently too strong for the "Ol' Ball Coach" to resist.

At the end of the 2004 season, then-head coach Lou Holtz hung up his coaching cleats once and for all. After six seasons in Columbia, Holtz had expected South Carolina's bowl game at the end of that season to be his swansong. However, during the final regular-season game inside the stadium we're sitting in, with Clemson cruising to a three-touchdown victory late in the fourth quarter, feathers began to fly on the visitors' sideline. This on-field brawl, which was precipitated by a shoving match during the exaggerated pregame entrance at the base of the grassy hill, had to be broken up by State Troopers.

Following the game, both universities announced self-imposed post-season bans upon their teams. At his final press conference, the resolute Holtz (whose head coaching career spanned 35 years at six different universities) recognized the irony that both he and Woody Hayes will be remembered for "getting into a fight at the Clemson game." Hayes's incident was during the 1978 Gator Bowl. With less than 2 minutes to go, the illustrious head coach at The Ohio State University cold-cocked backup nose guard Charlie Bauman as he raised the ball in celebration after intercepting the Buckeye's freshman quarterback. Clemson won the game 17-to-15. Hayes was immediately fired. He never coached another game. Anywhere.

At the start of the 2005 season, Spurrier was introduced as the head coach of the Gamecocks. In his eight years since, the former quarterback from Science Hill High School has never had a losing season.

Last year, in addition to trouncing the No. 21-ranked Cornhuskers from Nebraska in the Citrus Bowl, his fighting roosters conquered their cross-state rivals by the lopsided score of 34-to-13. His sophomore quarterback, Conner Shaw, passed for three touchdowns and scrambled for a score during this display of dominance. The beat-down cemented a ten-win season for only the second time in the 118-year history of football at the Southern university. Following the game, Spurrier boasted, "Historically, Clemson has owned this series. They don't own us now."

Given the unilateral outcomes of the three most recent meetings, the Ol' Ball Coach has a point.

The entire stadium is on its feet, albeit with a somewhat sozzled stance, as the perceived-to-be evenly-matched teams take the field.

With only one loss to the then fourth-ranked Seminoles, the home team fans tonight expect not only redemption for the past three games in this rivalry but also an invitation to a BCS bowl game in the weeks to come.

So confident are the Tigers that even though they won the coin toss, they choose to receive the opening kickoff. As the ball sails out of the end zone to our left, several South Carolina players jump and jeer around Clemson's return-man. Two referees break up the animated shove-fest in the northeast corner.

Tensions are already running high. And not just on the field. Fans surrounding us hurl angry expletives toward the all-white row of jerseys stretched across the sideline directly below our section.

More not-so-pleasant words emanate from our section after the first play from scrimmage. The 20-yard pass from junior quarterback Tajh Boyd is caught out-of-bounds by sophomore wide receiver Sammy Watkins. Following another incomplete pass on third down, the Tigers are forced to punt.

One of our section-mates attempts to calm his fellow fans by intoning, "It's awwrat! It's awwrat! It's still arrrly! It's still arrrly!"

The co-MVP of the U.S. Army High School All-American Bowl is met on the far sideline by Dabo Swinney, who appears to deliver this same repetitive chant.

Coming into this game, Clemson's starting quarterback has thrown 33 touchdowns this season. He's also rushed for eight more. Last week, in a 62-to-48 defense-optional victory over North Carolina State here inside Memorial Stadium, Boyd was responsible for all eight of the team's touchdowns, setting both an ACC and team record.

The "It's arrrly!" statement is correct. The "It's awwrat!" part might not be.

Catching the booming punt at his own 25-yard-line, the Gamecocks' return-man slices straight up the middle of the field. Ace Sanders, the 5'8" 175-pound speedster from Bradenton, Florida, loses his footing after 30 yards to give his team excellent field position for their first drive of the game.

Jogging onto the field, wearing No. 17 in white, is Connor Shaw's back-up. Even though the expected starter (who has sixteen wins and only three losses at South Carolina) wore full-pads during pregame warm-ups, Spurrier obviously decided the injury to his left foot is too severe. To add insult, the injury was incurred late in their home game versus an FCS team. Last week's contest was knotted at 7 points with less than 12 minutes to play against the much-better-than-expected Wofford Terriers. Shaw's back up, Dylan Thompson, rallied the SEC team to a 24-to-7 mistake-plagued win over the scrappy team from Spartanburg.

The 6'3" 212-pound sophomore got his first start following the season-opener when Shaw injured his same leg. In the Gamecocks' second game of the season, Thompson impressively threw for 330 yards and three touchdowns in their 38-point victory over the Pirates from East Carolina University.

On his first pass tonight, the second-stringer from Boiling Springs, South Carolina misfires. He then throws a bullet to Bruce Ellington on third down and 14 from the 48-yard-line. Thompson's sophomore wide receiver makes an incredible back-bending catch from his knees to secure this first down. With their hated rivals already in field goal range, fans surrounding our row begin to grumble in a Southern drawl.

After two plays for less than a yard, the Gamecocks line up for third down. With the blinding Jumbotron flashing "GET LOUDER" directly in his face, Thompson receives the shotgun snap and drops straight back in the pocket.

Sensing the magnitude of this threatening drive, defensive coordinator Brent Venables has dialed up a daring safety-blitz. From the right side, freshman Travis Blanks streaks toward the now scrambling Thompson. Rather than throw the ball away, the inexperienced quarterback turns to avoid the crashing blitz and runs face-first into defensive tackle Josh Watson.

Following this crushing sack, a loud tiger roar echoes across the stadium.

Valerie doesn't need to remind me that Venables, in his first year here at Clemson, was most recently in his thirteenth successful year as the heralded defensive coordinator at the public school in Norman, Oklahoma. But, she does anyway.

South Carolina's punter stands atop the tilted tiger paw at midfield. Following a fair-catch on their 15, the home team immediately goes to work. Fifteen methodical plays later, including two direct-snaps in the wildcat formation to senior running back Andre Ellington, a scramble out of the pocket for a first down by Boyd, and a 22-yard strike into the middle of the secondary to wide receiver Adam Humphries, Clemson lines up 3 yards outside of the goal line.

Staring at the white jackets of the Mighty Sound of the Southeast (the official name of the Gamecocks' marching band) in the stands to the right of the goalposts, Boyd receives the snap on this tense third down and goal. Immediately tucking the ball under his arm, the agile quarterback spins off a glancing blow on a student-body-right and strolls into the end zone for the game's first score.

As smoke dissipates from bursts of fireworks above his head, No. 10 struts to the far sideline with his helmet dangling in his right hand. The bruising drive takes more than 6 minutes off the play clock.

Since 1902, a rooster has been the official symbol of the University of South Carolina. It wasn't until almost 60 years later, however, that a gamecock became its official mascot.

During these six decades, students regularly attended athletic events wearing homemade costumes. One such outfit, worn by a first-year biology student in the early 70s, caught the eye of the athletic department. The rudimentary ensemble – handcrafted by the undergraduate's mother – featured a cardboard beak, torn fabric feathers, and foam spurs. Soon after its first appearance, the cartoon-like costume became the school's first mascot.

The trespassing rooster at the far end zone tonight was introduced during the 1980 homecoming game in Columbia against the University of Cincinnati and is wearing a black No. 01 jersey with "Cocky" across its back. As his team prepares to receive the kickoff following the 16-play scoring drive by the home team, the oversized bird with the jocular grin holds a large white sign above his head that simply reads: COCKS.

Catching the ball just inside the goal line, No. 23 in all-white races toward the far sideline. Running toward him is Damiere Byrd (who, with this perfect name, *is* playing on the correct team). With flawless timing, Bruce Ellington fakes a reverse to his fellow Gamecock and rambles to the 37-yard-line. Just under 4 minutes remain in the first quarter.

The energized visiting team strikes quickly with a 20-yard pass to tight end Justice Cunningham. This gain is immediately followed by a pass to Ace Sanders and burst by running back Kenny Miles to the 14-yard-line. On the final play of this drive – in less than 2 minutes of game time – Dylan Thompson drops back in the pocket. Taking advantage of great protection, the substitute quarterback flings the ball into the corner to our left. Diving away from cornerback Garry Peters, Bruce Ellington makes a spectacular back-shoulder catch to quickly tie the game.

Evidently, the Ol' Ball Coach still has some pep in his step. And a surprisingly adept quarterback behind a very proficient offense line.

After a touchback, Clemson wastes no time in regaining

momentum. Junior running back Roderick McDowell races 32 yards on first down along the far sideline. On the very next play, Tahj Boyd fakes a hand-off to running back Ellington, plants his right foot on the 50-yard-line, and launches a perfectly thrown pass into the arms of his streaking wide receiver, DeAndre Hopkins. With two defenders on his back, the junior receiver from Central, South Carolina summersaults into the end zone to once again put Clemson ahead by a touchdown.

Boyd hastily trots down the field to congratulate No. 6 in orange, who is being mobbed by his teammates. This stunning touchdown sets a school record of 34 scoring passes by the junior signal-caller this season.

The entire stadium is in a frenzy as the scoreboard glows 14-to-7. In just about 10 minutes of game time, the teams have scored three consecutive touchdowns. We cheer at the top of our lungs for the excitement to continue.

With a little more than 8 minutes until halftime, South Carolina puts together a methodical 12-play drive that begins on their 27-yard-line. The series, which includes five successful passes and four positive rushing plays by quarterback Thompson, culminates with a 27-yard field goal by fifth-year place-kicker Adam Yates. The visiting team now only trails by 4 points with 2:40 left until halftime as the frenzy in the stands turns to frustration. Tahj Boyd adds to this consternation on the ensuing possession.

After a 16-yard pass to senior wide receiver Jaron Brown and a 9-yard swing-pass to tight end Brandon Ford to midfield, the 6'1" 225-pound gunslinger commits the first turnover of the game. On first down, with a minute-and-a-half remaining, senior safety DeVonte Holloman snatches Boyd's mistimed pass and falls to the turf at the 24-yard-line.

Following a quick three-and-out by the visiting team, the Tigers are unable to mount an attack. Even though Dabo's squad is ahead 14-to-10 as both teams jog to the locker rooms, we can physically sense dissatisfaction from our row-mates.

Nothing a few halftime libations can't soothe.

As the ball sails through the night air into the arms of the Gamecock's return-man just outside the goal to our left, the residual effects of the home team's scoreless second quarter – along with hastily consumed high-octane beverages – linger across our section.

The well-oiled crowd lets out a loud "Ooooo!" as Bruce Ellington is slammed to the ground at the 15-yard-line by an ambush in orange ("ambush" being the *other* proper name for a group of tigers). Perhaps this jarring hit – and resulting field position – will set the tone for this second half.

Lamentably for the faithful surrounding us, this first series has a familiar ring. South Carolina moves down the field for what feels like the entire third quarter. An impressive 30-yard strike by Thompson to Nick Jones brings a deflating groan from our section. Five plays later, the visitors are facing a third down and 16 on the 34-yard-line.

Several rows below us, two fans in matching orange outfits wildly wave a white cardboard D and a cardboard picket fence above their heads. Just then, in spectacular fashion, Spurrier pulls a card from his sleeve – and it's an ace!

Standing in the pocket, Thompson fires a line-drive to Ace Sanders who is racing across the middle at the 10-yard-line. With a stop-on-a-dime move, the pivoting wide receiver causes three converging defensive backs to fly past him. Spinning away from the defenders, No. 1 in white sprints into the goal at the far end. The Mighty Sound of the Southeast blasts the school's fight song across the stunned arena. A little more than 3 minutes have transpired in this third quarter.

Following this fifth reception by Sanders, the scoreboard lights 17-to-14 in favor of the Gamecocks.

Adding to the Southern discomfort in our section, the home team is forced to punt to their loathed opponents after a quick three-and-out. On third down of this flaccid first series by Clemson, the fans in the stadium and across the nation witness an amazing display of tenacity from a rising young defensive star.

Shooting like a missile from his right defensive end position, sophomore Jadeveon Clowney flies past the massive left tackle and abruptly throws Tahj Boyd to the turf for a 10-yard sack.

As the 6'6" 272-pound former High School "Mr. Football" in South Carolina saunters to the sideline, I comment to Valerie that he reminds me of an All-American who once lined up across from me at Oklahoma State.

The Gamecocks again waste little time navigating the field after the 47-yard punt. Also, once again, their ponderous series seems to usurp the entire quarter.

If not for a holding penalty on third down and 1, the visiting team would have had a first down inside the 10. Following a pass over the head of wide receiver Nick Jones in the southwest corner, Spurrier judiciously opts to kick a field goal. From 43 yards away, his former walk-on placekicker, Adam Yates, splits the uprights to increase the lead 20-to-14. Once again, only about 3 minutes have ticked off the game clock.

Even though the natives in our section are now even more restless, their Tigers are only down by 6 points with 7 full minutes remaining in the third quarter. One quick score and they're right back in the lead.

On the first play of their second drive, Boyd launches a 38-yard spiral over the finger-tips of DeVonte Holloman and into the outstretched arms of his receiver, Jaron Brown. From the shotgun, he hands the ball to Andre Ellington, who scampers behind a superb seal-block from his 305-pound left tackle, Brandon Thomas, for another quick 12 yards. Unfortunately for the agitated home crowd, the typically poised QB is forced to hurry his pass to Sammy Watkins on third down. The former all-time leading receiver at South Fort Myers High School in Fort Myers, Florida (and No. 3 five-star recruit in the nation) catches the low-thrown ball and rolls to the 19-yard-line.

Reminiscent of the air-brakes at the end of tonight's pregame procession, fans in our section hiss in disapproval as Clemson's field goal team takes the field. Chandler Catanzaro, who's been perfect on all 10 tries from inside the 40-yard-line this season, sends the ball 37-yards into the middle of the stands at the east end.

With 5 minutes remaining in this quarter, a row of all-orange cheerleaders race across the end zone to our left with massive orange flags that spell: C-L-E-M-S-O-N. The Jumbotron above these seven swaying banners shows 17 points for the Tigers and 20 points for their rival.

The next two series are mirror images of each other. One, however, feels like a death nail in The Valley.

The Gamecocks' drive seems to once again expand time as they move 50 yards down the field to the 23-yard-line. After a tremendous sack by Xavier Brewer on a corner blitz, the visitors line up for third down with 18 yards for a first down. On this fifteenth play of the drive, Thompson drops deep in the pocket and throws an arcing pass into the northeast corner. Leaping high above the darting wide receiver in white, Brewer follows his crushing sack with an acrobatic interception for a touchback and the game's second turnover.

Our section-mates go wild as the defense mobs their cornerback in the end zone. The Ol' Ball Coach, directly in front of us in his garnet pullover jacket and black visor, slowly removes his headset.

With renewed vigor, Boyd scrambles 6 yards after being flushed out of the pocket to start the ensuing series. On second down from his 26-yard-line, the confident quarterback hands the ball to his running back, Ellington, on a well-executed end-around to the right side. Nine yards later, it happens.

Shooting across the field from his safety position, D.J. Swearinger sends a shudder through the crowd with a hit so hard it knocks the Clemson runner off his cleats. As Ellington lays at the feet of No. 36 in all-white, the safety with jet-black dreadlocks strikes a taunting muscleman pose. Even though the senior defensive back from Greenwood, South Carolina is immediately charged with an unsportsmanlike-conduct penalty, the crushing hit delivers a vicious message at the start of this fourth quarter. The first strike of the nail.

With boos still raining down from the home crowd, Boyd is only able to move the ball 3 yards from the middle of the field in two plays against the energized defense. Twelve minutes remain in the game. Jadeveon Clowney – from a standing position in front of Clemson's right guard – ferociously bull rushes Boyd on this crucial third down. Hastily, the talented trigger-man launches the ball, without setting his feet, down the middle of the field and directly into the arms of Brison Williams. The sophomore safety is tripped up at midfield as the fans in our section moan in disgust. The second strike of the nail.

Thirteen plays after this devastating interception by Williams, the interlopers from Columbia seal the coffin.

Their exhausting drive, which features a slashing 26-yard run on the opening play by true freshman running back Mike Davis and a successful quarterback-sneak on fourth down at the 19-yard-line, has taken more than seven-and-a-half minutes off the game clock. South Carolina's quarterback brings his team to the line of scrimmage on third down at the 6. The Jumbotron facing Thompson flashes wildly. From the left hash mark, the substitute quarterback rolls to the middle of the field. He confidently fires a bullet into the center of the east end zone where earlier the home team entered the field after touching Howard's Rock. No. 23 in all-white, Bruce Ellington, casually hands the ball to the referee. The final strike of the nail.

Trailing by two scores with only 4 minutes remaining on the game clock, the home team attempts to mount an attack against their dominating in-state foe. They've had the ball for 5 of the 25 minutes in this second half.

Following a touchback, No. 7 in white drops the hammer once again on Tahj Boyd. Racing untouched past first-team All-ACC left tackle Thomas, Clowney crashes into the blindside of the star quarterback to record his fourth sack of the night. The menacing defensive end (who is the third consecutive "Mr. Football" in the state to be recruited to Columbia) surpasses his team's single-season sack record of 12 with this shattering hit on Boyd.

The disgruntled fans around us begin to grasp the gravity of what's unfolding on the field. They also, suddenly, grasp each other. As fellow section-mates hurl curse words toward the visitors' bench, haymakers abruptly start hurling several rows below us. Spilling out into the aisle, two fans trade sloshy punches as the clock continues to run on the field.

This is not the first altercation we've witnessed on our annual pursuit. The World's Largest Cocktail Party, several seasons ago, is still fresh in our minds. Nevertheless, it is the first in-stadium brawl we've seen between fans of the *same* team.

Evidently, the evening has become too much for the two pudgy pugilists in orange and purple: too much frustration inside the stadium, too much libation outside. Several of the faithful in our section quickly separate the belligerent combatants and hold them at bay until stadium security shows up.

As if to add insult to the minor injuries incurred in the aisle to our left, on third down and 16 from their 19-yard-line, a wide-open DeAndre Hopkins, inexplicably drops a perfectly thrown 25-yard pass from Boyd. The fans in our section and throughout Memorial Stadium hang their heads.

The reality of a 10-point loss starts to sink-in as Ace Sanders calls for a fair-catch. Coming into this showdown, the Tigers have averaged almost 45 points per game. Tahj Boyd was a top contender for the trophy named after the former head coach here in Clemson. And Dabo had certainly been looking forward to a BCS Bowl Game.

Instead, following a final 6-play series by the Gamecocks and an insignificant 3-play drive by the Tigers – which ends with a fifth sack by Jadeveon Clowney – the visiting team wins their fourth consecutive victory in this rivalry. (South Carolina has only accomplished this feat one other time, from 1951 to 1954, during this second-longest consecutively played rivalry in the nation. Only Minnesota versus Wisconsin is longer with 106 uninterrupted seasons.) Steve Spurrier is now the winningest head coach in the history of varsity football at the University of South Carolina. Tonight is his 65th victory.

Looming over the Clemson quarterback following this final sack of the game, Clowney gets into a slight shoving match as the teams head toward each other for post-game handshakes. The scoreboard glows (just not as brightly), 17-to-27.

Obviously, this is not the outcome envisioned as the team prepared to run down the precarious hill into the balloon-filled stadium.

In addition to the almost 45 points per game, the hometown Tigers had, before this demeaning defeat, led their conference with an average of 535 yards per game – sixth-best in the nation. Tonight, they barely surpassed 300. In the second half alone, South Carolina ran 51 offensive plays. Clemson ran 19. Dabo Swinney lost his fourth game out of five to his rival from Columbia. And, his seniors on the field tonight never beat the Gamecocks.

College football has a way of eliciting a full range of emotions in even its most reserved fans. The highest of highs and lowest of lows are experienced every Saturday in every fall of every year.

Walking into the darkness surrounding Death Valley this evening, these emotions are on full display.

A very tall, seemingly very decorous individual is striding confidently alongside us, unaccompanied by any colleagues, through the hordes of ireful home team fans. Swinging his arms with each generous step, he hollers repeatedly into the damp night, "HOW . . . 'BOUT . . . THEM . . . FOOTBALL . . . FIGHTIN' . . . SOUTH CAROLINA . . . GAAAAMECOCKS!" A slightly swaying middle-aged woman in an orange Western-style hat curses at him to shut his mouth. And then challenges him to a fistfight.

Two South Carolina State Troopers stand over a handcuffed undergrad sitting on a curb arguing about how it was the other guy's fault. A young Southern belle with long blond curls is sobbing in her own sick on the same sidewalk.

An eerie silence, broken by the occasional car horn or yell of frustration, fills the parking lot as we search for Stevie's camp. We try, to no avail, to reach Boyd and Gina by cell phone.

Arriving at the large orange tent, Boyd's former roommate is packing up the remnants of our earlier revelry. He is by himself and informs us that our former partygoers have decided not to return to what was expected to be one of the school's biggest post-game celebrations. They're so upset that they left the stadium and never looked back.

Stevie's empty tent looks like a corpse. The canopy frame resembles skeletal bones. The only signs of life are the flying dots above the rotting food splayed across the folding tables.

Under her breath, Valerie says we may truly be in the shadow of Death Valley.

Adding to the misery, the wrong team was victorious in the first overtime game in the history of the Bedlam Series. Oklahoma State lost in Norman by the outrageous score of 48-to-51.

The orange team finished on the disappointing side of the scoreboard in both intrastate rivalries today.

CHAPTER FIFTEEN
Keeping the Faith
2013 Southern California | Notre Dame

Leaning against a wooden telephone pole, the kind that oozes pitch during the dog days of summer here in the Midwest, is an attractive woman with long straight brown hair.

Smartly dressed in a light-weight black jacket zipped to just below her chin and knee-high black leather boots, she appears to be waiting for fellow revelers outside of what looks like nothing more than two muddy-yellow trailer homes attached and perpendicular to each other. An unopened bottle of spiced rum, about the size of a gallon of milk, dangles from her right hand.

Strolling past an outmoded motorhome adorned with black and gold spray paint and a large Purdue logo at its rear, we see a small sign atop two faded blue poles. A tilted martini glass appears next to "the Linebacker INN" followed by "The Tradition Continues." Above this 1950s-style marquee sits a squatty goalpost with orange streamers. Turning to Valerie on this somewhat cloudy mid-October afternoon I say, "If we're gonna find revelry before this rivalry tonight, it's *gotta* be in here!"

It takes a couple moments for our eyes to adjust as we enter the overly crowded and overly cluttered tavern.

If not for several truckloads of Notre Dame memorabilia splattered across its chaotic walls, the bar feels a lot like any other slightly off-campus watering hole. Alongside several overstocked shelves hangs a green and white street marker that reads, "88 National Champions Avenue."

Valerie points out a collection of military patches on the mirror. A glowing cursive light blue neon reads The Linebacker above five or six rows of booze. Etched into the glass is "Linebacker Lounge, Across From Notre Dame, Est. 1962."

We're not sure if this establishment is The Linebacker Inn or Linebacker Lounge. We do, however, know that stenciled on the outside wall is simply: THE BACKER.

Having walked along East Angela Boulevard to this loutish if no less splendid lounge on this early afternoon before the 85th meeting between the University of Southern California and the hometown Fighting Irish, we begin to wonder if we'll ever fulfill the greatest desire of our annual pursuit. Over the past 14 years, we've always romanticized we'd chance upon the *perfect* tailgate party.

While many of our pregame festivities have been both memorable and enjoyable, we have never, to our regret, really experienced what it means to truly tailgate like a *local*. At a celebration that seems larger than life. Where we're accepted as one of the regulars. Where there are free-flowing libations and mounds of food and laughing and singing and costumes and celebrities and rock bands. Where we feel like we're in a light beer commercial!

This has been our goal – farfetched as it might be – since we began our wonderful quest.

Standing at the bar inside this rambunctious roadhouse across from the prestigious private university with overtly religious overtones, it seems unlikely this will be the year we stumble across our holy grail of college revelry. The predictable small gatherings alongside our trek to The Backer were nothing more than predictable trappings found on almost every campus across America. Folding picnic tables, chips and dips, cases of canned beer, cornhole, and the occasional logoed canopy.

After procuring two plastic cups of lager rivaling the size (and cost) of those at Stevenson's former fueling station, I turn to Valerie and smile. We still get to be a part of one of the most renowned clashes in all of sports today. Described over the years as the "Greatest Inter-Sectional Rivalry in College Football." At one of the most exalted venues in the nation.

And we get to experience it together.

Driving through the outskirts of South Bend on this midmorning before game day, Valerie comments it looks a lot like every other small town we've passed since entering Indiana.

On the corner of North Michigan Street and East Angela Boulevard, a rectangular block of dark marble announces we've arrived at the University of Notre Dame and that it was founded by the Congregation of Holy Cross in 1842. Our objective is to get eyes on tomorrow's venue and find a local bistro.

We check off the first box as we pass a lush field known as the Irish Green on the south side of Notre Dame Stadium. A quick right-turn and we see red awnings on a new brick building and a bright yellow sign that reads, "Best Specials. Most Fun."

Sounds perfect!

Brothers Bar & Grill turns out to be the newest outpost of a chain started a couple of decades ago in La Cross, Wisconsin. Inside, there are lots of patrons and lots of tap handles. Perfect. Our bubbly server boasts we have our choice of 40 draft beers. Even more perfect!

Finishing our deliciously messy pub food, I strike up a conversation with the table of blue and gold jerseys next to us. One of the soon-to-be fellow members of our game-day crowd tomorrow mentions that a campus pep rally is taking place in about 30 minutes outside the Joyce Center directly across the street. Polishing off our remaining few gulps, we settle our tab and head out toward Notre Dame Stadium.

Approaching the legendary arena, we see an animated crowd surrounding a group of coaches and players. Standing at a small podium with a microphone in his hand is a former linebacker from Kent State University. In addition to his years as a member of the Golden Flashes (yet another great team name), Lou Holtz was also the head football coach at The College of William & Mary, and North Carolina State University, and the University of Arkansas, and the University of Minnesota, and the University of South

Carolina. Talk about a legend. He's most honored, however, for holding this same position 11 illustrious years at this university in South Bend.

Dressed in a charcoal gray suit with a gray and black-striped tie and matching handkerchief, Holtz (who compiled 100 wins, 30 losses, and 2 ties at this school from 1986 to 1996) is in the midst of his commencement speech for this campus rally. This year's team flanks him on both sides as he passionately encourages the crowd of no more than several hundred students, faculty, and fans to root for these players this weekend.

Holtz has been a hero, here and across this Midwestern state, ever since his 1988 team finished their regular season unblemished and beat the undefeated-at-the-time Mountaineers from West Virginia in the Fiesta Bowl to claim the consensus National Championship. He does little to hold back his ardor for the home team – or his disdain for its opposition tomorrow.

All stand in reverence, including the Notre Dame Marching Band, cheerleaders, and goofy Leprechaun mascot, as the aging luminary with wispy golden-white hair and gold-rimmed glasses proclaims, "USC stands for University of Spoiled Children!" The crowd cheers. Without missing a beat, he adds, in his signature slurred delivery, "And most of their football players chose USC over UCLA because it's easier to spell." The crowd laughs and roars its approval. "I have great respect for Southern Cal and the people there, but it's not Notre Dame," he says. "We're Notre Dame – and they ain't. And that says it all."

After the applause from the energized flock dies down, Holtz shifts to a slightly softer tone and decrees, "Three things I want you to do tomorrow. Cheer louder than you ever have, and remember this, when people need love and understanding and support the most, it's usually when they deserve it the least. So, let's show everybody that we are the best fans in the world that you are, and cheer this team. Point number two, I want you to conduct yourself with class like you always do. I've had more people say to me, 'I went there with the opposition and I've never been treated any better than the Notre Dame fans,' and I'm proud of that, and you should be proud of that also." Then, with added

330 • THIS YEAR'S GAME

emphasis, he says, "The third thing I want you to do, and the last thing, I want you to go tell Southern Cal to bring a damn lunch because it's gonna be a long-ass day for them!"

He doesn't hold his arm out and drop the mic; it just seems like he does as he turns and walks away from the podium.

"Victory March," the school's instantly recognizable fight song, emanates from the stage as we set out to explore this fabled campus. Walking along Leahy Drive, we come upon a slightly-larger-than-life bronze statue of the man whose name is attached to this roadway.

Frank Leahy played on two national championship teams here under arguably the greatest head coach in all of college football. His former head coach, Knute Rockne, is the only coach in NCAA Division I football history to have finished his career with a higher winning percentage.

Leahy commanded the varsity squad in South Bend for 11 seasons from 1941 to 1953 (he was replaced by Edward McKeever in 1944 and Hugh Devore in 1945 while serving as a Naval lieutenant during World War II). He led the Fighting Irish to four national championships and six perfect seasons, a mind-boggling streak of zero losses in 39 games. Four (four!) of his players were awarded the Heisman Trophy during his tenure at the helm. The distinguished coach will always be remembered for his statement, "Notre Dame didn't kick field goals; Notre Dame was too tough to kick field goals."

Crossing the street named after this second most-famous coach, we stroll by an unassuming, two-story building that has the look of a modern church attempting to pass itself off as an antiquated cathedral. "Guglielmino Athletics Complex" is chiseled into the simple archway above its entrance.

No one is on the well-kept lawns surrounding the speckled-tan brick structure and we see no activity inside. Curious, we check to see if the doors are unlocked.

To our surprise, we walk into a vacant lobby of what we soon surmise to be the headquarters of the Fighting Irish football machine. On a dark blue wall next to an empty receptionist desk are the words: "Welcome to the Guglielmino Athletic Complex." We're not sure if "Athletic" is missing an "s", but we know how it's etched in stone above the building's entrance.

Recognized as "The Gug" (pronounced "goog"), this almost 100,000-square-foot facility is home to the football program's coaching offices, team locker room, and players' lounge. It also houses the training center for all scholarshiped athletes.

Commissioned in 2004 to be the "finest college football facility in the country," this $22 million hub of Notre Dame sports was a gift from an enterprising Southern California businessman who, in 1939, suited up along the Fighting Irish sideline under another famed head coach, Elmer Layden.

Upon announcing his generous gift, Don Guglielmino was invited to a special dinner hosted by Lou Holtz. The ever-gracious coach surprised the letterman with a field-pass for the rivalry taking place the next day in Notre Dame Stadium. After the hard-fought 24-to-20 victory over the University of Spoiled Children, Holtz presented the game ball to Guglielmino in the team's locker room.

This "house that Guglielmino funded" is more than just a state-of-the-art training facility. It's also a shrine to the storied history of Notre Dame football.

Slipping past the unoccupied reception desk, we're immediately greeted by a bronze rendition of the famous picture of the "Four Horsemen." Seated upon saddled steeds and wearing leather helmets and high-top cleats are the illustrious members of Knute Rockne's 1924 offensive backfield.

Originally formed two years earlier during all four players' sophomore season, quarterback Harry Stuhldreher, right halfback Don Miller, left halfback Jim Crowley, and fullback Elmer Layden won every game but two during their three seasons at the school. Even though Layden was the fastest of the quartet, it was Miller who proved to be the breakaway threat out of the backfield. In his later years, Rockne proclaimed that the 160-pound halfback from Defiance, Ohio was the greatest open-field runner he ever coached in his 16-year career.

The group's apocalyptic nickname was coined in 1924 by a

sportswriter at the *New York Herald Tribune* following their victory over the mighty Black Knights from West Point:

> "Outlined against a blue-gray October sky, the Four Horsemen rode again. In dramatic lore, their names are Death, Destruction, Pestilence, and Famine. But those are aliases. Their real names are: Stuhldreher, Crowley, Miller and Layden."

Across the lobby from these frozen equestrians are seven dark wood pedestals. Atop each is the instantly identifiable stiff-armed trophy presented to each season's most outstanding player. No other school has more of these awards.

Flanking these seven Heisman Trophies are three molded arches featuring blue-hued, larger-than-life photographs of each athlete in action. In the center cathedral-style arch is a life-sized picture taken during the 1987 Heisman ceremony.

Standing with three white-haired men in suits on his right and three on his left is the recipient of that year's most prestigious award. Above this photograph are the words: HEISMAN TROPHY WINNERS. Tim Brown, the first wide receiver to ever win the statue, smiles with his hands folded across his waist. To his right: Johnny Lujack ('47), Angelo Bertelli ('43), and Leon Hart ('49). On his left: Paul Hornung ('56), John Huarte ('64), and Johnny Lattner ('53). There may never be another time when seven living inductees of this most exclusive fraternity in sports, all from one university, assemble for a photo opportunity.

Remarkably, Frank Leahy not only coached Lujack, Bertelli, Hart, and Lattner, he also recruited Hornung to this Midwest university. Just as remarkable, Tim Brown played high school football at Woodrow Wilson High School in Dallas, Texas; the same institution that graduated 1938 Heisman Trophy winner Davey O'Brien. Even though O'Brien earned his varsity letter at Texas Christian University, this East Dallas high school is the only public high school to ever produce two Heisman Trophy recipients.

Inside a tall Plexiglas cylinder at the center of the lobby is the Gerrits/Pepsi-Cola Foundation UPI Coaches' Trophy. Etched on the shiny black base of this 4-foot tall block is, "1988 National Football Champion."

In that third season with Lou Holtz at the helm, the Fighting Irish won all 12 regular-season games, including the 31-to-30 upset over then-No. 1-ranked University of Miami. This victory, which to this day is known as "Catholics vs. Convicts," ended Miami's 36-game regular-season winning streak and is considered by many to be the greatest game ever played inside Notre Dame Stadium.

Commanded by my former head coach, Jimmy Johnson, the Hurricanes earned their derisive nickname attached to his game due to several players being arrested in the summer of that season. Following this only loss, the "Convicts" dominated the University of Nebraska in the Orange Bowl and finished No. 2 in both national polls. Undefeated Notre Dame, meanwhile, secured the crystal trophy in this clear plastic tube by easily handing the Mountaineers from Morgantown their only loss in the Fiesta Bowl.

Painted in gold leaf on the barrel-shaped stand in this lobby are the yearly dates of the 11 national championship titles won by the Fighting Irish. Two seasons, however, are not on this polished mahogany base. Apparently, Notre Dame only acknowledges national titles bestowed by the Associated Press and the Coaches Poll. Nevertheless, the Irish *were* recognized as the No. 1 team by every other national poll at the end of both the 1938 and 1953 seasons.

Whether or not these disputed titles are included, this small Midwestern school boasts more national championships than almost all other football programs in the nation. Due to the numerous (and seemingly ambiguous) ranking systems used since the birth of college football, the exact number of championships at each school will always be debatable. However, it's safe to say that Notre Dame easily ranks in the top-10.

"Excuse me." Startled, Valerie and I turn to see a portly, middle-aged woman with a shamrock-green lanyard around her neck walking toward us through the archway to our left.

"May I help you?" she asks in a stern voice.

We convey that we innocently stumbled upon this athletic (or athletics) complex on our self-guided tour of the campus.

Obviously perturbed, probably because no one was at the desk to prevent us from wandering around the adorned foyer, the corpulent staff member informs us this facility is only open to prospects and their families. Evidently, on this day before the showdown with its west coast rival, select high school players are invited to tour the campus and its training complex. Having no offspring of our own, we apologize for our indiscretion and hastily make our way out the door.

Crossing the street to the corner of Courtney Lane, we spot a familiar conveyance. Once again we've come across a flamboyant 18-wheeler used to transport equipment to and from away games.

The massive dark blue trailer is attached to an all-gold semi-truck. On the front of the trailer is an oversized golden logo, followed by the words "NOTRE DAME FOOTBALL." At the back is a photograph of the packed stadium here on campus with "Wake Up The Echoes" across its top. Valerie hangs from the side mirror and flashes an all too expected "Hook 'em" sign.

Inside "the Linebacker INN" on this gameday Saturday, with the Indiana Hoosiers embroiled in a surprising shootout in Ann Arbor on the flat-screen and an oversize draft beer in my hand, I feel a pat on my shoulder.

Expecting the fellow patron to ask if he can get by for a pregame libation, I'm surprised when he asks if we're from Oregon. Before I can ask how he knows, he mentions that his daughter goes to Oregon State University and that he saw the bright orange "O S U" on the back of my jacket. As I turn with a "hate to disappoint you, pal" expression, he sees the Cowboys' logo on my chest. Realizing he's about to admit his mistake, I tell him we *are* from Oregon and that this is our first visit to South Bend.

We strike up an instant bond as we talk about his daughter's university, and about our annual quest. Upon hearing about our many excursions in pursuit of rivalry and revelry, our new buddy, Dennis, says, "Boy, have I got a party for you!"

In his light grey sweatshirt embroidered with "Notre Dame" across the front, Dennis is out the door and heading west along East Angela Boulevard. The spray-painted Purdue motorhome is still parked alongside this classic college tavern. (Disappointingly, the attractive woman with the voluminous quantity of spiced rum is not.)

With about 3 hours until kickoff, not much has changed in the lots across from Notre Dame Stadium: same obligatory tailgating groups, same obligatory tailgating activities. Half a block into our trek, we veer right and into a neighborhood along Twyckenham Drive. Reflecting upon the prime barstools we surrendered, and that The Backer was just beginning to swell with pregame partiers, Valerie says just out of earshot of our escort, "Perhaps we should have stayed where the action was."

And then . . . BLAMMO! It happens!

On the corner at Ivy Court, directly across the street from Frank Eck Baseball Stadium, a crowd of a hundred or more raucous revelers – dressed in either navy-blue or kelly-green – is milling outside a small arch pinched between two oversized, over-used motorhomes. "JIM BEAM COUNTRY" is etched across the wooden entrance. Everyone in the street is attempting to join the hordes of tailgaters on the other side of this curved span. Dennis nods to a very large, very bald bouncer wearing a No. 3 Fighting Irish jersey who lets us pass under the wooden signboard.

As we shoulder our way through the crowd, BLAMMO aggressively belts out "Johnny B. Goode" over the heads of several hundred revelers confined in this corral formed by elongated recreational vehicles. Screaming along with this local cover-band, which has performed at weddings and special events since 1999, is Hank Schrader – Walter White's brother-in-law. Hank is the dedicated DEA agent on the hit television show *Breaking Bad*.

With reckless abandon, Dean Norris (the actor who played Hank) flails a half-full Solo cup into the crisp afternoon air as an encouragement to join him. BLAMMO seamlessly breaks into an uncanny rendition of The Killers' "Mr. Brightside." The faux-DEA agent, who graduated from Clay High School just a few miles down the road, pugnaciously bobs his head to the beat.

We hastily make our way past the 15-foot square canopy that serves as the stage for this surprisingly talented group of local musicians. To the left of the white tent is a shiny black vehicle. Above the front windshield, where the words "SCHOOL BUS" should be, is the word "GOODWRENCH." An awning juts from the side, and a wooden deck running the entire length of the converted kid-hauler is mounted on its roof. The Stars and Stripes, the flag of Ireland, and random NASCAR flags flutter above this homemade viewing platform.

Several partiers holler down to the crowd as agent Schrader pumps his fist to the cover-band's version of AC/DC's "You Shook Me All Night Long" and yells "Go IRISH!" to his fellow revelers.

The renovated bus anchors the south wall of this rectangular plot created by the five or six well-worn motorhomes. It's also the command center for this high-spirited fete. Dennis guides us toward its door where we see green and white stripes waggling above the crowd. Standing with his back to a flat-screen is a stocky, middle-aged man with a weighty look on his face – and one of the most outrageously fabulous tailgating costumes we've come across.

Fashioned in the style of the Mad Hatter, the thickset gentleman is wearing a ridiculously oversized green and white striped velvet hat with a bright green shamrock on its front. Around his neck dangle several strands of shiny green beads about the size of tree ornaments. A string of flashing plastic beer mugs also hangs across the front of his No. 88 navy-blue jersey. On his shoulder is a patch from last year's National Championship Game.

I surreptitiously whisper to Valerie it's probably best not to mention the final score of this most recent title game.

In addition to his flamboyant hat and beads, the obvious ringmaster of this pregame spectacle is wearing a plaid kilt that drapes below his knees. The tartan skirt is complemented by white and green ankle-high socks. In one hand are rapidly melting ice cubes atop an amber-colored liquid, in the other, a half-smoked cigarette.

Dennis introduces us to the bejeweled host and informs us he owns a building materials company here in South Bend. He may very well be a respected leader of the community every other day of the year; today he looks like a character from *Alice In Wonderland*.

Maybe best of all, his distinguished mustache and full-chin goatee are dyed bright green.

Welcoming us with open arms, he calls his wife over. She, too, has embraced the costume spirit of her congenial husband and is wearing a bright green Bavarian-style beer-serving outfit. Two glittered shamrocks spring from her head like cartoon antennae. With a bright smile, she points us in the direction of a tub full of beer and encourages us to take in the festivity from the balcony.

The grand scale of this game-day bash comes into view as we ascend to the roof of the recycled school transport.

BLAMMO crashes into out another pounding rendition while a couple hundred fans in multicolored athletic wear mill about. Smoke rises from several barbecue pits and into the slightly overcast sky. Clusters of revelers continue to gather outside the archway at the entrance to this unabashed celebration of everything Notre Dame. Flapping high above the motorhomes and renovated busses, dozens of Fighting Irish flags act as beacons for each party surrounding our rowdy encampment.

Standing along the railing, I notice a collage of names and dates, random sayings, and Notre Dame-themed graffiti etched into this sturdy wooden frame. Several fellow revelers are sitting around a table at the center of the perched patio. Soon we are arm-in-arm and singing along with them.

Decked out in bright green pullovers and various Fighting Irish jerseys, our newfound friends tell us they've been coming to this festivity for several years and that most of the partiers here today, including our Mad Hatter host, have no intention of going to the game this evening. Many have traveled from all over the state just to attend this tailgate party and to watch the game from inside its temporary compound.

As we gather for photos atop the game-day vehicle, I let a cute young lady in a dark blue sweater know we're writing a book to capture the wonderful experiences surrounding college football. Pointing in the direction of Notre Dame Stadium, the fresh-faced student with wonderfully high cheekbones exclaims we *must* stop by the Grotto of Our Lady of Lourdes and light a candle to ensure the success of our project. If only it were that simple! We do, however, take the advice of her easygoing boyfriend in a knitted Notre Dame beanie and make our way down the spiral staircase at the back of the bus toward the closest white awning inside the teeming bivouac.

Once under the tent, we are greeted by the sight of every kind of gooey, messy, crunchy, melty tailgate fare we can imagine, strewn across three or four oversized tables. Massive bread-loaf bowls. Overflowing spinach dip. Pizzas. Overstuffed Philly cheesesteak sandwiches. Dozens of crockeries with unidentifiable sauces. Bags and bins filled with chips and pretzels. Mounds of chicken wings soaking in tinfoil trays. Fresh smoked ribs and sausages. Veggie and cheese platters. White cupcakes frosted with Notre Dame logos. Home-baked blue and gold sheet cakes, all of it displayed as if poured from a dump truck.

With dozens and dozens of half-full red plastic cups and even more beer cans, the arrangement looks like the aftermath of a fraternity party. Valerie turns to me and says, "This is as good as it will ever get!" And she's right – except that two other same-sized tents with the same audacious culinary offerings are right next to this one!

My joyous mate strikes up a conversation with a stout young man sporting a closely cropped beard, and wearing a camo hunting jacket and weathered Notre Dame cap. Between bites and with buffalo sauce running down his fingers, he tells Valerie his name is Ryan and that he recently returned from two tours of active duty in the Middle East. He's back home in South Bend for good now.

Following another bite, he lets us know this tailgate party is one of the things that he most looked forward to while overseas serving our country. And I think: if there's anything to light a candle for, it's for young men and women like Ryan.

After several hours of over-eating and over-imbibing, our fellow merrymakers show no sign of winding down. With the sun beginning to set across campus, we inform Dennis – and our new favorite fans – we need to start making our way to the stadium.

Pressing through the tottering crowd toward the wooden whiskey archway, Valerie literally bumps into DEA agent Schrader. Turning around with a big grin beneath his navy-blue stocking cap, Dean Norris unnecessarily apologies for this in-crowd collision.

Wearing a faded green shirt and several strands of shiny gold beads, he and Valerie immediately fall into easy conversation. After several minutes of pleasantries – and one more can of low-calorie lager for the trek to Rockne's House – Valerie poses for a delightful photo with South Bend's most prominent thespian.

We also hastily extend sincere appreciation to our host who, having dealt with the hordes of rambunctious roisters all day, now looks more like Alice Cooper than Alice in Wonderland.

Valerie's affable Army Ranger friend Ryan extends best wishes for a great game. He and most all his buddies will be at this encampment well after the final gun sounds this evening.

With less than 30 minutes to kickoff, BLAMMO may have retired for the evening, but their energy continues to pulse through the welcome-with-open-arms folks who invited us into their celebration. It beats through us, as well. Crossing the street, we turn back and smile at the glowing white awnings inside the golden goblet of our annual pursuit.

As the last bit of light sinks in the west, we hurry toward the southeast curve of one of the most iconic venues in all of sports.

Notre Dame Stadium, built in 1930 at a cost of $750,000, acquired its well-known nickname not only because Knute Rockne was heavily involved in its planning; he also forced the reluctant administrators at the school to pony-up for its exorbitant cost. Revenues from gate receipts in 1928 brought almost $500,000 into the university's coffers. Even so, the overly cautious Congregation of Holy Cross priests weren't willing to finance the new stadium. Furious over their feet dragging, Rockne – the winningest coach in the 40 years Notre Dame had fielded a varsity football team – submitted his resignation letter.

The obstinate head coach had used this tactic several times earlier in his career, a fact not lost on the Catholic administrators.

Confident that ticket revenues the following season would easily swell their bank balance beyond its projected cost, the priests convinced Rockne to rescind his resignation in exchange for their commitment to construct the arena.

The "House That Rockne Built" was actually built by Sollitt Construction Company of South Bend and designed by Osborne Engineering in Cleveland, Ohio, which was selected because of its two other award-winning designs: Yankee Stadium and Fenway Park.

Residing just several miles south of the Michigan border, Rockne visited newly constructed Michigan Stadium in Ann Arbor ahead of the 1927 season. Impressed with its style and magnitude, he persuaded Osborne Engineering to model the new arena in South Bend after what was to become "The Big House." The only significant difference was the location of the tunnel onto the playing field. While Michigan players enter at the 50-yard-line on the east side of their stadium, the Fighting Irish race from the middle of the north end zone. Notre Dame stadium also held slightly fewer than 60,000 fans at its completion, whereas slightly more than 72,000 could be seated in Ann Arbor.

Floating on the southeast curve of this celebrated stadium is "Ara Parseghian Gate" in black letters. We ascertain this passageway is dedicated to the 23rd head coach at this school. Ara Parseghian, who played halfback and defensive end for the Cleveland Browns in the late 1940s, has been called the "savior of Notre Dame football. The former head coach at Miami University in Oxford, Ohio immediately returned the Irish to national glory when he took over in 1964.

Following years of futility, and a dismal two-win season under one-year coach Hugh Devore (in all fairness to Devore, he'd earlier coached Notre Dame to a 7-2-1 record during the time when Frank Leahy was the Navy), Parseghian directed the team to a No. 3 ranking in the nation. The Golden Domers' only loss that year came in their final game in Los Angeles Memorial Coliseum. Led by legendary head coach John McKay, the underdog Trojans from the "Children's University" in Los Angeles scored 13 points in the fourth quarter to upset the then-No. 2 team in the nation 20-to-17.

Parseghian would go on to lead the Fighting Irish to two National Championships; the first in 1966, followed by the second in 1973. Ever since, Rockne, Leahy, and Parseghian have been christened by many fans as the "Holy Trinity of Notre Dame Coaches."

Walking with high-spirited boosters from both schools, I comment that the dank underbelly of this antiquated structure is reminiscent of Harvard Stadium. Poorly lit cement passageways conjure up images of medieval dungeons during a millennium when religious institutions really *did* rule the civilized world. This evening, however, the battle isn't over ideology; it's for a medallion-studded, phallic-shaped piece of wood.

The Jeweled Shillelagh, first presented in 1952 after a 9-point shutout of USC in South Bend, is the spoils for the victor of this annual showdown. After each game, an emerald inlaid shamrock or ruby-adorned Trojan gets added to the shaft of this snake-like club. Not surprisingly, the first Jeweled Shillelagh quickly became chocked-full of these victory pins. Thus, following the 1995 defeat of Southern Cal inside this stadium, the original foot-long stick was replaced by a longer shillelagh made of blackthorn wood from County Leitrim, Ireland. Presented by the Notre Dame Club of Los Angeles, the alumni association proclaimed the new polished staff symbolizes "the high tradition, the keen rivalry, and above all the sincere respect which these two great universities have for each other."

We'll see how much sincere respect is left on the field by night's end.

Tonight's scrimmage may not have BCS National Championship implications; however, the energy inside this throwback stadium sure feels like it does.

Each team enters this game with two losses. The unranked visitors' four wins: University of Hawaii, Boston College, Utah State, and last week against the University of Arizona. Coming off a bye-week, Notre Dame has victories over Temple University, Purdue, Michigan State, and Arizona State. Both programs would very much like to claw their way back into the ranks of the Top 25.

Both also have something to prove.

Last season was Lane Kiffin's first as head coach at USC. At its start, his heralded Trojans were ranked No. 1. They finished with a 7-and-6 record that included a loss to Georgia Tech in the Hyundai Sun Bowl. (It also included a 13-to-22 defeat by Notre Dame in the Coliseum.) Kiffin's team was the first since the 1964 University of Mississippi Rebels to finish unranked after coming in as the nation's top team.

Following the first 5 games of this current 2013 season, Kiffin was fired. Even though his Trojans had three wins, the administration at the private university apparently perceived the program needed an abrupt change after the 41-to-62 loss at Arizona State. And abrupt it was! Six hours after fans stormed the field in Sun Devil Stadium, Kiffin was handed his walking papers as he stood on the tarmac to board the team's plane in Phoenix.

Ed Orgeron, USC's defensive line coach, was immediately promoted to interim head coach. Last week in Memorial Coliseum, the former assistant notched his first win as a head coach with a 38-to-31 victory in Tucson.

The fans wearing cardinal red and bright gold are acutely aware that a triumph this evening would go a long way toward calming the tumult of the past year and a half.

For Notre Dame, 2012 signaled the return to greatness – and a return to shenanigans.

After five years of mediocrity and opening the season unranked, the Irish finished, to the amazement of most all of college football, unblemished at the end of their regular-season schedule. Ranked No. 1 in the nation, they confidently prepared for the No. 2-ranked Crimson Tide in the National Championship Game. They had the best defense in the country – led by Butkus Award winner and Heisman Trophy finalist Manti Te'o – giving up only slightly more than 10 points per game. Third-year head coach Bryan Kelly looked to capture the program's first national championship since 1988.

Then Nick Saban did what Nick Saban is wont to do: the Alabama head coach captured his third national championship in only six years. Notre Dame never got off the bus. Halfway through the third quarter, the Crimson Tide were up 35-to-0. They finished with 529 total yards and 42 total points. Kelly's team scored 14.

This wasn't the only embarrassment to befall the Fighting Irish last season. Their entire fan-base had been shocked to learn Te'o lost his girlfriend to leukemia on the same day (September 11th) his grandmother passed away. Several pregame ceremonies complete with flowers and framed photographs were held inside this stadium. A charity fund was started. And, following the team's victory over Michigan one week after notification of this tragic death, Kelly awarded the game ball to his star linebacker with instructions to take it to Hawaii for her funeral.

There was only one problem: there was no funeral. There was no girlfriend. Te'o had been the innocent victim of an elaborate internet hoax. Much like their No. 1 ranking at the end of the regular season, the entire story was smoke and mirrors.

As I said, each team has a lot to atone for from last season.

From our weathered bench in the southeast corner, we notice not much has changed inside Rockne's house since the school's head coach took back his resignation at the end of the 1920s. If not for the small digital scoreboard to our right, this could be the kickoff to the inaugural clash between these teams in this stadium back in the fall of 1931. There is no Jumbotron. No replay screens of any size for that matter. The relatively small press box behind us is poorly lit. The playing field is the only well-lit part of the entire stadium, which creates a somewhat ominous vibe throughout our darkened section.

There's also very little room along the sidelines and behind each end zone. The four or five rows of dignitaries, players, and coaches fill the space between the white lines of the gridiron and the gray wall of the stadium. Rockne apparently desired the stands to be as close to the field as possible so fans could experience more than just the sights of the game.

From under a deep blue sign shouting "HERE COME THE IRISH," the home team shoots through the narrow tunnel at the center of the north end like a stream of bees from a hive. The 247th consecutive sellout crowd springs to its feet as the gleaming gold helmets race to our side of the field. The dark blue jerseys and gold pants come together at the sideline, buzzing and dancing like those same bees atop honeycomb.

Across the field, Ed Orgeron – who can join Paul Hackett and John Robinson as the only first-year head coaches at Southern California to defeat this team in their first scrimmage – instructs his players as they prepare for kickoff.

Dressed in bright white jerseys and bright yellow pants, the Trojans spread linearly across the 35-yard-line as the Irish spread across the field with their backs to the north end zone. The unadorned uniforms of both teams harken back to the early days of this rivalry. Even the end zones pay homage to the original gridiron at this Midwest university. Much like the home team's solid-gold helmets, which feature no ornamentation whatsoever, the scoring zones are nothing more than simple parallel slashes.

Everything about Notre Dame truly is "old school."

The ball sails from USC's kicker into the dark abyss above the stadium lights and out the far end zone. The 85th edition of the "Greatest Inter-Sectional Rivalry in College Football" is underway!

From his own 25-yard-line, senior quarterback Tommy Rees surveys the legendary field in this legendary arena and quickly hands the ball to Cam McDaniel. The junior running back is just as quickly stuffed at the line of scrimmage. On the next play, Rees finds wide receiver TJ Jones – who has slipped past the cornerback alongside the Trojans sideline – for a fabulous 25-yard reception. Ten methodical plays later, the Irish face a fourth down and goal less than 1 yard from the end zone.

Brian Kelly, whose defense last year stuffed the Trojans on four consecutive plays from their 1-yard-line to seal the victory with less than 2 minutes in the game, elects to roll the proverbial dice. A deafening moan carries across the stadium as USC's safety shoots through the line unblocked, pile-driving McDaniel behind the line of scrimmage.

The Trojans precariously start their first series just outside the end zone directly in front of us. An explosive 9-yard run by Silas Redd immediately opens the field. (The 5'10" 200-pound running back joined the team this July after the NCAA granted players at Penn State University the opportunity to transfer in the wake of sanctions levied upon the school for its complicity in the Jerry Sandusky child molestation scandal. During his sophomore season last year, Redd rushed for 1,188 yards; third-most in the Big Ten Conference.)

Following this burst, USC mounts a 10-play drive featuring five carries by the slashing running back for 40 yards, including a 15-yard blast from the Notre Dame 16-yard-line. On their 13th play, Redd plunges across the goal to put the visiting team up by 7 points.

The University of Notre Dame Band, which claims to be the oldest college band in continuous existence, assails the celebrating Trojans with sneers from the corner of the jam-packed end zone. Crammed several rows deep in their military-style navy blue and gold uniforms, the fresh-faced musicians will stand alongside this north scoring zone for the entire length of the game. The Spirit of Troy, the Trojans' famed marching band, will do the same at the opposite end.

The faithful in the stands are on edge as George Atkinson III is tackled at his 23-yard-line after receiving the kickoff just outside the goal line. Rees delivers a spark of confidence to the home crowd and his team with a 10-yard strike to wide receiver DaVaris Daniels. This spark becomes a blaze after the Irish move 70 yards in nine plays to the 7-yard-line. With perfect pocket protection, the senior quarterback fires a dart to tight end, Troy Niklas. The 6'7" junior from Fullerton, California, who all-but committed to USC before choosing South Bend, makes a spectacular grab just inside the goal to give Notre Dame its first score of the game.

Both Niklas and linebacker Hayes Pullard from Inglewood, California untangle themselves at the feet of the Trojan marching band. Several Spirit of Troy musicians hurl verbal spears in the direction of the celebrating Irish players.

The first quarter comes to an end on this game-tying touchdown. Valerie comments a replay would be great, given the pass to Niklas barely made it across the line. Alas, not in Rockne's House.

Fans surrounding us yell into the dark sky as Kevon Seymour cradles the kickoff and scampers to his 33-yard-line. They get even louder as Silas Redd quickly gains 16 yards on two gashes through Notre Dame's front four. On the next play, Cody Kessler artfully zips a 25-yard pass to his sophomore receiver, Nelson Agholor, for a first down. Following another 9-yard blast by Redd, the men of Greek mythology line up for second down on the 22-yard-line.

Unfortunately for the visiting warriors, Kessler throws two incomplete passes in the direction of Marquis Lee, his junior wide receiver from Inglewood, California. Their recently-christened head coach sends in his kicking team for a 40-yard field-goal-attempt. Orgeron immediately regrets this decision as he and 80,000-plus fans watch the ball sail wide-right of the goalpost.

Disappointingly for the local fans, the Domers squander this impressive defensive stand by gaining only 4 yards on the ensuing drive. Junior kicker Kyle Brindza sends the ball almost 50 yards downfield into the waiting arms of Agholor. No. 15 in white and yellow darts past the over-shooting coverage team and scampers 48 yards to just past the original line of scrimmage. Even more discouraging for the Irish, a 5-yard illegal-formation penalty is added to this electrifying run-back.

With just under nine-and-a-half minutes remaining in the first half, the traveling Trojans open with an 11-yard pass by Kessler to Marqise Lee from 20-yards outside the Notre Dame goal. The Irish, who just last week gave up an astonishing 34 points to the unranked Sun Devils from Arizona State in this same venue, need to dig down deep to keep *this* Pac-12 team out of the end zone.

A 3-yard rush up the middle by Justin Davis is a concerning start to this goal-to-go series. An incomplete pass, an offsides penalty, and a stifling tackle behind the line force Orgeron to once again send out his field goal team. This time, Andre Heidari sends the ball through the uprights to put his team ahead by 3. Even so, the home team fans send an appreciative cheer to their defense.

The faithful have something to really cheer about on the opening play of the next series. Receiving the shotgun snap after George Atkinson III returned the kickoff to the 31-yard-line, their seasoned quarterback from Lake Forest, Illinois lofts a perfectly thrown pass along the Irish sideline into the outstretched arms of tight end, Niklas, to the USC 39-yard-line. The promising drive stalls however and the home team is forced to punt. The ball fortuitously travels out-of-bounds at the 5.

After seven plays for positive yards, USC fails to convert a third down at midfield. With 2:42 left in the second quarter and a fair-catch on the ensuing punt, Notre Dame starts its next possession deep in their own territory.

Backed against his goal line, Rees opens the drive with another perfect strike to Niklas for 9 yards. Just as impressively, on second down his offensive line bursts a hole for McDaniel to ramble 24 yards. Following a pass-interference call, Rees again hands the ball to his running back; he makes a nifty stutter-step past blitzing cornerback Su'a Cravens off the left side. The junior ball carrier from Coppell, Texas streaks to the 11-yard-line.

With the stadium is on its feet, Rees steps back in the pocket. Just as the blitzing linebacker lunges into his face, the composed quarterback lobs an arc off his back foot into the northwest corner. His wide receiver – who is being mauled by 6'3" 220-pound linebacker Levi Jones – somehow snatches the ball out of the sky and falls at the feet of the Irish cheerleaders.

TJ Jones, who is all of 5'11" 190-pounds, jumps into the arms of his teammates as their Leprechaun mascot, in a bright pink Breast Cancer Awareness vest, launches into the celebration in the dark corner of the frenzied stadium.

The ensuing extra-point puts the Irish ahead 14-to-10 with

only a minute left in the half. The famed Notre Dame fight song is awoken and echoes across the historic stadium.

After a holding penalty on the kickoff, the Trojans are unable to mount any semblance of a drive. Following a punt, and two meaningless plays by the Irish, both teams head to the lone tunnel, the Notre Dame cheerleaders, in their short navy blue dresses with bright pink hair ribbons, wildly saluting their team as the shiny gold helmets disappear into the dark passageway.

A strange thing happens in the final two quarters. Just when it seems one team is about to burst the game wide open, the unexpectedly stingy defenses slam momentum shut.

USC's true freshman running back, Justin Davis, opens the third quarter with a 7-yard catch, followed by a 9-yard rush up the middle. On the Trojan's third play, another true freshman on the other side of the line also makes a name for himself. Outside linebacker Jaylon Smith steps in front of an errant throw by Kessler and intercepts the ball at the 40-yard-line. This hurried pass, which literally fell into the bright pink sleeves of Smith, sets the tone for the ensuing drives to come.

With this sudden turnover, favorable field position, and a 4-point lead, the Irish appear poised to unleash a charge at the start of this third quarter. Instead, after five quick plays, they're forced to punt. This is followed by a 3-play drive that nets 1 yard and a punt back to Notre Dame. Next, come three plays and a punt to the visiting team. After two incomplete passes and a false start, USC punts. A holding penalty and three plays for 9 yards force another punt back to the Trojans. Following three plays for 5 yards, USC punts again. Notre Dame gains 6 yards on the next three downs and punts back to the visitors.

This time, however, Agholor returns the kick 34 yards to just 33 yards outside the Golden Domers' goal line. The Trojans waste no time gaining 8 yards in three plays . . . and then losing 10 on a holding call! The third quarter mercifully comes to an end on this penalty.

No one in the dark stands surrounding us is dancing a jig after this unexpected stalemate of a third quarter. We see even more consternation on their faces as the punt following this stunted drive by USC – the eighth consecutive punt of this half – is downed on the 5-yard-line at the far end.

The Irish manage to move to their 21-yard-line on three plays. Alarmingly, on third down and 6, second-string quarterback Andrew Hendrix (who entered the game on his team's second possession of this half after Rees was unceremoniously knocked out of the game with a neck injury) fumbles as the pocket collapses. Fortunately for the Irish and their flock in the stands, the 6'2" 220-pound senior falls on the ball at his own 14-yard-line. Once again, however, they're forced to punt.

Agholor calls for a fair-catch of this ninth consecutive kick just inside the 50-yard-line. On first down, Silas Redd bursts ahead for 14 yards, only to have his team move 10 yards backward due to *another* holding penalty. Three plays later and only 28 yards away from the end zone, the Trojans face fourth down and 5.

With 9:25 left in the game, Orgeron once again opts to send his field goal team onto the field. Kessler kneels on the right hash mark to place the pigskin for his field goal kicker. Andre Heidari again sends the ball into the dark sky. The crowd erupts as it again sails to the right of the tunnel entrance. The score remains 14-to-10 in favor of the home team.

Taking over on the 28, Notre Dame attempts to chew time off the clock. After four consecutive runs and an incomplete pass by Hendrix, disaster strikes. On third down from their 41-yard-line, Hayes Pullard shoots the gap and stuffs Cam McDaniel in the backfield. The jarring tackle by the senior linebacker from Inglewood, California knocks the ball out of the running back's hands. Pullard's fellow linebacker, Su'a Cravens, recovers the loose ball just 34 yards from the goal line.

Six plays and 3 minutes of game time later, Southern California unfathomably squanders this fortuitous field position with two incomplete passes, another holding penalty, and a false-start on fourth and goal from the 15-yard-line. The parsimonious Irish defense forces a turnover-on-downs on the seventh play of this bungled drive.

With 2:42 left in this unruly contest between these illustrious programs, Notre Dame is only able to gain 9 yards in three rushing plays. They do, however, force their opposition to use their final two time-outs. Brian Kelly sends his punt team onto the field. Nelson Agholor catches the ball and falls forward to his 23-yard-line with only a minute-and-a-half remaining in this heavyweight slugfest.

As Cody Kessler awaits the shotgun snap on first down, the entire stadium is on its feet yelling a guttural "OHHH" into the chilly night air. Their howling abruptly changes to groans as the undaunted quarterback sends a 32-yard strike across midfield to Agholor. No. 6 in white immediately follows this portentous pass with another to his speedy sophomore wide receiver, who races out-of-bounds at the 36-yard-line with 1:05 on the game clock. Following an incomplete pass and (another!) false-start penalty on tight end Jalen Cope-Fitzpatrick, the defense that Kelly built lines up for USC's third down and 8 with only 57 seconds remaining.

From deep in the pocket, Kessler fires a perfect pass over the middle into the upstretched arms of Cope-Fitzpatrick. A jarring hit from Joe Schmidt, the former walk-on linebacker from Mater Dei High School in Southern California, knocks the ball to the turf. Fourth down.

The Irish faithful surrounding us frantically scream across the dark arena as the Spoiled Children line up in shotgun formation just 36 yards from the scoring zone.

On our endeavors across this great country, one thing we know for certain is winning *matters*.

It matters to the young alumnus in the dark blue sweatshirt tugging on my shoulder. It matters to the spirited student-section across the damp field from us. It matters to the members of the home team's marching band crammed in the far corner. It matters to a former combat soldier who never had any intention of attending the game who is watching these final 50 seconds from a converted school bus across campus. It matters to a wonderful host, his wonderful wife, and a wonderful guide who welcomed us as one of their own at a tailgate party that will forever live in our memories. It matters to all the living players from the past, regardless of the sport, from both these elite institutions of higher learning. It matters to anyone who admires the efforts and talents of young athletes and their coaches who strive to be their best.

And it's not just *winning* that matters. It's *how* you win. And *why* you win.

Tonight's grudge match has featured an amazing exhibition of speed, art, and violence. Seemingly gravity-defying leaps. Graceful cuts. Bone-jarring collisions. And dogged determination. It has also seen evenly matched squads play with respect for their adversary. The individuals on the field have pulled together to vanquish a storied rival. They've also pulled each other up off the turf after every play. And not just players wearing the same colors. It's truly evident to us *how you win* has been dutifully instilled into these young athletes.

Why you win has also been vividly displayed. To quote a favorite author of ours, "The creative man is driven by the desire to achieve; not to beat others." This spirit expressed by Ayn Rand can be seen in every player this evening. While they desperately want to win, they're also striving to be the best they can at their position. And in life.

When people say that the score doesn't matter, look into the eyes of each player setting their cleats for this most critical down of this hard-fought contest. Competition is the by-product of achievement. For without conquests, a team – and society – ceases to move forward. And, as the ball is snapped, achievement is what these players desire most.

With a roar that seems to suck the oxygen out of this jam-packed arena, Kessler drops back in the pocket at exactly midfield. Notre Dame's front four, led by senior defensive end Prince Shembo converge on the quarterback as he lets the ball fly toward wide receiver Agholor. The poorly timed pass sails over the head of No. 15 in white and into the black stillness of the night.

The small glowing numbers at the south end show first down for the home team.

With a jolt, both Valerie and I are raucously hugged around

the shoulders by several screaming fans behind us. The Fighting Irish proceed to run two perfectly executed "victory formations" as "Victory March" resounds across the fabled stadium. The final seconds drain from the small yet proud scoreboard that reads: IRISH 14 – USC 10.

It's just past midnight inside O'Rourke's Public House.

This bustling eatery, which claims to be "an authentic Irish Pub for football fans," is only several hundred yards from the south end of the "House that Rockne Built." And just down the street from Brothers Bar & Grill. It also claims to have Indiana's largest selection of Irish whiskey.

A steady parade of joyful fans tumbles through the Kelly-green archway leading to the copper-domed bar. Valerie has somehow commandeered two leather stools alongside this mahogany serving station. Surrounded by old-timey Guinness Stout posters and Jameson mirrors, we're soon in a wonderful conversation with several wonderful local boosters.

Tonight's hard-fought triumph, as conveyed by our boisterous bar-mates, not only sets the tone for the remainder of the schedule; in a small way, it atones for last season. It also snaps a five-game home losing streak to USC.

The green-clad alumnus next to Valerie bursts with laughter and buys another round of celebration for us all. It appears the sentiments expressed by Lou Holtz at yesterday's pep rally weren't just platitudes.

With frosty dark beverages in hand, Valerie and I reflect upon our amazing weekend. We also pause in reverence to our amazing pursuit of collegiate competition, ridiculous traditions, heartfelt passion, and true companionship. Every season, more than 140,000 plays are executed during the more than 800 games played in the Football Bowl Subdivision, and hundreds of thousands more in the collegiate levels below.

And every one of these plays involves an immeasurable number of hours behind them. Hours in practice drills. Hours in weight rooms. Hours in ice tanks. Hours in film sessions. Hours in team meetings. And every summer, as the days get a little shorter,

354 • THIS YEAR'S GAME

the two of us – and our nation – turn our attention to the season ahead, and to this year's game.

We have seen some of the greatest rivalries in the history of the sport on our quest. More importantly, we've been a part of the rich revelry surrounding each of these contests.

We have also met some of the most passionate, most accommodating, and most unusual characters along the way. Broadcasting personalities, Heisman trophy winners, bright-faced students, and mascots in all shapes and sizes. A four-star general. The families of All-Americans. Cheerleaders. Band-leaders. Song-leaders. Fan-leaders. A Big Dawg named Mike. A Malinois named Kevin. An elk named Elvis. A National League MVP. Hollywood stars. Old friends. New friends. And even the President of the United States.

This weekend, on our fourteenth excursion, our faith in the American spirit has been reaffirmed. Not the kind of blind faith associated with acceptance in the absence of evidence. Rather, genuine confidence based upon our confirmation over these years that Americans truly *are* wonderful in their ability to welcome outsiders into their communities, their customs, and their companionships. Not to mention their championships.

It's an ineluctable fact that college football is woven into the fabric of our country. The young men who wear colorful uniforms across every 100-yard field every season do so because of their love of the game. Love of camaraderie. Love of a sense of accomplishment. Love of themselves.

And all of them are heroes in their own way. Heroes to their family. Heroes to their teammates. Heroes to their alma mater. Heroes to their community. Heroes to our way of life in this great nation.

And some continue their heroism beyond the gridiron to real fields of battle.

Sitting in this charmingly teeming bar, I look into my bride's beaming face and raise a toast from a cherished Longfellow poem to each and every one of the heroes we have cheered for, cheered against, and reveled with over this past decade and a half:

"In the world's broad field of battle, in the bivouac of life, be not like dumb driven cattle, be a hero in the strife!"

To heroes! And to *this year's game.*

EPILOGUE

RIVALRIES WE'VE ATTENDED SINCE PUBLICATION

	Year	Game	Location
1.	2014	Mississippi State	Mississippi	Oxford, MS
2.	2015	Washington State	Washington	Seattle, WA
3.	2016	Clemson	Alabama (National Championship)	Glendale, AZ
4.	2017	Oregon	Washington	Seattle, WA
5.	2018	Georgia	Louisiana State	Baton Rouge, LA

RIVALRIES WE WISH WOULD RETURN

1. University of Texas | Texas A&M University
2. University of Missouri | University of Kansas
3. West Virginia University | University of Pittsburgh
4. University of Nebraska | University of Oklahoma
5. Boise State University | University of Idaho

LIVE MASCOTS & PERFORMING ANIMALS ON OUR QUEST (In order)

1.	*Bevo XIII*	University of Texas
2.	*Little White Ponies*	University of Oklahoma
3.	*Kevin*	Federal Employee
4.	*Traveler & Trouper*	U.S. Military Academy at West Point
5.	*Bill XXXI*	United States Naval Academy
6.	*Smokey XIII*	University of Tennessee
7.	*Challenger*	The Fiesta Bowl
8.	*Little White Ponies*	University of Oklahoma

9. *Uga VII*   University of Georgia
10. *Miss Rev (Reveille VII)*   Texas A&M University
11. *Parsons Mounted   Texas A&M University
    Cavalry*
12. *Bevo XIV*   University of Texas
13. *Handsome Dan XVII*   Yale University
14. *Military Working Dog*   United States Marine Corps
15. *Aurora*   United States Air Force Academy

FBS TEAM NAMES THAT DO NOT END IN 'S'

1. Cardinal   Stanford University
2. Crimson Tide   University of Alabama
3. Fighting Illini   University of Illinois
4. Fighting Irish   University of Notre Dame
5. Golden Hurricane   Tulsa University
6. Green Wave   Tulane University
7. Mean Green (Eagles)   University of North Texas
8. Midshipmen   United States Naval Academy
9. Minutemen   University of Massachusetts
10. The Orange   Syracuse University
11. Thundering Herd   Marshall University
12. Wolfpack   North Carolina State University
13. Wolfpack   University of Nevada, Reno

As prognosticated by Mel Kiper, Jr. . . . .
Matthew Stafford was the No. 1 pick in the 2009 NFL Draft. Write
that down.

ACKNOWLEDGMENTS

In addition to a work of love, *This Year's Game* is the culmination of many hours of outstanding work by many others. It wouldn't be in your hands if not for the amazing contributions from the dedicated professionals, family members, and friends recognized here.

Nancy Rommelmann, our editor and author of *To The Bridge*, for your ability to seamlessly weave our storyline into a compelling quest. Kimberly Colleen Willis (who goes by "Kacie") for your herculean accomplishment of editing our first (very rough!) draft. Our readers – friends who asked to simply be a part of a well-crafted tale – Boyd Pearson, Brett Walker, Frank Segale, Gary Spodnick, Jerry Wiant, Robert Wallace, Triston Dallas, and Zach Enlow. Your invaluable insight has made our book what it is today. Additional appreciation goes to Jerry Wiant for your superb contribution to the cover design and layout. Finally, thanks to Mary Sweigert for your astute proofreading of our completed story.

Many other experts and acquaintances also offered smart advice. Each of you has our sincere appreciation, as well.

Perhaps most notably, we extend a warm thanks to the wonderful fans mentioned (and not mentioned) in *This Year's Game* for welcoming us into your community, your traditions, and your stadiums. You are why there is no greater pastime in our great country than college football.

With heartfelt sincerity, I also wish to acknowledge my lovely bride. For without the unwavering support of Valerie McMahon, this book would still be nothing more than a dream. No other person has had a greater impact upon seeing it to completion . . . or upon who I am today.

NOTES

All Pages   All game statistics and scores, player backgrounds and statistics, team information and rankings (not cited in these Notes) are from major college football websites, respective university webpages, and other authoritative online sources; and, are as of the date of each rivalry in each chapter.

CHAPTER ONE   A CHILLING START TO A WONDERFUL QUEST
                         Texas | Oklahoma

Page

1   *"More than 75,000 adrenaline-fueled fans, . . ."* Linkowski, Jeff, *Oklahoma 63 – Texas 14*, SoonerStats.com, Sooner Stats, http://soonerstats.com/football/games/recap.cfm?GameID=1025

1   *"enormous waving cowboy known as "Big Tex," . . ."* State Fair of Texas, *Who is Big Tex*, 2006, BigTex.com, Official Site of the State Fair of Texas, http://www.yesterdayusa.com/BigTex_com%20Newsroom.htm

2   *"On a chilly night (for Southern California), . . ."* Zant, John, *Randall Cunningham's Don Pride Never Dies*, January 25, 2017, Independent.com, Santa Barbara Independent, Inc., https://www.independent.com/news/2017/jan/25/randall-cunninghams-don-pride-never-dies/

4   *"Way back in 1889, President Benjamin Harrison . . ."* Blochowiak, Mary Ann, *Sooners*, 2006, www.okhistory.org, Oklahoma Historical Society, https://www.okhistory.org/publications/enc/entry.php?entry=SO010

4   *"This "sooner clause" decreed that individuals . . ."* Blochowiak, Mary Ann, *Sooners*, 2006

4   *"Ever since their inaugural scrimmage in 1900, . . ."* Schnell, Lindsay, *A carnival on steroids: Oral history of the one-of-a-kind Red River Rivalry between Texas and Oklahoma*, October 06, 2016, Sports Illustrated, Time Inc, https://www.si.com/college-football/2016/10/06/red-river-rivalry-oral-history-texas-vs-oklahoma

4   *"seven years before Oklahoma joined the United States, . . ."* History.com, *Oklahoma*, November 9, 2009, A&E Television Networks, A&E Television Networks, LLC., https://www.history.com/topics/us-states/oklahoma

4   *"squad from Oklahoma, known then as the Rough Riders, . . ."* Schwartz, Evan S., *Team traditions: The story behind OU's Boomer Sooner nickname,*

October 13, 2014, Sports Illustrated, Time, Inc., https://www.si.com/college-football/2014/10/13/university-oklahoma-boomer-sooner

4   "*Rough Riders, traveled 500 miles by train . . .*" Dozier, Ray, *The Oklahoma Football Encyclopedia: 2nd Edition*, October 1, 2013, Skyhorse Publishing, Inc., p. 6

4   "*Arriving on the morning of the contest, the fledgling team. . .*" Hearst Chronical, *The 100-year football war: Texas-OU by the game*, October 7, 2005, HearstChronical.com, Hearst Chronical Archives, https://www.chron.com/sports/college-football/article/The-100-year-football-war-Texas-OU-by-the-game-1927889.php

5   "*Fittingly, the Austin American-Statesman referred to it . . .*" Austin American-Statesman, *Texas 28, Oklahoma 2*. 1900, Austin American-Statesman, Austin, Texas, https://wikivividly.com/wiki/Red_River_Showdown

6   "*Starting with the first game between these rivals . . .*" Hearst Chronical, *The 100-year football war: Texas-OU by the game*, October 7, 2005

6   "*officially changing it to the Red River Rivalry.*" Moriarty, Morgan, *Most people refer to Texas-Oklahoma as the Red River Rivalry, but Shootout is still popular, too*, October 14, 2017, SBNation, Vox Media, Inc., https://www.sbnation.com/college-football/2017/10/14/16467546/texas-oklahoma-name-red-river-rivalry-shootout

8   "*Constructed in 1937 at a cost of $328,000, . . .*" Everything2, *Cotton Bowl*, 2016, Everything2.com, Everything2 Media, LLC., https://www.everything2.com/title/Cotton+Bowl

8   "*its initial 46,000 capacity was increased . . .*" Maxwell, Lisa C., *Cotton Bowl*, June 12, 2010, TSHAonline.org, Texas State Historical Association, https://tshaonline.org/handbook/online/articles/xxc01

8   "*resulting in its current 75,000 seats.*" Maxwell, Lisa C., *Cotton Bowl*, June 12, 2010

8   "*Prior to the early 1990s, this annual contest . . .*" Horns 247, September 29, 2010, 247Sports.com, CBS Interactive, https://247sports.com/college/texas/Board/21/Contents/The-Tunnel-Texas-vs-OU-Pregame-Walk-1090999/

10   *"Coming into this 2000 season, the University of Oklahoma . . ."* Benke,
        Arthur, *2000 Football Season*, 2006, SoonerStats.com, Sooner Stats,
        http://soonerstats.com/football/seasons/schedule.cfm?SeasonID=2000

13   *"Charging through a hole wide enough for the 1,800-pound . . ."* Ebert,
        Wescott, *Five facts Texas fans need to know about Bevo XV*, September 4,
        2016, SBNation, Vox Media, Inc.,
        https://www.burntorangenation.com/2016/9/4/12795222/bevo-xv-
        facts-texas-longhorns-reveal-sunrise-spur

14   *"The normally triumphant blast from "Smokey the Cannon" . . ."* The
        University of Texas, *Smokey The Cannon*, October 22, 2004, UTexas.edu,
        The University of Texas at Austin,
        https://web.archive.org/web/20041022191012/http://www
        .utexas.edu/friends/fun.php?which=2

16   PHOTO: Cotton Bowl Stadium, Dallas, Texas, October 7, 2000, Left to
        right – Valerie McMahon, Sean McMahon, James Kruger, girlfriend of
        James Kruger

16   *"They have a right to be jubilant: today's 49-point massacre . . ."* Linkowski,
        Jeff, *Oklahoma 63 – Texas 14*, 2016, SoonerStats.com, Sooner Stats,
        http://soonerstats.com/football/games/recap.cfm?GameID=1025

19   *""Oh, I used to be disgusted, now I try to be amused," she says."* Costello,
        Elvis, *(The Angels Wanna Wear My) Red Shoes*, 2016, Universal Music
        Publishing Group, STANDS4 LLC,
        https://www.lyrics.com/lyric/27076436/Elvis+Costello/%28The+Ang
        els+Wanna+Wear+My%29+Red+Shoes

CHAPTER TWO   LIFE, LIBERTY, AND PURSUIT
                       Our Annual Quest

Page
20   *"The famed library tower reaches more than 300 feet into the sky."* University
        of Texas at Austin, *History of the UT Tower*, 2017, UTexas.edu, Official
        Site of The University of Texas at Austin,
        https://tower.utexas.edu/history/

20   *"Big Bertha, named after a massive World War I . . ."* Dural, Kevin, *UT-
        Austin's 'Big Bertha' drum literally has a radiant past*, April 12, 2018, Daily-
        TexanOnline.com, The Daily Texan,
        http://www.dailytexanonline.com/2018/04/12/ut-
        austin%E2%80%99s-%E2%80%98big-bertha%E2%80%99-drum-
        literally-has-a-radiant-past

21   *"The 15-to-15 contest remains one of only five ties . . ."* Linkowski, Jeff, *Oklahoma 15 – Texas 15*, 2018, SoonerStats.com, SoonerStats, http://soonerstats.com/football/games/recap.cfm?GameID=839

21   *"Barry Switzer, in his twelfth year as head coach, . . ."* Schurburtt, JC, *Barry Switzer still has the red ass over '84 Texas-OU Game*, October 8, 2014, 247Sports.com, CBS Interactive, https://247sports.com/Bolt/Barry-Switzer-still-has-the-red-ass-over-84-Texas-OU-Game-31853208/

23   PHOTO: 1980 Oklahoma State Football Media Press Guide, CFBmg12, P&R publications

24   *"that our dummy-O quarterback Rusty Hilger . . ."* SRCFB, *Rusty Hilger*, 2002, Sports-Reference.com, Sports Reference LLC, https://www.sports-reference.com/cfb/players/rusty-hilger-1.html

25   *"In her first couple months, the Ducks surprisingly . . ."* Martini, Pete, *Oregon Ducks: From 1917 to 2016, a complete bowl game history,* December 12, 2017, StatesmanJournal.com, Statesman Journal, https://www.statesmanjournal.com/story/spo rts/college/univ-oregon/2017/12/12/oregon-ducks-bowl-game-history/918427001/

25   *"Sitting in the luxurious sunshine with more than 102,000 . . ."* Gorman, Kevin, *Nittany Lions prove worth at 1995 Rose Bowl*, October 29, 2001, The Digital Collegian, Collegian Inc., https://web.archive.org/web/20011112115146/http://www.collegian.psu.edu/archive/2001/10/10-29-01cm/10-29-01dsports-11.asp

25   *"Due in part to this dominating performance, Carter . . ."* Pro Football Hall of Fame, *Draft History, 1995 National Football League Draft*, 2017, ProFootballHoF.com, Pro Football Hall of Fame, www.profootballhof.com/news/1995-national-football-league-draft/

25   *"In 1869, the Scarlet Knights of Rutgers College . . ."* Richmond, Sam, *College football history: Remembering the first game ever played in 1869*, November 6, 2017, Turner Sports Network, Turner Sports Interactive, Inc., https://www.ncaa.com/news/football/article/2017-11-06/college-football-history-heres-when-1st-game-was-played

CHAPTER THREE   SCHWARZKOPF ROCKS
                       Army | Navy

Page

29   *"Josh Heupel atoned for his second-place finish . . ."* SRCFB, *2000 Heisman Winner*, 2016, Sports-Reference.com, Sports Reference LLC, https://www.sports-reference.com/cfb/awards/heisman-2000.html

30   *"The United States Naval Academy first fielded a football team . . ."* Ruzicka, Joe, *The Brutal History Of The Army–Navy Football Game*, September 15, 2015, TaskAndPurpose.com, Lafayette Media Group, LLC, https://taskandpurpose.com/the-brutal-history-of-the-army-navy-football-game/

30   *"A year later, Army Cadet Dennis Mahan Michie . . ."* McLeroy, Carrie, *The Army-Navy game: 13 historical facts you probably don't know*, December 6, 2016, Army.mil, U.S. Army, www.army.mil/article/179134/the_army_navy_game_13_historical_facts_you_probably_dont_know

30   *"More than 270 Army cadets ponied up the exorbitant sum . . ."* McLeroy, Carrie, December 6, 2016

30   *"Seizing the moment, the officers-in-training . . ."* Wick, Joshua L., *Army-Navy Game: A Proud History of Tradition*, December 12, 2014, NavyLive.DoDLive.mil, Navy Office of Information, http://navylive.dodlive.mil/2014/12/12/army-navy-game-a-proud-history-of-tradition/

30   *"And ever since 1953, Army cadets attempt to clandestinely . . ."* Bogage, Jacob, *To prevent goat-napping, Navy ups security around mascots to protect against Army bandits*, December 8, 2018, WashingtonPost.com, The Washington Post, www.washingtonpost.com/sports/2018/12/08/prevent-kidnapping-navy-ups-security-around-goat-mascots-ahead-army-game/

30   *"Cadet Michie had to assume the roles of coach, field captain, . . ."* Crane, Dr. Conrad, *The First Army-Navy Game*, November 27, 2009, U. S. Army Military History Institute, www.army.mil/article/31068/the_first_army_navy_game

31   *"The first-ever crowd, approximately 500 fellow soldiers . . ."* Siggurdsson, *First Army-Navy Football Game Played; Navy Wins, 24-0*, November 30, 2011, The American Legion, www.burnpit.us/2011/11/first-army-navy-football-game-played-navy-wins-24-0

31   *"Cadet Kirby Walker was knocked out four times, . . ."* Siggurdsson, November 30, 2011

31   *"A spectacular touchdown run by Cadet Michie . . ."* Siggurdsson, November 30, 2011

34   *"Two rows down from us is Glen Davis, . . ."* Fimrite, Ron, *Mr. Inside & Mr.*

Outside, November 21, 1988, Sports Illustrated, Times, Inc., www.si.com/vault/1988/11/21/106779717/mr-inside—mr-outside

34   *"The other half of this unstoppable backfield, Felix "Doc" . . . "* Fimrite, Ron, *Mr. Inside & Mr. Outside*, November 21, 1988

34   *"That 1946 Heisman-winning season for Davis . . ."* Fimrite, Ron, *Mr. Inside & Mr. Outside*, November 21, 1988

34   *"Army gave up a total of only 46 points . . ."* SRCFB, *1945 Army Black Knights Schedule and Results*, 2016, Sports-Reference.com, Sports Reference LLC, https://www.sports-reference.com/cfb/schools/army/1945-schedule.html

35   *"This year's pair, Traveler and Trooper, . . ."* Army Sports Properties, *Traditions: Army Mules*, 2012, CBS Sports Interactive, https://web.archive.org/web/20120207000048/http://www.goarmysports.com/trads/army-mules.html

35   *"In 1899, an officer stationed at the Philadelphia . . ."* Army Sports Properties, 2012, CBS Sports Interactive

35   *"Since 1936, seventeen representatives . . ."* Army Sports Properties, 2012, CBS Sports Interactive

25   *"All have been male except Buckshot, who in 1964, . . ."* Army Sports Properties, 2012, CBS Sports Interactive

36   PHOTO: Veterans Stadium, Philadelphia, Pennsylvania, December 1, 2001, Holding sign: Sean McMahon

37   *"Gliding into the vast opening of Veterans Stadium . . ."* Gray, Amanda, *Elite Frogs fly over Lake Wawasee, raise money for SEALs*, Aug 26, 2012, GoshenNews.com, Goshen News, https://www.goshennews.com/news/elite-frogs-fly-over-lake-wawasee-raise-money-for-seals/article_a68c707b-e4a8-51cc-a92d-b38316726b50.html

37   *"Each has more than five years of jumps . . ."* Olson, N.H., USN, Retired, *The Leap Frogs-Origins of the Navy SEAL Parachuting Exhibition Team*, 2017, National Navy UDT-SEAL Museum, www.navysealmuseum.org/about-navy-seals/seal-history-the-naval-special-warfare-storyseal-history-the-naval-special-warfare-story/leap-frogs-origins-navy-seal-parachuting-exhibition-team

38   *"the almost 70,000 fans in Veterans Stadium . . ."* Klingaman, Mike, *America watched Army's last win over Navy, just months after 9/11*, December 9, 2011, BaltimoreSum.com, The Baltimore Sun, https://www.baltimoresun.com/sports/college/football/bs-sp-army-navy-1210-20111209-story.html

40   PHOTO: Veterans Stadium, Philadelphia, Pennsylvania, December 1, 2001, Descending stairs: General Norman Schwarzkopf

41   *"General Norman Schwarzkopf, the commander . . ."* Fadden, Robert D., *Gen. H. Norman Schwarzkopf, U.S. Commander in Gulf War, Dies at 78*, December 27, 2012, https://www.nytimes.com/2012/12/28/us/gen-h-norman-schwarzkopf-us-commander-in-gulf-war-dies-at-78.html?

41   *"With the world watching, Stormin' Norman . . ."* Fadden, Robert D., *Gen. H. Norman Schwarzkopf, U.S. Commander in Gulf War, Dies at 78*, December 27, 2012

41   *"The "football" he's referring to is the nuclear football . . ."* Gulley, Bill; Reese, Mary E., *Breaking Cover*, August 11, 1980, Simon & Schuster, New York, NY, p. 39

42   *"The contents of this ominous "football" include a black . . ."* Gulley, Bill; Reese, Mary E., *Breaking Cover*, August 11, 1980, p. 39

42   *""Twinkle" (her Secret Service code name) . . ."* Huppke, Rex W., *Renegade' joins 'Twinkle,' 'Rawhide,' 'Lancer' on list of Secret Service code names*, November 10, Chicago Tribune, www.chicagotribune.com/news/chi-secret-service-code-names-obama-story.html

42   *"mother's sorority Kappa Alpha Theta in Austin . . ."* Biography, *Jenna Bush Biography*, April 2, 2014, Biography.com, A&E Television Networks, LLC. https://www.biography.com/people/jenna-bush-244190

42   *"Barbara, is clandestinely called Turquoise)."* Huppke, Rex W., November 10, Chicago Tribune

44   *"second-longest kickoff return in the 102-year history "* Feinstein, John, *The Rivalry: Mystery at the Army-Navy Game*, 2010, p. 264

44   *"Only a runback during the 1901 game by Army's . . ."* Feinstein, John, *The Rivalry: Mystery at the Army-Navy Game*, 2010, p. 264

46   *"today's Army-Navy game was the most-watched game . . ."* National September 11 Memorial & Museum, *A Look Back at the Army-Navy*

Football Game Following 9/11, December 6, 2018, 911memorial.org, National September 11 Memorial & Museum, https://www.911memorial.org/blog/look-back-army-navy-football-game-following-911

47   *"The following morning, the Baltimore Sun . . ."* Klingaman, Mike, *America watched Army's last win over Navy, just months after 9/11*, Dec. 9, 2011

CHAPTER FOUR   SWAMPED IN KNOXVILLE
                                 Florida | Tennessee

Page

48   *"The Art of War identifies five factors . . ."* Griffith, Samuel B., *Sun Tzu The Art of War*, 1963, Oxford University Press, London, England, p. 40

48   *"In 1950, The Ohio State Buckeyes hosted . . ."* Sauer, Patrick, *The Coldest College Football Game Ever*, November 27, 2015, Sports.Vice.com, Vice Sports, https://sports.vice.com/en_us/article/z4ab45/the-coldest-college-football-game-ever

48   *"The thermometer peaked at 10 degrees . . ."* Sauer, Patrick, *The Coldest College Football Game Ever*, November 27, 2015

48   *"With a kickoff temperature of 5 degrees . . ."* Speltz, Bill, *Coldcocked – Coastal Carolina knocks out Montana*, December 7, 2013, Missoulian, https://missoulian.com/sports/college/montana/football/coastal-carolina-knocks-out-montana/article_fd32c1e2-5f69-11e3-97ea-001a4bcf887a.html

49   *"According to school records, attendance was . . ."* SoonerStats, *1985 Football Season*, 2016, SoonerStats.com, Sooner Stats, http://www.soonerstats.com/football/seasons/schedule.cfm?seasonid=1985

51   *"The University of Tennessee was established . . ."* University of Tennessee, *Our History*, 2012, UTK.edu, Official Site of the University of Tennessee Knoxville, https://web.archive.org/web/20121201051930/http://www.utk.edu/aboutut/history/

51   *"Appropriately, the new learning institution drew upon . . ."* State Symbols USA, *The Volunteer State*, 2017, StateSymbosUSA.org, State Symbols USA, https://statesymbolsusa.org/symbol-official-item/tennessee/state-nickname/volunteer-state

51   *"It's said The Volunteer State moniker originated . . ."* 50States.com,

Tennessee, 2017, 50States.com, Digital Properties, LLC, https://www.50states.com/bio/nickname5.htm

51   *"Knoxville formed its first varsity football team in 1891."* Neely, Jake, *The Birth of Tennessee Football*, September 3, 2015, Knoxville Mercury, The Knoxville History Project, http://www.knoxmercury.com/2015/09/03/the-birth-of-tennessee-football/

51   *"Unfortunately, the Volunteers' maiden scrimmage . . ."* Neely, Jake, *The Birth of Tennessee Football*, September 3, 2015

51   *"This now pre-kindergarten through grade-12 school . . ."* Tennessee School for the Deaf, *The Birth of Tennessee Football*, September 3, 2015, TSDeaf.org, Tennessee School for the Deaf, https://www.tsdeaf.org/

51   *"In the second game of that season, fans witnessed . . ."* Rucker, Wes, *Tennessee's biggest blowout wins in history,* September 3, 2015, Knoxville News Sentinel, https://247sports.com/college/tennessee/LongForm-Article/Tennessee-Vols-footballs-biggest-blowout-wins-in-history-121831087/#121831087_1

52   *"Established during the 1890s in a rural valley . . ."* Batesel, Paul, *America's Lost Colleges – Profiles of 270 closed or merged colleges*, 2017, *American Temperance University*, LostColleges.com, www.lostcolleges.com/american-temperance-university

52   *"In the storied history of the sport, only 40 teams . . ."* Neely, Jake, *College football championship history*, December 8, 2018, Turner Sports Interactive, Inc., NCAA.com, https://www.ncaa.com/news/football/article/college-football-national-championship-history

52   *"In 1967 – the final year that the National Championship . . ."* National Collegiate Athletic Association (NCAA), *National Poll Champions*, 2011, NCAA.org, NCAA Division I Football Records, p. 74., http://fs.ncaa.org/Docs/stats/football_records/2011/FBS.pdf

52   *"In 1889, the president of the university's athletic association . . ."* University of Tennessee, *Tennessee Traditions*, 2016, University of Tennessee Athletics, University of Tennessee, https://utsports.com/sports/2017/6/14/history-traditions-html.aspx

52   *"Charles Moore is said to have selected these distinctive shades . . ."* University of Tennessee, *Tennessee Traditions*, 2016

53 *"Mack Brown, who restored prominence . . ."* National Football Foundation, Hall of Fame – *Mack Brown*, 2018, National Football Foundation & College Football Hall of Fame, Inc., https://footballfoundation.org/hof_search.aspx?hof=2431

53 *"In the 85 years since their first game in 1916, . . ."* Von Hagen, Blake, *Tennessee vs Florida: A historical breakdown*, September 17, 2018, utdailybeacon.com, University of Tennessee Daily Beacon, http://www.utdailybeacon.com/sports/tennessee-vs-florida-a-historical-breakdown/article_219ee278-bab8-11e8-b6d9-2309e1546061.html

53 *"approximately 100 miles east of Knoxville in Johnson City . . ."* Heisman Trophy, *Steve Spurrier 1996*, 2016, Heisman.com, Heisman Trophy, https://www.heisman.com/heisman-winners/steve-spurrier/

54 *"In a certified Category 5 storm, . . ."* Bagnato, Andrew, *Florida 35, Tennessee 20*, September 22, 1996, ChicagoTribune.com, Chicago Tribune, https://www.chicagotribune.com/news/ct-xpm-1996-09-22-9609220281-story.html

54 *"His Gators scored more points against the Vols . . ."* Associated Press, *COLLEGE FOOTBALL : Tennessee Loses Game of Wuerffel Ball : SEC: No. 4 Florida, after trailing, 30-14, scores 48 points in a row against No. 8 Volunteers.*, September 17, 1995, LATimes.com, Los Angeles Times, http://articles.latimes.com/1995-09-17/sports/sp-46979_1_danny-wuerffel

54 *"Spurrier famously quipped during a booster dinner . . ."* Rapaport, Daniel, *Steve Spurrier's Best Insults, Ranked*, August 09, 2017, SI.com, Sports Illustrated, www.si.com/extra-mustard/2017/08/09/steve-spurrier-quotes-insults-best-lines-ranked

54 *""He wants to be a three-time Citrus Bowl MVP," he said."* Rapaport, Daniel, *Steve Spurrier's Best Insults, Ranked*, August 09, 2017

55 *"Named "Best Bar in America" by Playboy magazine . . ."* Mapicurious, *The Strip – University of Tennessee – Knoxville*, 2016, Mapicurious.com, Mapicurious http://mapicurious.com/maps/176

55 *"Built in 1921, Neyland Stadium is nestled . . ."* University of Tennessee, *Neyland Stadium*, 2017, University of Tennessee Athletics, University of Tennessee, https://utsports.com/facilities/?id=8#section-6

56 *"Dockage is on a first come, first serve basis."* VOL Navy Boaters

Association, *The official online harbor for VOL fans and boating enthUsiastTs*, 2016, VolNavyBoaters.com, VOL Navy Boaters Association, http://volnavyboaters.com/

56   *"the relocation site of the university in 1828."* University of Tennessee Athletics, *A "Salute" to Tradition*, November 7, 2012, UTSports.com, University of Tennessee, https://utsports.com/news/2012/11/2/A_Salute_to_Tradition.aspx

57   *"ESPN's GameDay first aired in 1987 . . ."* ESPN MediaZone, *ESPN College GameDay*, October 28, 2009, ESPNMediaZone.com, ESPN MediaZone, https://web.archive.org/web/20111030144644/http://www.espnmedi azone3.com/us/2009/10/28/corso_lee/

57   *"In 1993, the show was broadcast outside Notre Dame . . ."* Rocky Mountain News, *College GameDay study in marketing*, November 18, 2006, Bonham.com, The Bonham Group Sports & Entertainment Marketing, Newshttps://web.archive.org/web/20071011111126/http://www.bon ham.com/NewsDetails.aspx?NID=12

57   *"fifth time the countdown-to-kickoff TV show . . ."* University of Tennessee, *ESPN College Gameday on Rocky Top*, September 20, 2016, University of Tennessee Athletics, University of Tennessee, https://utsports.com/news/2016/9/20/ESPN_College_GameDay_on _Rocky_Top.aspx

57   *"the three horsemen of college football pregame . . ."* ESPN MediaZone, *Chris Fowler*, 2015, ESPNMediaZone.com, ESPN MediaZone, https://espnmediazone.com/us/bios/fowler_chris/

58   *"(First recorded in 1967 by the Osborne Brothers, . . ."* WBIR-TV, *Rocky Top: The history behind the song*, August 26, 2014, WBIR.com, WBIR-TV, https://www.wbir.com/article/life/music/rocky-top-the-history-behind-the-song/51-95130035

58   *"Neyland Stadium, the largest of all stadiums in the SEC . . ."* University of Tennessee, *Neyland Stadium*, 2017, University of Tennessee Athletics, University of Tennessee, https://utsports.com/facilities/?id=8#section-6

58   *"Fittingly, Neyland was also a brigadier general . . ."* Lester, Connie L., *Robert Reese Neyland*, October 8, 2017, TennesseeEncyclopedia.com, Tennessee Historical Society, https://tennesseeencyclopedia.net/entries/robert-reese-neyland/

59   *"The Seven Maxims of Football are the most well-known . . ."* University of Tennessee, *Neyland: 50 Facts on 50th Anniversary*, March 28, 2012, University of Tennessee Athletics, University of Tennessee, https://utsports.com/news/2012/3/28/Neyland_50_Facts_on_50th_Anniversary.aspx

60   *"(Florida's Athletic Director awkwardly acknowledged . . ."* Schlabach Mark, *Gators Fire Zook, Keep Spurrier in Mind*, October 26, 2004, p. D03, WashingtonPost.com, Washington Post, http://www.washingtonpost.com/wp-dyn/articles/A61014-2004Oct25.html

61   *"Earlier this week, the 6'1" 215-pound signal-caller. . ."* Dooley, Pat, *Grossman knew it, then proved it at UT*, September 22, 2002, Gainesville.com, The Gainesville Sun, https://www.gainesville.com/sports/20020922/grossman-knew-it-then-proved-it-at-ut

64   *"Marveling at the 1-in-108,722 odds . . ."* Associated Press, *Gators give Zook needed big-game victory*, September 22, 2002, ESPN.com, ESPN, http://www.espn.com/college-football/recap?gameId=222642633

64   *"The first Rex Grossman was an outstanding college quarterback . . ."* Newell, Nat, *Where are the Mr. Football now?*, February 16, 2015, IndyStar.com, USA Today Network, https://www.indystar.com/story/sports/high-school/2015/02/16/from-the-archives-where-are-the-mr-football-now/23504401/

64   *"He capped off his senior year by commanding the Panthers . . ."* Newell, Nat, *Where are the Mr. Football now?*, February 16, 2015

65   *"Following this state title, the third-generation Rex . . ."* Newell, Nat, *Where are the Mr. Football now?*, February 16, 2015

67   PHOTO: Neyland Stadium, Knoxville, Tennessee, September 21, 2002, Standing in stadium: Sean McMahon

68   *"17-point loss was the largest deficit at the jaws . . ."* Associated Press, *Gators give Zook needed big-game victory*, February 16, 2015, ESPN.com, ESPN, http://www.espn.com/college-football/recap?gameId=222642633

CHAPTER FIVE   WELCOME TO THE TERRORDOME
Miami (FL) | Virginia Tech

Page

69   *"It's been proven they can have up to a 20% . . ."* Moskowitz, Tobias J.;
Wertheim, L. Jon, *Scorecasting: The Hidden Influences Behind How Sports
Are Played and Games Are Won*, 2011, Random House, Inc., p. 65

69   *"co-authors Tobias J. Moskowitz and L. Jon Wertheim . . ."* Moskowitz,
Tobias J.; Wertheim, L. Jon, *Scorecasting: The Hidden Influences Behind
How Sports Are Played and Games Are Won*, p. 65

69   *"A study by Bleacher Report revealed, between 2001 . . ."* Spicer, Ben, *Home
Field Advantage and Sport: Does It Truly Exist?*, October 12, 2008, Bleacher
Report, Turner Broadcasting System, Inc.,
https://bleacherreport.com/articles/68147-home field-advantage-and-
sport-does-it-truly-exist

69   *"Sunshine Forecast Enterprises also discovered . . ."* Repole, Warren, *College
Football*, September 9, 2014, Repole.com, Sunshine Forecast Enterprises,
http://www.repole.com/sun4cast/data.html

70   *"Through 2003, the following teams in this top division . . ."* Howell, James,
Winning Percentage, 2016, James Howell's Database,
http://football.stassen.com/records/h-win-pct.html

70   *"Stewarded by former Oklahoma State offensive . . ."* Haisten, Bill, *It all
started in Stillwater*, August 12, 2001, TulsaWorld.com, BH Media Group,
Inc., https://www.tulsaworld.com/archives/it-all-started-in-
stillwater/article_b2710fd9-a554-57f4-8258-507053734d22.html

71   *"According to school archives, a student in that year's . . ."* Virginia Tech,
History and Traditions, 2016

71   *"The senior, O.M. Stull, was awarded $5.00 . . ."* Virginia Polytechnic
Institute and State University, *History and Traditions*, 2017,
https://vt.edu/about/traditions.html

71   *"Founded as a land-grant military institute in 1872, . . ."* Virginia
Polytechnic Institute and State University, *Factbook: About the University*,
2014, VT.edu, Virginia Tech University,
https://web.archive.org/web/20140527005122/http://www.vt.edu/a
bout/factbook/about-university.html

71   *"Ostensibly since the school's name just wasn't . . ."* Virginia Polytechnic
Institute and State University, *History and Traditions*, 2017

71 *"As one legend has it, the name "Gobblers"..."* Bithell, Sherri, *Life behind the beak*, Fall 2002, University Relations, Virginia Polytechnic Institute and State University, https://www.vtmag.vt.edu/fall18/Fall02-HokieBird.php

72 *"1913 is certainly when their mascot made its first appearance."* Bithell, Sherri, *Life behind the beak*, Fall 2002

72 *"That year, the student body elected Fred Meade..."* Virginia Polytechnic Institute and State University, *History and Traditions*, 2017

72 *"ability of his oversized bird to gobble on command."* Virginia Polytechnic Institute and State University, *History and Traditions*, 2017

72 *"Virginia Agricultural and Mechanical College played..."* Virginia Tech, *History and Traditions*, 2016, VT.edu, Virginia Polytechnic Institute and State University, 2016, https://vt.edu/about/traditions.html

72 *"The newly formed team handed the mighty prep school..."* Pieper, Lindsay, *From wheat to Worsham: The history of Lane*, September 2, 2006, Collegiate Times, Educational Media Company at Virginia Tech, https://web.archive.org/web/20070927104307/http://www.collegiatetimes.com/news/23/ARTICLE/7367/2006-09-02.html

72 *"10-point shutout over the same gray-clad Lutheran Boys..."* Pieper, Lindsay, *From wheat to Worsham: The history of Lane*, September 2, 2006

72 *"Thus, in the same year that the school changed its name..."* Pieper, Lindsay, *From wheat to Worsham: The history of Lane*, September 2, 2006

72 *"Ironically, the inaugural scrimmage on this field..."* Pieper, Lindsay, *From wheat to Worsham: The history of Lane*, September 2, 2006

72 *"In 1965, the first scrimmage took place at the site..."* Pieper, Lindsay, *From wheat to Worsham: The history of Lane*, September 2, 2006

73 *"Completed in 1968, the 35,000-seat arena..."* Virginia Tech, *Lane Stadium/Worsham Field*, 2016, VT.edu, Virginia Polytechnic Institute and State University, https://vt.edu/about/locations/buildings/lane-stadium-worsham-field.html

73 *"Decibel levels in modern football stadiums..."* Virostek, Paul, *Sound Effects Decibel Level Chart*, November 1, 2011, CreativeFieldRecording.com, Creative Field Recording, https://www.creativefieldrecording.com/2017/11/01/sound-effects-

decibel-level-chart/

73   *"Even though it's relatively small, only seating up to 54,000 . . ."* Newcomb, Tim, *Stadium Spotlight: What makes Oregon's Autzen Stadium so loud?*, September 5, 2014, SI.com, Sports Illustrated, https://www.si.com/college-football/2014/09/05/stadium-spotlight-autzen-stadium-oregon

73   *"an effect dubbed the "Autzen bounce.""* Newcomb, Tim, *Stadium Spotlight: What makes Oregon's Autzen Stadium so loud?*, September 5, 2014

73   *"Bronco Stadium sits at more than a half-mile . . ."* Rains, B.J., *Notebook: Elevation at Wyoming Not a Concern for Boise State*, October 27, 2016, IdahoPress.com, Idaho Press, https://www.idahopress.com/blueturfsports/notebook-elevation-at-wyoming-not-a-concern-for-boise-state/article_e2fded50-dc07-501c-aea1-0b8d0d8fe44e.html

74   *"To this point, British scientist Patrick J. Kiger . . ."* Kiger, Patrick J., *Why Does Home Field Advantage Matter?*, October 4, 2013, Seeker.com, Seeker, https://www.seeker.com/why-does-home field-advantage-matter-1767908680.html

74   *"In his 2013 article titled Why Does Home Field Advantage . . ."* Kiger, Patrick J., *Why Does Home Field Advantage Matter?*, October 4, 2013

74   *"Moskowitz and Wertheim were able to verify . . ."* Dubner, Stephen J., *"Football Freakonomics": How Advantageous Is Home Field Advantage? And Why?*, December 18, 2011, Freakonomics, LLC, http://freakonomics.com/2011/12/18/football-freakonomics-how-advantageous-is-home field-advantage-and-why/

74   *"The 2011 article "Football Freakonomics", . . ."* Dubner, Stephen J., *"Football Freakonomics": How Advantageous Is Home field Advantage? And Why?*, December 18, 2011

75   *"the city formerly known as Big Lick."* American Studies at the University of Virginia, *Roanoke*, September 1, 2009, Virginia.edu, University of Virginia, http://xroads.virginia.edu/~HYPER/VAGuide/roanoke.html

75   *"The Rotunda is exactly half the height and half the width . . ."* Patton, John S., *Jefferson, Cabell and the University of Virginia*, 1906, The Neale Publishing Company, p. 186, http://xtf.lib.virginia.edu/xtf/view?docId=2005_Q4_1%2FuvaBook%2

Ftei%2Fb000206392.xml&chunk.id=d25&query=pantheon#5

75   *"While residing on this 5,000-acre plantation, . . ."* Monticello.org, *Monticello – One of the South's Best*, 2017, Monticello.org, Monticello and the University of Virginia in Charlottesville, https://home.monticello.org/

75   *"In deference to this expedition, a private liberal . . ."* Lewis & Clark, *About Lewis & Clark*, 2018, LClark.edu, Lewis & Clark, https://www.lclark.edu/about/history/

76   *"Virginia Tech is more than just a member . . ."* The Association of Military Colleges and Schools of the United States, *Great Schools Changing the World*, 2017, Association of Military Colleges and Schools United States, https://amcsus.org/

76   *"The campus also has an instantly identifiable . . ."* Virginia Polytechnic Institute and State University, *Hokie Stone*, 2017, VT.edu, Virginia Polytechnic Institute and State University, https://vt.edu/about/traditions/hokie-stone.html

76   *"Formed by more than 450 million years of pressure, . . ."* Virginia Polytechnic Institute and State University, *Hokie Stone*, 2017

76   *"In 1872, active military training was mandatory . . ."* Virginia Tech, *A History of the Corps of Cadets*, 2016, VTCC.vt.edu, Virginia Polytechnic Institute and State University, https://www.vtcc.vt.edu/about/history.html

76   *"During this founding year, however, its Corps of Cadets . . ."* Virginia Tech, *A History of the Corps of Cadets*, 2016

76   *"Colonel John Alexander Harman, Commandant of Cadets . . ."* Virginia Tech, *A History of the Corps of Cadets*, 2016

77   *""highty tighty" were originally embedded in a spirit cheer . . ."* Virginia Tech, *The Highty-Tighties: Our History*, VTCC.vt.edu, Virginia Polytechnic Institute and State University, 2017, https://www.vtcc.vt.edu/band/band-history.html

77   *"the name to an elaborate series of events in 1919, . . ."* Virginia Tech, *The Highty-Tighties: Our History*, VTCC.vt.edu, Virginia Polytechnic Institute and State University, 2017

77   *"Virginia Tech has another officially recognized . . ."* The Marching

Virginians, *About The Band: History*, 2017, SpiritOfTech.com, The Marching Virginians - Virginia Polytechnic Institute and State University, https://www.spiritoftech.com/history/

77 *"This 352-member assemblage (which, no surprise, . . ."* The Marching Virginians, *About The Band: History*, 2017

78 *"According to the Virginia Tech chapter of Tau Beta Sigma . . ."* The Marching Virginians, *About The Band: History*, 2017

78 *"Conceived by Al and Shirl Edwards in 1977, . . ."* Murphy, Donal, *Big Al's and Poor Billy's up for sale*, November 14, 2012, Collegiate Times, http://www.collegiatetimes.com/news/virginia_tech/big-al-s-and-poor-billy-s-up-for-sale/article_6ac4dd0e-2cc6-5075-8e53-b39963085412.html

79 PHOTO: Big Al's Grill & Sports Bar, Blacksburg, Virginia, November 1, 2003, Sitting in crowd: Sean McMahon, Valerie McMahon

80 *"Though it officially holds only slightly more than 65,000 . . ."* Virginia Tech, *Lane Stadium/Worsham Field*, 2017, VT.edu, Virginia Polytechnic Institute and State University, https://vt.edu/about/locations/buildings/lane-stadium-worsham-field.html

80 *"In early 1990, the politically charged rap group Public Enemy . . ."* Virginia Tech, *Welcome to the Terrordome by Public Enemy*, 2017, Songfacts.com, Songfacts, LLC, https://www.songfacts.com/facts/public-enemy/welcome-to-the-terrordome

80 *"This heavily-sampled song was their response . . ."* Durham, Aisha, *Behind Beats and Rhymes: working class from a Hampton Roads hip hop homeplace*, November 2, 2009, Policy Futures in Education, p. 223, https://journals.sagepub.com/doi/pdf/10.2304/pfie.2009.7.2.217

80 *"Ten years later, Virginia Tech's senior defensive end, . . ."* Jones, Matt, *Welcome to the Terror Dome*, November 7, 2012, Collegiate Times, www.collegiatetimes.com/sports/welcome-to-the-terror-dome/article_77edeae8-1b2f-5ad2-81c6-9729cba4508d.html

80 *"Looking directly at the national television audience, . . ."* Jones, Matt, *Welcome to the Terror Dome*, November 7, 2012

81 *"For the past three seasons, the Hokies have used . . ."* Moriarty, Morgan, *The 11 greatest things about Virginia Tech's 'Enter Sandman' tradition*, October 6, 2018, SBNation, Vox Media, Inc., www.sbnation.com/college-

football/2017/9/30/16381936/virginia-tech-enter-sandman-entrance-history-metallica

81   *"Just before the 2000 season, a high-tech video screen . . ."* Moriarty, Morgan, *The 11 greatest things about Virginia Tech's 'Enter Sandman' tradition,* October 6, 2018,

82   *"The first officially-recognized costumed mascot . . ."* Bithell, Sherri, *Life behind the beak,* Fall 2002, University Relations, Virginia Polytechnic Institute and State University, https://www.vtmag.vt.edu/fall18/Fall02-HokieBird.php

82   *"That year, a young engineering student held a campus . . ."* Bithell, Sherri, *Life behind the beak,* Fall 2002

82   *"Nine years later, the school modified the mascot's neck . . . "* Bithell, Sherri, *Life behind the beak,* Fall 2002

82   *"The towering burgundy bird became known as . . . "* Bithell, Sherri, *Life behind the beak,* Fall 2002

82   PHOTO: Original HokieBird, Virginia Tech University mascot, Dan Askers, Virginia Tech class of 1963

82   *"Tonight's turkey-like mascot, which is haunting . . ."* Bithell, Sherri, *The 11 greatest things about Virginia Tech's 'Enter Sandman' tradition,* Fall 2002

83   *"Virginia Tech first challenged the University of Miami . . ."* Canes Warning, *History Lesson: Miami Hurricanes vs. Virginia Tech Hokies,* October 20, 2014, CanesWarning.com, Fansided, Inc., https://caneswarning.com/2014/10/20/history-lesson-miami-hurricanes-vs-virginia-tech-hokies/

84   *"Frank Beamer, who played for the Gobblers . . ."* Bithell, Sherri, *The 11 greatest things about Virginia Tech's 'Enter Sandman' tradition,* Fall 2002

84   *"His reputation for taking risks on these plays . . ."* Murray State University Athletics, *Racers Honor Beamer Ball - Frank Beamer Returns To Campus Saturday,* October 11, 2018

86   *"(Miami's quarterback tonight was one of the most . . ."* Richards, George, *What ever happened to all those former UM quarterbacks?,* August 27, 2017, MiamiHerald.com, Miami Herald Media Company, https://www.miamiherald.com/sports/college/acc/university-of-miami/article168616282.html

86   *"If not for the proficiency of Rex Grossman, III, . . ."* Richards, George, *What ever happened to all those former UM quarterbacks?*, August 27, 2017

86   *"For the first time in five years, the Hurricanes . . ."* SRCFB, *1997 Miami (FL) Hurricanes Schedule and Results*, 2002, Sports-Reference.com, Sports Reference LLC, https://www.sports-reference.com/cfb/schools/miami-fl/1997-schedule.html

87   *"Whether this sound from the innovative noise-making . . ."* Virginia Tech, *Students and Alumni – Traditions*, 2016, Unirel.vt.edu, Virginia Polytechnic Institute and State University, https://www.unirel.vt.edu/history/students_alumni/traditions.html

89   *"Tonight's dominating performance by the Hokies . . ."* Associated Press, *Hokies defense scores twice*, November 3, 2003, ESPN.com, ESPN, http://www.espn.com/college-football/recap?gameId=233050259

CHAPTER SIX   FANS AND FORMATIONS
                            Michigan | Ohio State

Page

91   *"Selected in the first round of the 1983 Major League . . ."* Baseball Reference, *Rob Dibble*, 2016, Baseball-Reference.com, Sports Reference LLC., https://www.baseball-reference.com/players/d/dibblro01.shtml

91   *"The right-handed hurler was also voted . . ."* ESPN.com, *MLB Awards - NLCS MVP*, 2016, ESPN.com, ESPN Internet Ventures, http://www.espn.com/mlb/history/awards/_/id/18

91   *"Wright Flyer I fabricated by Orville and Wilbur Wright . . ."* Honious, Ann, *What Dreams We Have – The Wright Brothers and Their Hometown of Dayton, Ohio*, 2003, https://web.archive.org/web/20070816072152/http://www.nps.gov:80/history/history/online_books/daav/chap3.htm

92   *"more than a decade playing Major League Baseball . . ."* Baseball Reference, *Rob Dibble*, 2016, Baseball-Reference.com, Sports Reference LLC., https://www.baseball-reference.com/players/d/dibblro01.shtml

94   *"The two squads also played to a draw six times . . ."* Kinney, Greg, *Michigan vs Ohio State All-Time UM-OSU Results*, 2002, Bentley Historical Library, The Regents of the University of Michigan, https://bentley.umich.edu/athdept/football/umosu/results.htm

94   *"border dispute known as the Toledo War . . ."* State of Michigan, *The Toledo War*, 2016, Michigan Department of Military & Veterans Affairs, State of

Michigan, https://www.michigan.gov/dmva/0,4569,7-126-
2360_3003_3009-16934—,00.html

95   *"Beginning in 1835, for almost two years, . . ."* State of Michigan, *The Toledo War*, 2016

95   *"zero casualties, one injury, and the ceding . . ."* State of Michigan, *The Toledo War*, 2016

95   *"Ohio Stadium, with its distinctive U-shape, . . ."* Munsey, Paul; Suppes, Cory, *Stadiums by Munsey & Suppes*, 1996-2017, BALLPARKS.com, http://football.ballparks.com/NCAA/OhioState/index.htm

95   *"Upon completion in 1922, The Horseshoe, . . ."* Ohio State University, *Ohio Stadium*, 2017, OhioStateBuckeyes.com, Ohio State University, https://ohiostatebuckeyes.com/sports/m-footbl/facilities/ohio-stadium/

95   *"With an original capacity of slightly more than 66,000 . . ."* Munsey, Paul, and Suppes, Cory, Stadiums by Munsey & Suppes, 1996-2017

95   *"Slightly more than 25,000 fans . . ."* Thomas, Jeanna, *Ohio State football history: Oct. 7, 1922*, October 9, 2014, SBNation, Vox Media, Inc., https://www.landgrantholyland.com/2014/10/9/6934745/ohio-stadium-history-ohio-wesleyan

96   *"On October 21, 1922, an estimated 72,000 . . ."* Munsey, Paul, and Suppes, Cory, *Stadiums by Munsey & Suppes*, 1996-2017

96   *"The most recent facelift, in 2001, added 81 luxury suites . . ."* College Gridirons, *Ohio Stadium*, 2004, CollegeGridirons.com, College Gridirons, https://www.collegegridirons.com/stadiums/ohio-stadium/

96   *"Constructed to resemble the famed Pantheon . . ."* Newcomb, Tim, *Stadium Spotlight: Everything centers on the horseshoe at Ohio Stadium*, November 25, 2014, SI.com, Time Inc., https://www.si.com/college-football/2014/11/25/ohio-stadium-spotlight-ohio-state-buckeyes

96   *"Like many marching bands, "TBDBITL" . . ."* The Little Band Man Company, *College Band History*, 2016, LittleBandMan.com, The Little Band Man Company, http://littlebandman.com/college-band-history

96   *"In 1878, much like the Highty-Tighties at Virginia Tech . . ."* Bitzel, Danielle, *History of the OSUMB*, 1997, 50megs.com, B Row,

http://betarho.50megs.com/history.html55

97 *"It wasn't until 1907, however, that a band . . ."* Illinois Distributed Museum, *Marching Band Field Show*, 2016, Illinois.edu, University of Illinois in Urbana-Champaign, https://distributedmuseum.illinois.edu/exhibit/marching-band-field-show/

97 *"Later that same year, Paul Spotts Emrick, . . ."* Purdue Bands & Orchestras, *Purdue "All-American" Marching Band*, 2016, Purdue.edu, Purdue University, https://www.purdue.edu/bands/aboutus/history/

97 *"Observing geese flying overhead, Emrick similarly . . ."* Purdue Bands & Orchestras, *Purdue "All-American" Marching Band*, 2016

97 *"Introduced in Ann Arbor after newly christened . . ."* Bentley Historical Library, *University of Michigan Football – Michigan's Winged Helmet*, February 23, 2015, The Regents of the University of Michigan, https://bentley.umich.edu/athdept/football/helmet/mhelmet.htm

97 *"The "winged" portion also had the functional purpose . . ."* Bentley Historical Library, *University of Michigan Football – Michigan's Winged Helmet*, February 23, 2015

98 *"Proclaimed by famed composer John Philip Sousa . . ."* Kryk, John, *Who's No. 1? Fight Songs*, 2004, Natural Enemies: Major College Football's Oldest, Fiercest Rivalry—Michigan vs. Notre Dame. Lanham, MD: Taylor Trade Publication, pp. 242–245, https://bentley.umich.edu/athdept/football/umosu/images/krykchi1898.pdf

98 *"1898 by University of Michigan student Louis Elbel."* Daughters, Amy, *Ranking the Top 50 College Football Fight Songs*, October 11, 2011, Bleacher Report, Turner Broadcasting System, Inc., https://bleacherreport.com/articles/891006-power-ranking-the-top-50-college-football-fight-songs#slide50

98 *"'There'll be a Hot Time in the Old Town Tonight' . . ."* Dickson, James, *Talk of the Town: Hail to the Victors - a borrowed song?*, November 4, 2009, The Ann Arbor News, MLive Media Group, http://www.annarbor.com/entertainment/the-deuce/talk-of-the-town-classic-u-m-songs-in-retrospect/

99 *"The former star quarterback of the undefeated 1967 . . ."* The Regents of the

University of Michigan, *University of Michigan Football Coaches – Lloyd Carr*, April 10, 2006, Bentley Historical Library, The Regents of the University of Michigan, https://bentley.umich.edu/athdept/football/coaches/lcarr.htm

100   *"in 1940 by Ohio State graduate, James Thurber."* Columbus Alive, *17 Ohio State traditions that (probably) won't get anyone fired ... and the stories behind them*, 2006-2018, GateHouse Media, LLC., GateHouse Entertainment, http://www.columbusalive.com/content/stories/2014/08/28/17-ohio-state-traditions-that-probably-wont-get-anyone-fired———and-the-stories-behind-them.html

101   *"first on-field formation of "Ohio" in script . . ."* Bovenzi, Giustino, *"The unlikely history behind "Script Ohio:" One of college football's most iconic, longstanding traditions*, November 20, 2015, Sports Illustrated, https://www.si.com/college-football/2015/11/20/history-behind-ohio-states-legendary-script-ohio-routine

101   PHOTO: Ohio Stadium, Columbus, Ohio, October 15, 1932, Original formation of 'Ohio' in script by Michigan Marching Band.

101   *"Script Ohio, as we know it today, . . ."* Bovenzi, Giustino, *"The unlikely history behind "Script Ohio:" One of college football's most iconic, longstanding traditions*, November 20, 2015

101   *"According to then band-leader Eugene J. Weigel, . . ."* Aambarchive, *Purdue "All-American" Archive*, 2016, weebly.com, AAMB Archive, https://aambarchive.weebly.com/history.html

101   *"Composed in 1879 by Robert Planquette, . . ."* IMSLP, *Le régiment de Sambre et Meuse (Planquette, Robert)*, 2016, IMSLP.org, International Music Score Library Project, https://imslp.org/wiki/Le_r%C3%A9giment_de_Sambre_et_Meuse_(Planquette,_Robert)

102   *"It's been the signature number . . ."* The Ohio State University Marching and Athletic Bands, *Traditions: Ohio Script*, 2017, OSU.edu, The Ohio State University, https://tbdbitl.osu.edu/marching-band/traditions

102   *"When originally choreographed by Eugene Weigel, . . ."* The Ohio State University Marching and Athletic Bands, *Traditions: Ohio Script*, 2017

103   *"Since that fortuitous gaff, more than 800 sousaphone . . ."* The Ohio State University Marching and Athletic Bands, *Traditions: Ohio Script*, 2017

103   *"No span during the 100 games . . ."* Pennington, Joel, *The Ten Year War: Ten Classic Games Between Bo and Woody*, September 1, 2005, p. 33

103   *"During almost three decades at the helm in Columbus, . . ."* Kinney, Greg, *Michigan vs Ohio State – Woody vs Bo*, November 23, 2013, Bentley Historical Library, The Regents of the University of Michigan, https://bentley.umich.edu/athdept/football/umosu/woodyvbo.htm

103   *"Following the beatdown of the Wolverines in 1968, . . ."* Orr, Tom, *Did Woody Hayes Really Say 'I Couldn't Go For Three'?*, June 13, 2018, TheOZone.net, Ozone Communications, LLC, https://theozone.net/2018/06/did-woody-hayes-really-say-i-couldnt-go-for-three/

104   *"Over the 21 years as commander in Ann Arbor, . . ."* Kinney, Greg, *Michigan vs Ohio State – Woody vs Bo*, November 23, 2013

104   *"Even Hayes hinted Michigan deserved an invitation . . ."* Cleveland.com, *OSU-Michigan 1973: 10-10 tie leaves Buckeyes, Wolverines drained and deadlocked atop Big Ten standings*, March 11, 2012, Cleveland.com, Advance Local Media LLC https://www.cleveland.com/osu-michigan/2012/03/osu-michigan_1973_10-10_tie_le.html

104   *"Nevertheless, the Big Ten powers-that-be decided, . . ."* Cleveland.com, *OSU-Michigan 1973: 10-10 tie leaves Buckeyes, Wolverines drained and deadlocked atop Big Ten standings*, March 11, 2012

105   *"They also earned him four Coach of the Year awards."* White, Mike, *Jim Tressel: More Than a Football Coach*, October 25, 2006, Yahoo Voices, Yahoo Sports and Yahoo News, Networkhttps://web.archive.org/web/20140729002112/http://voices.yahoo.com/jim-tressel-more-than-football-coach-98394.html

105   *"Somehow, the lifelong assistant coach rallied his team . . ."* The Regents of the University of Michigan, *University of Michigan Football Coaches – Lloyd Carr*, April 10, 2006, Bentley Historical Library, The Regents of the University of Michigan, https://bentley.umich.edu/athdept/football/coaches/lcarr.htm

105   *"would not have been elevated to this position . . ."* The Regents of the University of Michigan, *University of Michigan Football Coaches – Lloyd Carr*, April 10, 2006

105   *"As the massive edifice fills to more than 101,000 , . . ."* OhioStateBuckeys.com, *Ohio Stadium*, 2016, OhioStateBuckeys.com,

Ohio State University, https://ohiostatebuckeyes.com/sports/m-footbl/facilities/ohio-stadium/

106   *"In 1953, the Ohio buckeye . . ."* Ohio History Central, *Ohio's State Tree - Buckeye*, October 16, 2006, Ohio History Connection, http://www.ohio-historycentral.org/w/Ohio%27s_State_Tree_-_Buckeye

106   *"Three years earlier, the university selected the tree's . . ."* The Ohio State University, *What is a Buckeye*, 2017, OhioStateBuckeyes.com, The Ohio State University, http://ohiostatebuckeyes.com/what-is-a-buckeye/

106   *"Complementing this somewhat silly name, . . ."* The Ohio State University, *Brutus Buckeye*, 2016, OhioStateBuckeyes.com, The Ohio State University, https://ohiostatebuckeyes.com/brutus-buckeye-2/

106   *"Several art students that year created . . ."* The Ohio State University, *Brutus Buckeye*, 2016

106   *"Most fans here today know, in the 100-year history. . ."* Nicols, Jay, *Leach, Henne, Forcier: Three True Freshman, One Manly Feat*, October 1, 2009, Bleacher Report, Inc. Turner Broadcasting System, Inc., https://bleacherreport.com/articles/264721-leach-henne-forcier-three-true-freshman-one-manly-feat

111   *"Having shown their appreciation, they then . . ."* The Ohio State University Alumni Association, *Skull Session on the Road in NYC*, November 1, 2018, The Ohio State University Alumni Association, The Ohio State University, https://www.osu.edu/alumni/activities-and-events/events/2018/skull-session-on-the-road-in-nyc.html

114   *"Just before their 31st meeting in 1934, . . ."* The Ohio State University – University Libraries, *Gold Pants Club*, 2017, OSU.edu, https://library.osu.edu/blogs/osuvsmichigan/gold-pants-club/

115   *"When asked by local reporters as to how well . . ."* The Ohio State University – University Libraries, *Gold Pants Club*, 2017

115   *"Originally designed by two local businessmen, . . ."* Thomas, Jeanna, *Gold pants: An Ohio State football tradition*, Jun 3, 2013, SB Nation, Vox Media, Inc., https://www.landgrantholyland.com/2013/6/3/4381740/gold-pants-an-ohio-state-football-tradition

115   *"At the end of that same season, the Gold Pants Club . . ."* Thomas, Jeanna, *Gold pants: An Ohio State football tradition*, Jun 3, 2013

CHAPTER SEVEN   THE BIG GAME
                       California | Stanford

Page

117   *"Proclaimed as "the greatest college football play of all time"..."* The Best
        Damn Sports Show Period, *Best Damn Top 50: Outrageous Moments In
        Sports*, May 24, 2012, The Best Damn Sports Show Period, Fox Sports
        Network, https://www.youtube.com/watch?v=-7wbhEOa0Ow

118   *"After the University of California – also known simply..."* Krentzman,
        Jackie, *And the Band Played On*, November/December 2002, Stanford
        Magazine, Stanford University,
        https://stanfordmag.org/contents/and-the-band-played-on

119   *"University of California radio broadcaster Joe Starkey..."* Goldman, Tom,
        Key Players from Stanford and Cal Relive 'The Play', November 20, 2007,
        NPR.com, National Public Radio, Inc.,
        https://www.npr.org/templates/story/story.php?storyId=16442781

119   *"Remembering back to a favorite practice drill..."* Lee, Phillip, *Moen made
        "The Play" in the "Big Game"*, November 19, 2003, ESPN Classic,
        http://www.espn.com/classic/s/Where_now_moen_kevin.html

119   *"Like the rest of his Cardinal bandmates, Gary Tyrell..."* History.com, *Cal
        beats Stanford as band blocks field*, November 16, 2009, History.com, A&E
        Television Networks, LLC., https://www.history.com/this-day-in-
        history/cal-beats-stanford-as-band-blocks-field

119   *"As screaming fans swarm the field, Joe Starkey..."* Wallach, Dan, *The Play:
        Joe Starkey's Call of the 1982 Cal/Stanford Big Game*, October 27, 1998, CS
        Department, Rice University,
        https://www.cs.rice.edu/~dwallach/the_play.html

119   *"Cal inadvertently received the kickoff..."* Migdol, Gary, *Stanford: Home of
        Champions*, September 7, 1997, Sports Publishing LLC, p. 184

119   *"Following the inaugural meeting..."* Satterlee, Cameron, *Stanford vs Cal:
        A Brief History of the Big Game*, November 14, 2017, SB Nation, Vox
        Media, Inc.,
        https://www.ruleoftree.com/2017/11/14/16652110/history-big-game-
        stanford-cal

120   *"Recognized by many as the "Father of American Football"..."* Bishop,
        LuAnn, *11 historic tidbits about The Game*, November 18, 2013, YaleNews,
        Yale University, https://news.yale.edu/2013/11/18/11-historic-tidbits-
        about-game

120   *"These innovations evolved the game . . ."* Bishop, LuAnn, *11 historic tidbits about The Game*, November 18, 2013

120   *"The now-annual showdown in the Bay Area . . ."* Satterlee, Cameron, *Stanford vs Cal: A Brief History of the Big Game*, November 14, 2017

120   *"Beginning in the mid-1890s, a vocal faction . . ."* Klein, Christopher, *How Teddy Roosevelt Saved Football*, September 6, 2012, History, A&E Television Networks, LLC., https://www.history.com/news/how-teddy-roosevelt-saved-football

120   *"An 1892 article in The New York Times . . ."* Volk, Greg, *The Time Teddy Roosevelt Saved Football*, December 1, 2012, Mental Floss, Minute Media, http://mentalfloss.com/article/31657/time-teddy-roosevelt-saved-football

120   *"During the 1905 season, football had become . . ."* Klein, Christopher, *How Teddy Roosevelt Saved Football*, September 6, 2012

121   *"Lesser in severity, if not in prominence: Theodore . . ."* Volk, Greg, *The Time Teddy Roosevelt Saved Football*, December 1, 2012

121   *"In early October of that year, the elder Roosevelt . . ."* Volk, Greg, *The Time Teddy Roosevelt Saved Football*, December 1, 2012

121   *"During this forced hiatus, the two institutions . . ."* Elliott, Orrin Leslie, *Stanford University – The First Twenty Five Years 1891–1925*, 1937, Stanford, California: Stanford University Press, pp. 231–233

121   *"Fortuitously, the adoption of the new rules . . ."* Volk, Greg, *The Time Teddy Roosevelt Saved Football*, December 1, 2012

121   *"We know this organization today . . ."* Klein, Christopher, *How Teddy Roosevelt Saved Football*, September 6, 2012, History, A&E Television Networks, LLC., https://www.history.com/news/how-teddy-roosevelt-saved-football

122   *"University of the Pacific elected to drop football . . ."* Gilbert, Lori, *Ten Years Ago, the Final Horn Sounded for Pacific*, December 18, 2005, https://www.recordnet.com/article/20051218/OPED0303/512180337

122   *"The Tigers from Stockton first fielded a team in 1895."* Fandom, *Pacific (CA) Tigers*, 2016, FANDOM Lifestyle Community, Wikia, Inc., http://americanfootball.wikia.com/wiki/Pacific_(CA)_Tigers

122   *"However, it wasn't until the 1930s, when Amos . . ."* Wulf, Steve, *ESPN: The Mighty Book of Sports Knowledge,* June 9, 2009, Random House Publishing Group, Sports & Recreation Press, p. 24

122   *"Stagg introduced several innovations, . . ."* Wulf, Steve, *ESPN: The Mighty Book of Sports Knowledge,* June 9, 2009

122   *"To this day, even though it sits idle . . ."* Pacific Athletics, *Stagg Stadium to Close While University Conducts Feasibility Study,* February 26, 2012, PacificTigers.com, University of the Pacific, https://www.pacifictigers.com/genrel/Stagg_Stadium_to_Close_While_University_Conducts_Feasiblity_Study

122   *"In 1989, he became head coach of his alma mater . . ."* Edwards, Josh, *Hue Jackson, Jon Gruden used to share an office at tiny Pacific,* 2016, 247sports.com, CBS Sports Interactive, https://247sports.com/nfl/cleveland-browns/Article/Hue-Jackson-Jon-Gruden-shared-off-Pacific-122551831/

123   *"Following the inaugural victory . . ."* Stanford University, *On Campus,* 2016, GoStanford.com, Stanford University, https://gostanford.com/sports/2013/4/17/208445366.aspx

123   *"It wasn't until the 1930s that the university . . ."* Stanford University, *On Campus,* 2016

123   *"By unanimous vote, the Executive Committee . . ."* Stanford University, *On Campus,* 2016

123   *"In 1972, however, the powers-that-be . . ."* Woodward, Denni D., *The Removal of the Indian Mascot of Stanford,* 2017, Stanford University, Native American Cultural Center, https://nacc.stanford.edu/about-nacc/history-timelines/stanford-mascot-timeline/removal-indian-mascot-stanford

123   *"Citing pressure from 55 Native American students . . ."* Woodward, Denni D., *The Removal of the Indian Mascot of Stanford,* 2017

123   *"nicknames were suggested: The Railroaders. . . ."* Stanford University, *What is the history of Stanford's mascot and nickname?,* 2017, On Campus – Athletic Department, https://gostanford.com/sports/2013/4/17/208445366.aspx

123   *"This last proposed label was so well received . . ."* Stanford University, *What is the history of Stanford's mascot and nickname?,* 2017

123   *"the next president of the school, Donald Kennedy, . . ."* Stanford University, *What is the history of Stanford's mascot and nickname?*, 2017

123   *"Thus, in 1981, Kennedy announced that Stanford . . ."* Stanford University, *What is the history of Stanford's mascot and nickname?*, 2017

124   *"Originally constructed in 1921, the horseshoe-shaped . . ."* Spokane Daily Chronicle, *Stanford Stadium nears completion,* August 3, 1921, p. 18, https://news.google.com/newspapers?id=brxXAAAAIBAJ&sjid=U_Q DAAAAIBAJ&pg=6443%2C384486

124   *"(Its 60,000 seats, however, paled in comparison . . ."* Berkeley Daily Gazette, *Huge Stanford Stadium, with seating of 60,000,* June 13, 1921, p. 8, https://news.google.com/newspapers?id=TlciAAAAIBAJ&sjid=eqcFA AAAIBAJ&pg=826%2C5007039

124   *"bowl-shape with a capacity of 89,000, in 1927."* Berkeley Daily Gazette, *Stanford Stadium to have addition,* May 24, 1927, p. 11, https://news.google.com/newspapers?id=0VAyAAAAIBAJ&sjid=VeQ FAAAAIBAJ&pg=3149%2C4588931

124   *"Leland Stanford, and his wife, Jane, . . ."* Stanford University, *The Farm,* 2017, Stanford Speak, https://www.stanford.edu/campus-life/stanford-speak/

124   *"Affectionately known as The Red Barn, . . ."* Stanford Equestrian, *Welcome to Stanford Equestrian,* 2017, Stanford Equestrian, Stanford University, http://equestrian.stanford.edu/

125   *"In its place will be a 50,000-seat dual-deck octagon . . ."* College Gridirons, *Stanford Stadium,* 2016, CollegeGridirons.com, College Gridirons https://www.collegegridirons.com/stadiums/stanford-stadium/

126   *"Originally formed in 1893, the Stanford marching . . ."* Stanford University, *History,* 2016, Stanford.edu, Stanford University, https://lsjumb.stanford.edu/history.html

126   *"Jules Schucat, was suddenly relieved of his duties."* Stanford University, *History,* 2016

126   *"Carrying the original title of Interim Band Director, . . ."* Meigs, James B., *Band on the Run,* September 24, 1987, Rolling Stone, p. 153

126   *"Unofficially, according to a 1987 Rolling Stone article . . ."* Meigs, James B., *Band on the Run,* September 24, 1987

128   *"private school with the nobly-named athletic teams . . ."* Stanford
        University, *What is the history of Stanford's mascot and nickname?*, 2017

129   *"Stanford Tree has informally assumed the role . . ."* Sullivan, Kathleen J.,
        Retired Stanford Trees have found a home in Green Library, April 11, 2018,
        Stanford Libraries, Stanford University,
        https://news.stanford.edu/2018/04/11/retired-stanford-trees-found-
        home-green-library/

129   *"Originally constructed that year by then-student . . ."* Sullivan, Kathleen J.,
        Retired Stanford Trees have found a home in Green Library, April 11, 2018

129   *"After the LSJUMB held inaugural tryouts . . ."* Wikipedia.com, *Stanford
        Tree*, 2016, https://en.wikipedia.org/wiki/Stanford_Tree

129   *"In his article for Rolling Stone, James B. Meigs . . ."* Meigs, James B., *Band
        on the Run*, September 24, 1987, Rolling Stone, p. 153

129   *"Kelly's first-year tree costume was purloined . . ."* Mulhauser, Dana, *Tree
        relinquished by Cal captors; revered mascot safely back on campus*, November
        2, 1998, The Stanford Daily, The Stanford Daily Publishing Corporation,
        https://web.archive.org/web/20080310005542/http://daily.stanford.e
        du:80/article/1998/11/2/treeRelinquishedByCalCaptorsReveredMas-
        cotSafelyBackOnCampus

129   *"In their words, the Stanford Tree was . . ."* Trei, Lisa, *Tree costume kidnapped
        from Band Shak; Bears claim responsibility*, October 28, 1998, Stanford
        Report, Stanford University,
        https://news.stanford.edu/news/1998/october28/treenap1028.html

133   *"(These official team colors are said to have . . ."* Berkeley University of
        California, *Traditions of Berkeley*, 2017, UC Regents,
        https://www.berkeley.edu/about/traditions

134   *"Parading onto the field from the north end . . ."* University of California,
        Marching Band – Tradition, 2016, University of California Marching
        Band, University of California, http://calband.berkeley.edu/about-
        us/university-of-california-marching-band/

136   *"Stanford Axe was first presented to the winner . . ."* Stanford Axe
        Committee, *The Tale of the Majestic Blade*, 2016, Stanford.edu, Stanford
        Axe Committee, https://web.stanford.edu/group/axecomm/cgi-
        bin/wordpress/?page_id=139

136   *"(Introduced as a prop in 1899, this woodsman's tool . . ."* Stanford

University, *The Story of the Stanford Axe*, 2016, Stanford.edu, Stanford University, http://axecomm.stanford.edu/history/calaxe.html

138 PHOTO: Stanford University, Palo Alto, California, November 19, 2005, Standing with the Leland Stanford Junior Marching Band outside of Stanford Stadium: Valerie McMahon

138 *"Stanford University has refused to accept they lost in 1982."* DeCourcy, Michael, *Look: The strange tradition of the Stanford Axe*, 2016, TheScore.com, Score Media Ventures Inc., https://www.thescore.com/ncaaf/news/1160190

CHAPTER EIGHT   FEAR THE THUMB
                            Auburn | Alabama

Page
140 *"To this day, we recall USC running back Reggie Bush . . ."* Kersey, Jason, *Worst losses of the Bob Stoops era: No. 4, USC 55, OU 19 (2005 Orange Bowl)*, August 10, 2012, NewsOK.com, The Oklahoman, https://newsok.com/article/3777075/worst-losses-of-the-bob-stoops-era-no-4-usc-55-ou-19-2005-orange-*bowl*

140 *"Trojans remained in the top position of both polls . . ."* NCAA.com, *College football rankings: Here is who has been No. 1 in the AP preseason poll most often and how they finished*, August 21, 2018, NCAA.com, Turner Sports Interactive, Inc., https://auburntigers.com/sports/2018/6/11/trads-12-auburn-tiger-walk-html.aspx

140 *"AP opted to disallow their national poll as a component . . ."* Thamel, Pete, *Associated Press Football Poll Is Pulled From B.C.S. Equation*, December 22, 2004, NYTimes.com, The New York Times, https://www.nytimes.com/2004/12/22/sports/ncaafootball/associated-press-football-poll-is-pulled-from-bcs.html

141 *"This tradition, known as Tiger Walk, . . ."* Auburn University Athletics, *Traditions – Tiger Walk*, 2016, Auburn University Athletics, Auburn University, https://auburntigers.com/sports/2018/6/11/trads-12-auburn-tiger-walk-html.aspx

141 *"Though a handful of other schools – including Stanford . . ."* Maisel, Ivan, *The best Walk in America*, 2016, ESPN.com, ESPN, http://www.espn.com/page2/s/maisel/031120auburn.html

141 *"Avid boosters arrive on Friday evenings . . ."* Maisel, Ivan, *The best Walk in America*, 2016

142   PHOTO: Bryant-Denny Stadium, Tuscaloosa, Alabama, November 18, 2006, Standing in front of Tiger Walk banner: Sean McMahon

142   *"On February 22, 1893, a crowd of more than 5,000 fans . . ."* Causey, Donna R, *Do you know how many people attended the first Iron Bowl game in 1893?*, 2016, AlabamaPioneers.com, Alabama Pioneers, https://www.alabamapioneers.com/know-many-people-attended-first-iron-bowl-game-1893/

142   *"Oddly, the University of Alabama recognizes . . ."* Bolton, Clyde, *Alabama, Auburn football teams played 1st Iron Bowl on Feb. 22, 1893*, February 22, 2016, NCAA.com, Turner Sports Interactive, https://www.ncaa.com/news/football/article/2016-02-21/alabama-auburn-football-teams-played-1st-iron-bowl-feb-22-1893

142   *"In 1868, during the Civil War Reconstruction Era . . ."* Cox, Dwayne; Steward, Rodney J., *The New South*, 2016, They Auburn University Digital Library, Auburn University, http://diglib.auburn.edu/auburnhistory/newsouth.htm

143   *"(This Confederate invasion of northern Maryland . . ."* History.com, Rodney J., *McClellan lets Lee retreat from Antietam*, November 13, 2009, History.com, A&E Television Networks, LLC., https://www.history.com/this-day-in-history/mcclellan-lets-lee-retreat-from-antietam

143   *"Over the next four years, they petitioned the state . . ."* Lee, Larry, *A Unique Perspective On The Iron Bowl*, LarryEducation.com, Larry Lee Education Blogger, November 20, 2017, http://www.larryeducation.com/a-unique-perspective-on-the-iron-bowl/

143   *"After the 1906 game, Auburn's head coach . . ."* Fravel, Jonathan, *Alabama-Auburn Rivalry: In Dead Period, Political Football Takes Center Stage*, March 11, 2011, Bleacher Report, Inc., Turner Broadcasting System, Inc., https://bleacherreport.com/articles/630912-alabama-auburn-rivalry-the-dead-period-political-football-takes-center-stage

143   *"Doc Pollard ceased using "unsportsmanlike tactics" . . ."* Groom, Winston, *The Crimson Tide – An Illustrated History*, 2000, The University of Alabama Press, p. 16

143   *"At the end of their 1907 contest, these threats . . ."* Fravel, Jonathan, *Alabama-Auburn Rivalry: In Dead Period, Political Football Takes Center Stage*, March 11, 2011

143   *"Two official reasons were given: the inability to agree . . ."* Fravel, Jonathan, *Alabama-Auburn Rivalry: In Dead Period, Political Football Takes Center Stage*, March 11, 2011

144   *"For the next 41 years, the upstart Tigers . . ."* Fravel, Jonathan, Alabama-Auburn Rivalry: In Dead Period, Political Football Takes Center Stage, March 11, 2011

144   *"Mechanical College of Alabama more than quadruple."* Olliff, Martin T., *Auburn University (AU)*, August 18, 2008, The Encyclopedia of Alabama, Alabama Humanities Foundation, http://www.encyclopediaofalabama.org/article/h-1649

144   *"In 1947, the Alabama House of Representatives . . ."* Rocky Mountain Auburn Club, *The Auburn-Alabama Rivalry*, 2006, https://web.archive.org/web/20070821050549/http://www.coloradotigers.com/concourse/traditions_ironbowl.htm

144   *"Begrudgingly, the trustees at each institution voted . . ."* Rocky Mountain Auburn Club, *The Auburn-Alabama Rivalry*, 2006

145   *"This bludgeoning on December 4, 1948 stands . . ."* AL.com, *Iron Bowl history: Scores*, November 26, 2010, AL.com, Advance Local Media LLC., https://www.al.com/ironbowl/index.ssf/2010/11/iron_bowl_history_scores.html

145   *"Beginning with this rout, the Crimson Tide . . ."* Taylor, Drew, *It's been 20 years since Iron Bowl was played in Birmingham*, November 23, 2018, TuscaloosaNews.com, GateHouse Media, LLC, https://www.tuscaloosanews.com/news/20181123/its-been-20-years-since-iron-bowl-was-played-in-birmingham

145   *"As unfathomable as it seems, it wasn't until 1989 . . ."* AL.com, *Iron Bowl history: Scores*, November 26, 2010 https://www.al.com/ironbowl/index.ssf/2010/11/iron_bowl_history_scores.html

145   *"It was the largest-ever crowd at an Auburn game."* ColoradoTigers.com, *The Auburn-Alabama Rivalry "The Iron Bowl"*, August 21, 2007, ColoradoTigers.com, Rocky Mountain Auburn Club, https://web.archive.org/web/20070821050549/http://www.coloradotigers.com/concourse/traditions_ironbowl.htm

146   *"Rama Jama's opened its doors in September 1996."* Mason, Carolyn, *Rama Jama's*, September 8, 2009, TuscaloosaNews.com, GateHouse Media,

LLC, https://www.tuscaloosanews.com/news/20090908/rama-jamas

147 *"In 1929, the Crimson Tide christened this hulking . . ."* Alabama Humanities Foundation, *Bryant-Denny Stadium*, 2016, The Encyclopedia of Alabama, Alabama Humanities Foundation, http://www.encyclopediaofalabama.org/article/m-4153

147 *"Slightly more than 6,000 fans attended this inaugural game."* Tubb, Donald, *Alabama Gets 6 Touchdowns by Swift Play in First Half,* September 29, 1929, The Tuscaloosa News, https://news.google.com/newspapers?id=29A-AAAAIBAJ&sjid=gkwMAAAAIBAJ&pg=5474%2C5147177

147 *"the imposing structure will hold more than 92,000 . . ."* Rolltide.com, *Bryant-Denny Stadium,* 2017, Rolltide.com, University of Alabama, https://rolltide.com/sports/2016/6/10/facilities-bryant-denny-html.aspx

148 *"As their in-state showdown in 1964 approached, . . ."* Bonesteel, Matt, *How the Iron Bowl got its name, and other stories behind college football's rivalry trophies,* Nov. 28, 2014, The Washington Post, Early Lead, https://www.washingtonpost.com/news/early-lead/wp/2014/11/28/how-the-iron-bowl-got-its-name-and-other-stories-behind-college-footballs-rivalry-trophies/

148 *"This poignant statement was the first time . . ."* Bonesteel, Matt, *How the Iron Bowl got its name, and other stories behind college football's rivalry trophies,* Nov. 28, 2014

149 *"At the end of that season, due in large part to sanctions . . ."* Saban, Rainer, *Looking back at Dennis Franchione's stunning move from Alabama to Texas A&M,* October 20, 2016, AL.com, Advance Local Media LLC., https://www.al.com/alabamafootball/index.ssf/2016/10/looking_back_at_the_coach_who.html

149 *"In May 2003, after the immediate hiring . . ."* Whiteside, Kelly, *Price fired as coach of Alabama football,* Nov. 28, 2014, USA Today, Gannett Co. Inc., http://usatoday30.usatoday.com/sports/college/football/sec/2003-05-03-price-fired_x.htm

149 PHOTO: Bryant-Denny Stadium, Tuscaloosa, Alabama, November 18, 2006, Spirit flag of Auburn University

150 *"Legend has it, their officially recognized moniker . . ."* Pow, Chris, *UA's Million Dollar Band marks 100 years of tradition this weekend,* September

20, 2012, Alabama Media Group, Advance Local Media LLC.,
http://blog.al.com/tuscaloosa/2012/09/uas_million_dollar_band_mar
ks.html

150   *"the sportswriter asked William C. Pickens, . . ."* Eureka Humboldt
         Standard, *William Champ Pickens Dies,* September 19, 1963, Eureka
         Humboldt Standard, Times Standard Newspapers, p. 26
         https://www.newspapers.com/clip/3285223/eureka_humboldt_stand
         ard/

151   *"Hired as the youngest head coach in the nation, . . ."*
         SaturdayDownSouth.com, *Mike Shula,* 2016, SaturdayDownSouth.com,
         Saturday Down South,
         https://www.saturdaydownsouth.com/coaches/mike-shula/

151   *"recognized as the "Deep South's Oldest Rivalry.""* University of Georgia
         Athletics, *Georgia and Auburn Renew Deep South's Oldest Rivalry,*
         November 08, 2010, University of Georgia,
         https://georgiadogs.com/news/2010/11/8/Georgia_and_Auburn_Re
         new_Deep_South_s_Oldest_Rivalry.aspx

158   *"Just then, the-instantly recognizable first chords . . ."* Genius.com, *Sweet
         Home Alabama,* 2017, Genius.com, Genius Media Group Inc.,
         https://genius.com/Lynyrd-skynyrd-sweet-home-alabama-lyrics

158   *"the stadium hollers in unison, "Roll, Tide, Roll!""* IMG College Licensing,
         Roll Tide, Role, 2019, Collegiate Licensing Company, IMG College
         Licensing, http://www.imgcollegelicensing.com/

CHAPTER NINE   FIESTA TIME
                       West Virginia I Oklahoma
Page
163   *"The Tigers from Columbia are outside the top-25 . . ."* Williams, Gene,
         Preseason magazine reviews - Phil Steele, June 26, 2007, Warchant.com,
         Oath, Inc., https://floridastate.rivals.com/news/preseason-magazine-
         reviews-phil-steele

163   *"Immediately following the thumb-raising loss . . ."* WSFA12 News, *Mike
         Shula Fired,* November 27, 2006, WSFA.com, WSFA 12 News,
         http://www.wsfa.com/story/5731202/mike-shula-fired/

164   *"The controversial Bowl Championship Series . . ."* BCSFootball.org, *The
         Bowl Championship Series: A Golden Era,* December 20, 2013,
         BCSFootball.org, Bowl Championship Series,
         http://www.bcsfootball.org/news/story?id=10172026

164   "*Big XII Conference has been contractually obligated . . .*" BCSFootball.org, *BCS chronology*, October 8, 2013

165   "*This highest-ever initial standing . . .*" Elliott, Bud, *Why 2007's preseason college football rankings fell apart, making room for chaos*, 2017, SBNation, Vox Media, Inc., https://www.sbnation.com/a/2007-college-football-season/preseason-rankings

165   "*Courted by the likes of Auburn, Mississippi State, . . .*" Townes, Devaughn, *Where Are They Now?: Pat White and Steve Slaton*, July 31, 2018, UnfilteredAccess.com, Unfiltered Access, https://unfilteredaccess.com/2018/07/31/where-are-they-now-pat-white-and-steve-slaton/

167   "*White and Slaton, who came to be known as . . .*" Townes, Devaughn, *Where Are They Now?: Pat White and Steve Slaton*, July 31, 2018

167   "*Hosting this year's game is a civic arena . . .*" Associated Press, *U. of Phoenix buys naming rights to Cardinals stadium*, September 26, 2006, ESPN.com, ESPN Internet Ventures, http://www.espn.com/nfl/news/story?id=2603052

167   "*University of Phoenix Stadium features a football field . . .*" LloydEngineers.com, *Portfolio: University of Phoenix Stadium*, 2015, LloydEngineers.com, Lloyd Civil & Sports Engineering, http://www.lloydengineers.com/professional-international/

167   "*If the massive silver-clad dome is recognized . . .*" FANDOM, *University of Phoenix Stadium*, 2016, American Football Wiki, FANDOM Lifestyle Community, http://americanfootball.wikia.com/wiki/State_Farm_Stadium

168   "*Following his senior year at Daphne High School, . . .*" Furfari, Mickey, *White has no regrets for rejecting rich baseball offer*, August 7, 2006, timeswv.com, Times West Virginian, https://www.timeswv.com/sports/white-has-no-regrets-for-rejecting-rich-baseball-offer/article_e9a511e6-26b8-5203-809b-1ed779227ead.html

171   "*(The team traveled 90 miles to the small town . . .*" Sparks, Patrick, *West Virginia- The One Rival Missing From Marshall's Schedule (Part 1)*, SBNation, Vox Media, Inc., November 28, 2014, https://www.underdogdynasty.com/2014/11/28/7277429/the-rivalry-thats-affecting-the-playoff-committee

174   "*Sports Illustrated in their article "Behind the Scenes . . .*" Markazi, Arash,

Behind the Scenes with Boise, January 2, 2007, CNN/Sports Illustrated, A Time Warner Company,
https://web.archive.org/web/20070104022040/http://sportsillus-trated.cnn.com/2007/writers/arash_markazi/01/02/inside.boise/index.html

175   *"Aptly named Challenger, the majestic raptor . . ."* The American Eagle Foundation, *Celebrity Eagle Challenger Earns Historic Place*, 2008, https://www.eagles.org/bald-eagle-challenger-earns-historic-place-on-u-s-half-dollar-commemorative-coin-2/

176   *"The former assistant head coach, hired by Don Nehlen . . ."* Baum, Bob, *Bill Stewart promoted to West Virginia football coach*, January 3, 2008, StarNewsOnline.com, GateHouse Media, LLC, https://www.starnewsonline.com/news/20080103/bill-stewart-promoted-to-west-virginia-football-coach

176   *"Two weeks following the stunning loss . . ."* Baum, Bob, *Rodriguez leaving West Virginia to coach Michigan*, December 16, 2007, ESPN.com, ESPN, http://www.espn.com/college-football/news/story?id=3157227

180   *"Crossing the goal, No. 35 in white not only . . ."* Hertzel, Bob, *Beware of WVU's next big moment in bowl*, December 27, 2016, WVNews.com, WVNews, https://www.wvnews.com/sports/wvu/beware-of-wvu-s-next-big-moment-in-bowl/article_0798b493-5e58-5544-bb9e-b2c016e426bf.html

181   PHOTO: University of Phoenix Stadium, Glendale, Arizona, January 2, 2008, Standing to receive snap from center: Pat White, Photo courtesy of Andrea Joliet, Wild and Wonderful Tailgating

183   *"And, once again, this is not lost on the 70,000 . . ."* FiestaBowl.org, *37th Annual Fiesta Bowl*, 2016, FiestaBowl.org, Fiesta Bowl, https://fiestabowl.org/game-history/fiesta-bowl/37th-annual-fiesta-bowl/

186   *"Devine unknowingly just bested Schmitt's . . ."* Hertzel, Bob, *Beware of WVU's next big moment in bowl*, December 27, 2016, WVNews.com, WVNews, https://www.wvnews.com/sports/wvu/beware-of-wvu-s-next-big-moment-in-bowl/article_0798b493-5e58-5544-bb9e-b2c016e426bf.html

187   PHOTO: University of Phoenix Stadium, Glendale, Arizona, January 2, 2008, Final score on stadium scoreboard, Photo courtesy of Andrea Joliet, Wild and Wonderful Tailgating

CHAPTER TEN   WORLD'S LARGEST COCKTAIL PARTY
                     Georgia | Florida
PAGE

189   *"Even though its star quarterback was nursing . . ."* ESPN.com, *Georgia upsets Florida for just third win in last 18 meetings*, October 28, 2007, ESPN Internet Ventures, http://www.espn.com/college-football/recap?gameId=273000061

190   *"Vern Lundquist, calling the game for CBS Sports, . . ."* RedStripeDawg, *Georgia Celebrates After TD Against Florida - 2007*, October 30, 2007, https://www.youtube.com/watch?v=mJAQjqZg_zI

191   *"The University of Georgia contends its first . . ."* University of Georgia, *2011 Georgia Football Media Guide*, October 10, 2011, University of Georgia Athletic Department, Athens, Georgia, pp. 157 & 158, https://issuu.com/georgiadogs/docs/uga_football_web-final4

191   *"Their interstate rival asserts they didn't even have . . ."* University of Florida, *2011 University of Florida Football Media Guide*, 2011, University of Florida Communications Department, University Athletic Association, Inc., p. 116, https://web.archive.org/web/20120402035222/http://web.gatorzone.com/football/media/2011/media_guide.pdf

191   *"Both colleges do agree that 11 years after this game . . ."* University of Georgia, *2011 Georgia Football Media Guide*, October 10, 2011, University of Georgia Athletic Department, Athens, Georgia, p. 158, https://issuu.com/georgiadogs/docs/uga_football_web-final4

191   *"Early in the 1950s, a reporter for The Florida Times-Union . . ."* DiRocco, Michael, *Georgia-Florida game needs a name and a trophy*, October 28, 2010, Jacksonville.com, The Florida Times-Union, https://www.jacksonville.com/sports/college/florida-gators/2010-10-28/story/revisiting-cocktail-party-georgia-florida-needs-name

192   *"city officials announced they would no longer . . ."* DiRocco, Michael, *Georgia-Florida game needs a name and a trophy*, October 28, 2010, https://www.jacksonville.com/sports/college/florida-gators/2010-10-28/story/revisiting-cocktail-party-georgia-florida-needs-name

192   *"The SEC followed suit when the moniker was dropped . . ."* DiRocco, Michael, *Georgia-Florida game needs a name and a trophy*, October 28, 2010

192   *"Eighty combined points – the most-ever in its 103-year . . ."* MCubed.net, *Texas is (62-47-5) against Oklahoma*, 2013, MCubed.net, MCubed,

http://www.mcubed.net/ncaaf/series/tx/ok.shtml

194   *"In 1992, head coach Steve Spurrier . . ."* English, Antonya, *100 things about 100 years of Gator football,* August 27, 2006, Tampa Bay Times, https://web.archive.org/web/20160904141255/http://www.sptimes.c om/2006/08/27/Sports/100_things_about_100_.shtml

196   *"At the press conference after the game, a teary-eyed . . ."* Associated Press, *Snead tosses two TDs, runs for one as Ole Miss stuns Florida,* September 28, 2008, ESPN Internet Ventures, http://www.espn.com/college-football/recap?gameId=282710057

196   *"Completed just three months ago, Heavener Football . . ."* Apple, Dan, *James W. "Bill" Heavener Football Complex Opens Doors,* August 30, 2008, University of Florida, University Athletic Assoc., Inc., FOX Sports Sun & IMG College, https://floridagators.com/news/2008/8/30/14380.aspx

197   PHOTO: Ben Hill Griffin Stadium, Gainesville, Florida, November 1, 2008, Outside of Heavener Football Complex with statue of Bull Gator: Sean McMahon

197   *"Homeschooled all his life, he took advantage . . ."* Strauss, Valerie, *Tim Tebow's unusual education,* January 14, 2012, The Washington Post, WP Company, LLC, https://www.washingtonpost.com/

199   *"Izhevsk, Russia, a former Soviet military city . . ."* Vershinin, Alexander, *Izhevsk: 200 years at the forefront of Russian rifle production,* June 15, 2015, https://www.rbth.com/defence/2015/06/15/izhevsk_200_years_at_th e_forefront_of_russian_rifle_production_46919.html

200   *"Home to three naval bases and a submarine base . . ."* World Port Source, *Port of Jacksonville – Review and History,* 2016, WorldPortSource.com, World Port Source, http://www.worldportsource.com/ports/review/USA_FL_Port_of_Ja cksonville_225.php

200   *"1995 to be the home field for the NFL Jacksonville . . ."* Jacksonville Jaguars, *Stadium History,* 2016, Jacksonville Jaguars Public Relations, Jacksonville Jaguars, https://www.jaguars.com/stadium/

200   *"It has also hosted every Cocktail Party ever since."* Verney, Stewart, *Money, not tradition keeps Florida-Georgia game in Jacksonville,* October 5, 2009, Jacksonville Business Journal, American City Business Journals, https://www.bizjournals.com/jacksonville/stories/2009/10/05/story

1.html?b=1254715200%255E2197241

200   *"According to the Jacksonville Business Journal, . . ."* Verney, Stewart,
      Money, not tradition keeps Florida-Georgia game in Jacksonville, Oct. 5, 2009

202   *"Mike "Big Dawg" Woods is also proudly sporting . . ."* May, Jed,
      Remembering Mike 'Big Dawg' Woods, January 12, 2017, The Red&Black,
      RedAndBlack.com,
      https://www.redandblack.com/sports/remembering-mike-big-dawg
      woods/article_b3e9bcf0-d862-11e6-9c64-3b5dc8e3843b.html

202   PHOTO: Alltel Stadium, Jacksonville, Florida, November 1, 2008, Inside
      stadium with Mike "Big Dawg" Woods: Sean McMahon

203   *"Before he ever played a down in college, ESPN Radio . . ."* Kowalski, Tom,
      ESPN's Mel Kiper lauded Matthew Stafford as a high school QB, January 29,
      2009, MLive Media Group, Advance Local Media LLC.,
      https://www.mlive.com/lions/index.ssf/2009/01/heres_one_reason_
      why_mel_kiper.html

205   *"As he stated in his autobiography . . ."* English, Antonya, *Meyer, Florida
      Gators want to move past Georgia's end zone celebration*, October 27, 2008,
      St. Petersburg Times,
      http://www.tampabay.com/sports/college/article872965.ece

210   *"Starting the next drive on their 40-yard-line, . . ."* Austro, Ben, *Chronology
      of kickoff rules changes*, May 17, 2018, FootballZebras.com, Football
      Zebras, http://www.footballzebras.com/2018/05/chronology-of-
      kickoff-rules-changes/

211   *"With encouragement from his handler, the 56-pound . . ."* University of
      Georgia Athletics, *Uga - The Georgia Bulldog*, 2017, University of Georgia
      Athletics, University of Georgia,
      https://georgiadogs.com/sports/2017/6/16/uga.aspx

211   *"In 1956, the Southern trial lawyer . . ."* University of Georgia Athletics,
      Uga - The Georgia Bulldog, 2017

211   *"And each wrinkle-faced canine has received a varsity . . ."* University of
      Georgia Athletics, *Uga - The Georgia Bulldog*, 2017

CHAPTER ELEVEN   MIDNIGHT YELL
                        Texas | Texas A&M

Page
218   *"Founded in 1974 by two local business partners, . . ."* Salazar, Andrea,

Dixie Chicken to celebrate 40 years of business on Northgate, June 12, 2014, The Eagle, BH Media Group, Inc., https://www.theeagle.com/news/local/dixie-chicken-to-celebrate-years-of-business-on-northgate/article_8db35b47-2611-5818-ae60-4c2cd2c2c47e.html

218   *"It's said Lyle Lovett and several other country music . . ."* Hlavaty, Craig, *College Station's legendary Dixie Chicken celebrates a milestone*, June 14, 2014, Houston Chronical, Hearst Newspapers, https://www.chron.com/news/houston-texas/texas/article/Dixie-Chicken-College-Station-5550574.php

218   *"From an initial investment of $7,000, . . ."* Salazar, Andrea, *Dixie Chicken to celebrate 40 years of business on Northgate*, June 12, 2014

218   *"Three years ago, Playboy On-Campus claimed . . ."* Playboy.com, *College Bar of the Month: Dixie Chicken Texas A&M*, April 28, 2006, Playboy.com On Campus, https://web.archive.org/web/20060428080550/http://www.playboy.com/on-campus/collegebars/dixie/

219   *"This community-wide pep rally got its humble beginning . . ."* Texas A&M University Traditions Council, *Aggie Traditions – Midnight Yell*, June 4, 2006, Texas A&M University Traditions Council, Texas A&M University, https://web.archive.org/web/20000604131510/http://aggietraditions.tamu.edu/midnight.shtml

219   *"In the early 1930s, as the legend goes, . . ."* Texas A&M University Traditions Council, *Aggie Traditions – Midnight Yell*, June 4, 2006

219   *"In the mid-1880s, an all-male pep squad at Princeton . . ."* Varsity Spirit, *Cheerleading*, 2016, Varsity.com, Varsity Spirit, LLC, https://www.varsity.com/news/cheerleader-history-cheerleading/

219   *"Thomas Peebles, a former member of that squad, . . ."* Varsity Spirit, *Being a Cheerleader – History of Cheerleading*, October 20, 2014

219   *"In 1923, at the same university, women joined . . ."* Varsity Spirit, *Being a Cheerleader – History of Cheerleading*, October 20, 2014

219   *"introduction of synchronized routines . . ."* Golden, Suzi J., *Best Cheers: How to Be the Best Cheerleader Ever!*, WA: Becker & Mayer, 2004, p. 5.

220   *"During this era, Lawrence "Herkie" Herkimer, . . ."* Varsity Spirit, *Being a Cheerleader – History of Cheerleading*, October 20, 2014

220   *"Credited with introducing pom-poms . . ."* Varsity Spirit, *Being a Cheerleader – History of Cheerleading*, October 20, 2014

220   *"In 1961, Herkimer formalized his organization . . ."* Varsity Spirit, *Being a Cheerleader – History of Cheerleading*, October 20, 2014

220   *"Instead, the school – which officially changed . . ."* Texas A&M University, *History of the University*, tamu.edu, Texas A&M University, 2016, https://www.tamu.edu/about/history.html

220   *"Each year, the all-male troupe of three seniors . . ."* Texas A&M University, *History of the Yell Leaders*, 2015, Department of Student Activities, Texas A&M University College Station, https://yell.tamu.edu/

220   *"This tradition of masculine Yell Leaders . . ."* The Eagle, *The yell leaders: How Texas A&M's loudest tradition got its start*, June 8, 2013, myaggienation.com, My Aggie Nation, https://www.myaggienation.com/history_traditions/yell_leaders/the-yell-leaders-how-texas-a-m-s-loudest-tradition/article_7b9ca3c0-e7e4-11e2-96fd-0019bb2963f4.html

220   *"The freshmen reportedly snuck into a maintenance . . ."* The Eagle, *The yell leaders: How Texas A&M's loudest tradition got its start*, June 8, 2013

221   *"Aggie Rings, we are told, are given out . . ."* Tresaugue, Matthew, *Gift has nice ring to it*, July 7, 2007, Houston Chronicle, p. A1, A8

221   *"On these Ring Days, students flock to this fowl-named . . ."* Janik, Jenna,*Unofficial tradition of ring dunking began on accident*, September 26, 2005, thebatt.com, The Battalion, https://web.archive.org/web/20070929111513/http://media.www.thebatt.com/media/storage/paper657/news/2005/09/26/News/Unofficial.Tradition.Of.Ring.Dunking.Began.On.Accident-997822.shtml

221   *"(As of four years ago, the state of Texas no longer . . ."* Janik, Jenna, *Unofficial tradition of ring dunking began on accident*, September 26, 2005

221   *"During his commencement speech at last year's . . ."* The Washington Post, *Bush Delivers Commencement Address at Texas A & M University*, December 12, 2008, WashingtonPost.com, The Washington Post, http://www.washingtonpost.com/wp-dyn/content/article/2008/12/12/AR2008121202727_pf.html

221   *"The 43rd Commander in Chief at the time made . . ."* The Washington Post, *Bush Delivers Commencement Address at Texas A & M University*,

December 12, 2008

222 *"Started in 1954 by a student activity director . . ."* The Austin American-Statesman, *Higher Education, GateHouse Media, LLC.,* July 25, 2008, p. B02

222 *"Last year, almost 6,000 high school graduates . . ."* KBTX.com, *Texas A&M's Fish Camp Begins Tuesday, with about 6,000 New Aggies To Participate,* July 25, 2013, KBTX.com, KBTX-TV Channel 3, https://www.kbtx.com/home/headlines/Texas-AMs-Fish-Camp-Begins-Tuesday-With-About-6000-New-Aggies-To-Participate-216974981.html

226 *"If an underclassman is caught performing . . ."* Connolly, Mike, *Open your mouth and yell!,* September 1, 2000, Notre Dame Observer, https://web.archive.org/web/20070301044235/http://www.nd.edu/~observer/09012000/Scene/0.html

227 *"The former head coach unceremoniously resigned . . ."* Davis, Brian, *Texas A&M finds violations in newsletters,* Oct. 12, 2007, Dallas Morning News, https://web.archive.org/web/20071116053214/http://www.dallasnews.com/sharedcontent/dws/dn/latestnews/stories/101207dnspotamulede.86c1dc.html

228 *"Yell Leaders let out a "horse laugh yell" . . ."* Greenwald, Michael L., *Crash course in rooting for Aggies,* December 24, 2006, The San Diego Union-Tribune, Union-Tribune Publishing Co., https://web.archive.org/web/20081216051618/http://www.signonsandiego.com/uniontrib/20061224/news_1s24am.html

229 PHOTO: Kyle Field, College Station, Texas, November 26, 2009, Valerie McMahon with Yell Leader after Midnight Yell Practice

229 *"The Agricultural and Mechanical College of Texas . . ."* Texas A&M, *History of the University,* tamu.edu, Texas A&M University, 2016

229 *"It wasn't until 1904, when a professor of . . ."* Perry, George Sessions, *The Story of Texas A. and M.,* 1951, McGraw Hill, New York, p. 127

229 *"Using $650 of his own money . . ."* Perry, George Sessions, *The Story of Texas A. and M.,* 1951, p. 127

229 *"The Corps of Cadets christened it two seasons . . . "* Perry, George Sessions, *The Story of Texas A. and M.,* 1951, p. 128

230 *"Early in the morning of November 18ᵗʰ, . . ."* CNN.com, *Unlit bonfire*

collapse at Texas A&M kills at least 4, injures 25, November 18, 1999, CNN.com, Cable News Network, https://web.archive.org/web/20070210031853/http://www.cnn.com/US/9911/18/students.crushed.03/

230   *"At 2:42am, the unthinkable happened."* CNN.com, *Unlit bonfire collapse at Texas A&M kills at least 4, injures 25,* November 18, 1999

230   *"Rescue operations took more than 24 hours . . ."* CNN.com, *Unlit bonfire collapse at Texas A&M kills at least 4, injures 25,* November 18, 1999

230   *"A&M football team rushed to the polo field . . ."* Bowen, Larry, *Football Players Assist in Rescue,* November 19, 1999, theeagle.com, The Bryan-College Station Eagle, https://archive.is/20070930200950/http://www.theeagle.com/bonfire/storyarchive/november1999/191199e.htm

230   *"Five years ago, a circular memorial . . ."* Mfon, Tosin, *A&M remembers bonfire tragedy,* November 19, 2004, theeagle.com, The Daily Texan Online, The Daily Texan and Texas Student Publications, https://archive.is/20070930200950/http://www.theeagle.com/bonfire/storyarchive/november1999/191199e.htm

230   *"On Thanksgiving Day in 1956, the Texas A&M varsity . . ."* The Eagle, *1956,* July 25, 2013, myaggienation.com, My Aggie Nation, https://www.myaggienation.com/athletics_history/football/year_by_year/year_by_year_2/article_7c4d2e58-f544-11e2-a882-0019bb2963f4.html

231   *"After this first-ever victory in the Austin arena, . . ."* The Eagle, *1956,* July 25, 2013

231   *"Ranked No. 1 in the country, coach Bryant proclaimed, . . ."* The Associated Press, *John David Crow, Heisman Winner at Texas A&M, Dies at 79,* June 18, 2015, The New York Times, The New York Times Company, https://www.nytimes.com/2015/06/19/sports/ncaafootball/john-david-crow-heisman-winner-at-texas-am-dies-at-79.html?_r=0

231   *"On December 3rd of that same year, he became . . ."* Heisman.com, *1957–23rd Award: John David Crow Texas A&M Back Dies at 79,* July 7, 2006, HeismanTrophy.com, All Things Media LLC, https://web.archive.org/web/20110706234204/http://www.heisman.com/winners/j-crow57.php

231   *"Unbeknownst to us, this 2009 season is the 75th year . . ."* Sass, Erik, *Nissan,*

SI Celebrate Heisman's 75th Birthday, July 27, 2009, Media Daily News, MediaPost Communications, https://www.mediapost.com/publications/article/110545/nissan-si-celebrate-heismans-75th-birthday.html

232   PHOTO: Kyle Field, College Station, Texas, November 26, 2009, *Sports Illustrated* photo-journalist outside of Texas A&M football stadium

233   *"In 1921, this second-year student became the source ..."* The Eagle, *The 12th Man: How E. King Gill started Texas A&M's identity of teamwork and support,* August 12, 2013, myaggienation.com, My Aggie Nation, https://www.myaggienation.com/history_traditions/12th_man/the-th-man-how-e-king-gill-started-texas-a/article_3d5df82c-0394-11e3-95ab-001a4bcf887a.html

233   *"After quitting the varsity football team, ..."* The Eagle, *The 12th Man: How E. King Gill started Texas A&M's identity of teamwork and support,* August 12, 2013

233   *"At the end of the season, the five-win, one-loss ..."* Schoor, Gene, *The Fightin' Texas Aggies: 100 Years of A&M Football,* Sept. 1, 1994, Taylor Publishing Company, p. 3

233   *"During that scrimmage, the undefeated Praying Colonels ..."* The Eagle, *The 12th Man: How E. King Gill started Texas A&M's identity of teamwork and support,* August 12, 2013

233   *"After the game, the reserve player stated ..."* The Eagle, *The 12th Man: How E. King Gill started Texas A&M's identity of teamwork and support,* August 12, 2013

233   *"In 1983, head coach Jackie Sherrill added ..."* The Eagle, *The 12th Man: How E. King Gill started Texas A&M's identity of teamwork and support,* August 12, 2013

234   *"E.A. McGowan, in a 1912 edition of The Iowa Alumnus, ..."* McGowan, E.A., *The Twelfth Player,* November 1912, The Iowa Alumnus, University of Iowa Alumni Association 10, p.30, http://digital.lib.uiowa.edu/cdm/compoundobject/collection/uap/id/5706/rec/10

234   *"The olive-green cannon has been fired ..."* Robbins, Kevin; Janner, Jay, *Those who go risk vertigo in Aggies' towering stadium,* The Austin American-Statesman, GateHouse Media, LLC., Nov. 24, 2007, p. B9

234   *"A total of 68 equine – 61 horses and 7 mules . . ."* Fieldler, Rebecca; Janner, Jay, *Parsons Mounted Cavalry a proud tradition at Texas A&M,* The Associated Press, The Seattle Times, October 15, 2017, https://www.seattletimes.com/nation-world/parsons-mounted-cavalry-a-proud-tradition-at-texas-am/

235   *"Recognized as the "First Lady of Aggie Land," . . ."* Heathman, Claire, *How a stray dog became Reveille, the First Lady of Aggieland,* July 5, 2013, myaggienation.com, My Aggie Nation, https://www.myaggienation.com/history_traditions/reveille/article_b7842f1c-e59f-11e2-b6a2-0019bb2963f4.html

235   *"Reveille VII, wearing a replica of the cape worn . . ."* Peshek, Sam, *Former Texas A&M Mascot Reveille VIII Dies At Age 12,* June 25, 2018, tamu.edu, Texas A&M University, https://today.tamu.edu/2018/06/25/former-texas-am-mascot-reveille-viii-dies-at-age-12/

235   *"sporting hound was introduced last season . . ."* Heathman, Claire, *How a stray dog became Reveille, the First Lady of Aggieland,* July 5, 2013

235   *"Prior to 1960, each mascot roamed freely..."* Heathman, Claire, *How a stray dog became Reveille, the First Lady of Aggieland,* July 5, 2013

235   *"As tradition has it, if the coddled canine barks . . ."* Heathman, Claire, *How a stray dog became Reveille, the First Lady of Aggieland,* July 5, 2013

236   *"(Ten years ago, an imposing presidential library . . ."* George H.W. Bush Center, *Presidential Library & Museum,* 2016, George H.W. Bush Presidential Library Foundation, George H.W. Bush Center, https://www.bush41.org/about/presidential-library-and-museum

236   *"the almost 83,000 fans inside Kyle Field . . ."* College Gridirons, *Kyle Field,* 2016, CollegeGridirons.com, College Gridirons https://www.college-gridirons.com/stadiums/kyle-field/

238   *"The adage behind this being, "When the team scores . . ."* Lyght, Daniel, *Cultivating that Aggie Spirit: Tradition goes beyond football, binds fans, players, alum,* Sept. 7, 2007, The Fresno Bee, Fresno, California, p. D1 https://www.myaggienation.com/history_traditions/reveille/article_b7842f1c-e59f-11e2-b6a2-0019bb2963f4.html

238   *"In 1985, the Student Aggie Club erected kiosks . . ."* OMICS International, *Traditions of Texas A&M University,* 2014, OMICSGroup.org, OMICS International, http://research.omicsgroup.org/index.php/Traditions_of_Texas_A%2

6M_University

242   *"(We did later learn that during the ten seasons ..."* Bowie, James I.,
       Longhorn Logo Turns 50, April 30, 2013, The Alcalde, Texas Exes,
       https://alcalde.texasexes.org/2011/08/longhorn-logo-turns-50/

244   *"Tonight's shootout is the highest-scoring game ..."* San Antonio Express-
       News, *Texas vs. Texas A&M, 1894-2011: A complete history*, November 23,
       2011, Hearst Newspapers, Hearst Communications Inc.,
       https://www.expressnews.com/sports/college_sports/big_12/article/
       Texas-vs-Texas-A-M-1894-2011-A-complete-history-2283658.php

245   *"It is true that early in the morning on February 12, 1917 ..."* Schraeder,
       Jordan, *Bevo's the Name: Debunking the Aggie Myth [Proof]*,
       September/October 2011, The Alcalde, Texas Exes,
       http://alcalde.texasexes.org/2013/04/bevos-the-name/

245   *"This, the Aggies faithful claim, is how the bovine got its name."* Schraeder,
       Jordan, *Bevo's the Name: Debunking the Aggie Myth [Proof]*,
       September/October 2011

245   *"Nonetheless, two months before this nefarious searing ..."* Schraeder,
       Jordan, *Bevo's the Name: Debunking the Aggie Myth [Proof]*, April 30, 2013

245   *"Stephen Pinckney, suggested a steer would better symbolize ..."* The
       University of Texas, *"Pig's Dead ... Dog gone": UT Austin students lead
       effort to pay tribute to first varsity mascot*, April 24, 2001, Office of Public
       Affairs, The University of Texas at Austin,
       https://web.archive.org/web/20060629033039/http://www.utexas.edu
       /opa/news/01newsreleases/nr_200104/nr_pig010424.html

245   *"Bevo XIV, whose predecessor was at the Red River blowout ..."* Roberts,
       Roxanne, Zachary, *The Inauguration of George W. Bush*, January 21, 2001,
       The Washington Post, WP Company LLC,
       https://www.washingtonpost.com/archive/lifestyle/2001/01/21/the-
       inauguration-of-george-w-bush/91536bba-9a26-4272-95a8-
       00fe3fedbb32/?noredirect=on&utm_term=.8abb9031df72

245   PHOTO: Original Bevo mascot, University of Texas, 1917, Prints and
       Photographs Collection, di_02241, The Dolph Briscoe Center for
       American History, The University of Texas at Austin

246   *"horns that measure 72 inches from tip to tip."* Ayala, Christine; Strain,
       Zachary, *14 Things you didn't know about Bevo XIV*, September 15, 2013,
       The Daily Texan, Texas Student Media,

http://www.dailytexanonline.com/news/2013/09/15/14-things-you-didnt-know-about-bevo-xiv

CHAPTER TWELVE   THE FIGHT IN THE DOG
                  Yale | Harvard

Page

247   *"Built in 1903, the horseshoe-shaped arena . . ."* Harvard University,
       Harvard Stadium, August 2017, GoCrimson.com, The Official Website of
       Harvard Athletics,
       https://www.gocrimson.com/information/facilities/harvardstadium

247   *"To address the savagery of the game, the presidential . . ."* Harvard
       University, *Harvard Stadium*, August 2017

248   *"More than 37 million pounds of concrete . . ."* Sisson, Patrick, *How Harvard
       Stadium's concrete construction changed the rules of football,* January 20,
       2017, Curbed.com, Vox Media, Inc.,
       https://www.curbed.com/2016/2/1/10871942/harvard-stadium-first-
       football-stadium

248   *"To avoid having to rebuild the hulking stadium, . . ."* Given, Kare, *Football
       Deaths, The Forward Pass And 250K Cubic Feet Of Concrete,* December 15,
       2017, WBUR.org, WBUR,
       https://www.wbur.org/onlyagame/2017/12/15/harvard-stadium-
       forward-pass

248   *"In 1923, the prestigious university expanded . . ."* Skenderian, Tanner;
       Wong, Justin C., *A Stadium For the Ages,* 2014, The Harvard Crimson,
       The Harvard Crimson, Inc.,
       https://www.thecrimson.com/article/2014/11/20/harvard-stadium-
       scrutiny/

248   *"seats in the north end were removed after the 1951 season."* Harvard
       University, *Harvard Stadium*, August 2017, GoCrimson.com, The Official
       Website of Harvard Athletics

248   *"Even with its size, the Romanesque structure . . ."* Harvard University,
       Harvard Stadium, August 2017

248   *"was a gift from the Class of 1879 on their 25th graduation . . ."* Harvard
       University, *Harvard Stadium*, August 2017

248   *"The New York Times described in 1903 . . ."* New York Times
       (Newspaper), *A Stadium for Harvard,* March 17, 1903, New York, New
       York, p. 7, https://newspaperarchive.com/new-york-times-mar-17-

1903-p-7/

249   *"In 1978, this highest stratum was divided . . ."* Berkman, Justin, *What Are NCAA Divisions? Division 1 vs 2 vs 3*, August 21, 2015, PrepScholar.com, PrepScholar, https://blog.prepscholar.com/what-are-ncaa-divisions-1-vs-2-vs-3

249   *"Along with consideration given to enrollment, . . ."* Berkman, Justin, *What Are NCAA Divisions? Division 1 vs 2 vs 3*, August 21, 2015

249   *"The "big boy" schools in the FBS . . ."* Berkman, Justin, *What Are NCAA Divisions? Division 1 vs 2 vs 3*, August 21, 2015

250   *"The Ivy League (where both of today's contestants reside) . . ."* Berkman, Justin, *What Are NCAA Divisions? Division 1 vs 2 vs 3*, August 21, 2015

250   *"Planting ivy was an annual tradition . . ."* The Harvard Crimson, *Class Day-Old and New.*, June 3, 1893, The Harvard Crimson, Inc., https://www.thecrimson.com/article/1893/6/3/class-day-old-and-new-it-is/?print=1

250   *"Others, however, claim the moniker is a nod . . ."* Yazigi, Monique, *At Ivy Club, A Trip Back to Elitism*, May 16, 1999, The New York Times, https://www.nytimes.com/1999/05/16/style/at-ivy-club-a-trip-back-to-elitism.html?

250   *"Memorialized by F. Scott Fitzgerald . . ."* Fitzgerald, Francis S., *This Side of Paradise*, 1920, New York: Charles Scribner's Sons, p. 49

250   *"On October 14, 1933, sportswriter Stanley Woodward . . ."* Woodward, Stanley, *Sports – College Football*, October 14, 1933, New York Tribune, New York

250   *"However, it wasn't until the formation of Division I . . ."* McCaulley, John, *The History of the Ivy League*, 2017, Best College Reviews.org, Best College Reviews, https://www.bestcollegereviews.org/history-ivy-league/

250   *"Prior to the start of the 1981 season, . . ."* Pennington, Bill, *Ivy Football and Academics Strike an Uneasy Balance*, November 17, 2006, The New York Times, The New York Times Company, https://www.nytimes.com/2006/11/17/sports/ncaafootball/17ivy.html

251   *"(Columbia University is the last Ivy League college . . ."* Steinman, Bill, *75 Years Ago: Columbia wins Rose Bowl!*, January 1, 2009, Columbia-Barnard

Athletic Consortium, Columbia University in the City of New York, https://gocolumbialions.com/news/2009/1/1/3637120.aspx?path=fo otball

251 *"In addition to this self-imposed ban, scholarships . . ."* Pennington, Bill, *Ivy Football and Academics Strike an Uneasy Balance,* November 17, 2006

251 *"Harvard and Yale are squaring off on the gridiron . . ."* Ivy Rugby Conference, *1875 The Game: Harvard vs. Yale,* 2017, IvyRugby.com, https://www.ivyrugby.com/news/1875-game-harvard-vs-yale

251 *"Slightly more than 2,000 fans . . ."* Halpern, Joe, *The Game: Harvard-Yale, by the numbers,* November 14, 2012, Boston Business Journal, American City Business Journals, https://www.bizjournals.com/boston/blog/bbj_research_alert/2012/11/harvard-yale-football-by-the-numbers.html

251 *"The visiting team won the rugby-style scrimmage . . ."* Ivy Rugby Conference, *1875 The Game: Harvard Vs. Yale,* 2017, IvyRugby.com, Ivy Rugby Conference, https://www.ivyrugby.com/news/1875-game-harvard-vs-yale

251 *"(During the seven seasons the teams played ahead of 1883, . . ."* The Harvard Crimson, *Harvard-Yale Football Scores,* November 25, 1905, The Harvard Crimson, The Harvard Crimson, Inc. https://www.thecrimson.com/article/1905/11/25/harvard-yale-football-scores-pfollowing-are-the/

251 *"On November 12, 1881, the fighting Elis from Yale . . ."* The Harvard Crimson, *Harvard-Yale Football Scores,* November 25, 1905

251 *"The Bulldogs – who are also called the "fighting Elis" . . ."* Anthony, Mike, *College Nicknames Can Leave You Scratching Your Head,* December 24, 2013, Courant.com, Hartford Courant, https://www.courant.com/sports/hc-xpm-2013-12-24-hc-ct-college-nicknames-1225-20131224-story.html

252 *"The Methodists from Wesleyan – and all of Yale's . . ."* SRCFB, *1888 Yale Bulldogs Schedule and Results,* 2002, Sports-Reference.com, Sports Reference LLC, https://www.sports-reference.com/cfb/schools/yale/1888-schedule.html

252 *"only two teams on its nine-game schedule crossed . . ."* Harvard University, *1920 Harvard Football Schedule,* August 2017, GoCrimson.com, The Official Website of Harvard Athletics,

https://www.gocrimson.com/information/facilities/harvardstadium

252   *"Harvard and Yale were the first institutions . . ."* Veneziano, John, *America's Oldest Intercollegiate Athletic Event,* April 29, 2011, Harvard University, Havard.edu, https://web.archive.org/web/20110429031611/http://www.hcs.harvard.edu/~harvcrew/Website/History/HY/

252   *"In May 1843, the Elis established the nation's first . . ."* Veneziano, John, *Great Moments in Yale Sports,* March 2001, Yale Alumni Magazine, Yale Alumni Publications, https://web.archive.org/web/20121114113135/http://yalealumni-imagazine.com/issues/01_03/sports.html

252   *"Originally a recreational sport, the rowing team . . ."* Veneziano, John, *America's Oldest Intercollegiate Athletic Event,* April 29, 2011

252   *"This first-ever intercollegiate sporting event . . ."* Veneziano, John, *America's Oldest Intercollegiate Athletic Event,* April 29, 2011

252   *"crimson-colored scarves were given to the boat mates . . ."* Harvard University, *History – Why Crimson?,* 2017, The President and Fellows of Harvard College, Havard.edu, https://www.harvard.edu/about-harvard/harvard-glance/history

253   *"(which Facebook founder and CEO Mark Zuckerberg . . ."* Grossman, Lev, *Person of the Year 2010: Mark Zuckerberg,* Aug. 17, 2013, Time, Time, Inc., https://web.archive.org/web/20130817081156/http://www.time.com/time/specials/packages/article/0,28804,2036683_2037183_2037185,00.html

254   *"The Whiffenpoofs, founded in 1909 . . ."* The Whiffenpoofs of Yale, *History,* https://www.whiffenpoofs.com/about

254   *"Evidently, the spirited ballad, titled "Boola," . . ."* Shapiro, Fred R., *You can quote them,* September/October 2009, Yale Alumni Magazine, Yale Alumni Publications, Inc.https://web.archive.org/web/20101202105307/http://yalealumni-imagazine.com/issues/2009_09/arts_quot057.html

254   *"Hirsh admitted, in a 1930 letter, the obscure word . . ."* Shapiro, Fred R., *You can quote them,* September/October 2009

254   *"The fur-draped orator explains it's been adopted . . ."* Scarponi, Diane, *'Boola: Yale's fight song marks 100ᵗʰ Anniversary ,* November 19, 2000,

SouthCoastToday.com, Gatehouse Media, LLC, https://www.south-coasttoday.com/article/20001119/LIFE/311199944

255   PHOTO: Harvard Stadium, Boston, Massachusetts, November 20, 2010, Students singing Yale fight song outside of stadium

255   *"The plot of land it occupies, now called Soldiers Field, . . ."* Harvard University, *Education, bricks and mortar: Harvard buildings and their contribution to the advancement of learning,* 1949, Harvard University Press, Cambridge, MD

255   *"Following the heralded victory by the crew in red scarves . . ."* GoCrimson.com, *Harvard-Yale Regatta - 150 Years of Tradition,* 2015, GoCrimson.com, Harvard University, https://www.gocrimson.com/sports/mcrew-hw/tradition/harvard-yale-regatta

255   *"their 17-year head coach, Tim Murphy . . ."* GoCrimson.com, *Football – Tim Murphy,* 2017, GoCrimson.com, Harvard University, https://www.gocrimson.com/sports/fball/coaches/murphy_tim?view=bio

257   *"Handsome Dan XVII is the latest in a long line . . ."* Kim, Ruth, *Handsome Dan term no longer lasts a lifetime,* November 16, 2007, Yale Daily News, https://web.archive.org/web/20071118085010/http://www.yaledailynews.com/articles/view/22483

257   *"Born in Johnson City, Tennessee . . ."* Kim, Ruth, *Handsome Dan term no longer lasts a lifetime,* November 16, 2007

258   *"Nonetheless, Sherman's predecessor evidently . . ."* Kim, Ruth, *Handsome Dan term no longer lasts a lifetime,* November 16, 2007

258   *"The original Handsome Dan was spotted by Yale's . . ."* The Official Website of Yale University Athletics, *Handsome Dan I – 1889-1898,* 2017, YaleBulldogs.com, Yale University, News, http://www.yalebulldogs.com/information/mascot/handsome_dan/I

258   *"offered $5.00 to the shop owner for the brown-faced puppy."* The Official Website of Yale University Athletics, *Handsome Dan I – 1889-1898,* 2017

258   *"Yale students quickly adopted Handsome Dan . . ."* The Official Website of Yale University Athletics, *Handsome Dan I – 1889-1898,* 2017

258   *"The local paper questioned the appropriateness . . ."* The Official Website of

Yale University Athletics, *Handsome Dan I – 1889-1898,* 2017

258 *"Factually, he was one of the finest representatives . . ."* The Official Website of Yale University Athletics, *Handsome Dan I – 1889-1898,* 2017

260 *"These practical jokes, known as "hacks," . . ."* Carrillo, Carolina, *5 Best Harvard-Yale Pranks,* November 19, 2015, TheBoola.com, The Boola, http://theboola.com/5-best-harvard-yale-pranks/

261 *"In 1934, staff members from The Harvard Lampoon . . ."* The Harvard Crimson, *First Eli Bulldog Barked at Opponents In 1890; Second Licked Harvard's Feet,* November 25, 1950, The Harvard Crimson, Inc., https://www.thecrimson.com/article/1950/11/25/first-eli-bulldog-barked-at-opponents/

261 *"Although the white bulldog was returned . . ."* The Harvard Crimson, *First Eli Bulldog Barked at Opponents In 1890; Second Licked Harvard's Feet,* November 25, 1950

261 *"Prior to the 1961 scrimmage, The Harvard Crimson . . ."* Wong, Justin C., *The Game Boasts A Colorful History of Pranks,* November 15, 2012, The Harvard Crimson, The Harvard Crimson, Inc., https://www.thecrimson.com/blog/the-back-page/article/2012/11/15/harvard-yale-mit-pranks/

261 *"Standing at midfield during halftime, the president . . ."* Carrillo, Carolina, *5 Best Harvard-Yale Pranks,* November 19, 2015

261 *"One year later, at 3:00 in the morning . . ."* Carrillo, Carolina, *5 Best Harvard-Yale Pranks,* November 19, 2015

261 *"Much to the displeasure of the sleepy coastal town . . ."* Greenburg, Zack O., *The '04 Prank gave Yale the ultimate win,* November 16, 2005, yaledailynews.com, Yale Daily News, https://yaledailynews.com/blog/2005/11/16/the-04-prank-gave-yale-the-ultimate-win/

261 *"The seemingly simple prank required more than a year . . ."* Greenburg, Zack O., *The '04 Prank gave Yale the ultimate win,* November 16, 2005

261 *"The clever duo came up with the non-existent . . ."* Greenburg, Zack O., *The '04 Prank gave Yale the ultimate win,* November 16, 2005

262 *"On each square were the instructions . . ."* Greenburg, Zack O., *The '04 Prank gave Yale the ultimate win,* November 16, 2005

262   *"Across the field, the Yale faithful squealed . . ."* Greenburg, Zack O., *The '04 Prank gave Yale the ultimate win,* November 16, 2005

263   PHOTO: Harvard Stadium, Boston, Massachusetts, November 20, 2010, Halftime presentation by Yale Precision Marching Band

267   *"They also give no notice to the small white banner . . ."* Chicago Sunday Tribune, *30,000 expected to see Harvard-Oregon battle at Pasadena,* December 28, 1919, https://chicagotribune.newspapers.com/

268   *"In 1920, the Crimson traveled by train to Pasadena . . ."* Chicago Sunday Tribune, *30,000 expected to see Harvard-Oregon battle at Pasadena,* December 28, 1919

268   *"Grendel's Den was established in 1971."* Sun, Grace, *Grendel's Den Reaches 40th,* April 1, 2011, The Harvard Crimson, The Harvard Crimson, Inc., https://www.thecrimson.com/article/2011/4/1/grendels-club-cake-restaurant/

268   *"Grendel's Restaurant was named after . . ."* Party Earth, *Grendel's Den Review – The Scene,* 2017, PartyEarth.com, World Travel Media LLC., https://www.partyearth.com/boston/restaurants/grendels-den-2/#review

269   *"The eatery is well known locally for successfully . . ."* United States Supreme Court, *Larkin v. Grendel's Den, Inc.,* April 1, 2011, FindLaw.com, Thomson Reuters, https://caselaw.findlaw.com/us-supreme-court/459/116.html

269   *"In 1982, the United States Supreme Court . . ."* United States Supreme Court, *Larkin v. Grendel's Den, Inc.,* April 1, 2011

269   *"Upstart craft breweries, such as Boston Beer Company . . ."* BostonVoyager, *Meet Kari Kuelzer of Grendel's Den Restaurant & Bar in Harvard Square,* 2015, BostonVoyager.com, Voyage Group of Magazines, http://bostonvoyager.com/interview/meet-kari-kuelzer-grendels-den-restaurant-bar-harvard-square-cambridge/

269   *"Almost 100,000 no doubt raucous fans . . ."* ESPN.com, *Texas Versus Florida Atlantic Gamecast,* November 20, 2010, ESPN Internet Ventures, http://www.espn.com/college-football/game/_/gameId/303240251

269   *"Slightly more than the 30,000 . . ."* ESPN.com, *Harvard Versus Yale,* November 20, 2010, ESPN Internet Ventures, http://www.espn.com/college-football/game/_/gameId/303240108

CHAPTER THIRTEEN   FLIGHT AND FIGHT
Texas Christian | Air Force

Page

271   *"A massive block of gneiss – a steely gray stone . . ."* Railsback, Bruce, *Gneiss at West Point*, 2017, Department of Geology – Franklin College of Arts and Sciences, University of Georgia, http://www.gly.uga.edu/railsback/BS-WP.html

271   *"Recognized simply as "The Plain,"" . . ."* ArmyGameDay.com, *Get To The Game*, 2017, ArmyGameDay.com, Army West Point Athletics, https://www.armygameday.com/gamedayevents/

273   *"home of the Superintendent of the Academy, . . ."* Students Veteran Center, *Franklin L. Hagenbeck*, 2017, Veterans.fsu.edu, Veterans Alliance Florida State University, https://veterans.fsu.edu/donate/veterans-advancement-board/franklin-l-hagenbeck/

273   PHOTO: United States Military Academy, West Point, New York, May 21, 2010, United States Military Academy Band at graduation ceremony on The Plain

274   *"As we approach Buffalo Soldiers Field, . . ."* Buffalo Soldiers Association of West Point, *Welcome*, 2017, Official website of the Buffalo Soldiers Association of West Point, Buffalo Soldiers Association of West Point, Inc., http://www.buffalosoldiersofwestpoint.org/

274   *"coordinator of the Executive Flight Detachment."* United States Marine Corps, *Marine Helicopter Squadron One*, 2017, HQMC.Marines.mil, United States Marine Corps, https://www.hqmc.marines.mil/hmx-1/About/

275   *"Boeing CH-46 Sea Knights."* United States Marine Corps, *Marine Helicopter Squadron One*, 2017

275   *"Directed by the White House Military Office, . . ."* United States Marine Corps, *Marine Helicopter Squadron One*, 2017

275   *"one of these matching dark green SH-3 Sea Kings, . . ."* US Navy, *H-3 Sea King Helicopter*, February 18, 2009, Navy.mil, Official Website of the United States Navy, https://www.navy.mil/navydata/fact_display.asp?cid=1200&tid=300&ct=1

275   *"(The other white-capped aircraft will be used as a decoy.)"* Keene, R.R., *HMX-1: There's More Than Flying Off the White House Lawn*, July 1996,

Volume 79, Issue 7, Leatherneck, Marine Corps Association &
Foundation, https://www.mca-
marines.org/leatherneck/1996/07/hmx-1-theres-more-flying-white-
house-lawn

276 *"Executive Flight Detachment calls a "cage tour.""* Keene, R.R., *HMX-1:
There's More Than Flying Off the White House Lawn,* July 1996

276 PHOTO: Stewart Air National Guard Base, Orange County, New York,
May 21, 2010, Standing in front of Marine One helicopter: Valerie
McMahon, Sean McMahon

277 *"The former Continental Army quarters . . ."* Palka, Eugene; Malinowski,
Jon C., *Historic Photos of West Point,* February 1, 2008, Turner Publishing
Company, Nashville, TN, p. VIII

277 *"The central complex of the campus, . . ."* Palka, Eugene; Malinowski, Jon
C., *Historic Photos of West Point,* February 1, 2008, p.27

277 *"Half a century later, architects commissioned . . ."* Palka, Eugene;
Malinowski, Jon C., *Historic Photos of West Point,* February 1, 2008, p.27

277 *"General Tadeusz Kościuszko, the original designer . . ."* Crackel, Theodore,
The Illustrated History of West Point, September 1, 1991, Harry N.
Abrams, Inc., Boston, MA, p. 44

277 *"James Joyce stated that for an object . . ."* Joyce, James, *A Portrait of the
Artist as a Young Man,* December 29, 1916, B. W. Huebsch, New York
City, NY, p. 204

278 *"Following an assessment by President Eisenhower . . ."* Spokesman-
Review, *Air Force Academy Act signed by Eisenhower,* April 2, 1954,
Associated Press, Spokesman-Review, Spokane, Washington, p.1,
https://news.google.com/newspapers?id=9G8pAAAAIBAJ&sjid=VeY
DAAAAIBAJ&pg=6899%2C3318710

278 *"During its four-year construction, these 306 students . . ."* Spokesman-
Review, *Air Force Academy dedicated at Lowry,* July 12, 1955, p.1

278 *"Instructed by Air Training Officers, . . ."* Joiner, Stephen, *Class of '59,*
August 2016, Air & Space Magazine, Air & Space/Smithsonian,
https://www.airspacemag.com/history-of-flight/the-59ers-180960072/

279 *"the illustrious Hollywood director Cecil B. Demille.) . . ."* Nauman, Robert
A., *On the Wings of Modernism: The United States Air Force Academy,*

February 24, 2004, University of Illinois Press, Champaign, IL, p.127

279   *"Originally controversial, this modern-day cathedral . . ."* Som.com, *Walter Netsch Interviewed by Detlef Mertins,* May 21, 2001, Som.com, Skidmore, Owings & Merrill LLP, https://web.archive.org/web/20100408014230/http://www.som.com/content.cfm/walter_netsch_interview

279   *"The Terrazzo is a sprawling, square piece of land . . ."* Cambridge Dictionary, *terrazzo,* 2017, Cambridge University Press, https://dictionary.cambridge.org/us/dictionary/italian-english/terrazzo

280   *"The aircraft closest to us, in the northwest corner, . . ."* United States Air Force Academy, *The Terrazo,* 2017, USAFA.edu, https://www.usafa.edu/academics/facilities/terrazzo/

280   *"Across from this single-tailed jet is a much larger F-105 . . ."* United States Air Force Academy, *The Terrazo,* 2017

280   *"this fighter has been on permanent display here since 1968 . . ."* United States Air Force Academy, *The Terrazo,* 2017

280   *"This black-nosed attack jet is the only United States aircraft . . ."* United States Air Force Academy, *The Terrazo,* 2017

280   *"Completing the quadrant, a 1976 twin-tailed, dark gray . . ."* United States Air Force Academy, *The Terrazo,* 2017

280   *"This newest addition to the Terrazzo was flown on intercept . . ."* United States Air Force Academy, *The Terrazo,* 2017

280   *"Known as Honor Court, this upper plaza . . ."* United States Air Force Academy, *Air Force Academy history,* January 18, 2012, USAFA.edu, https://www.usafa.af.mil/News/Fact-Sheets/Display/Article/428274/air-force-academy-history/

280   *"statue of America's first jet ace, Jimmy Jabara, . . ."* Nauman, Robert A., *Aerial Victories of the Jet Era,* 2005, Lulu.com, Raleigh, NC, p. 12

280   *"Shooting down 15 Russian-built MiG fighters, . . ."* Nauman, Robert A., *Aerial Victories of the Jet Era,* 2005, Lulu.com, Raleigh, NC, p. 12

281   *"This twisted beam from the wreckage . . ."* United States Air Force Academy, *9/11 Memorial on the Terrazzo,* 2017, USAFA.org,

https://www.usafa.org/Heritage/Memorial_911

281   "Home to the 4th Infantry Division . . ." MyBaseGuide, Fort Carson, 2017,
       MyBaseGuide.com, MARCOA Media, LLC,
       http://www.mybaseguide.com/army/40-658/fort_carson_units

281   "The famed NORAD aerospace surveillance . . ." MyBaseGuide, Fort
       Carson, 2017, MyBaseGuide.com, MARCOA Media, LLC,
       http://www.mybaseguide.com/army/40-658/fort_carson_units

282   PHOTO: Falcon Stadium, United States Air Force Academy, Colorado
       Springs, Colorado, September 10, 2001, Standing with the Air Force
       mascot: Sean McMahon, Valerie McMahon

282   "Constructed three years after the Academy . . ." Associated Press, Air Force
       will dedicate stadium, October 17, 1962, Florence Times, Florence, AL, p. 2
       https://news.google.com/newspapers?id=GCcsAAAAIBAJ&sjid=Ip8F
       AAAAIBAJ&pg=5960%2C5092586

283   "One year after this Academy was commissioned, . . ." Volk, Pete, The 15 best
       service academy football teams since 1776, July 4, 2014, SBNation, Vox
       Media, Inc., https://www.sbnation.com/college-
       football/2014/7/4/5860616/navy-army-air-force-football-history-best-
       seasons

283   "Dubbed the Falcons by this inaugural squad, . . ." Volk, Pete, The 15 best
       service academy football teams since 1776, July 4, 201

283   "All "home games" that season . . ." United States Air Force Academy, Air
       Force Football 2013, September 25, 2013, United States Air Force, 2013 Air
       Force Media Guide, p. 125,
       http://grfx.cstv.com/photos/schools/afa/sports/m-
       footbl/auto_pdf/2013-14/misc_non_event/HistorySection2013.pdf

284   "(Horned frogs are wide-mouthed amphibians . . ." Frost, Darrell,
       Ceratophrys cranwelli Barrio, 1980, Research.amhn.org, American
       Museum of Natural History,
       http://research.amnh.org/vz/herpetology/amphibia/Amphibia/Anu
       ra/Ceratophryidae/Ceratophrys/Ceratophrys-cranwelli

284   "while horned lizards are spiked-back reptiles . . ." Seymour, George; Royo,
       A.R., Horned Lizards Genus Phrynosoma, 2016, DesertUSA.com, Digital
       West Media, Inc., p. 111, https://www.desertusa.com/reptiles/horned-
       lizard.html

284   *"Ever since its earliest days, this private university . . ."* Texas Christian University, *2016 TCU Football Fact Book*, August 21, 2016, TCU Athletics Communication Office, Texas Christian University, p. 111, https://issuu.com/tcu_athletics/docs/full_book

284   *"In 1896, the inaugural football squad . . ."* Texas Christian University, *2016 TCU Football Fact Book*, August 21, 2016, p. 111, https://issuu.com/tcu_athletics/docs/full_book

284   *"A couple years before the institution became known . . ."* Texas Christian University, *2016 TCU Football Fact Book*, August 21, 2016, p. 111

285   *"Known rather airily as Flight of Sound, . . ."* Lundy, Harry, *A Flight of Sound: Academy Drum & Bugle Corps performs at Denver halftime show*, November 22, 2013, Academy Public Affairs, United States Air Force Academy, https://www.usafa.af.mil/News/Features/Display/Article/619783/a-flight-of-sound-academy-drum-bugle-corps-performs-at-denver-halftime-show/

285   *"The troupe also competes against the U.S. . . ."* Drum Corps International, *Air Force edges Navy at Interservice Academy Drum & Bugle Corps Competition*, October 3, 2011, DCI.org, https://www.dci.org/news/air-force-edges-navy-at-interservice-academy-drum-bugle-corps-competition

286   *"During their third year at the Academy, . . ."* United States Air Force, *Soaring Programs at USAFA*, October 3, 2011, Air Education and Training Command, United States Air Force, https://www.aetc.af.mil/About-Us/Fact-Sheets/Display/Article/261039/soaring-programs-at-usafa/

286   *"pilots one of 19 German-made DG Flugzeugbau . . ."* DG Aircraft News, *US Air Force Academy Pilot visits DG Flugzeugbau*, July 18, 2017, DG Group, DG Flugzeugbau GmbH, https://www.dg-flugzeugbau.de/en/dg-aircraft-news/pilotin-us-air/14664

286   *"These lightweight gliders are towed into the sky . . ."* United State Air Force, *Cadet Airmanship Programs,* January 8, 2010, USAFA.af.mil, Official United States Airforce Website, https://www.usafa.af.mil/News/Fact-Sheets/Display/Article/428280/cadet-airmanship-programs/

287   *"Since 1967, the Wings of Blue . . ."* Wings of Blue, *History*, 2017, WingsOfBlue.com, U.S. Airforce Skydiving Team, http://wingsofblue.com/about/

287   *"Having exited a DeHavilland UV-18B Otter . . ."* United State Air Force, *Cadet Airmanship Programs,* January 8, 2010

287   *"Another successful jump, of the more than 600 . . ."* Wings of Blue, *History,* 2017

288   *"Calhoun was named 2007 Mountain West Conference . . ."* SRCFB, *MWC Coach of the Year Winners,* 2002, Sports-Reference.com, Sports Reference LLC, https://www.sports-reference.com/cfb/awards/mwc-coy.html

289   *"Legend has it this logo was selected . . ."* TigerNet.com, *Why would the Air Force Falcons have lightning bolts on their helmets?,* Dec 29, 2012, TigerNet.com, USA Today, https://www.tigernet.com/forum/thread/Why-would-the-Air-Force-Falcons-have-lightning-bolts-on-their-helmets***-1195457

290   *"Known as the Cadets in Section 8, . . ."* United States Air Force, *Falcons rally in 2nd half, overcome Demons,* October 3, 2011, USAFA.af.mil, Official United States Air Force Website, https://www.usafa.af.mil/News/Photos/igphoto/2000328895/

291   *"Ever since its formation in the late 1950s, . . ."* Kekis, John; Ginsburg, David, *Triple option helps level playing field at service academies,* December 5, 2017, The Associated Press, USAToday, https://www.usatoday.com/story/sports/ncaaf/2017/12/05/triple-option-helps-level-playing-field-at-service-academies/108324706/

291   *"Cadets at these showdowns are known to chant, . . ."* Lidz, Franz, *Woofers & Tweeters,* October 28, 1991, Sports Illustrated Vault, Time Inc., Sports Illustrated Group, https://www.si.com/vault/1991/10/28/106783277/woofers—tweeters

292   *"Live falcons do perform a series of bombing runs . . ."* United States Air Force, *Our Majestic Mascots – Falconry,* 2017, United States Air Force Academy, https://www.usafa.edu/cadet-life/clubs/falconry/

292   *"Falconry at the Academy, an extracurricular activity . . ."* United States Air Force, *Our Majestic Mascots – Falconry,* 2017, United States Air Force Academy

292   *"In October 1955, this first student body . . ."* United States Air Force, *Academy Falcons and Falconry,* September 27, 2011, United States Air Force Academy, https://www.usafa.af.mil/News/Fact-Sheets/Display/Article/428277/academy-falcons-and-falconry/

292 *"Today, a dozen or so flying predators . . ."* United States Air Force, *Our Majestic Mascots – Falconry,* 2017

293 *"A team of 12 falconers maintains the modern aviary facility."* United States Air Force, *Academy Falcons and Falconry,* September 27, 2011

293 *"Each bird requires more than 300 hours of training . . ."* United States Air Force, *Our Majestic Mascots – Falconry,* 2017

293 *"female white-phase gyrfalcon named Aurora . . ."* United States Air Force, *Our Majestic Mascots – Falconry,* 2017

293 *"Aurora is one of only two performing live mascots . . ."* The Best of America, *Best College Mascots (Live),* 2017, AmericasBestOnline.com, https://www.americasbestonline.com/cmascots.htm

293 *"The 12-year-old eagle, whose actual name is Nova, . . ."* McCoy, Janet, *Nova, War Eagle VII, sidelined for 2017 football season,* June 26, 2017, Auburn University, OCM.Auburn.edu, http://ocm.auburn.edu/newsroom/news_articles/2017/06/nova,-war-eagle-vii,-sidelined-for-2017-football-season.php

295 *"(Two seasons ago, during the lopsided 72-to-0 victory . . ."* Branum, Don, *Football: Air Force blasts Nicholls State 72-0 in home opener,* September 5, 2009, United States Air Force Academy Public Affairs, United States Air Force Academy, https://www.af.mil/News/Article-Display/Article/119246/football-air-force-blasts-nicholls-state-72-0-in-home-opener/

296 *"Zoomies (yet another creative nickname for the cadets) . . ."* United States Air Force Academy, *Learn The Lingo,* 2017, airforce.com, United States Air Force Academy, https://www.academyadmissions.com/what-to-expect/how-to-speak-academy/

297 *"Originally titled "Army Air Corps" . . ."* United States Air Force, *History of the U.S. Air Force Song,* January 29, 2007, Hill.af.mil, Official United States Air Force Website, https://www.hill.af.mil/About-Us/Fact-Sheets/Display/Article/397525/history-of-the-us-air-force-song/

297 *"Recognized by all military branches as the "Toast to . . ."* United States Air Force, *History of the U.S. Air Force Song,* January 29, 2007

297 *"With the sun setting over the edge of Falcon Stadium, . . ."* United States Air Force, *History of the U.S. Air Force Song,* January 29, 2007

CHAPTER FOURTEEN   A SOBERING AFFAIR
South Carolina | Clemson

Page

298   *"Tiger Town Tavern, situated inside Clemson's . . ."* Ordereze, *About Tiger Town Tavern*, 2018, TigerTownTavern.com, http://www.tigertowntavern.com/Aboutus

299   *"of this second-largest university in the Palmetto State, . . ."* SCIWAY.net, *Clemson, South Carolina*, 2018, SCIWAY.net, LLC, https://www.sciway.net/city/clemson.html

299   *"William Christopher Swinney got his nickname as an infant."* foxsports, *Clemson head coach Dabo Swinney didn't know his real name until 3rd grade*, January 5, 2016, Fox Sports Interactive Media, LLC., https://www.foxsports.com/college-football/story/clemson-head coach-dabo-swinney-didn-t-know-his-real-name-until-3rd-grade-010516

299   *"His elder brother, before the age of two, . . ."* foxsports, *Clemson head coach Dabo Swinney didn't know his real name until 3rd grade*, January 5, 2016

300   *"Many long-time boosters questioned the decision . . ."* Couch, Greg, *How Dabo Swinney Went from Bad Hire to Hot Seat to National Championship Game*, January 6, 2016, Bleacher Report, Inc., Turner Broadcasting System, Inc., https://bleacherreport.com/articles/2605558-how-dabo-swinney-went-from-bad-hire-to-hot-seat-to-national-championship-game

300   *"Many fans, along with members of the regional press, . . ."* Couch, Greg, *How Dabo Swinney Went from Bad Hire to Hot Seat to National Championship Game*, January 6, 2016

301   *"Swinney boasted during a pregame interview on ESPN, . . ."* Merriman, Sean, *Chick-fil-A Bowl 2012: Les .Miles and Dabo Swinney's 5 Best Presser Moments*, December 27, 2012, Bleacher Report, Inc., Turner Broadcasting System, Inc., https://bleacherreport.com/articles/1459146-chick-fil-a-bowl-2012-les-miles-and-dabo-swinneys-5-best-presser-moments#slide0

301   *"West Virginia scored the most ever points in a quarter . . ."* Associated Press, *West Virginia routs Clemson in record-setting Orange Bowl*, August 20, 2012, ESPN.com, http://www.espn.com/college-football/recap?gameId=320040228

302   *"Home to Clemson's soccer teams, historic Riggs Field . . ."* Clemson

University, *Historic Riggs Field Renovation Update*, 2016, ClemsonTigers.com, https://clemsontigers.com/hitstoric-riggs-field-renovation-update/

302   *"The namesake of this first home football field, . . ."* Kantor, Ryan; WelbornTiger, *Greatest Football Coaches in Clemson History: #10 Walter Riggs*, August 6, 2017, SBNation, Vox Media, Inc., https://www.shakinthesouthland.com/2017/8/6/16088808/greatest-football-coaches-in-clemson-history-10-walter-riggs

302   *"Riggs was also president of Clemson University . . ."* Clemson University, *Walter M. Riggs and S.C. State*, 2017, ClemsonTigers.com, The Official Website of Clemson University Athletics, https://clemsontigers.com/walter-m-riggs-and-s-c-state/

302   *"(Early in this second game, both squads agreed . . ."* Blackman, Sam; Bradley, Bob; Kriese, Chuck, *Where the Tigers Play*, 2001, Sports Publishing LLC, p. 4, https://books.google.com/books?id=zPugTuXMEq8C&pg=PA4#v=onepage&q&f=false

302   *"The 51-to-nil final score remains the largest margin . . ."* Post and Currier, *South Carolina-Clemson Rivalry Results*, November 25, 2017, The Post and Currier, Evening Post Industries Company, https://www.postandcourier.com/sports/south-carolina-clemson-rivalry-results/article_ac82bbfe-cfc6-11e7-865f-2f6ce6b8918d.html

302   *"Heisman won the conference title . . ."* Blackman, Sam; Bourret, Tim; Swinney, Dabo, *If These Walls Could Talk: Clemson Tigers: Stories from the Clemson Tigers Sideline, Locker Room, and Press Box*, August 15, 2016, Triumph Books, p. 46, https://books.google.com/books?id=zPugTuXMEq8C&pg=PA4#v=onepage&q&f=false

302   *"Fittingly, his memorial at the College Football Hall of Fame . . ."* Football-Foundation.org, *Hall of Fame John Heisman*, 2017, National Football Foundation & College Football Hall of Fame, https://footballfounda-tion.org/hof_search.aspx?hof=1297

303   PHOTO: The 1903 Clemson Tigers football team, (Oconeean 1904), marked as public domain, John Heisman standing second from the left in back row

303   *"this 110th meeting between these prominent . . ."* ThePalmettoBowl.com, *Results from past Clemson vs. South Carolina Games*, 2017, ThePalmetto-

Bowl.com, https://thepalmettobowl.com/results/

303   *"Back in the 30s and 40s, when this highway . . ."* Bell, Candice; Brown, David, *Our History – The Legend of The Esso Club*, 2017, TheEssoClub.com, The Esso Club, https://theessoclub.com/pages/our-history

304   *"In 1933, James A. Stevenson opened his service station . . ."* Bell, Candice; Brown, David, *Our History – The Legend of The Esso Club*, 2017

304   *"During the late 1950s, Stevenson's station . . ."* Bell, Candice; Brown, David, *Our History – The Legend of The Esso Club*, 2017

304   *"In the early 1970s, Standard Oil Company . . ."* Bell, Candice; Brown, David, *Our History – The Legend of The Esso Club*, 2017

304   *"ceased selling gasoline altogether in 1985."* Bell, Candice; Brown, David, *Our History – The Legend of The Esso Club*, 2017

304   *"CBS's play-by-play announcer Brent Musburger . . ."* Bell, Candice; Brown, David, *Our History – The Legend of The Esso Club*, 2017

306   *"Abdullah was selected in the second round . . ."* ProFootballReference.com, *Rahim Abdullah*, 2017, ProFootballReference.com, Sports Reference LLC, https://www.pro-football-reference.com/players/A/AbduRa20.htm

306   *"The Esso Club bills itself as being "In the Shadow . . ."* Bell, Candice; Brown, David, *Our History – The Legend of The Esso Club*, 2017

306   *"Officially christened as Clemson Memorial Stadium in 1942, . . ."* Clemson University, *2001 Clemson Football Media Guide*, 2001, Clemson.edu, Clemson University Department of Athletics, https://tigerprints.clemson.edu/cgi/viewcontent.cgi?article=1030&context=fball_media

306   *"The nickname apparently came from the town's first . . ."* Bradley, Bob, *Death Valley Days*, 1991, Longstreet Press, Inc., Atlanta, Georgia, p. 11, https://tigerprints.clemson.edu/cgi/viewcontent.cgi?article=1030&context=fball_media

306   *"Former head coach of Presbyterian College . . ."* Bradley, Bob, *Death Valley Days*, 1991, p. 11

307   *"During its 1972 renovation, aluminum benches . . ."* Feher, George N., *Death Valley at Memorial Stadium & Frank Howard Field – Clemson*

University, October 13, Playin Your Dreams, 2017, http://playinyour-dreams.com/?p=3138

308 *"For the first time in the 107-year history, . . ."* Tramel, Berry, *Bedlam by the numbers: Breaking down the series history,* November 19, 2012, NewsOK.com, The Oklahoman, https://newsok.com/article/3730087/bedlam-by-the-numbers-breaking-down-the-series-history

308 *"Brent Musburger described as the "twenty-five . . ."* Marshall, Thomas, *The Most Exciting 25 Seconds in College Football: An Open Letter to the Hill,* September 5, 2016, TheTigerNews.com, The Tiger, http://www.thetigernews.com/sports/the-most-exciting-seconds-in-college-football-an- open-letter/article_487beac0-72ef-11e6-8a04-8bd5f49df6c3.html

308 PHOTO: Memorial Stadium, Clemson, South Carolina, November 24, 2012, Standing in tailgate tent outside of Death Valley stadium: Boyd Pearson, Sean McMahon

309 *"The ubiquitous tiger paw, with its consistent 30-degree . . ."* MacRay, Robert, *Setting the Record Straight,* January 7, 2015, ClemsonInsider.com, USA Today Sports Digital Properties, https://theclemsoninsider.com/2015/01/07/setting-the-record-straight/

310 *"What began as a simple suggestion . . ."* Clemson University, *The Hill,* 2016, ClemsonTigers.com, The Official Website of Clemson University Athletics, https://clemsontigers.com/the-hill/

310 *"Coach Ingram decided to make Anderson's suggestion . . ."* Clemson University, *The Hill,* 2016

311 *"In the early 1960s, a large piece of white flint . . ."* Hyland, Tim, *Howard's Rock at Clemson University,* 2017, ThoughtCo., Dotdash publishing family, https://www.thoughtco.com/howards-rock-clemson-university-791830

312 *"Up until the 1966 season, the cantankerous coach . . ."* Hyland, Tim, *Howard's Rock at Clemson University,* 2017

312 *"Recognizing its novelty, Willimon had it mounted . . ."* Hyland, Tim, *Howard's Rock at Clemson University,* 2017

312 *""From Death Valley, CA to Death Valley, SC.""* Associated Press, *College*

FB Package: Clemson players "rub the rock", September 20, 2006, ESPN.com, ESPN Internet Ventures, http://www.espn.com/espn/wire/_/section/ncf/id/2596355

313   *"After 12 years of orchestrating the "Fun 'n' Gun" . . ."* Pells, Eddie, *Spurrier calls it quits as Florida head coach,* January 4, 2002, AZDailySun.com, Arizona Daily Sun, https://azdailysun.com/spurrier-calls-it-quits-as-florida-head-coach/article_06b0066f-7703-5763-85ec-b72bd502bc57.html

313   *"At the end of the 2004 season, then-head coach . . ."* GamecocksOnline.com, *Lou Holtz Announces Retirement From Coaching,* Nov. 22, 2004, GamecocksOnline.com, South Carolina Gamecocks, https://gamecocksonline.com/news/2004/11/22/Lou_Holtz_Announces_Retirement_From_Coaching.aspx?path=football

313   *"At his final press conference, the resolute Holtz . . ."* Scheib, Samuel L., *Horseshoes at the Old Ball Coach's Club,* August 1, 2014, Tomahawk Nation, Vox Media, Inc., https://www.tomahawknation.com/2014/8/1/5959169/horseshoes-at-the-old-ball-coach-s-club

313   *"With less than 2 minutes to go, the illustrious . . ."* Rosenberg, Michael, *December 23, 2016, Woody Hayes's last stand: Ohio State, Clemson and the punch that ruined Hayes,* 2017, Sports Illustrated, Time, Inc., https://www.si.com/college-football/2016/12/23/woody-hayes-punch-clemson-ohio-state

314   *"Following the game, Spurrier boasted, "Historically, . . ."* Low, Chris, *December 23, 2016, SEC Power Rankings: Week 14,* November 28, 2011, ESPN.com, ESPN, http://www.espn.com/blog/ncfnation/post/_/id/54404/sec-power-rankings-week-14-2

317   *"Since 1902, a rooster has been the official symbol . . ."* Nauright, John, *The South Carolina – Clemson Football War of 1902,* 2005, Gridiron Greats, https://www.academia.edu/1578479/The_South_Carolina_Clemson_Football_War_of_1902

317   *"One such outfit, worn by a first-year biology student . . ."* Hunt, Kimberly,*First USC mascot 'The Rooster' led way for Big Spur, Cocky,* 2000, USC, University of South Carolina, http://www.datelinecarolina.org/story/5521416/first-usc-mascot-the-rooster-led-way-for-big-spur-cocky

317   *"The rudimentary ensemble – handcrafted by . . ."* Hunt, Kimberly, *First USC mascot 'The Rooster' led way for Big Spur, Cocky,* 2000

322   *"(who is the third consecutive "Mr. Football" . . ."* Staples, Andy, *Top 2011 recruit Clowney ends suspense, picks South Carolina,* February 14, 2011, Sports Illustrated, Time, Inc.

323   *"second-longest consecutively played rivalry in the nation."* Inabinett, Mark, *Countdown to Football: 31 Days — College football gets new oldest rivalry,* August 3, 2011, The Press-Register, Advance Local Media LLC., https://www.al.com/sports/index.ssf/2011/08/countdown_to_football_31_days.html

323   *"(Only Minnesota versus Wisconsin is longer . . ."* Inabinett, Mark, *Countdown to Football: 31 Days — College football gets new oldest rivalry,* August 3, 2011

323   *"Steve Spurrier is now the winningest head coach . . ."* Malone, Christian, *Report: Steve Spurrier considering new position at South Carolina,* 2016, SaturdayDownSouth.com, Saturday Down South, https://www.saturday-downsouth.com/south-carolina-football/spurrier-considering-ambassador-role-south-carolina/

CHAPTER FIFTEEN   KEEPING THE FAITH
                       Southern California | Notre Dame
Page
327   *"85th meeting between the University of Southern . . ."* Reign of Troy, *USC vs Notre Dame 2013 Gameday Preview: Lineups and Links,* October 19, 2013, ReignOfTroy.com, Fansided Inc., https://reignoftroy.com/2013/10/19/usc-vs-notre-dame-2013-gameday-preview-lineups-links/

328   *""Greatest Inter-Sectional Rivalry in College Football.". . ."* LaMare, Amy, *Notre Dame vs. USC: Greatest Intersectional Rivalry in College Football 2012,* November 22, 2012, Bleacher Report, Inc. Turner Broadcasting System, Inc., https://bleacherreport.com/articles/1418818-notre-dame-vs-usc-greatest-intersectional-rivalry-in-college-football-2012

328   *"Brothers Bar & Grill turns out to be the newest . . ."* Brothers Bar & Grill, *Brothers Story,* 2017, Brothers Bar & Grill, https://www.brothersbar.com/

329   *"Holtz (who compiled 100 wins, 30 losses, and 2 ties . . ."* University of Notre Dame, *2016 Media Guide – Notre Dame Football,* 2016, Fighting Irish Media, University of Notre Dame, 2016., p. 217,

http://grfx.cstv.com/photos/schools/nd/sports/m-footbl/auto_pdf/2016-17/misc_non_event/16-media-guide.pdf

329   *"Holtz has been a hero, here and across this Midwestern . . ."* College Poll Archive, *Notre Dame 1988 AP Football Rankings,* October 19, 2013, College Poll Archive, http://www.collegepollarchive.com/football/ap/teams/by_season.cfm?teamid=7&seasonid=1988#.XB1hOlxKhPY

330   *"Frank Leahy played on two national championship teams . . ."* The Bulletin, *Frank Leahy dies at Portland home,* June 21, 1973, The Bulletin (Bend), A Western Communications Company, https://news.google.com/newspapers?id=LDcVAAAAIBAJ&sjid=G_gDAAAAIBAJ&pg=5105,4878496

330   *"His former head coach, Knute Rockne, is the only coach . . ."* The Bulletin, *Frank Leahy dies at Portland home,* June 21, 1973, p. 12

330   *"(he was replaced by Edward McKeever in 1944 . . ."* The Bulletin, *Frank Leahy dies at Portland home,* June 21, 1973, p. 12

330   *"Four (four!) of his players were awarded . . ."* UHND.com, *Frank Leahy, College Football's Greatest Coach,* January 2, 2014, UHND.com, USAToday Sports Media Group, https://www.uhnd.com/football/college-footballs-greatest-coach/

330   *""Notre Dame didn't kick field goals; . . ."* RareNewspapers.com, *Frank Leahy at Notre Dame...,* September 28, 1941, RareNewspapers.com, Timothy Hughes Rare & Early Newspapers, http://www.rarenewspapers.com/view/564337

331   *"Recognized as "The Gug" (pronounced "goog") . . ."* Leonard, Pat, *ND Athletics: Gug' gives Notre Dame new look,* August 24, 2005, The Observer, https://ndsmcobserver.com/2005/08/nd-athletics-gug-gives-notre-dame-new-look/

331   *"Commissioned in 2004 to be the "finest college football . . ."* Leonard, Pat, *ND Athletics: Gug' gives Notre Dame new look,* August 24, 2005

331   *"Upon announcing his generous gift, Don Guglielmino . . ."* Leonard, Pat, *The Guglielmino Complex,* October 14, 2005, UND.com, The University of Notre Dame, https://und.com/news/2005/10/14/The_Guglielmino_Complex.aspx

331   *"After the hard-fought 24-to-20 victory . . ."* Leonard, Pat, *The Guglielmino*

Complex, October 14, 2005

331   *"the famous picture of the "Four Horsemen"* The University of Notre
       Dame, *October 18, 1924 The Four Horsemen Arrive*, 2017, 125.nd.edu, The
       University of Notre Dame, https://125.nd.edu/moments/october-18-
       1924-the-four-horsemen-arrive/

331   *"Seated upon saddled steeds and wearing leather helmets . . ."* The University
       of Notre Dame, *The Four Horsemen*, 2017, UND.com, The University of
       Notre Dame, https://und.com/sports/2018/8/7/trads-horse-
       html.aspx?id=2038

331   *"In his later years, Rockne proclaimed that the 160-pound . . ."* The
       University of Notre Dame, *The Four Horsemen*, 2017

331   *"The group's apocalyptic nickname was coined in 1924 . . ."* Rice, Grantland,
       The Four Horsemen, October 18, 1924, New York Herald Tribune,
       University of Notre Dame Archives,
       http://archives.nd.edu/research/texts/rice.htm

332   *"No other school has more of these awards."* Heisman Trophy Trust,
       Heisman Trophy Winners List, 2017, Heisman.com, Heisman Trophy
       Trust, https://www.heisman.com/heisman-winners/

332   *"Tim Brown, the first wide receiver to ever win the statue, . . ."* University of
       Notre Dame, *Heisman Trophy Winners List*, 2017, Department of
       Athletics, University of Notre Dame,
       https://125.nd.edu/moments/notre-dames-seventh-heisman-trophy-
       tim-brown-1987/

332   *"Remarkably, Frank Leahy not only coached Lujack, . . ."* UHND.com, *Frank
       Leahy, College Football's Greatest Coach*, January 2, 2014

332   *"Just as remarkable, Tim Brown played high school football . . ."* Weber, Paul
       J., *Dallas school boasts pair of Heisman winners*, September 4, 2006,
       MyPlainview.com, Hearst Newspapers, LLC,
       https://www.myplainview.com/news/article/Dallas-school-boasts-
       pair-of-Heisman-winners-8683372.php

332   *"East Dallas high school is the only public high school . . ."* Weber, Paul J.,
       Dallas school boasts pair of Heisman winners, September 4, 2006

333   *"This victory, which to this day is known as . . ."* Johnson, Richard,
       *'Catholics vs. Convicts' was an imperfect nickname back then, and definitely
       doesn't fit now*, November 11, 2017, SBNation, Vox Media, Inc.,

https://www.sbnation.com/college-football/2017/11/11/16626580/catholics-vs-convicts-rivalry-miami-notre-dame-2017

333   *"Hurricanes earned their derisive nickname . . ."* Johnson, Richard, *'Catholics vs. Convicts' was an imperfect nickname back then, and definitely doesn't fit now*, November 11, 2017

333   *"Apparently, Notre Dame only acknowledges national titles . . ."* Trietley, Greg, *Trietley: Pitt can claim nine titles*, September 5, 2011, The Pitt News, University of Pittsburg, https://pittnews.com/article/15992/archives/trietley-pitt-can-claim-nine-titles/

333   *"Nevertheless, the Irish were recognized as the No. 1 team . . ."* Trietley, Greg, *Trietley: Pitt can claim nine titles*, September 5, 2011

335   *"BLAMMO aggressively belts out "Johnny B. Goode". . ."* Facebook, *Blammo*, 2017, Facebook.com, https://www.facebook.com/pg/blammoband/about/?ref=page_internal

335   *"Dean Norris (the actor who played Hank) . . ."* Harrell, Jeff, *As 'Breaking Bad' ends, Norris moves to 'Dome'*, August 11, 2013, SouthBendTribune.com, South Bend Tribune, https://www.south-bendtribune.com/entertainment/inthebend/entertainmentnews/as-breaking-bad-ends-norris-moves-to-dome/article_2171ade8-026d-11e3-a350-001a4bcf6878.html

337   PHOTO: Notre Dame Stadium, South Bend, Indiana, October 19, 2013, Tailgate party outside stadium: The Mad Hatter host and his wife

340   PHOTO: Notre Dame Stadium, South Bend, Indiana, October 19, 2013, Tailgate party outside stadium: Dean Norris, Valerie McMahon

340   *"Notre Dame Stadium, built in 1930 . . ."* The Milwaukee Journal, *Notre Dame Dedicates New Stadium and Is Victor Over Southern*, October 5, 1930, Sports, Recreation, Markets, The Milwaukee Journal, https://news.google.com/newspapers?id=vKZQAAAAIBAJ&sjid=tCEEAAAAIBAJ&pg=4845%2C5309050

341   *"Revenues from gate receipts in 1928 brought . . ."* Sperber, Murray A., *Shake Down the Thunder: The Creation of Notre Dame Football*, 2002, Indiana University Press, p. 270

341   *"Furious over their feet dragging, Rockne . . ."* Sperber, Murray A., *Shake*

Down the Thunder: The Creation of Notre Dame Football, 2002, p. 270

341   *"Confident that ticket revenues the following . . ."* Sperber, Murray A., *Shake Down the Thunder: The Creation of Notre Dame Football*, 2002, p. 270

341   *"The "House That Rockne Built" was actually . . ."* The George Sollitt Construction Company, *History*, 2017, The George Sollitt Construction Company, http://www.sollitt.com/history.html

341   *"by Osborne Engineering in Cleveland, Ohio, . . ."* The Osborn Engineering Company, *History*, 2017, The Osborn Engineering Company, http://www.osborn-eng.com/History

341   *"Residing just several miles south of the Michigan . . ."* Sperber, Murray A., *Shake Down the Thunder: The Creation of Notre Dame Football*, 2002, p. 271

341   *"Notre Dame stadium held slightly fewer than 60,000 . . ."* StadiumDB, *New stadiums: Old Gray Lady and others*, September 25, 2015, StadiumDB.com, StadiumDB http://stadiumdb.com/news/2015/09/new_stadiums_old_gray_lady_and_others

341   *"72,000 could be seated in Ann Arbor."* Kryk, John, *What makes the Big House so unique, and so special?*, December 27, 2013, Toronto Sun, Postmedia Network Inc., https://torontosun.com/2013/12/27/what-makes-the-big-house-so-unique-and-so-special/wcm/65d15265-fb0f-4ca1-ad80-bc658039c5bf

341   *"Ara Parseghian, who played halfback . . ."* NYTimes.com, *Ara Parseghian, Coach Who Returned Notre Dame Football to Greatness, Dies at 94*, August 2, 2017, The New York Times, New York, NY, https://www.nytimes.com/2017/08/.../notre-dame-coach-ara-parseghian-dead-at-94.html

342   *"(in all fairness to Devore, he'd earlier coached . . ."* NYTimes.com, *Ara Parseghian, Coach Who Returned Notre Dame Football to Greatness, Dies at 94*, August 2, 2017, The New York Times, New York, NY, https://www.nytimes.com/2017/08/.../notre-dame-coach-ara-parseghian-dead-at-94.html

342   *"The Jeweled Shillelagh, first presented in 1952 . . ."* Satzman, Darrell, *Sticking Point – Toluca Lake Man Held the Club in USC-Notre Dame Brouhaha*, April 19, 2017, LATimes.com, Los Angeles Times, http://articles.latimes.com/1997-04-19/local/me-50201_1_notre-dame

342   *"Following each game, an emerald inlaid shamrock . . ."* Satzman, Darrell, *Sticking Point – Toluca Lake Man Held the Club in USC-Notre Dame Brouhaha,* April 19, 2017

342   *"the first Jeweled Shillelagh quickly became . . ."* Satzman, Darrell, *Sticking Point – Toluca Lake Man Held the Club in USC-Notre Dame Brouhaha,* April 19, 2017

342   *"Thus, following the 1995 defeat of Southern Cal . . ."* Satzman, Darrell, *Sticking Point – Toluca Lake Man Held the Club in USC-Notre Dame Brouhaha,* April 19, 2017

342   *"Presented by the Notre Dame Club of Los Angeles, . . ."* University of Southern California, *Jeweled Shillelagh,* 2017, USCTrojans.com, University of Southern California Athletics, https://usctrojans.com/sports/2018/7/25/usc-history-traditions-jeweled-shillelagh-notre-dame-rivalry.aspx

343   *"Kiffin's team was the first since the 1964 . . ."* Whitely, David, *Sorry, USC coach Lane Kiffin doesn't deserve fast track out of L.A.,* November 19, 2012, USCTrojans.com, Sporting.News.com, Media Sporting News Media, http://www.sportingnews.com/us/ncaa-football/news/4332979-sorry-kiffin-doesnt-deserve-fast-lane-out-of-la

343   *"Following the first 5 games of this current 2013 . . ."* Klein, Gary, *USC fires Lane Kiffin in the middle of the night,* September 30, 2013, LosAnglesTimes.com, Los Angeles Times, http://articles.latimes.com/2013/sep/30/sports/la-sp-0930-usc-lane-kiffin-20130930

343   *"Kiffin was handed his walking papers . . ."* Klein, Gary, *USC fires Lane Kiffin in the middle of the night,* September 30, 2013

344   *"Their entire fan-base had been shocked to learn Te'o . . ."* Burke, Timothy; Dicky, Jack, *Manti Te'o's Dead Girlfriend, The Most Heartbreaking And Inspirational Story Of The College Football Season, Is A Hoax,* January 16, 2013, DeadSpin.com, Gizmodo Media Group, https://deadspin.com/manti-teos-dead-girlfriend-the-most-heartbreaking-an-5976517

344   *"A charity fund was started."* Burke, Timothy; Dicky, Jack, *Manti Te'o's Dead Girlfriend, The Most Heartbreaking And Inspirational Story Of The College Football Season, Is A Hoax,* Jan. 16, 2013

344   *"Kelly awarded the game ball to his star linebacker . . ."* Burke, Timothy;

Dicky, Jack, *Manti Te'o's Dead Girlfriend, The Most Heartbreaking And Inspirational Story Of The College Football Season, Is A Hoax,* Jan. 16, 2013

344   *"Te'o had been the innocent victim of an elaborate . . ."* Burke, Timothy; Dicky, Jack, *Manti Te'o's Dead Girlfriend, The Most Heartbreaking And Inspirational Story Of The College Football Season, Is A Hoax,* Jan. 16, 2013

344   *"inaugural clash between these teams in this stadium . . ."* Fiutak, Pete, *The Ten Greatest College Football Rivalries,* November 17, 2006, CollegeFootballNews.com, Scout.com, https://web.archive.org/web/20070309013228/http://cfn.scout.com/2/591649.html

345   *"Rockne apparently desired the stands to be as close . . ."* UHND.com, *Notre Dame Stadium,* May 24, 2007, UHND.com, IMG College, https://www.uhnd.com/history/notre-dame-stadium/

345   *"The 247th consecutive sellout crowd springs to its feet . . ."* Heisler, John, *Irish Sellout Streak Reaches 250 Mark,* September 8, 2016, UND.com, The University of Notre Dame, https://und.com/news/2016/9/8/Irish_Sellout_Streak_Reaches_250_Mark.aspx?path=football

345   *"Across the field, Ed Orgeron – who can join . . ."* Klien, Gary, *USC's Ed Orgeron doesn't want big deal made of playing Notre Dame,* October 14, 2013, LATimes.com, Los Angeles Times, http://articles.latimes.com/2013/oct/14/sports/la-sp-1015-usc-football-20131015

346   *"NCAA granted players at Penn State University . . ."* Cable News Network, *Penn State Scandal Fast Facts,* March 28, 2018, Cable News Network, Turner Broadcasting System, Inc., https://www.cnn.com/2013/10/28/us/penn-state-scandal-fast-facts/index.html

346   *"The University of Notre Dame Band, which claims . . ."* Heisler, John, *History of the Notre Dame Band,* 2014, Notre Dame Bands, University of Notre Dame Band, http://www.ndband.com/about-the-nd-band/history.cfm

352   *"The creative man is driven by the desire to achieve; . . ."* Rand, Ayn, *The Ayn Rand Letter,* 1971, AynRandLexicon.com, Ayn Rand Institute, p.1, http://aynrandlexicon.com/lexicon/competition.html

353   *"It also claims to have Indiana's largest selection . . . ."* O'rourke's Public

House, *O'rourke's*, 2017, ORourkesSouthBend.com, O'rourke's Public
House, https://orourkessouthbend.com/

353   *"Every season, more than 140,000 plays . . ."* Konkle, BJ, *ND vs. National
        Champions Advanced States*, July 22, 2016, HerLoyalSons.com, Foodie Pro
        & The Genesis Framework,
        https://www.herloyalsons.com/blog/2016/07/22/advanced-stats-
        indicate-ndfb-good-2015-not-great/

354   *""In the world's broad field of battle, . . ."* Longfellow, Henry W., *A Psalm of
        Life*, 1838, The Knickerbocker, p.189, (or, New-York Monthly Magazine,
        Том 12),
        https://books.google.bg/books?id=6pQ0AQAAMAAJ&pg=PA199#v=
        onepage&q&f=false

357   *"As prognosticated by Mel Kiper, Jr. . . ."* Associated Press, *Stafford goes
        No. 1, but Jets' trade to pick Sanchez shakes up draft*, April 26, 2009,
        http://www.nfl.com/draft/story/09000d5d80ffab1f/article/stafford-
        goes-no-1-but-jets-trade-to-pick-sanchez-shakes-up-draft

BIBLIOGRAPHY

All sources of game scores and statistics, player backgrounds and statistics, team information and rankings (not cited in this Bibliography) are from major college football websites, respective university webpages, and other authoritative online sources.

Boyles, Bob; Guido, Paul. The USA Today College Football Encyclopedia 2009–2010. New York, New York. Skyhorse Publishing. 2009

Bradley, Bob. Death Valley Days. Atlanta, Georgia. Longstreet Press, Inc. 1991

Dozier, Ray. The Oklahoma Football Encyclopedia: 2nd Edition. New York, New York. Skyhorse Publishing, Inc. 2013

Elliot, Orrin Leslie. Stanford University – The First Twenty Five Years 1891 – 1925. Stanford, California. Stanford University Press. 1937

Fitzgerald, Francis Scott. This Side of Paradise. New York, New York. Charles Scribner's Sons. 1920

Griffith, Samuel B. Sun Tzu The Art of War. London, England. Oxford University Press. 1963.

Groom, Winston. The Crimson Tide – An Illustrated History. Tuscaloosa, Alabama. The University of Alabama Press. 2000

Gulley, Bill; Reese, Mary E. Breaking Cover. New York, New York. Simon & Schuster. 1980

Harvard University. Education, bricks and mortar: Harvard buildings and their contribution to the advancement of learning. Cambridge, Maryland. Harvard University Press. 1949

Honious, Ann. What Dreams We Have – The Wright Brothers and Their Hometown of Dayton, Ohio. Ft. Washington, Pennsylvania, 2003

Joyce, James. A Portrait of the Artist as a Young Man. New York, New York. B. W. Huebsch. 1916

Migdol, Gary. Stanford: Home of Champions. Champaign, Illinois. Sports Publishing LLC. 1997

Moskowitz, Tobias J.; Wertheim, L. Jon. Scorecasting: The Hidden Influences Behind How Sports Are Played and Games Are Won. New York, New York.

Random House, Inc. 2011

Nauman, Robert A. On the Wings of Modernism: The United States Air Force Academy. Champaign, Illinois. University of Illinois Press. 2004

Nauman, Robert A. Aerial Victories of the Jet Era. Raleigh, North Carolina. Lulu. 2005

Palka, Eugene; Malinowski, Jon C. Historic Photos of West Point. Nashville, Tennessee. Turner Publishing Company. 2008

Pennington, Joel. The Ten Year War: Ten Classic Games Between Bo and Woody. Pullman, Washington. Ulyssian Publications. 2005.

Perry, George Sessions. The Story of Texas A. and M. New York, New York. McGraw Hill. 1951

Rand, Ayn. The Ayn Rand Letter. Irvine, California. Ayn Rand Institute. 1971

Schoor, Gene. The Fightin' Texas Aggies: 100 Years of A&M Football. Dallas, Texas. Taylor Publishing Company. 1994

Sperber, Murray A. Shake Down the Thunder: The Creation of Notre Dame Football. Bloomington, Indiana. Indiana University Press. 2002

Steele, Michael R. Miracle Moments in Notre Dame Fighting Irish Football History: Best Plays, Games, and Records. New York, New York. Skyhorse Publishing Inc. 2018

Wulf, Steve. ESPN: The Mighty Book of Sports Knowledge. New York, New York. Random House Publishing Group. 2009

INDEX

ABOUT THE AUTHORS

Having contributed to the founding teams of several successful technology-based companies, Sean and Valerie McMahon have been successfully married for more than twenty-five seasons. And, each one of those years has seen an excursion to a new college football rivalry. They live along the scenic Columbia River just outside of Portland, Oregon.
